THIS IS VOLUME III

IN

The Pioneer Heritage Series

SOUTH PASS, 1868

JAMES CHISHOLM'S JOURNAL

OF THE

WYOMING GOLD RUSH

Introduced and edited by

LOLA M. HOMSHER

Director, Wyoming State Archives
and Historical Department

UNIVERSITY OF NEBRASKA PRESS
LINCOLN • LONDON

First Bison Book printing: 1975
Most recent printing indicated by the first digit below:
3   4   5   6   7   8   9   10

CONTENTS

PART I : *THE STORY*

PART II : *THE JOURNAL*

[v]

Contents

SUPPLEMENTARY NOTES

Maps of Wyoming and of South Pass Gold Fields
appear on page 48 and page 58 respectively.
A picture section follows page 58.

PART I

THE STORY

I

THE STORY BREAKS

JUNE 1867. *In a windswept solitude on the crest of the Rockies, a little group of men began cutting up logs for a cabin. Fifteen miles to the southwest the Oregon Trail approached the broad and sandy expanse of a great pass. On the north and south sides of the pass, snow-covered mountain peaks cut the sky; within it rose two streams. That which flowed to the east ultimately discharged its waters into the Gulf of Mexico; the west-running stream emptied into the Pacific Ocean. This was South Pass, landmark and gateway for emigrants marching to fortune and freedom in the bountiful lands of the West.*

But the men building the cabin were not planning on going anywhere; the territory beyond the pass held no allure for them. They were gold prospectors, and they had found what they were looking for.

URING THE RESTLESS, exciting summer of 1867, the heads of state of three North American nations took turns in making news. Down in Mexico in June a firing squad terminated Emperor Maximilian's three-year reign; in July a sovereign who had ruled ten times that long was toasted by her subjects in the newly established Dominion of Canada. And in Washington, during August, the seventeenth President of the United States suspended his Secretary of War, thereby initiating the chain of events which would lead to his own impeachment.

Amid such headline-making stories and others connected with the problems of reconstruction in the South and with the nation's expansion westward, the sketchy reports of a gold strike in a remote corner of Dakota Territory at first commanded little attention. In fact the first news story to cross the Mississippi and reach Chicago erroneously announced the "Discovery of Rich Gold Mines in Utah." According to this despatch, which appeared in the Chicago *Times* on Saturday, July 13, 1867, and was sent from Omaha on July 12,

> Salt Lake papers of July 1, received here, give accounts of rich gold discoveries in the mines of that territory. Three men brought in 40 ounces of quartz dust, which assayed over $700. These mines are located in the Green river country, 200 miles distant from Salt Lake.

On the following Wednesday, under the heading "A Rush to the Green River Mines," the *Times* printed a second, even briefer item:

[4]

Omaha, July 16}

Salt Lake papers of July 6 state that large numbers of people are flocking to the new mines discovered recently on Green river.

During the rest of the month the reports persisted, confirming the story but adding little concrete detail. Within one ten-day period four despatches appeared in the Chicago *Tribune.*

Omaha, July 20}

A Salt Lake letter says the excitement about the new gold mines continues, although the exact locality on the Green River is not made public. People, principally Mormons, continue abandoning their vocation and rushing for the mines. It is feared that the crops will suffer for want of harvesting . . .[1]

July 23}

Salt Lake papers report late gold discoveries by Lewis and Robinson located at the head of the Sweetwater. The excitement still continues.[2]

Omaha, July 29}

The Salt Lake mines near South Pass are still drawing a large number of Gentiles and Mormons. Their richness is undoubted.[3]

Omaha, July 30}

A despatch from Salt Lake, of the 20th, says that William Munsey, the discoverer of the celebrated Munsey and Morgan lode on [Horse] River, has fitted out an expedition and leaves for the new mines on Green River today with full faith of their richness.[4]

News of a second rich strike in September was slow in reaching the eastern papers, but by November reports on the gold fields near South Pass again were appearing at frequent intervals.

> Salt Lake, Nov. 6—Late arrivals from the Sweet Water mines report one company taking out $40 in gold per day to each hand. Judge Carter * has built a new road to the mines from Fort Bridger, shortening the distance 15 miles.[5]

> *Omaha, Neb., Nov. 21*}
> A gentleman just from the Green River mines bring fine specimens of gold nuggets. Quartz was also found as rich as any in the country.[6]

> The Salt Lake correspondent of the 20th says fifty houses and several mills are erected at the Sweetwater mines, near Wind River mountains. The ledges there are gold bearing from one to twenty feet wide. Wood and water are abundant. The Indians are hostile, and prospectors have to go in large numbers. No one is allowed to locate lode claims except for himself.[7]

> *Omaha, Dec. 17*}
> Reports from the Sweetwater mines state that the Indians are quiet. It is expected that a large number of miners will be there early in the spring. Several quartz mills are also expected to arrive.[8]

> *Omaha, Neb., Dec. 26*}
> The late arrival from the new Wind river mines reports a general stampede from the Sweetwater mines to the new diggings which are found to be very rich.[9]

* Judge W. A. Carter of Fort Bridger, a well-known figure in Wyoming preterritorial history. He accompanied the U.S. Army under Colonel A. S. Johnston to this country in 1857, and became post sutler of Fort Bridger that winter when it was taken over by the Army and established as a military post.

Obviously the mines were not a flash in the pan; and with memories of Sutter's Mill, Pikes Peak, and the Comstock lode still fresh, it was equally obvious a rush could be expected when the season opened in the spring. Such a story could not be adequately covered in two- and three-line despatches via Salt Lake and Omaha: it would be necessary to have a man on the spot. At least this was the decision of the Chicago *Tribune*, and they made arrangements to send out a correspondent.

II

THE CORRESPONDENT

THE MAN TO WHOM the assignment was offered, James
Chisholm, had been on the staff of the rival *Times* for
about four years. A Scotsman, he had emigrated to the
United States toward the end of the Civil War. Born on
February 18, 1838, in Turriff, in the county of Aberdeen
in northeast Scotland, Chisholm was one of the nine children
of Captain Alexander Chisholm and Mary Davidson Chisholm. "Jeames," as he was called, was particularly close to
his brother Harry, five years older than he, and all his life
was warmed by memories of their boyhood—of rambles
with Harry and their dog Norah to the "brig o' Castleton"
across the river Deveron, and in the countryside around
Turriff, which lies inland from Banff on the shores of the
North Sea.

Presumably Chisholm learned the three R's at home or in

the village school, and he received some formal education at the Elgin Academy in Edinburgh. He had been destined for the law, but after beginning his studies decided that it was not his true vocation and took a job as bookkeeper in a large Edinburgh shop. Harry was with him—"writing poems and tragedies that were to astonish the world"—and together the two young men lived a semi-bohemian life, reading much and arguing the merits of favorite authors with their friends, going to the theatre as often as they could afford it, and diverting themselves at "glorious evening parties of which [Harry] was the accepted lion." There was an unhappy interval—probably during the abortive period of law apprenticeship—which James spent in Glasgow; a "dismal year" in which the only bright spots were visits from Harry, who "had dropped temporarily from his high pedestal to the practical level of Commercial Traveller and . . . was often in the city."

Up until this time, if James "cherished . . . secret aspirations . . . they were buried deep down in [his] inmost consciousness." Clearly he felt himself outshone by his brilliant elder brother. He was content to act as "corrector and refiner," and despite Harry's encouragement "never once attempted literary composition till [he] came to do so for a living." Nevertheless, his fluent and graceful style and his frequent and easy use of literary allusions show that he must have absorbed a great deal during those "obscure, hard but happy" Edinburgh years.

The future careers of both brothers appear to have been determined by a pamphlet on Burns which Harry published in Glasgow. It brought him "into the sphere of newspaper life," and he drew James after him. No more bookkeeping for James: he found work as a journalist, first in Edinburgh, later in London. Meanwhile Harry emigrated to Canada, and after a period on the Toronto *Globe*, went on to Chicago where he was employed by the *Times* as drama, music, and art critic. (The eldest Chisholm brother, John, also came to America but whether at this period or later is not known.) Finally, in 1864, at Harry's urging James left London for Chicago where he too secured a position on the *Times*.[1]

The two most influential Chicago papers at this date were the *Tribune*, whose editor-in-chief was Joseph Medill, and the *Times*, owned and edited by the erratic but forceful Wilbur F. Storey. The *Tribune* was vehemently abolitionist and Republican—in fact, Medill gave the name of Republican to the party which came into being in 1854—whereas the *Times* was the semiofficial spokesman for the local Democrats, and its editorial policy was notoriously Copperhead. (In 1863 Storey's criticisms of President Lincoln had led General Ambrose E. Burnside to order the paper's suppression—an order which was quickly revoked by Lincoln.) Storey's philosophy, which he followed to the letter, was "to print the news and raise hell." Under his aegis the *Times* announced an execution with what has been called American journalism's most famous headline, "Jerked to Jesus"; and there was the same classic—or barbaric—simplicity in Storey's instructions to his war correspondents: "Telegraph fully all the news you can get and when there is no news, send rumors." [2]

Fresh from the somewhat more placid purlieus of Fleet Street, Chisholm must have found Storey quite as much a contrast to his British opposite number as was the raw, brawling, lusty lake city—half frontier town, half metropolis—to Queen Victoria's London. But he had Harry to show him the ropes, and when Harry left the *Times* to become city editor of the Chicago *Evening Post*, "Jeames"—now Jim—stayed on, serving as an editorial writer and dramatic critic as well as carrying out reportorial assignments.

He made a good many friends in and out of his profession,

among them the well-known photographer Joseph Battersby, a competitor of Brady and of Hessler. A photograph taken by Battersby in 1865 shows Jim with Charles Wright, city editor of the *Times*, Harry Griffiths, described as "a brilliant and versatile writer upon any theme which he was assigned," and Sam Medill, younger brother of Joseph Medill, who later on was city editor and managing editor of the *Tribune*.* Curiously enough, it was another photograph taken by Battersby which proved to be the starting point of Jim's great romance.[3]

During the years immediately after the Civil War, prominent Chicagoans were engaged in various good works whose object was to help out veterans and their families. Fairs held in churches and halls were favorite money-raising devices, and as the "society photographer," Mr. Battersby was often called on to help publicize such projects by displaying pictures of the young women participants. When making notes on one of these affairs which he was covering for the *Times*, Jim was much struck by the photograph of a young lady who he learned was Miss Mary Evelyn Garrison, daughter of Judge and Mrs. Andrew Garrison. He contrived to meet her and her parents at a Sunday afternoon tea at Mr. and Mrs. Battersby's, asked the privilege of calling, and soon thereafter was a guest at a birthday party at the Garrison home.

From then on, the Garrison household saw a good deal of Jim. The particular attraction, of course, was Mary (nicknamed "Mate"), but Mrs. Garrison was the essence of hos-

---

* An article accompanying a later reproduction of the photograph states that Medill, Wright, and Chisholm were "inseparable companions, largely because they were congenial spirits, imbued with a love of their profession, and partly because they were always intent on 'scooping' each other, keeping a jealous guard over each other's whereabouts. The sensational department of the newspaper was confided to these subordinates, and their manner of handling such material was either a feather in their cap or a black eye. But it was always a friendly rivalry" (Chicago *Tribune*, n.d.).

pitality, and Jim found the whole atmosphere congenial. "Mr. Garrison knew Lincoln well," Chisholm wrote to his daughter many years later. "They were very much akin in spirit and political principles, and were lawyers together, all working in the same groove, so to say, and they had many confabs and conferences both here [Chicago] and in Springfield. Mr. Garrison never went deeply into politics, but clung to law. . . ." [4] Although it is unlikely that Jim became acquainted with the Garrisons until after Lincoln's death, the past association was an enriching one and many a Lincoln anecdote must have found its way into the conversation.

Despite the handicaps imposed by the conventions of the period—a young lady could not receive a "gentleman caller" or go about with him unchaperoned—Jim's courtship of Mary seems to have proceeded in fairly untrammelled fashion. There were duets in the parlor at 65 Park Avenue— Mate had a fine soprano voice and Jim played the flute—and there were enough outside excursions to leave Jim with nostalgic memories of "matinees, sunshiny days, and paper collars": theatre parties, perhaps, and visits to Colonel Joseph H. Wood's renowned museum, which contained "150,000 curiosities of every kind" including (in 1866) "the largest woman in the world weighing near 900."

The one jarring note was parental disapproval of any more serious commitment than friendship. Although Mrs. Garrison was fond of the young Scotsman, she did her best to discourage Mary's interest in him. After all, as she pointed out, a reporter's income was meager; the people of his world might be interesting but they were unreliable; and the wife of a man on a morning paper could expect to spend her evenings alone.

It was welcome news to Mrs. Garrison when Jim told the family that he had been offered an assignment which would take him west to investigate the much-heralded Sweetwater mines. She was less pleased when he added that since it might be a long absence, he hoped Mate's parents would consent to an engagement. The consent was not forthcoming; and on top of this disappointment, Judge Garrison, prompted by his wife, asked Jim's promise "not to write Mary or correspond with her in any way" for a year.

It is not known precisely when Horace White (who had replaced Joseph Medill as editor of the *Tribune*) approached Jim with the offer of the assignment. Nor do we know what impelled the *Tribune* management to go outside their own staff for a correspondent. However, it was no more uncommon then than it is now to "hire away" useful personnel from a rival establishment, and in the absence of any sort of contractual agreement there was certainly nothing unethical about it.

No doubt the impasse Chisholm had reached in his relations with the Garrisons played a part in his decision to accept the offer. Since he had agreed not to see or communicate with Mary for a year, it would be easier to wait out the time if there was a sizable hunk of geography between them. He had recently become a United States citizen, and he felt that this was a golden opportunity to see a little-known area of his adopted country. And—who could say? anything was possible in the fabulous West—perhaps there was a pot of gold with his name on it waiting for him out there in those mountains beyond the plains.

Although there is some reason to suppose that Jim's "hour of decision" came around Christmas 1867—he planned to return to Chicago in time for Christmas the following year [5] —still, the date of the *Tribune* offer and of his departure for the West must remain matters for conjecture. All that can

[13]

be said for certain is that a second rich strike in the South
Pass region was reported in September 1867; that the Union
Pacific reached Cheyenne in November; and that in mid-
March 1868 Jim was in Omaha, Nebraska, en route to the
gold fields.

III

CHEYENNE

WHEN JIM BOUGHT HIS TICKET from Omaha to Cheyenne, he was heading for a town that was listed in the timetables before it ever appeared on official maps—a town that had not even been on the drawing board a year before. On July 4, 1867, the chief engineer of the Union Pacific, General Grenville M. Dodge, designated a point on Crow Creek, Dakota Territory, as a rail terminal, and named it Cheyenne for the Indian tribe nearby. He recalled that

While we camped there, the Indians swooped down out of the ravine of Crow Creek and attacked a Mormon grading train and outfit that had followed our trail and killed two of its men; . . . but we saved their stock and started the graveyard of the future city.[1]

Several buildings were up before the official survey was completed on July 19, and during that summer of '67 three or four hundred businesses were opened and the population swelled to ten thousand. But as the railroad construction forged westward, the construction crews and transients moved on with it, and on the March evening Jim stepped off the Omaha train—some eight and a half months after Cheyenne had been born—the population was down to five thousand and still shrinking. Not so the graveyard, however. Almost before he had time to unpack his valise, Jim was reporting the details of a double lynching to the Chicago *Tribune*.

From Our Own Correspondent.

Cheyenne, D.T., March 21 }

"It is a sign of good times," they say here, "when people begin to do a little hanging." And it would appear, to judge from the terrible events of the past night, that the good times have come upon the Magic City with a vengeance. The *Vigilantes* have been "doing a little hanging" over night, and today there is an excitement such as we do not witness every day, even in Cheyenne. The spectacle of a human being suspended in the air, with blue, swollen features, tongue and eyes protruding in a horrible manner, and fists clenched in the last convulsive struggle, is not a pleasing object to encounter in your morning ramble. Such was the ghastly sight presented to the eyes of the Cheyennese at sunrise this morning, near the east end of the principal street. A little to the westward of the city, near Crow Creek, was a companion picture, and rumor had it that three more were hanging somewhere in the vicinity. The two bodies were cut down by order of the authorities and deposited in the City Hall. From thence they were soon conveyed in a wagon—the rope still round their necks —to the Coroner's office, where an inquest was held, the jury having no difficulty in arriving unanimously at the conclusion that they had both come to their death by strangulation.

THE VIGILANTES AT WORK.

These stern and summary proceedings have produced a profound impression on the minds of the citizens, and all day long the place has been in a perfect hubbub of excitement. The roughs are visibly panic-stricken, not knowing how soon another blow may be struck. The respectable citizens are divided in opinion regarding the action of the Vigilance Committee, some commending it, (with a subdued kind of protest, of course, against mob law,) while others denounce the "Vigies" as midnight assassins. The civic authorities accept the situation in passive silence, and apparently look upon the event as one of those accidents that will happen in such an ill-regulated family. All are agreed in this, that it is a serious business. One of the unfortunate wretches thus strangled to death was a man of desperate character, Charles Martin by name, who had been arrested on a charge of murder, tried before the United States District Court, and acquitted by a jury of his countrymen. The other is said to be one of a gang of horse-thieves who are a pest to this community.

RUFFIANS ON THE RAMPAGE.

Perhaps the present condition of society in Cheyenne, and the difficulty of applying legitimate remedies, may offer some palliation for the commission of such acts. Notwithstanding the efforts of the police to amend it by prohibiting the carrying of concealed weapons, and other measures, it is plain that the rowdies have still the control. The wildest roughs from all parts of the country are congregated here, as one may see by glancing into the numerous dance-houses and gambling hells—men who carry on the trade of robbery openly, and would not scruple to kill a man for ten dollars. This class is decidedly in the majority, and they

[17]

have carried matters with a high hand for sometime past. Strangers are beset and robbed, and honest traders leaving the city with their mule teams are often waylaid and rendered penniless at a moment's warning.

THE LAST OF A ROWDY.

A fair representative of this rowdy element was Charles Martin, one of last night's victims. A fellow who never knew fear himself, he was a terror to every community, and had already signalized himself by more than one murder before his arrival in Cheyenne. Sometime since he, and a fellow named Andy Harris, with other congenial spirits, succeeded in robbing a stranger of a considerable sum of money, and the proceeds were devoted to the purchase of a dance house, which was carried on under their joint management. But about five weeks ago the thieves fell out about the division of the spoil, and Martin, being the most expert shot of the two, killed Harris by putting a line of five bullets into him from his chin downwards. He was arrested and lodged in the jail, and his trial has occupied the attention of the district court for four days. On Thursday evening the jury brought in a verdict of acquittal, which appeared to create not a little dissatisfaction throughout the community, and, had Martin been possessed of ordinary prudence, he would have profited by the ominous murmur of disapproval expressed on all hands, and departed. On the contrary, he had no sooner regained his liberty, than his demeanor became more insolent and defiant than ever. That evening he put on a gay suit of clothes and swaggered around his accustomed haunts, at some of which he was saluted with cheers, while he openly intimated his purpose to "Furnish another man for breakfast" and very soon. Yesterday (Friday) he was still seen around, and, little dreaming of the terrible doom which awaited him, was enjoying life with his companions in his old reckless fashion. Late in the evening he entered one of his favorite resorts—a dance-house called the "Keystone"— one of about a score of such places in Cheyenne, where amusement of a questionable kind is offered to the citizen. They are generally crowded to the door all night long, and the sound of fiddles and banjoes, mingled with the voice of the master of ceremonies. "Only two more gentlemen wanted for the next dance," as you hear it from the various halls, conveys the idea of a whole city being one huge rustic festival—an impression which is by no means sustained on entering the halls of mirth. A space in the centre is devoted to the terpsichorean art, where females of the lowest type may be secured as partners in the dance, while faro tables, keno, and all imaginable games constitute the side dishes.

A MIDNIGHT SURPRISE BY THE VIGILANTES.

In such a den was Charley Martin last evening, surrounded by a circle of sympathizers, and enjoying himself to the full, when about midnight an individual entered the house and privately asked him to step to the door to see a friend. Nothing doubting, he obeyed the invitation, and was ushered into the street. A policeman, who was standing near the bar at the moment, observed that the door was suddenly closed after him and secured from the outside. Immediately there was an uproar in the saloon, and forty revolvers were pulled, while a rush was made for the door to ascertain what was the matter. Then the door was flung open. On the outside stood fifteen men in black masks, with revolvers in each hand, pointing in a determined and threatening aspect to the interior. The forty revolvers were suddenly sheathed, and a supressed murmur of "The Vigilantes" intimated that Martin's fate was fixed. Some effort was made by the men to follow and rescue the unhappy wretch, but the black masks divided into two squads, and disappeared in the darkness.

Martin had fought dearly for his life. He was insensible to fear, and even the suddenness of the surprise had not disconcerted him. As he was dragged away from the saloon he was heard to ejaculate "My God, men, what are you going to do with me," and there were ghastly wounds upon his head when found in the morning, and other evidences of a bitter and deadly struggle. They had dragged him to a spot near the east end of the city. There a rude gallows was hastily erected by placing three poles in the ground, and the victim was suspended from the centre by a piece of bed cord.

THE PITIFUL PART OF THE TALE.

Whatever feeling may exist as to the violence of the proceeding, the community are unanimously glad to be rid of such a knave. Martin belonged to a respectable family in Lexington, Missouri, where he has a wife and two little children. In his pocket was found a letter from this poor wife of his, containing a touching appeal to him to forsake his evil ways and return to his family, but it had apparently no effect. He has been from his youth a desperado, and he died the death of one.

OTHER VICTIMS.

But the Vigilantes had not yet completed their night's work. Other victims awaited their approach at the other end of the town. These were two men by name Morgan and Kelly, who were connected with a gang of horse thieves in the vicinity, and who had just been captured. It appears that a large number of mules had recently been stolen, and among others a four-mule team belonging to a Mr. W. G. Smith. All efforts to find the missing property had been fruitless, until one night the terrible

"Vigies" seized upon a fellow known as "Wild-horse" Smith—a species of Roaring Ralph Stackpole—and strung him up by the neck three times. They did not quite strangle him, however, and the fellow revealed the hiding-place of the stolen mules, a "dug-out," or underground den, near the creek.

THE ROWDIES' RETREATS.

Your correspondent was induced to visit some of these dug-outs one day, and found them quite interesting places of their kind, suggesting curious reminiscences of the famous robbers' cave in Gil Blas. They are not all occupied by bandits, however. In the face of the bluff overlooking the creek are a variety of holes, large enough to admit a man to crawl into. In the interior the clay has been scooped out, forming quite a habitable abode, while a chimney is improvised by boring another hole upwards to the surface, and into this is stuck a barrel to carry off the smoke. These places are mostly occupied by very poor men, reduced to very desperate circumstances, who are probably waiting for something to turn up. One would scarcely have dreamed of searching in such holes for stolen mules. Yet in one of these very dug-outs denoted by the horse-thief was found no less than 15 animals. Thither [had] Mr. Smith's mules been taken, and sold to Morgan and Kelly, the latter of whom started with them to Denver. The owner received information of their whereabouts, and at once went in pursuit. At Denver he learned that Kelly had gone up into the mountains; so he followed, and at length overtook him at Guy Hill. Kelly was brought back to Denver, and delivered into the custody of Mr. Smith, who started back towards Cheyenne.

"HUNG FOR A WARNING."

On the way he was met by Morgan, who was on his way to join Kelly on an expedition to Sweetwater. Morgan was also arrested, and at an early hour this morning both of the men were brought to the city. Before they could be secured in jail, the secret committee were upon them, and they were never seen again alive. About daylight the body of Morgan was cut down by Marshal Land, who found the poor wretch suspended by the neck, with his feet trailing on the ground. A placard was pinned upon his back with the inscription; "This man was hung by the Vigilance committee for being one of a gang of horse-thieves." His companion, Kelly, is said to have been shot or hanged at a distance of several miles beyond the city, but up to this time his body has not been found.

THE FEELING IN THE COMMUNITY.

These midnight doings have created, naturally, great excitement in the city—an excitement "not loud but deep." People are collected in little groups all through the streets, and talk with bated breath of the hangings. Even Sweetwater [the South Pass gold fields were commonly known as the Sweetwater mines] is for the time forgotten. Some claim that Morgan was innocent, and that his companion had borrowed the money from a friend wherewith to purchase the mules, which is probably the case. It is conceded, however, that he purchased them in the dug-out cavern aforesaid, for about half their real value, so he must have known them to be stolen property. Much feeling is manifested on this point, but the argument is conducted rather in undertones. One thing is particularly to be noted as a result of last night's work. The city is remarkably quiet and well-behaved. The rowdy element suddenly manifests a very retiring disposition, and the gambling houses are not nearly so crowded as they were yesterday. It is by no means certain that the committee have finished their labors yet, and no one in the community would be surprised to awaken on the sabbath day, and find another victim or two with the fatal placard on their backs dangling in the sun. There are several prisoners now in jail who have committed worse offenses than Morgan, and the jail is but a frail tenement of timber. The anticipations of these prisoners will not be of a very pleasing character under the circumstances.

As the day closes the city is restored, not to its wonted state, but to a state of tranquility, and the gloomy subject of the morning's excitement gradually gives place once more to the all-absorbing topic of Sweetwater.

J. C.

Cheyenne, March 22}

The body of the man Kelly has not yet been found, and it is conjectured that the Vigilantes have permitted him to escape. A few shots were heard just about the time that his comrade was hanged, probably fired by some of the committee with a view to accelerate his flight from the neighborhood.

The bodies of Morgan and Martin, which lay all day on the floor of the dusty back room of the Coroner's store were this evening carried out to the prairie and buried. I looked at Morgan's hair, which had been of a yellowish color, and it was nearly white. It is not improbable that the poor fellow may have died of terror before be was strangled by the rope!

A FRESH EXCITEMENT

has just been started, and the temporary calmness of the city is again ruffled, restoring it to something of its usual bustle. Two gamblers, Butters [Burtis] and Dodge had a quarrel—about a woman, of course. Dodge followed Butters armed all day, seeking for a settlement of the difficulty. In the evening Butters was seated at supper in the Ford House, when Dodge entered, fully armed, and said, "Come outside and let us settle this matter."

"No," replied Butters, "better settle it here." And in the same breath he drew his revolver and shot Dodge in the head, through the skull. They are now carrying the dead man to the Coroner, in a wagon, followed by a large crowd, and Butters is in the custody of Mr. Land, the United States Marshal of the Territory.

J. C.[2]

The Cheyenne *Daily Leader* devoted considerably less space than the Chicago *Tribune* to the lynching of Morgan and Martin (the one-column story was headed VIGILAN-TES AGAIN—TWO MEN HUNG),[3] but the local scribes were not nearly so blasé in reporting what Jim called the "fresh excitement."

ADDITIONAL CRIME!

Continuation of the Carnival of Blood!

A. G. BURTIS SHOOTS H. W. DODGE!

A Woman at the Bottom of it!

FULL DETAILS OF THE AFFAIR!

It would seem from the occurrences of crime within the past few days, that Cheyenne was about to realize the truth of assertions which have been made by her enemies that it was becoming a place of the worst name for its tragic scenes of blood and riot. It shall be no part of our purpose to gloss over the state of morals here, but to portray in truthful colors events as they may transpire, at the same time hoping, trusting and praying that our young city may be spared the further opprobrium of deeds of violence and bloodshed.

Hardly have the bodies of Martin and Morgan become rigid in the arms of death, before we are called upon to chronicle another shooting affair, wherein the soul of H. W. Dodge was hurried, with but a second's warning, into eternity. . . .

Translated into the language of the theatre, the story which emerged from the testimony of the witnesses might have been classified as a melodrama in two acts and three scenes. The setting for Act One was "a house on Ferguson street"; the time Sunday afternoon. "Burtis had been talking with a woman; [Dodge] had come in and offered to bet with Burtis; and finally . . . attacked Burtis." He was forthwith ejected from the house by a Negro bouncer, "and went away saying he wouldn't stand it to be called a — — — — nor a liar." Act Two opened twenty-four hours later on a street "near the Gold Room," with Dodge telling a man named Montgomery that "he would never take an unfair advantage of Burtis, but that Burtis might go out and make the fight and he would meet him." The final scene was played out at Ford's Restaurant, where John M. Thompson, one of the witnesses,

saw two men standing in the aisle between the tables; heard one of them make the request to go out and settle the matter, to which answer was given, that this was the place to settle; next heard a shot fired, and saw deceased fall; think deceased had his hands in his pockets all the time; saw revolver in the hands of Burtis . . .[4]

Dodge's death, the jury found, was "occasioned by a pistol shot fired by A. G. Burtis," and they were "not satisfied that it was a justifiable act." The *Leader* had learned from "authentic sources" that the deceased "was an officer in the volunteer force, during the rebellion, and attained the rank of Brigadier General by Brevet. He had only resided in Cheyenne six weeks."

If a seasoned soldier—a man who had performed so intrepidly as to win his stars on the battlefield—could last only six weeks in Cheyenne, what was the life expectancy of a greenhorn newspaper chap who seldom had heard a shot fired except in make-believe? While Jim's experience as a drama critic came in handy in reporting these real-life theatricals, he may well have wondered if it was the ideal training to enable him to survive them. Book-learning and aesthetic formulae had their uses, but, as he noted drily in a letter written a few days after his arrival, "the far West is not favorable to the cultivation of the Muses—not at least in the higher branches." [5] Nothing in his previous experience, not even his stay in Omaha, could have prepared him for life in Cheyenne.

Just why Jim stopped over in Omaha and how long he remained there are questions which cannot be answered; he could have made the trip direct from Chicago to Cheyenne in fifty-two hours. [6] In any event, a letter to Mrs. Andrew Garrison (apparently the ban on correspondence did not extend to Mate's mother) indicates a stay of some days. He speaks of the high cost of living in Omaha, and mentions that he had "frequently" seen a friend of the Garrisons', General Augur, "without knowing it was he until the day I left." *

* General Christopher C. Augur (1821-1898), a West Point classmate of General Ulysses S. Grant, distinguished himself as a Union commander. Prior to the Civil War he saw active service in the Mexican War and in the territories of Washington and Oregon. Having been brevetted major general during the Civil War, he reverted to colonel's rank on being mustered out of the volunteer service, and was promoted to brigadier general by President Grant in 1869.

"The building of the Union Pacific Railroad and the migration of thousands of home seekers to the West aroused the Indian tribes to

Another passage in the same letter does at least provide a clue as to the date of his departure: "During my residence in Omaha a young poetess there, I remember, gave to the world a lyrical rhapsody on Mud; and it was painfully apparent that she could soar no higher." The poem referred to, "Omaha in Mud" by F. Alice B., appeared in the Omaha *Herald* of March 18, 1868. The trip from Omaha to Cheyenne took twenty-two and a half hours—the Union Pacific Passenger Express left Omaha at 8:30 P.M. and reached Cheyenne at 7:00 P.M.[7]—and since Jim could hardly have arrived in Cheyenne later than the evening of March 20 and still had time to gather the details for the *Tribune* story written next day, he must have left Omaha either March 18 or March 19.*

During Jim's first days in the Wild West, it certainly more than lived up to its advance billing. After the lynchings and the Burtis-Dodge shooting, Cheyenne—still on its worst behavior—was hit by a blizzard, and what with one thing and another, "A Rambler in the Far West" soon had ample

the defense of their hunting grounds. Augur commanded various military departments during that period and directed operations against nearly every one of the hostile tribes in the years from 1867 to 1885." *(Dictionary of American Biography)*

* If Chisholm's only reading matter on a train journey of nearly twenty-three hours was the Omaha *Herald*, one can see how the "Mud" rhapsody might make an impression that not even the lively happenings of the next week could efface. The first two of the poem's six verses are:

> Some towns are famed for beauty,
>   And others for deeds of blood,
> But say what you may of "Omaha,"
>   It beats them all for MUD.

> Oh! What a pleasing sensation
>   When pedestrians cross the street,
> To stop at every corner
>   And shovel off their feet.

In fairness, it should be noted that the "young poetess" was aged twelve.

material for a letter to Mrs. Garrison and other members of the "happy family at 65 Park Avenue."

Cheyenne, D.T. March 27, 1868

Tis pleasant, believe me, in the midst of the riot and excitement which prevails around me, to escape for an hour or two in this manner, and fly off on the wings of a goose quill, (literally, a steel pen, Mrs. James) back to your hospitable fireside again . . . .

I am now located temporarily in Cheyenne, where we are effectually snowed in. It was only owing to the merest chance that I do not happen to be snowed *out*. Choked and frozen among the hills. The changes in the weather here are inconceivably violent and sudden. One day the flies were buzzing around the doors, and next morning the deadly snowdrifts were up to the eaves. Everything looked lovely for Sweetwater and the streets were alive with traders packing their mule wagons. I had arranged to go out with a party of Southerners that evening when I was suddenly prostrated by a violent attack of sickness—cramps, spasms, fever and I know not what, so that I could not stir. My friends went on without me, and I fear to think of their fate.

Never did I realize the terrors of a snow storm till now. All that night and next day the blinding drift continued, until it seemed as if the city would actually be buried. Partially recovered from my sickness in the afternoon, I attempted to cross the street to dine, and was lost—literally lost, blinded, senseless and half suffocated, and staggered into a snowdrift up to the chin. I was rescued by a Jew who drew me into his clothing store, and there I lay down on some buffalo robes and had a relapse; nor could I get out again, for in a few hours the doors were effectually barricaded by the snow. That night I began to think my bark had foundered, and I mentally made my will, bequeathing my good wishes to my friends, my forgiveness to mine enemies. My Hebrew friend was very kind, and I felt like the wounded knight of Ivanhoe, only it was Isaac, and not the gentle Rebecca, who tended me. Fortunately my sickness was of a transitory nature, attributable to local causes, and in the morning I made a vigorous effort and shook it off. (No man was ever known to die a natural death in Cheyenne.)

We had to dig our way through the snow to breakfast—a task of several hours—and in this work I exhibited such prowess in the use of the shovel as to earn the applause of all my co-laborers. Now the storm is over and the city is partially disinterred. The citizens, rejoiced to see the world again, are all engaged in a riotous tournament of snowballing. This frolic they carry to excess like everything else, and 'tis but a step from snowballs to pistol balls. An hour ago a luckless nigger, mounted upon a mule was riding along, when he encountered such a volley that his beast went down under him, and he was precipitated into a deep drift headlong.

But how fares it with my hapless comrades out on the plains? Today accounts come in from all points, of travellers found dead or half frozen, coaches upset, and horses riderless. No living thing without shelter could have survived such a night. This thought has haunted me all day, and I shudder to think that my friends may have met such a fate. They went away as joyous and hopeful on that sunny afternoon with their mule team loaded with merchandize, and I was to rejoin them at the mines. Heaven pity them then if the cruel storm was loosed upon their unsheltered heads, for they are by this time as silent as the hills—hushed to sleep by the deadly snow kisses. Thus far nature has bidden us but a surly welcome to the West.

The Eastern train is snowed up about thirty miles down the track, so we are quite isolated. No mail, no news. But a deputation is getting ready to go out to the relief of the passengers. They say there are four hundred Mormons on board the cars—Converts from the old world on their way to the New Jerusalem. I will go and have a look at the saints if it be true.*

---

* "We have just passed through one of the worst snow storms ever known here. It commenced on Tuesday, the 24th, and snowed constantly for forty-eight hours accompanied by a terrible gale. Huge drifts are piled up in the streets and against the houses. The stages from Denver did not arrive until yesterday—nearly three days late.

And now since I have button-holed you all, let me say a few words on this marvellous city. I do not share the sanguine hopes of its citizens that Cheyenne will ever grow to be a great metropolis. It may be that it is even now about at the zenith of its prosperity. It may even vanish like Jonah's gourd, as Julesburg has done. Yet take it as it stands today with its astonishing vitality, pluck, and enterprize, its astonishing wickedness if you will, and the world has not its equal to show. Scarcely eight months old, it is already a compact well built city full of good hotels, and spacious stores well stocked with wares of every kind, and with a daily living tide flowing through its streets such as one could not find in a city of ten times the size and age. This is its distinctive peculiarity: It is full to the brim. No scraps and patches of building, tapering off into suburbs, but a clearly defined square dot on the prairie, and busy as a bee hive, as if one had miraculously cut out a chunk from the heart of Chicago and planted it—people and all—in the wilderness. One might say a single step carries you at once from the barren plain right into the midst of a stirring spirited community, and that is Cheyenne.

All day alive with the murmur of trade and traffic, and all night still more alive with murmurs of a less attractive kind— "Sore given to revel and ungodly glee", and the black sheep greatly outnumber the white. There is no such thing as domestic life, no friendship, no hospitality. People are too much occupied to think of it. 'Tis all a rough battle for gain, and a stranger sees at once on entering the place that he must fight and fight boldly to maintain his own ground. What a monstrous fuss, after all, do we Lilliputian mortals make just to keep our little souls in our bodies for a few years, and then we have to give them up in the long run, and much the worse for wear. I think you, of the gentler sex have by far the best of the game. You stand aside and watch the

Two of the drivers got lost and were badly frozen, but at length succeeded in reaching this place. The passenger train due here from the east on Tuesday night has not yet arrived, but is expected at 12 tonight. It has been lying with its two hundred passengers, in a huge snow drift, forty miles east of this place, between Pine Bluffs and Hillsdale Station."—Chicago *Tribune*, April 3, 1868, 2:7. Dated March 26, 1868.

game till a trump turns up, and so with a smile you win. Well, as soon as you get your "rights" secured, so that you can do your own fighting (and who shall say you may!) come out West and see how you like it.

When people speak of Seeing *life* out here, I think they must allow a wide latitude in the interpretation of the phrase. My own experience in Cheyenne would lead me to infer that Seeing life means seeing a good deal of death. But that is an unpleasant topic and I will skip it.

The condition of the town is very unsettled, the Vigilantes are abroad, and there may soon be a necessity of putting the city under martial law. I am rooming with the U. S. Marshal of the territory, who on account of his prisoners is an object of dislike to these Vigilantes, and we have each to keep a double barreled shot gun at the head of our couch besides revolvers. This looks very warlike, but there is no immediate danger, and when it does approach, why I will contrive some means of getting round it. I always alight on my feet somehow, like a cat, and I have a supreme reliance in the belief that when I am wanted I will be called hence, and not till then. When a man gets hanged or shot or stabbed here, the people say "he is out of luck."

I would it were in my power, now, to entertain or horrify you (which is all the same) with the recital of some thrilling adventure, something that might look romantic and probably half true. Know however, that there is not a shadow of romance about me or my travels, the romantic having been crushed out of me many years ago, when—but I wonder. You would not think there is much romance in these grey dreary plains if you saw nothing else from day to day. If those sublime souls "whose spirit walks not with the souls of men" and who love to commune with nature, would come here and "commune" awhile alone, they would be glad to get under the gaslight again.

Perhaps when I return from Sweetwater I may be enabled to give you a few personal experiences (together with a lock of my hair). Yet I have had a sample of Camp life, and I may as well give you a peep at it, although I am conscious already of trespassing on your patience (I advise you to take this letter in separate doses, and you will get to the end of it in the course of time.)

[31]

A few days ago I was desired by some friends, who were encamped at a considerable distance on the plains, to take charge of a team with some provisions and go out. I did. Imagine the sight. Two tough gaunt horrid looking nags, their hair standing on end all over, hitched to a long deep box like a coffin on wheels, with a high seat in front. *Me* driving—"wh-ha-huddup"—Thus I left Cheyenne. Besides the provisions I had with me a drunk man and his wife, and an Indian girl. The drunk man belonged to the team somehow, and the wife and the Indian girl belonged, I suppose to the man. All I know about the matter was that I was to take the inanimate portion of the freight to a certain point, and then leave the animates to take care of themselves and the team.

We started off in the evening at a jolly pace and were soon encompassed by the bare dreary melancholy plains, partially snow clad, and looking like vast winding sheet considerably ripped—crawling over the heights, driving into the hollows, bumping into unexpected prairie dog holes, and passing innumerable dead mules, which appeared to be laid down at regular intervals, like milestones.

I will not tell you—for I fear Mate's ridicule of my horsemanship—what mishaps occasionally befel—how often our team got stuck in the treacherous hollows full of snow—how the two Rozinantes paced it till they foamed again—how the old wagon tossed like a ship at sea, till Minnehaha's teeth chattered, and the inebriate rolled about promiscously among flour sacks, loaves, hams and tin pans. By the aid of the good woman—who pointed out the way, I reached my destination sometime after dark.

"Childe Roland to the dark tower came". It was a dilapedated looking hut half log, half mud, hard by a little creek on the face of a windy slope. A pair of shaggy beings crept out of the dismal habitation and welcomed me (with the provisions) to their "ranch". So here I abode for two days and nights. The furniture of the cabin consisted of an old anvil and some barrels with the ends out, to sit upon. In the middle of the floor, which was a kind of rolling prairie, were a few Buffalo robes and blankets to sleep in, while at one corner was a sheet iron portable stove where we did our cooking. We had good ventilation, for one end of the hut had never been quite finished. For the privilege of inhabiting this dwelling my friends paid one dollar per day to the owner.

On the second morning while the occupants were out looking for antelope and I was attending to the coffee pot, an excited individual rushed in upon me and without ceremony commenced to detail his domestic history. He had just escaped from Cheyenne where the police were chasing him. He informed me how his wife after six years marriage, had gone off with another, how he had attempted to kill her and the other, how she had sworn her life against him, how he had but deferred vengeance by running away, and how he was nearly crazy, which I fully believed. Endeavered to console him by reminding him that a wife was but a woman after all and subject to violent changes like western weather.

Presently he drew forth a knife and asked me to look at it. I did so. "Now look here" he said "You are going back to Cheyenne. You go to that woman and tell her, the very first time I see her I will send this to her heart so help me, will you do it?" I said I would be delighted. "Now then can you write?" Yes "Then I will dictate some letters". I produced paper and pencil and he dictated four letters; one to the wife's brother and three others. The most insane compositions I ever penned. And you may be sure they lost nothing in going through my hands. That done I began to have my doubts whether this crazy husband might not take a fancy to cut me off in the flower of my youth. So I told him privately that our *boss* who was just coming over the hill there, was the Captain of the Vigilantes and would hang him if he knew of these threats. Whereupon the man decamped. On reaching Cheyenne again I found that his story was true, but I did not deliver the message—That was not a very romantic adventure but it is not my fault.

One thing more. My letter would surely be incomplete without some mention of your old friend and favorite the flute. It was an old request that I should never fail to bring my flute with me when I called, and I have not forgotten it. It is still my constant companion, but a mute one, for I never ask it to talk. Indeed I wish I had left the poor thing at home. The howling wilderness is not congenial, and I believe it sighs and moans in secret, pinning for the land of the dead. Not that music is altogether despised and rejected in Cheyenne. There is a fiddle scraping and drumming and organ grinding enough to furnish a small Babel. The strains are by no means of an Arplic character—not the tones of Apollo's lyre which built the towers of Ilion, but rather suggestive of the Ramshorns which blew down the walls of Jericho.

The other day I took out the flute to give it an airing when the leader of a band happened to see it. On hearing its tones he immediately offered me an engagement to play at a concert hall at seven dollars a night and seemed offended when I declined the offer. Yet that was a fair opportunity to convert musical notes into greenbacks.

As soon as the snow melts I depart for the Sweetwater region where I have a little project in hand. Meanwhile I am exploring Cheyenne, familiarising myself with the leading personages, and quietly pulling wires—uncertain as yet, however, whether there is a bell to ring at the other end. The great objection to this spot is the extravagant price of living. Omaha was bad enough but this is a degree worse. When we get out we must live by the rifle. Probably I shall write a few letters on Sweetwater to the Tribune in a few weeks. I mailed one the other day regarding certain disturbances here, but whether it ever reached I know not, and care less.

It may be a bit of news to Mate that I met an acquaintance of hers the other day—Mr. Mankham who went on to Colorado. And by the way there is an old friend of hers living here—the fat woman from the museum.* At least she was an acquaintance of mine. It makes me sigh to look at her, for then I think of matinees, and sunshiny days, paper collars, and a clean shave, and such things are affecting.

But enough now, and more than enough I fear. There is a limit to human patience, and I think I have taxed yours sufficiently for once. And since I have written so much to the "girls" let me not forget the boys. I desire you will present my good wishes to them all, to Mr. Garrison, Green,

---

* Probably a reference to the fat woman at Wood's Museum (see page 12).

Southworth, McCarthy, and Murray. With this I bid you adieu till we meet again.

Respectfully
James Chisholm [8]

Assuming that "the happy family at 65 Park Avenue"—or one member of it, at least—had been keeping an eagle eye on the columns of the *Tribune,* a story with the dateline "Cheyenne, D. T., March 26" surely would not have passed unnoticed. Signed "Western," it appeared in the *Tribune* on April 3, and bore out much of what Jim said in his letter.*

> Cheyenne may almost be called one of the wonders of the world. Its growth has been rapid. Last July there was not a house here; now they can be numbered by hundreds, and its inhabitants by thousands, although there is undoubtedly a large floating population.
>
> The town site was first located by Engineer Brown, of the Union Pacific Railroad, who was shortly after killed by Indians near the town.
>
> The first building was erected on the 27th of July, 1867, and at this date the population is said to exceed five thousand. It is situated on the Union Pacific Railroad, 517 miles west of Omaha and 527 miles east of Salt Lake City, 110 miles north of Denver and 85 miles south of Fort Laramie. Fort D. A. Russell is about two miles northwest of the city and is garrisoned by about 1,100 troops under the command of General J. D. Stevesen. The fort is situated on Crow Creek, which runs through the city. The United States Arsenal will be built at the fort this summer. Cheyenne is located at the eastern base of the Laramie Mountains, or Black Hills, at an elevation of 6,000 feet above the sea level. The Union Pacific Railroad Company, it is said, expect to em-

---

* Since the correspondent states that "it is only four years since I walked from Atchison to Denver, and it took me twenty-three weary days," the account could not have been written by James Chisholm.

ploy 5,000 men on their works in this city during the coming summer.

The floating population, as you may suppose, is decidedly "mixed," consisting of miners, mule drivers, "bullwhackers," Gamblers, and a sprinkling of Eastern men on their way to the mines. The former class are a rough, noisy set, who can throw themselves outside of more whiskey than you can imagine.

Our amusements are varied and entertaining. We have a museum, theatre, dance houses, gambling halls, dog fights and man fights—the latter very prevelent, and I think closely allied to the former. Two hundred of the "fair, but frail," persuasion occupy quarters here. Take it all in all, it is a very gay place.

The "Vigilants" are still at work. Two men were hung in the streets a week ago. Street fights are almost of daily occurrence. Four men have been shot within six days.

There is a great deal of excitement at present in regard to the Sweetwater mines, about two hundred miles northwest of here. We are constantly receiving almost fabulous news concerning their richness. There will be a big rush for that point as soon as the season opens. The Sweetwater mines are all, or nearly all, confined to goldbearing leads, and those who go to that country in search of mines will find that, by obtaining possession of good leads and thoroughly developing them, they will always find a ready demand and good prices for their property, and fortunes will be made again in that country as they have been in others. The railway will be near this locality next fall, and machinery and provisions will be delivered at low costs, and no doubt exists that in another year Sweetwater will be one of the most extensive mining districts in the United States. The telegraph company will extend their wire to South Pass City, Sweetwater district, this spring.

IV

SWEETWATER BRIEFING

"As soon as the snow melts," Jim had written, "I depart for the Sweetwater where I have a little project in hand." Though no doubt they would have expressed themselves differently, similar intentions might have been voiced by a goodly percentage of Cheyenne's male inhabitants. "A large number of trains are fitting to go to the Sweet Water mines," it was reported from Cheyenne via Denver on March 28. "Several trains start on April 1st." [1] *Weather permitting*, the despatch should have added—the gold rush season was to be a little late that year. In fact, as late as May 5 the Union Pacific Express was snowbound six miles east of Cheyenne.[2]

Impatient though he might be to get under way on his "little project," Jim at least could make use of the delay to brief himself about developments on the Sweetwater to date. He would have found no lack of informants: at the mere mention of the word *Sweetwater*, every public place for loafing or entertainment would sprout a panel of experts, self-styled and genuine. The problem was to separate the wheat from the chaff, the firsthand from the rumored, to distinguish between the true tale and the yarn—not always easy in a land of natural wonders that strained credibility, and where men, simply in order to survive, routinely lived through adventures that might have fazed mythological heroes. It was a land famed, too, for tall tales and veteran tale-tellers, and as that traditional target, the tenderfoot from the East, Jim must have found that the drinks were on him a good many times.

Another clearing house for rumor and report was the press of the region. In Cheyenne there were the *Argus* and the *Leader*, and Jim also must have been acquainted with the itinerant papers: the *Sweetwater Mines*, then being published at Fort Bridger, and the *Frontier Index*, the "press on wheels" which came west with the railroad and which in April 1868 emanated from Laramie after a stand at Fort Sanders, D. T.[3]

A useful background piece on the gold fields at South Pass was reprinted in the Cheyenne *Leader* (March 11, 1868). It had appeared originally in the March 7 *Sweetwater Mines* and was passed along to "our readers, so that they may in time of peace prepare for war. The *Mines* is the advocate of the mines right along! and its editors will leave no stone unturned to attract to that 'summer resort' this season, many millions of inhabitants. Here is what they say about mines and things . . . ."

THE SWEETWATER COUNTRY.

Having had brought to our notice many erroneous and, in some instances, highly romantic ac-

counts of the first discoveries of gold in the
Sweetwater country (that are now going the
rounds of the press), we think it advisable to lay
before our readers a condensed and reliable history
of the first discoveries and the subsequent excitement in relation to them.

Ever since 1849, when the first overland emigration to California set in, rumors have from time to
time reached the ear of the mining public of a remarkable rich mineral belt lying somewhere in the
Wind River range of mountains, to the east of what
is known as the South Pass, on the old emigrant
overland route.* Trappers, Indians, and others,
have at different times, since the period above indicated, brought into the settlements specimens of
gold and gold-bearing quartz, which they stated
were picked up in the section of country watered
by the Sweetwater and its tributaries; and small
parties of prospectors have occasionally ventured
a trip into that region to hunt up the locality of
the new Eldorado, but in almost every instance
they were driven out by the Indians before fully
determining the truth or falsity of the rumors.
Some few went in that never came out, having had
their hair raised by "Sherman's pets" and induced
by them to take up a *quiet* residence there.

In 1864 some parties went in and commenced
mining on Willow Creek, near what is now South
Pass City, but were, like those who had preceded
them, driven out by the Indians, leaving behind
them evidences of their work in the shape of some
cabins and small prospect holes.

In June, 1867, a party consisting of Redell, Harris
B. Hubbell, Joshua Terry, and a few others went
in and discovered the now far-famed Caresa
[Carissa] Ledge, situated about one half mile north-
east of Willow Creek and 15 miles northeast of
Pacific Springs on the South Pass emigrant road.

* Actually, gold was first reported in this region in 1842. See
"South Pass Gold Fields," page 216.

These gentlemen hastily threw up a log cabin, lining it on the outside with turf, as a protection against Indians, and commenced pounding out the gold in their rock. . . .

During Jim's first week in Cheyenne, the *Mines* published a letter from its correspondent at South Pass City, the first of the towns to spring up in the gold fields. Located a half mile below the Carissa mine, it came into being during the summer of 1867, following the Carissa strike. By October a number of substantial cabins had gone up, and on December 27 it was designated by the Dakota Legislature as the county seat of the recently organized Carter County.

SOUTH PASS CITY,
March 16th, 1868.

EDITOR SWEETWATER MINES:—I do not deem it necessary at this time, to speak of the extent or richness of our mineral veins. That we have them of extraordinary value both in gold and silver is now, I believe, a well established fact. There have been several ledges discoverd since my last letter . . . all of them pronounced well defined, rich ledges. This city will soon take rank among the magic cities of the West. A number of commodious buildings are already up, awaiting the finishing touch of the painter before being occupied. Billy Wilson's hotel and saloon are nearly ready to receive the public. . . . Lightburn & Co.'s large store is nearly finished, as is also the warehouse of Joseph Marion, besides many other buildings of less dimensions.

The correspondent then commented on the weather—he spoke of several men who were nearly snow-blind after breaking road in the vicinity of Oregon Springs—and gave "a table of distances or rather time occupied at this season of the year in making the trip" from Granger's (near Green River) to South Pass City. "As you will perceive, it takes about eleven days . . . when the same distance can, and has been made, in the summer season, by loaded wagons inside of three days." [4]

More word about the effect of weather on mining came in a Cheyenne *Leader* story of April 1, derived "from a private letter, dated South Pass City, March 7th."

I may not be able to forward this for several days, owing to the severity of the weather; the expressman, for aught we know, being laid up on his way in here, but we are generally looking for a "break up" of winter soon.* *

As for prospecting for placers [mines where gold could be obtained by washing], there are two things at present which interfere with it. One is the total absence of gum boots, without which it is almost impossible to do any work, and another is that the weather will hardly admit of it. So far as Rock Creek has been prospected, it is believed to be ten to twenty dollar diggings, and extensive; pay dirt being supposed to extend for fifteen miles in length on that stream.

Sufficient gold has been taken from the Atlantic gulch to satisfy the discoverers, that it will pay from ten to twenty-five dollars per day. . . . There are several other gulches that are supposed to be good, while there are three gulches which were discovered before I came in last fall, that are good and no mistake.

As for quartz, judging from what men of experience say, we have one of the richest camps that has ever been discovered. The country is as yet unprospected, and hundreds of ledges lay untouched, which bear every evidence of being equally as good as any of those which have been located. The belt in which these leads exist, is about fifteen miles in width; length unknown. . . .

I do not tell these things through excitement, nor to excite you, but I think there is no chance for this country to prove a "bilk." Should the placer

diggings not turn out good, it will be a year or two
before there is much money in circulation here;
during which time many that come here with the
expectation of making a fortune in a single night,
will go away disappointed and damning the country, while those who remain and do what they may
will undoubtedly prosper. This (South Pass) city
has many resources besides gold and silver. . . .

A somewhat fruitier communication, evoked by the vex-
ing question of adequate mail service, appeared in the
"Local Matters" column of the *Mines* on March 28. During
the course of a long and mellifluous letter to the editor, the
Special Agent of the Post Office Department at Salt Lake
City, Jno. W. Clampitt, saw fit to quote in full a letter he
had addressed to the Postmaster General, with the object of
securing a post office at South Pass City.

. . . South Pass City is situated within eighteen
miles of the South Pass of the Rocky Mountains,
and distant from Cheyenne, D. T., two hundred
and fifty miles, and from Fort Bridger one hundred and forty miles, which are the nearest points
for Postal facilities. It has a population today of one
thousand *bona fide* residents, who have laid off the
town in streets and squares and erected a large
number of houses. . . . At present their only communication is by a private express—the cost of a
single letter being not less than one dollar. The
population of South Pass City in one or two months
from the present date will be at least three thousand, and judging from other reports presumed to
be reliable by 4th of July next [1868], there will
be a population of ten thousand persons to cele-
brate, at that point, the nation's anniversary. Miners, merchants, lawyers, physicians, sons of toil and
the hardy pioneer, who, amid storms and snow,
and the wilds of unbroken nature, part the way to
a civilization that reflects honor upon our race and
land—are flocking thither. From the El Dorado

upon the Pacific, the Sierras of Nevada, from
Idaho, Montana, Utah and Colorado, they are
"marching on" to Wyoming. The cause of this
emigration is that . . . a gold mining country has
been discovered . . . near the South Pass, which,
from reliable report, is unsurpassed in richness by
any gold region on the continent. . . . Independent
of the rich bearing quartz ledges, there is another
source of wealth. . . . I allude to agriculture. This
section of country contains some of the finest and
richest agricultural valleys. . . . The fertility of the
soil is such, watered by pure mountain streams,
that in a short period, it will yield in return for the
labors of the farmer, a rich harvest. . . . As soon as
the spring dawns, Wells Fargo & Co. will place a
line of stages from the end of the Railroad to South
Pass City and from thence to connect at Hams
Fork with the great overland route, over which
the United States Mails are now being trans-
ported. . . .

Possibly as a result of this outburst of organ music from
his Special Agent, Postmaster General A. W. Randall
shortly called "for bids for a weekly and tri-weekly postal
service between Fort Bridger and South Pass City, D. T.,"
according to the April 15 *Sweetwater Mines*. The same issue reported that

☞ A new city [Atlantic City] has recently been
laid out on the north side of Rock Creek, distant
4½ miles northwest of South Pass City. There are
already several buildings up, including one store,
and many more in course of erection. The town
site is eligibly situated, and located nearly in the
centre of the mining districts. It was laid out by
Messrs. Tozer, Collins, Thompson, and others,
who are confident that it will become the metropolis of the Sweetwater country.

Although snow was still on the ground in mid-May, reports from South Pass City began to take on a somewhat

brisker, more businesslike tone. But—perhaps owing to "cabin fever"—a few sour notes could be discerned. A Mr. W. G. Smith, returning from the Sweetwater, stated that

☛ There are now congregated in the new mining region, between three and four thousand people. But few goods have yet arrived, and provisions are high, flour $30 per cwt., bacon 50c, sugar and coffee 75c, etc. There are some eight or ten buildings partially completed at South Pass City, and the chief occupation of those there consists in the endeavor to sell lots or quartz lodes to the new comers. The Nye Forwarding Co.'s teams, bound for Sweetwater, had taken the Sage Creek road, and were encountering much hardship for lack of water. Travelers will do well to avoid this route, as there is a single stretch of seventy-five miles destitute of water on this road. . . .[5]

SOUTH PASS CITY, D. T. }
May 15, 1868. }

. . . This should have been named the City of Rumors; . . . Every day there is a new report and excitement about "placers," and everybody, as in duty bound, "rushes," but thus far no surface diggings of importance have been found. We are daily looking for the entrance of Wells, Fargo & Co.'s coaches; and from all accounts we are led to believe the line will be transferred to this road by next week, at the farthest. This city is located on the bank of a little stream the marshy banks of which are lined with willows which are looking tolerably well now, but during the winter and early spring they flung their bare, lean, crooked, skeleton branches about in a manner that was shockingly repulsive. This city is neither very attractive itself, nor has its location any extraordinary natural beauties; "but the quartz is good," as

every old settler says to every new comer. . . .
Everybody insists placer diggings will be discovered, and if hard work and enterprising prospecting
does any good they may be found at any moment.
Strangely enough, everybody is excited about them,
and I believe half the men in the camp sleep with
their blankets tied in a roll on their backs, and their
coffee-pot in one hand and a tin cup in the other,
so as to be ready to jump up and run at the first
whisper of a new thing being struck.

There are not many goods here yet, but plenty
are expected. At present Mr. John McGlinchey
has the only store of any consequence, and he is
doing a remarkably good business. Flour is now
held at $35 per cwt. and is scarce at that. Owing
to the high price of lumber, $135 per thousand de-
livered, and difficult to get, owing to the snow and
trifling character of the saw mill—only one in the
county—building has not progressed very rapidly.
. . . When the snow disappears, we expect many
changes in everything. At present it is almost impossible to get about.

. . . Everybody thinks this will be a good camp
for the next ten years, but of course that is only
conjecture at present. Large numbers of miners
continue to come in from the west. Most of them
think well of this country, and, as is always the
case, some say its a dead beat, and leave at once
without knowing much about it. . . .[6]

An earlier item referring to the second great strike of the
preceding year, the Miner's Delight, also concerned a man
whom Jim eventually came to know well.

☞ Among the Californians who may be said to
have "struck it rich" here, is Major Patrick Gallagher, formerly of the California Volunteers. The
Major is largely interested in the "Miners Delight"
ledge, in the California District, and there is no
discount on the richness of the vein. The ledge was
located last September by Frank McGovern and

others, and has turned out some of the richest gold specimens yet obtained in this section of the country. The vein is about two feet wide, and, to use a miner's phrase, is "lousy" with gold. Major Gallagher bought into the claim, and has made arrangements to have a mill erected as soon as the weather and roads will permit. When their mill gets under way, you will be apt to hear of the Miners Delight often.[7]

Miner's Delight was the locale of the third of the three South Pass towns, which was founded sometime during these late spring months. Located on Spring Gulch seven hundred feet below Miner's Delight, it originally was given the same name but soon was rechristened Hamilton City. By early summer, according to the *Sweetwater Mines* (now being published at South Pass City), the new town was "growing apace."

> . . . some thirty buildings are up, and more in course of construction. Spring Gulch is turning out the bright ore in very comfortable quantities and more dust can be seen there, and in the two adjacent gulches, Yankee and Meadow, than in any other locality in the Sweetwater country. Ten companies are at work in Spring Gulch . . . and all appear content with the result of their labors. In answer to our enquiries, most of them assured us that they could make $100 per *diem* to each hand, if they had 250 inches of water to wash with. Before another season rolls around an abundance of water will be brought in when we prophesy the yield of gold will astonish all tender-foot-dom.[8]

But before the summer's end the Sweetwater mines had been labelled a humbug, and when Jim visited the mining camps in September the South Pass gold rush was already a thing of the past.

V

WHERE WAS JIM?

FOR REASONS WHICH PROBABLY never will be known, James Chisholm did not carry out his plan to go from Cheyenne to the gold fields as soon as he was able to get through. The sole concrete clues to his whereabouts between March 27, when he wrote Mrs. Garrison that he was intending to visit the Sweetwater country, and September 7, when he left Green River for South Pass City, are passing remarks in the journal he began on the latter date. From it, we know that in the five months which had passed since his arrival in Wyoming he had become tolerably familiar with "the roaring hells of railroad towns," and he had had "so much of camp life" crossing the plains from Laramie to Green River that it gave him "a kind of seasickness to resume it."

The fact that a letter mailed in Chicago toward the end

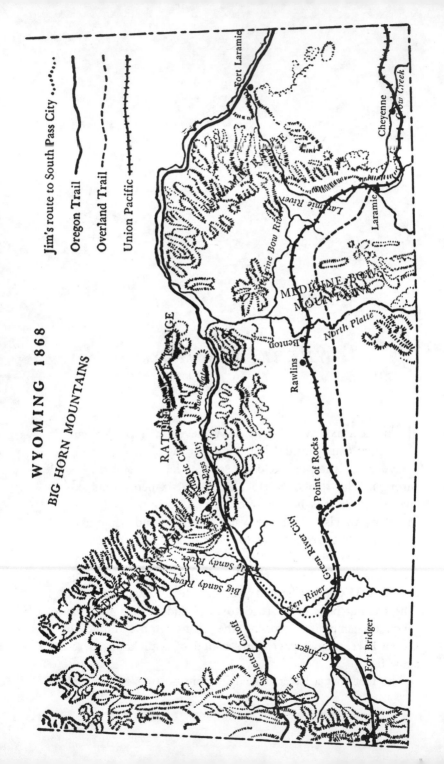

of June did not reach Jim until October suggests that he had no definite itinerary.[1] His eldest brother, John, was a miner in the Salt Lake City area, but if Jim visited him it was not during the months in question.[2] The one reference to James Chisholm that can be found in the Wyoming papers says of his activities only that he had "spent the entire summer in the territory."[3]

In the Chicago *Tribune*—nothing.

Frustrating though it may be to those tracing Jim's Wyoming career, there is nothing to wonder at in his being lost to sight amid the large, ever-shifting, transient population in the boiling turmoil of towns along the Union Pacific right-of-way. Laramie, short-lived Benton, Rawlins, Green River, Evanston, all came into being between the time of Jim's arrival in Cheyenne and his departure for the east, each town marking a stage in the westward progress of the railroad. Grading crews which might number as many as 10,000 men requiring 300 freighters to carry supplies, 400 to 500 track-layers, and a floating population of gamblers, saloon-keepers, prostitutes, and sharpers of all kinds moved along with the rail construction. At the same time, gold prospectors bound for the Sweetwater or the Big Horn Buttes (where a strike had been rumored in April) and new settlers, lured by accounts of cheap land and the new towns so glowingly described in railroad brochures, streamed into the region, adding to the ebb and flow of population.

On May 10 the first train reached Laramie; in July the Platte was bridged at Brownsville, a town soon completely deserted for the next end-of-track, Benton. Described by C. G. Coutant in his *History of Wyoming* as "the one bad town along the line of the Union Pacific," Benton

> at once took high rank as a saloon, gambling and sporting town. In two or three days it had from 1,000 to 1,500 inhabitants, and there being no such

thing as law and order the rough element ran things to suit themselves. Murder was an every day occurence and peaceably disposed people soon learned that protesting against violence was something that would not be tolerated by those in control of affairs. . . . Prize fighting and all that goes with it was patronized, and the place became the rendezvous of outlaws of every description. It was a city of portable houses and tents stretched over wood frames (pp. 614-615).

A report from Benton, with an August 9 dateline, characteristically opens with an account of the "excitement created in this city last night by the shooting of a man in a private row," but devotes much more space to complaint about the alkali dust that has caused

a number of our citizens to move on to Green River. This alkali is almost as fine as flour, and it lies to a depth of about four inches on the level. Owing to the wind which blows here continually, it is a circulating medium of the most marked character. . . . Many here are bleeding at the lungs from inhaling the alkali, which . . . permeates [us] to such an extent as would lead any person to believe that by swallowing a small amount of tartaric acid we would all be brought to a state of effervescence, and the community of Benton, in the new Territory of Wyoming would resemble one immense foaming seidlitz powder. . . .*

The track is making tracks across the trackless waste towards Green River at a rapid rate. Moonlight nights and Sundays are drafted into service for extra hours whenever the material is on hand in sufficient quantities to keep the men at work. Towns along the road from Laramie west are engaged in a game of leap frog. From Big Laramie to

---

* The Wyoming Organic Act, creating Wyoming Territory, was signed by President Andrew Johnson on July 25, 1868.

> Little Laramie; from Little Laramie to Rock Creek;
> from Rock Creek to Carbon; from Carbon to Ben-
> ton; from Benton to Rolling Springs [Rawlins],
> where more shops are to be built; from there to
> Green River; and from Green River to Ham's
> Fork, Echo Canon, Weber, Salt Lake—anywhere
> at all so as to be going somewhere and taking one
> jump farther than the town which was the last in
> the lead. . . .[4]

On August 17, end-of-track was seventy miles west of
Benton amid what the correspondent called "the monotonous surroundings of Bridger's pass."

> The course of the railroad from Benton westerly
> is for some forty miles through slightly undulating
> country, with here and there low ridges . . . en-
> tirely destitute of timber, unless indeed you dignify
> the sage brush with the name of timber. As you
> near the point where the waters divide and a por-
> tion seeks the Atlantic and the rest the Pacific
> coast, the country assumes the appearance of an
> immense water shed plain, without mountainous
> peaks nearer than some twenty miles on either side
> of where the railroad crosses the summit. . . .
> The Casement Brothers are laying the track
> down a dry valley which is tributary to the famed
> Bitter creek, and they are now about twenty miles
> from that valley. . . . About three hundred and fifty
> men and sixty teams are employed in the construc-
> tion force, and they average four miles of work
> per day. . . .[5]

It could not have been too long after this was written that
Jim passed the end-of-track en route to Green River City,
which he reached in late August or early September 1868.
Staked out by H. M. Hook, first mayor of Cheyenne, in
July of that year, the town that Jim saw already had an
appearance of permanence: many substantial wood and

adobe buildings housed a population of about 2,000.* In August the *Frontier Index* had set up shop in Green River, and perhaps Jim stopped in to pay his respects.

It can be stated with certainty that at some point during his stay he made the acquaintance of A. L. Houghton, of the firm of Houghton and Cotter, dealers in miners' supplies, which built the first store in South Pass City. On September 7, in the company of Houghton—who probably was taking a load of merchandise to South Pass City—Jim left Green River on the last lap of his trip to the Sweetwater mines.

* The Union Pacific ignored the original town, and spanned the river when the railroad reached this point. Later the railroad company sold lots at the site of present Green River, across from what is now called "Old Town" on the eastern side of the stream, and made Green River a division point. According to word from Omaha in the October 5, 1868, Chicago *Tribune*, the railroad "was finished yesterday [October 2] to Green River, to which point passenger trains will commence running next week."

REFERENCE NOTES

1. THE STORY BREAKS

1. Chicago *Tribune*, July 21, 1867.
2. Chicago *Tribune*, July 24, 1867.
3. Chicago *Tribune*, July 30, 1867.
4. Chicago *Tribune*, July 31, 1867.
5. Chicago *Times*, November 15, 1867.
6. Chicago *Times*, November 22, 1867.
7. Chicago *Tribune*, November 28, 1867.
8. Chicago *Times*, December 19, 1867.
9. Chicago *Times*, December 27, 1867.

II. THE CORRESPONDENT

1. The preceding biographical information was derived from letters and interviews with Chisholm's daughter Myra (Mrs. George Carson Moon); from the Chicago *Tribune*, June 22, 1868, 4:5; and from Chapter VIII of Chisholm's journal (q.v.). All quotations are from Chapter VIII.
2. See Emmett Dedmon, *Fabulous Chicago* (New York: Random House, 1953), pp. 63-65; and Wayne Andrews, *Battle for Chicago* (New York: Harcourt, Brace and Company, 1956), pp. 47-55, 67-70.

3. Information on James Chisholm's courtship of Mary Garrison is derived from an unpublished account, "Jim's Romance," by Mrs. George Carson Moon.
4. Letter from James Chisholm to his daughter Myra (Mrs. George Carson Moon), undated, but probably written in the late 1890's. See page 226.
5. See page 147.

III. CHEYENNE

1. Grenville M. Dodge, *How We Built the Union Pacific Railway and Other Papers and Addresses* (Council Bluffs: The Monarch Printing Co., 1910), p. 23.
2. Chicago *Tribune*, March 27, 1868.
3. Cheyenne *Daily Evening Leader*, March 21, 1868. The text of the story is given in full on pages 208-209.
4. Cheyenne *Daily Evening Leader*, March 23, 1868.
5. Letter of March 27, 1868, to Mrs. Andrew Garrison. Unless otherwise specified, the quotations which follow are from this letter.
6. Chicago *Tribune*, April 3, 1868. 2:7.
7. Schedule in the Cheyenne *Daily Evening Leader*, March 6, 1868.
8. The opening passages of the letter are given on pages 224-225.

IV. SWEETWATER BRIEFING

1. Chicago *Times*, March 31, 1868. 1:5.
2. Cheyenne *Daily Evening Leader*, May 7, 1868.
3. For a note on the *Sweetwater Mines* and the *Frontier Index*, see "The Peripatetic Press," pages 234-235.
4. *Sweetwater Mines*, March 25, 1868.
5. Cheyenne *Daily Evening Leader*, May 21, 1868.
6. Cheyenne *Daily Evening Leader*, May 23, 1868.
7. *Sweetwater Mines*, April 1, 1868.
8. *Sweetwater Mines*, July 3, 1868.

v. WHERE WAS JIM?

1. See page 162.
2. See page 147.
3. See page 200.
4. Cheyenne *Daily Evening Leader*, August 10, 1868.
5. Cheyenne *Daily Evening Leader*, August 19, 1868.

PART II

THE JOURNAL

The transcription which follows is the complete text of James Chisholm's journal except for two lost pages. Descriptive headings which Chisholm placed on each page for approximately two-thirds of the journal are listed at the end of the Supplementary Notes.

The dashes and blanks here and there in the text do not indicate editorial deletions; they appear thus in the original. Obvious omissions in punctuation—closing quotation marks, commas, periods—have been supplied and the entries have been paragraphed, but otherwise the text remains unchanged. Chapter divisions and titles have been added. All other editorial additions are indicated by brackets.

A note on the dating of the entries is given on page 233.

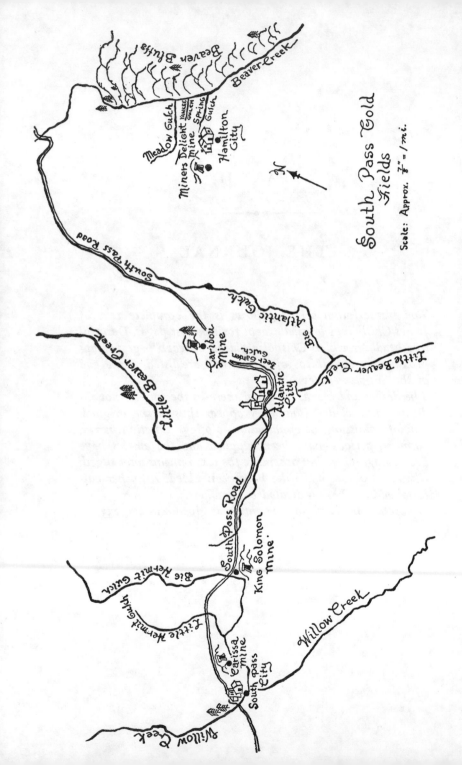

South Pass Gold Fields

Scale: Approx. ½" = 1 mi.

PENCILLING BY THE WAY. KING SOLOMON MINE.

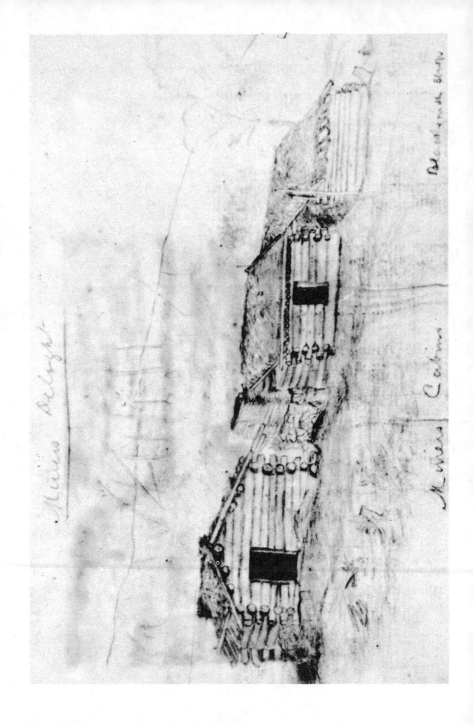

MINER'S DELIGHT: MINERS' CABINS.

MINER'S DELIGHT: SOCIETY WOMAN

the Dutchman in a fix

THE DUTCHMAN IN A FIX

Mountain Bill (Dutch Bill)

Bill Rhodes

MOUNTAIN BILL RHODES

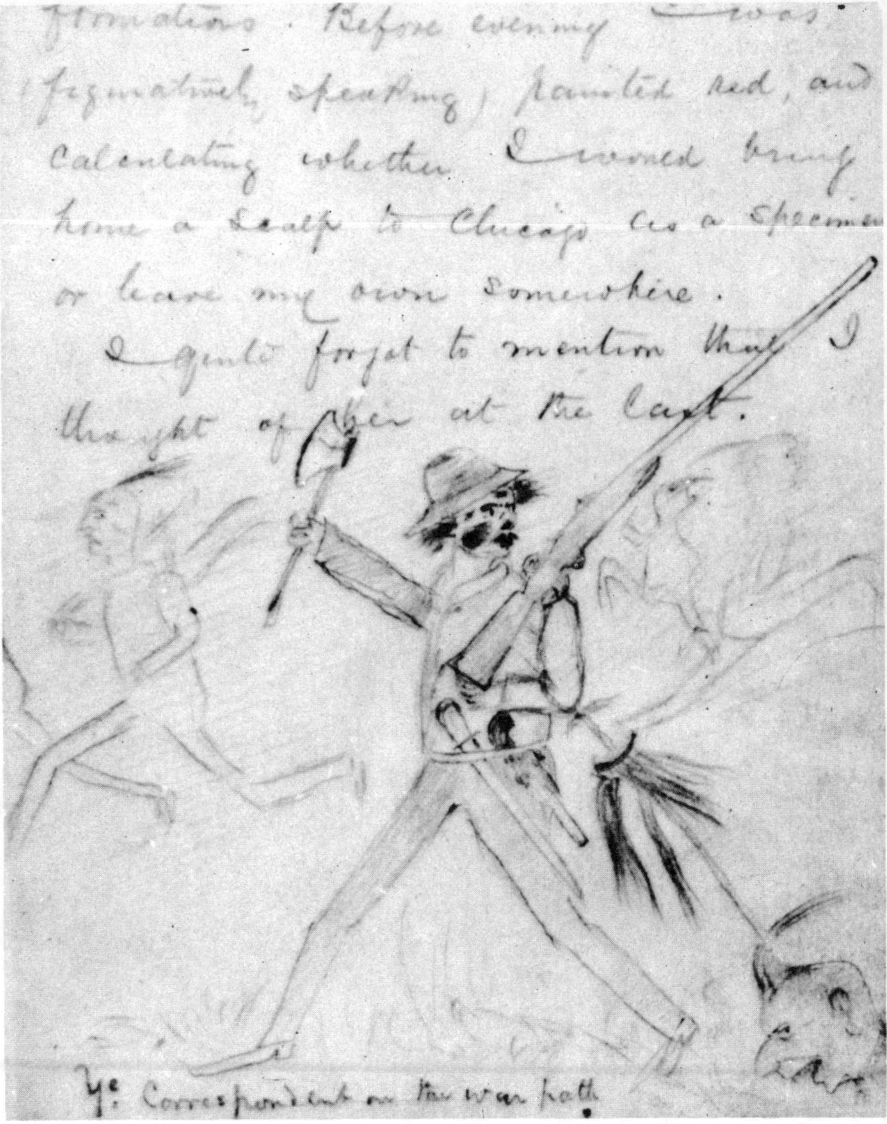

YE CORRESPONDENT ON THE WAR PATH

I

GREEN RIVER TO SOUTH PASS

1868—September 8th

LEFT GREEN RIVER FOR SOUTH PASS in company with A. L.
Houghton with a light spring wagon and two ponies,
a third pony being attached to the rear. A rather trouble-
some appendage he proved for the first few miles, and as he
caught all the dust in his white bald face, he looked a very
sorry spectacle indeed.

The flourishing city of Green River is soon out of sight
and we face the wilderness of hills which stretch away to
the Northward. Our path keeps the river in view all the way
although it makes wild deviations round slopes of the hills,
now running by the face of tall cliffs whose white sides rise
up like the wall of a house till their giddy summits seem to

be brushed by the downy white clouds that sail over them, now through narrow, rocky passes, and again over the bare hills and down into dry hollows. The river gleams upon our sight at intervals as it comes down in serpentine curves amid the hills and, although the scenery along its banks is mostly of a barren description, there are occasional patches of timber in the bottoms, and some islands "with verdure clad." This road to Sweetwater might be greatly shortened, but at an immense outlay.

We passed major grading work where they are cutting into the face of the rock by the river side, and the progress of their work was announced by several successive thunder-claps accompanied by eruptions of rocks which fell in spray to earth again. Further up the valley to the westward was Tom Malloy's camp—a considerable settlement.[1]

Another bend of our crooked road sweeps all the railroading and other signs and sounds of human life out of our sight and hearing. My companion proceeds to entertain me by an account of the luckless adventure of Bill Rose who was killed the other day at South Pass by the Indians. Bill was slightly bald on the top of the head; so for a trophy the Indians had to cut off his side hair and one ear. They cut out the sinews of his arms which they use for tying the steel heads to their arrows, and they cut out the sinews of

1. The railroad construction camp. Progress of the work in the vicinity of Green River was reported by the *Frontier Index*. On August 28, the editor wrote: "In returning from Bryan, the other day, we called at the camp of Tom Maloy, contractor, and from this conversation we were led to believe that the heavy work along and through the bluffs, intervening between here and Bryan will be completed and the track laid, in forty days time. Maloy is working double sets of hands, and blasts are sent off every hour of the day and night." On September 11: "Mr. Thos. Maloy has just returned from the east with reinforcement of men for his heavy work in the rock cuts across the river. Mr. Maloy informs us that he expects to have his grading ready for the ties in thirty days' time." On September 18: "Maloy has been reinforced by five hundred men armed with picks and drills, in support of the artillery blasts that are set off every hour of the week days, Sundays and nights in the bluffs on the west side of the river."

his back for bowstrings. In fact poor Bill seems to have been pretty much used up.

[Bill Rose was killed about August 9, 1868, in a running fight when he and three other men attempted to rescue a teamster, Dave Hayes, who had been wounded in an earlier skirmish with the Indians. They found Hayes dead and the Indians lying in wait for the rescue party. Rose and Hayes were buried together a few miles east of South Pass City (*Sweetwater Mines*, April 7, 1869). Rose, a part owner of the Empire State Mine, was one of the first county commissioners of Carter County, Dakota Territory; he was appointed by the Dakota Legislative Assembly on December 27, 1867. Previously, on December 18, he had been elected chairman and deputy recorder of the Pacific Mining District in the South Pass area.]

I have had so much of camp life lately that it gives me a kind of seasickness to resume it, but this trip is vastly different from that across the plains from Laramie. Here we meet no wagons loaded with merchandize,—come to no roadside ranches—we are all alone. Once, looking down by the foot of a slope, we discovered two Indian Tepees, while a few cattle dotted the side of the hill. Probably it was white men, many of whom have adopted the Indian habits of forming tents. A pleasant breeze was blowing in our faces all the way and soon the road descended toward the river again. We camped for the night in a grassy bottom where a few clumps of timber afforded a grateful shelter from the wind. Supped on a piece of cold beef, sardines, bread and tea, and went to sleep with the day.

September 9

Just about daybreak the clouds began to gather darkly overhead and we were awakened by the first, faint sprinkling of a coming shower upon our faces. This caused us to start up and exclaim "hello!" simultaneously. "I think we had better be moving," was the first proposition. "I think we had better get under that wagon" was the amendment, and finally a compromise was effected by hauling the wagon over us. This partially kept us from the rain, and we slept on till sunrise, then swallowed a hasty lunch and went on our way.

Turning from the river we once more entered the hills. The ascents were more gradual than heretofore and the road on the whole tolerably good. We were now about thirty miles from the town of G. R. and this was our point of departure from the river [2]—a long, dry ride before us, till we reach the first crossing of the Big Sandy, and over a series of desolate moors of whitish, clayey soil, covered with the sage brush—a chirping ground squirrel or a scudding rabbit here and there the only living thing to be seen.

Early in the day we encountered an Irishman from South Pass who had a great deal of fearful warning to give us regarding the Indians, and cautioned us against going on alone. Tom Carter (whom we expect to overtake) was up at Big Sandy, scared to go on, and a message had been sent for three men to come out and conduct him to South Pass. Thus comforted by Mike we examine our pistols and rifle and proceed. Nothing occurs to intercept our expedition, and we both make up our minds never to be afraid of Indians till we meet them.

After toiling over the hills for several hours we come to a kind of limit and the face of the country assumes a different aspect. Its monotony is broken by a group of grey rounded mounds of considerable height that seem to be composed of soft sandstone or clay, and generally rising

---

2. This would be below the old Lombard Ferry crossing of the Oregon Trail and south of the mouth of the Big Sandy. They probably struck the old stage road and followed along the north edge of the Bad Lands and Hills south of Big Sandy.

into cones like huge anthills, as if the rains had washed them into that shape. [The area known as Bad Land Hills, lying east of Green River and south of Big Sandy Creek.] The ground around their base is baked and polished into a hard whitish clay. Beyond these sand hills which occupy but a speck in the great lonely waste a broad level country stretches away as far as the eye can follow. To the Northward a line of high rocky cliffs is plainly visible, and beyond them all, at an immense distance—and scarcely distinguishable from the clouds—are the high, blue shadowy ranges of the Sweetwater Hills.[3] Afar off they seem to be in the realms of cloudland—an Eldorado in the sky, and many a poor pilgrim, no doubt, who travelled this very road last spring, built his airy edifice upon just such an exalted foundation.

Well, the excitement has all died away and Sweetwater has been voted by the unanimous voice of hundreds of disappointed bummers—a humbug. Still yonder it lies, waiting a proper inspection, waiting for capital and human energy to develop its resources. Sweetwater was not so much the humbug, however, as the inexperienced incapables who went there, with no money and no knowledge, the crowds of busted individuals who thought gold could be gathered like pebbles, the traders who brought goods to a market where nothing was to be had in exchange—they were the humbugs. That was the trouble. I am told that numbers came there who simply lay around the camp for a week drinking whisky and were too indolent even to look at the ledges—then departed, preaching humbug.

The apparent lack of good placer diggings drove back all the immigration and South Pass soon became a deserted camp. Yet from what I could learn from Major Lyon there

3. From this distance Chisholm probably saw the south end of the Wind River Range which rises to the highest elevation in the state of Wyoming at Gannett Peak, altitude 13,785. The Sweetwater Hills or Rocks were not yet in sight. The hills south of the Sweetwater River in the vicinity of South Pass are known as Oregon Buttes.

would appear to be rich gulch diggings, but poor men cannot reach them. Thirty men with, say, $1000 each to start with could make gulch digging pay handsomely. So much I gather by the way.

[Chisholm must have talked with Major Lyon, a geologist, only a few days before. According to the *Frontier Index* of September 8:

> Major Sydney S. Lyon, just in from South Pass City, informs us that the little six stamp mill there cleaned up $14,000 from last week's run of 103 tons of ore from the Miners Delight lead. The Major assures us that there are a number of other leads that will yield richly so soon as mills can be gotten up there. He thinks Sweetwater is to be the best camp in the mountains.

A previous item (August 21) reported that the Major was on his way to Sweetwater to investigate the mines, and would furnish the *Frontier Index* with a scientific report on the ledges in the vicinity of South Pass City. Editor Freeman stated that the Major was formerly of the State of Nevada, and had left the regular army for reasons of health.]

Night has almost fallen by the time we reach the first crossing of the Big Sandy. Being a good camping place we would remain there over night, but determine to push on to the second crossing—25 miles—for fear of a surprise by Indians; so we only want an hour or so here to rest and feed our horses.

The Sandy is a clear shallow stream running in a very sandy bed, and fordable almost at any point. In this green dell there is a fragment standing of an old stage station which was burnt by the Indians. Here too was the scene of an old Mormon raid.[4]

4. Chisholm is probably referring to the Mormon raid of October 1857 during which the raiders burned a U. S. Army supply of twenty-six wagons under command of Captain Lew Simpson. Although this

Houghton thinks he saw a Bar up the valley and goes after him with his gun. No Bar thar only a Jack Rabbit. The skies are threatening as we hitch up and the lightning is quivering on all sides of the horizon.

September 10th

Passed a fearful night—my young remembrance hath not its parallel.

As we left the crossing the wind began to blow from the East. The clouds gathered heavily and soon shut down over the heavens like a lid leaving not a gleam of light in the sky although it was hardly yet the hour of sunset. The rain pelted thick and fast in our faces, the thunder growled behind and around us, and the lightning grew more and more frequent. It was a dreary prospect, a ride of 25 miles in the night through such a storm as was evidently approaching, and over a dreary moor. But as well ride as sleep in it, we argued. Encountered a party of men, just at starting, bound for Green River, who had more precautionary yarns about Indians. "Darn the Indians," was the polite rejoinder.

Darker and darker it grew. Heavens, how dark! The road was straight and the ground even, or we could never have kept upon it. As it was we had to trust to luck pretty much. The darkness deepened into a midnight that was positively appalling. Martin's hells were nothing to it. Fast the road vanished from our sight—then the dim outline of the hills began to blend with the skies and soon [they] were indistinguishable. Our superfluous third horse we hitched to the

site has since been known as Simpson's Hollow, the actual location of Simpson's Hollow is on the old emigrant road about fifteen miles southwest of Big Sandy Stage Station.

Big Sandy Station at the crosssing of Big Sandy on the old Oregon Trail was destroyed by Indians when they attacked all stations in this area in 1862. It was at this time that the Overland Stage Company abandoned its route along the Oregon Trail and moved south to the Overland Trail.

other two in front, and they too became mere phantoms of horses. That part of the roan that was nearest to us preserved a kind of faint glimmer for a time, but that too *went out*. Still we went jogging onward through the blind darkness for an hour or so, lashed by the pelting rain and feeling that our path was getting more rugged.

The lightning had been playing around the horizon and we were enabled now and then to obtain a glimpse of the road. But now the storm broke in all its terror directly overhead as if ten thousand furies had been suddenly set loose. The lightning quivered madly through the black sky, and a terrific storm of hail came down—hail "like hens eggs" as one is accustomed to hear it described, but in reality as large as a man's thumb.

Both of us hastily threw a buffalo robe over our heads for protection, but at that instant the horses, maddened by the rattling shower of ice, took fright and went off at a frantic gallop through the bushes. It was impossible to check them and all our efforts were concentrated on keeping our seat. We must have gone in this mad dance for two miles, plunging through the murky blackness, and momentarily expecting a horrible dive into some ravine, when we at length succeeded in checking their flight. The hail storm had ceased, but the rain still continued to descend in torrents, and the lightning was growing more vivid. How to find the road again was a puzzle. We knew not which was East or West or South, and every step would lead us farther astray.

Houghton left me with the horses and went off through the soft, plashy clay to seek our lost path. Naturally he became lost in a few minutes, and there I sat for a weary time, powerless to act. Suddenly there was a glare of lightning more terrible than anything I ever saw. I shut my sight in dread, and when I opened my eyes again there was a still red glow before them. I looked up to the sky, down to the earth, and all round, and there was the same still fiery glow. I thought, now sure I am struck blind, what is to be done? I am struck by lightning—here's a pretty fix. Just then Houghton shouted to me to come on—he thought he had found a kind of road. I pushed forward in the direction of his voice, but just as I have felt in a nightmare, the horses, the more I urged them, seemed to be going backward with all their might. To test the reality of the thing I wheeled them round, and then the wagon seemed to be gliding sideways. Finally I sprung from the wagon, thoroughly alarmed, and called to Houghton to take the horses. He came up and as he approached very close I could just perceive his form, which gave me inexpressible relief.

As we mounted the wagon again a kind of rift opened in the clouds towards the horizon, and through it appeared a dull, hazy blurr of red fire. At first sight I took it to be some startling horror of a meteor, but it proved to be the Moon—a very ghastly looking satellite, which shed no ray of light. In a few minutes the clouds closed over it again. We had found out, however, by means of this apparition which was the East; so we turned the horses heads in the proper direction and went on.

Another hour or more of blind groping through the drenched bushes and we stopped again. The bronchos had run down a slope and came to a dead stand beside a creek which we traced into a kind of semi-circle. Again Houghton went off in search of a road, and this time he wandered for nearly an hour, which seemed a long night to me. The rain poured all the while with never a pause.

I whistled, shouted, and fired off my pistol to call him back, but no answer came, and an eerie feeling crept over me in spite of myself. All kinds of monstrous shapes seemed to be crowding round me in the gloom, the rain falling among the bushes sounded sometimes like running footsteps, and the distant cry of a bird or cayote was full of dread.

Then a dread of the Indians seized me. I thought my companion might have fallen into the hands of the savages and that made me afraid to make any noise again.

It was a blessed relief when I heard Houghton's voice shouting for guidance. He had been wandering around in circles without finding an indication of a path, and so we both threw up our hands and confessed ourselves beaten. There was nothing for it but to lay down under the wagon for the rest of the night. So we disposed ourselves the best way we could by rolling out our robes and blankets on the wet mud, tucked our heads well under, and, both being wearied out, we actually slept.

When we awoke the moon was shining through white, scudding clouds, and we were enabled to push on once more. We had to trace back the wheel tracks to the point whence we first diverged from the road, and by these means we succeeded, after much toil, in regaining the right road. On examining the bronchos we found one of them cut through the hair and slightly bleeding. Such was the size and force of some of these hail bullets.

We travelled on till daybreak when we came to the second crossing of the Big Sandy. Hard work to strike a fire from such damp materials, but we did it and boiled some tea which refreshed us exceedingly. After such a dreary night I thought the rising sun was a beautiful and cheerful sight. The poor animals found sweet refreshment in the green hollow. Birds were chirping in the willow bushes— everything looked fresher after the rain and the sky bespoke a pleasant day.

We made 65 miles yesterday not counting our mad witch dances on the blasted heath. From the Big Sandy to the Little Sandy is a drive of eight miles, and we are here now. Another ride of 15 miles will carry us on to the Dry Sandy. And now for a fresh start.

September 11th

At South Pass City—another such adventure as that of last night would in all probability prove one too many. I am suffering from a severe cold which I caught at Green River and the past two nights' experience has not improved it.

Leaving the Little Sandy, we had a pleasant drive over a road which for the most part was as smooth and level as a turnpike. The weather kept up dry and agreeably cool all day with the exception of a few trifling showers. Country mostly level or gently undulating, with here and there long, low, smooth hills. We seemed to be approaching very near to the Sweetwater hills,[5] but the road makes another wide sweep away from their direction and round by the foot of several minor ranges before it reaches them. Again a long, long stretch of smooth road and we camped at noon by a little well near the Dry Sandy.

Next we came to the Pacific Springs where I saw delightful patches of green grass.[6] We were now among the hills again. It was near sundown and the evening was unusually lovely. The sight of the grand old hills which were now not far off was truly sublime. The west looked stormy, and the sunset streamed in long rays of glory through their misty crags. Beyond the loftiest range, whose splintered summits are flecked with snow, I beheld the grandest perspective of high, rocky summits, towering aloft like the spires and domes of some great city of the gods, all bathed in a kind of dusky splendor. I think had I been alone the sublime

5. This would be either the Oregon Buttes or Wind River Range, rather than the "Sweetwater Hills."

6. Pacific Springs was a favorite camp site on the Oregon Trail. In 1860-1861 a Pony Express station which also served as a stage station on the first Overland Stage Route was located here. The springs lie three miles west of the Continental Divide at South Pass. South Pass City is approximately fifteen miles northeast of this point.

beauty of such a scene would have struck me with fear.

We did not pause long to look back upon this majestic sight, for the night was fast approaching and we hastened down the track that led us toward the Sweetwater river. We had ten miles yet to make and we were determined to make it if possible. Houghton dreaded, he said, to lay over at the river, much as the horses needed rest as that locality afforded a good ambush for Indians. After passing that point there was but little to fear. We soon came to the place.— A brisk run down the back of a long hill brought us to the valley, covered with long grass and thick with willow bushes. Through these we drove slowly and cautiously, peering anxiously on every side.

The Sweetwater comes down in a sleepy murmur over innumerable spreading shallows, and almost hidden by the bushes. We crossed the stream and began to ascend the hill, when "Baldy", our superfluous appendage, whom we had trained to run along ahead of our team, took a fancy to emancipate himself, and went off through the valley in the full enjoyment of glorious freedom and the grass. This annoying circumstance hindered us considerably. A long and toilsome climb of about two miles to the brow of the hill. Darkness was coming on again. The western sky was growing ominously black, and the clouds were trailing slowly over the heavens. The rain commenced to patter among the sage brush, mild at first, but slowly and surely increasing. A distant growl of thunder, then a flash of lightning.

It was plain we were in for another storm, and in fact we soon perceived to our dismay that we were likely to have a second rehearsal of the previous night's performance. Down drooped the vapors over the hills, the orchestra struck up its deafening notes, the rain hissed, and ere we had proceeded two miles from the valley, the same inky blackness that I have already described, overspread the earth. If possible it was even more impenetrable than before. I know of no superlatives that would convey any idea of it. There was no hail and no wind, but mercy on us, how the rain came down —not in fitful dashes, but one steady continuous torrent— rushing, pelting, hissing into our very bones.

We were rapidly drenched to the skin, and every blanket and robe in the wagon was soaking wet. The roan pony being a resident of South Pass, was pretty well acquainted with all the roads, so we entrusted him with unlimited powers, and entertained a blind hope that we might possibly reach our destination at some hour of the night. Whether he proved entirely worthy of our confidence I cannot say. Certainly he led us for some hours through strange ways, into many mudholes, and down a variety of steep places. All the while the deluge of rain never once abated. At length we crossed a stream and when we reached the other side the ponies came to a dead stand as if they had said "we give it up". A few inneffectual gropings satisfied us that we were astray again, so we abandoned all hope of reaching South Pass that night.

The situation was a most distressing one. Our horses were already half dead with fatigue and exposure. My limbs were stiff with cold, and the rain still came down in madening force. Such unqualified, unmitigated misery I never endured before. One might suffer such a trial with some degree of patience if he has the prospect of a bright fire and a warm supper ahead. But we had no such hope before us then, and it was with a chilly feeling as if I was digging my grave that I wrapped myself, all soaked with the rain, in a wet blanket and lay down under the wagon on the wet ground. Houghton did the same, and we lay there for two hours in a kind of stupor—I could not call it sleep.

Although I endeavored to accept the situation as cheerfully as possible, I began to entertain grave apprehensions as to the results of this kind of tampering with my constitution. The strangest fancies crowded into my mind as I lay in my slushy bed, which a physician might have called the first symptoms of Delirium Tremens. Hideous witch faces, goblin faces, corpses, and all unimaginable shapes of monstrous beasts, became distinctly present to my vision. Strangely too, an endless crowd of faces of long forgotten acquaintances, contorted into ghastly expressions, seemed to pass before me. I was sure I was not asleep, for all the while I could hear the horses breathing and slobbering by the wagon, and yet I must have dozed considerably.

Houghton started up at last saying he would be dead if he lay there longer. The rain was over and there was now a faint greyish light sufficient to show the way. We both crept out of our blankets utterly wretched and shivering and stiff, and hitched up the ponies, resumed the journey.

We had been travelling very nearly in the right direction, and in an hour we at last found ourselves descending a steep place into South Pass City. It is a deserted village at the best, but at that hour of the morning it looked as still as a churchyard. It consists of two streets in the form of the letter T and lies in a kind of ravine between two hills—altogether a snug, sheltered nook. There we found a roof to cover us, a good warm cup of tea, a glass of whisky, and a roaring fire by the side of which I slept in dry Buffalo robes and dreamed that I dwelt in marble halls.

I have not moved out of doors all day hoping to cure my cold. I had it before I left Green River and put it out at interest among the hills, yet I must confess, to my surprise, that my original stock has not sensibly increased. I was so ill at Green River as to be confined to bed a good deal. After that first night in the rain I felt much better than I had done. In fact I am not so well under the influence of comfort and warmth, as I was while facing "the power of the night, the press of the storm".

II

THE GOLD FIELDS

[A glossary of mining terms used in the journal begins on page 211.]

September 12

BETWEEN SOUTH PASS CITY at 3 o'clock in the morning and South Pass City at 3 o'clock in the afternoon there is but little difference. The actual residents number not over 50 or 60. [A large per cent of the population, according to the August 18 *Frontier Index*, had moved to Green River City to work on the railroad construction crews.] There are some 50 dwellings but the greater part of them are either forsaken, or were never inhabited. Recently when the place was believed to be threatened by an Indians raid they endeavored to drum up volunteers to act as a guard, and the greatest number they could raise was fifty men. I see a number of stores in the main street, with attractive fronts all bran new—not one of which seem to have been occupied. One has to seek for the inhabitants principally among the humble looking dwellings built of logs or rubble stone which dot the back of the hill.

This morning I took a stroll around the vicinity. From the neighboring heights I could obtain a very pleasing prospect of hills crowned with timber, valleys and swelling uplands. Willow Creek runs through winding ravines of wild rugged aspect. But few green spots are to be seen. All is wild rock and ragged brush and desolation. A rude cheerless life this is to lead, and few there be that take real delight in it.

It is an established fact I believe that sailors never like the sea, and the same might apply to the restless rovers in this country. I have talked on the subject with all kinds of men who have passed the fairest portion of their lives in the West, and the unanimous opinion of all is that it is "a dog's life". Why is it, one would ask, that so many of these men, when they do go East again, come back dissatisfied, and resume their western life. A thorough western man, who has lived in the mountains for years, speculating in mines, bull whacking, ranch keeping, making piles of money one day and losing it the next, will go back to the States in a poorer plight than he left them, with the notion of striking into some steady business, and restoring himself to society. But he will rarely remain there long. No, he wanders back to the mountains again. He says, "O damn the States I couldn't live there again". Not because he has quite lost the relish for civilized comfort, or prefers the rude life of the plains, but because he finds himself an alien in that more refined company, and the artificial restraints of society are too burdensome to him.

Nor is this life of hardship and privation very often compensated by the acquisition of riches. In 999 cases out of a thousand the men who pursue the varied avocations of western life, do not even acquire a decent competence. They would have done better (and they know it) to remain where they came from, practising a wise economy with the modest earnings of their trade or profession. The populations in the States are on the average better off than the floating populations out in the mountains. One hears a very general regret unconsciously expressed, as in the case of sailors, that they ever adopted this kind of life. And yet they hang on to it, partly from habit, partly because they are reluctant to return to their friends in a state of poverty, and partly because there is always a hope that they will make a "big strike" some day. One man in the thousand makes the big strike, and the 999 linger on, upheld by the expectation of doing the like.

I have been obliged to waste a whole day in this place on account of indisposition—severe headache and cold. My friend Houghton is temporarily laid on the shelf and I myself ought to be in bed with a nurse to attend me, but I must not give way.

Miners dropping in from time to time discussing the prospects and chances, and the value of the different claims. "Miners Delight" seems to carry off the palm at present, although some affect to disparage it.[1] They say several new

---

1. Miner's Delight, located on Spring Gulch, was discovered in September 1867. Although Frank McGovern is generally credited with the discovery, James Carpenter, pioneer resident of Atlantic City, relates that an associate of McGovern's, Jonathan Pugh, told him that he (Pugh) discovered the original ledge while hunting work oxen belonging to his mining party. Pugh said the quartz vein stood out so that he could see the gold fifty feet away.

Pugh lived in the Atlantic City area for many years. There was a dance hall and saloon at the mouth of Beer Garden Gulch, and the story is that on occasion Pugh would stop in and tell the proprietor, "Turn her loose, and I'll pay the bill in the morning"—an expansive gesture which usually cost him twelve to fifteen hundred dollars. The U. S. Census of 1870 lists him as living at Willow Creek Gulch, a miner, aged forty-three, born in Virginia, and owning real estate valued at $13,000.

ledges have been discovered within a few days which are considerably richer. Met Colonel Williams, an old California man, who showed me some fine pure gold dust obtained from the gulch diggings at Miners Delight.

Major Gallagher came down from Miner's Delight and it was my intention to ride up with him in the evening, but I am incapable of the exertion and must put it off till tomorrow, when I *will* recover in spite of ——. The Major with whom I got acquainted at Green River is a lawyer, and a soldier who has seen some service.[2] He is largely interested, with Frank McGovern and others, in the Miner's Delight.

Among other new acquaintances, I encountered a German, the owner of the Young American, who has the most indescribable accent I ever heard. He desired me to pay a visit to his claim and exhibited some specimens of "yolltt which he yott out of itt".[3]

2. According to the *Sweetwater Mines* (April 4, 1868), Major Patrick A. Gallagher of the California Volunteers held the command at Fort Bridger in the fall of 1863. On May 27 the same paper called attention to the professional card of Henry Black and P. A. Gallagher, attorneys at law with an office on Eddy Street, two doors east of Dakota Street in South Pass City. The editor informed his readers that the Major had had a great deal of experience in law.

The U. S. Census Report of 1870 listed Gallagher as aged thirty-three, originally from the state of New York, a miner who held real estate to the value of $15,000 and personal property of $1,000.

3. Zerreuner and Arnot were the owners of the Young American Mine, located one and a half miles from South Pass City, according to the *Sweetwater Mines* (June 6, 1868). A subsequent (July 3) issue gives the spelling of the one as F. Zerenner. In C. G. Coutant's *History of Wyoming,* the names are given as Francis Zernier and George Arnett. Coutant states that Zernier, called Vinegar, was killed by Sam Fairfield in 1869.

On November 25, 1868, the *Sweetwater Mines* reported that the Young American Mine was sold in Chicago for $50,000.

September 13

Boisterous and stormy all morning. No chance of a team to take me to Miner's Delight, so I concluded to walk the eight miles. I started about 3 o'clock in the afternoon expecting to reach the place by sundown. Struck over the hill in the direction indicated to me, passing the Young American on the point of a hill overlooking the village, where a number of men were engaged working a shaft and taking out rock.

Following the trail, as I thought, I wandered for several miles over long bare hills, and finally descended by a path which led me into a clump of timber. Here the road came to an end and I found I had mistaken the trail. I encountered a man who was just emerging from the wood leading a pony, to who I exclaimed "turn gentle hermit of the dale and guide my lonely way" to Miner's Delight. "Miner's Delight!!" quoth the hermit compassionately, "you are far off the road to Miner's Delight." "Then tell me where I can strike it". "Well that would be difficult too, unless you know the country". But he directed me towards a height near which the road passed, so I struck across the hills, keeping it before my eye, and finally reached the pathway.

Miner's Delight lies in a North Easterly direction from South Pass, over a broken rocky country through which winds a faintly traced wagon road. The great range of mountains which first attracted my notice at the distance now lay almost behind me. They are not properly speaking a part of the Sweetwater district, although I called them so, as being the most prominent range.

Plodding slowly over this long road, climbing heights and dipping into lonely woody hollows, I passed a number of empty log cabins, very few of which have the appearance of ever having been occupied. I suppose they were built in expectation and never realized. The mountain streams cross the path very frequently and consequently the green patches are numerous. As you ascend the higher hills, magnificent views of high rolling mountain lands are disclosed, stretching away in the direction of the Wind River Valley which is only about thirty miles distant. At intervals I passed on the top of some ridge a shaft sunk for the distance of a few feet and apparently abandoned, the owners being too poor to carry on the work. The claims are rendered good, however, by sinking to a certain depth, and the proprietors will doubtless return to them when they can make a raise. Occasionally a solitary prospector would be visible far up the hill picking liesurely at the rock.

A walk of four miles—long ones I fancied—brought me within sight of Atlantic City. Rock Creek where good gulch diggings are believed to exist, flows through the bottom of the ravine. Most of the hills bristling with pointed black slate rock. The pathway passes along the back of a high bald ridge which ends abruptly and you look far down into an irregular valley where the settlement lies.

There are about sixty good log cabins, and at first sight one would say, here is a considerable settlement. But when you descend and pass through the silent city, very few of the huts bear any traces of a housewarming. In fact they were all built on speculation. I saw at least one family—a mother and a few flaxen-haired children, and further on I came to a cabin labelled "Atlantic Hotel" and another near it "Saloon". From outward appearance I might conjecture that it would not take a very smart man to run that hotel. I saw from a distance an Arasta "swashing and circling", but deferred a visit to it till afterwards.

I was by no means certain of keeping the right road and should I fail in reaching the right place before sundown, there was no saying what might be the consequences. So I kept a jealous eye upon the luminary as I saw him slowly approaching the hills, and pushed on. The next four miles were very long, very lonely, and with many a stiff climb. Not a living thing in sight all the way—a wind-swept solitude. The trail, too, grew so faint at times that I had the utmost difficulty in tracing it. Occasionally it forked over the hill, and caused me much trouble and vexation of spirit. It was a race now between me and the sun. He knew *his* road well enough and had no hills to climb, and my shadow was tapering out every minute. There was something in these lenghtening shadows and this growing stillness, which, in connection with the uncertainty ahead, increased my anxiety. However, just as he dipped over *his* hill, I succeeded in dipping over the crest of my last one, and the cheerful sound of wood-chopping announced the vicinity of human beings.

A few minutes brought me round the face of a rocky slope, and down into a valley where a number of log houses nestled snugly enough near a field of young trees and bushes. A large house dog came up the hill barking to give me a welcome, and presently some friendly voices which I knew, and some friendly hands extended a miner's welcome. This was Miner's Delight. I was all at home in a few minutes and felt quite refreshed by such a hearty reception as I met with from all the men.

I was proceeding to look around for Major Gallagher when I saw him—now attired in mining costume—coming towards me carrying a panful of black dirt, from which he was engaged in eliminating the gold. It was obtained from the last cleaning up at Toger's Mill [4] and there seemed to be some difficulties in the way of separating the particles of precious metal from the iron. So he gave it over to another party who employed himself for the evening in trying another process, by grinding it into a fine dust on a flat rock, then washing carefully, and separating the gold by quick-

4. This probably should be Tozer. Messrs Tozer and Eddy erected a mill in this area in July 1868 (*Sweetwater Mines*, June 13 and July 25, 1868).

silver. In this way they succeeded in producing a small gold bullet equal in value to $5 odds—while from the remainder another three dollars worth could be taken by dusting off the iron with salt. This primitive process was the first I had happened to see of gold making and therefore I note it down here.

The major soon conducted me to his modest cabin and introduced me to his excellent young wife who prepared for my benefit a hearty supper of venison stew.[5] Here was a picture of domestic comfort under the most unpromising circumstances. It did not need that blythe smiling face to reveal to me that I was sitting in something better than a rough bachelor hut. The presence of a woman (with a capital W.) was touchingly manifest in all the little household arrangements—in the clean swept hearth, the little curtained window, the arrangement of a side table, on which were books and photograph albums and other reminiscences of civilized life, and in various tender efforts to cozify and adorn the naked logs. Who but woman, with a capital W, would have had the consideration to carpet the bare floor with Buffalo skins, to hang a protecting canvas under the rafters, to construct an ottoman under that wee window, and to decorate the rude fireplace with old newspapers?

But apart from Woman in the abstract, for whom I entertain an unspeakable veneration, I could not help regarding this lady in the desert with unfeigned admiration. A poor Irish lass, born and raised in a shieling might not find anything very new or hard in such a life. But she must be a brave soul who, accustomed to the refinements of life, can voluntarily front the hardships and perils of a mining camp like this, far in the remote wilderness, that she might be the

5. Major Gallagher had brought his wife to South Pass City from Salt Lake City in July (*Sweetwater Mines,* July 11, 1868). The U. S. Census Report of 1870 records that Mrs. Gallagher was originally from Massachusetts, named Frances E., aged twenty-six. This would place her age at twenty-four at the time Chisholm met her.

sharer of her husband's fortunes for better for worse. A good many considerate people have told me they would not on any account, permit their better half to undertake such a life as they have to lead. May it not be that they would not, because they did not happen to get the kind of better half that would consent to it!

After supper came pipes and a lively interchange of talk on many topics for the reminder of the evening. The Major is an entertaining companion, after the first slight barrier of polite reserve is broken down—courteous, intelligent and conversant with many subjects. He has been a brave soldier and a prosperous miner, and although temporarily under a cloud,[6] like Mr. Micawber, there appears to be something "turning up" for him pretty soon and fast. They propose to brave out the winter here, and on the whole I have come to the conclusion that there is something to be envied even in a life passed amid such desolations.

From the Major's domicile we adjourned late in the evenings to Mr. John Means' store where I was invited to pass the night.[7] Here I met a number of miners, some of whom were engaged at a friendly game in a corner by the ample fireplace. The conversation reverted to railroad matters, the Union Pacific and their slovenly put down grading work, the Western Company [Central Pacific Railroad] and their chances of becoming a mere branch of the Union should the latter get past the meridian, and finally to the chinamen who were voted by unanimous consent as a curse to the labor of California.

The bed stands invitingly in the corner, and as my cold is by no means cured, and my head aches somewhat, I silently disappear into the regions of Nod.

6. James Carpenter states that Gallagher was probably "bob-tailed" (dishonorably discharged) out of the Army.

7. John Means' store was located in Hamilton City, about seven hundred feet below the actual site of Miner's Delight Mine.

September 14

Eight o'clock had been announced as the Major's breakfast hour, but I slept on for full thirty minutes beyond the time when the Major himself came up to arouse me. After breakfast I went forth to view my surroundings.

The land slopes from the North West to S. East in a gradual incline, until it closes by a line of high limestone cliffs which rise abruptly through a steep slope to a towering height and effectually shut out the view to the Eastward. Adown this spacious incline which is thinly covered with slender trees and shrubbery, there run several rocky ridges at a slight elevation from the surface, while a small mountain stream finds its way to the hollow. The rock found on the surface of these ridges are of the common black slate and granite, and it is here that the gold indications are generally found. It is generally understood that these sand stone rocks interrupt the course of the quartz ledges, although some hold that the ledges dip under them. I saw some specimens of float rock found among the loose slate which exhibited rich indications of gold.

It is at the head of one of these ridges that the first discovery was made, and lower down the two principal shafts are being sunk. I was lowered into each of these successively, while the men were occupied in clearing away the wall rock. In the first, the ledge, after descending a short distance below the surface, was found to dip at an angle of about forty-five degrees, while an elbow runs in, almost at right angles. Specimens of the rock, picked up at random, seemed to be quite rich in gold. Very little has yet been done, however, to develop either of these, principally for lack of adequate means. Indeed the entire district has never been half prospected. The few experienced miners who have remained behind, undaunted by the universal stampede, and are working at five dollars a day, can do little more than prove the undoubted richness of the mine. But more of this anon, as I have extended my knowledge as yet but imperfectly.

Mr. Means is exceedingly hospitable entertained me at dinner to an elk steak—very savory. It was brought in by a pair of hunters whose appearance arrested my attention. Hard, weather-beaten visages, a couple of veritable, natty leather stockings, of taciturn demeanor, and clad in the ordinary buckskin garb with fringy decorations. They came into the camp silently, made their trade, and stalked silently forth into the hills again. What a strange solitary life to lead, wandering aimlessly to and fro, and camping wherever night happens to overtake them.

A great many are decamping from here to the Wind River Valley where game is abundant and where the Buffalo are now coming in. Wash-ke [Washakie, Chief of the Shoshoni Indians] and part of his band are also believed to be there. He is the friendly chief of the Snakes and seems to be highly respected by all the miners.

Spring Gulch, Yankee Gulch, and Meadow Gulch—these are the principal gulches in this district. They run parallel with each other down the slope, and from the indications, it is believed that they are traversed by a still undiscovered ledge of surpassing richness. In Spring Gulch where four men are now working—two by day and two by night—they are washing out at an average of $25 to the hand per day. This, too, with a scarcity of water which renders gulch digging a very limited field of operation. They have taken out as high as 20 ounces of dust from this gulch in one day, while nuggets have been found ranging in size from twenty to a hundred dollars value.

No great outlay would be needed to bring a liberal supply of water through all these gulches, and thus make gulch digging a profitable work. A feasible enough plan was at one time projected to carry a stream from the Little Beaver to the hill, but it has not been put in practice.

[83]

September 15

"He who ascends to mountain tops shall find" that things assume a different aspect from what they had, as viewed from the vale. Such was my experience to-day. Having obtained a view of this country from an exalted stand point, I have to declare that my former description of it is a total failure. I simply made the mistake of noting down the appearance of one insignificant corner as if it were the whole. But everything is on such a gigantic scale that one must get well elevated before he can gain a correct impression.

I have been ruralizing all day—soaring very high indeed—and I found in my rambles much to interest. Mr. Means proposed a walk after breakfast and without much preparation we set out. It was a clear morning but a strong wind was blowing. Striking off at an Easterly direction from Spring Gulch round the face of the ridge, we descended a dry gulch [probably Yankee Gulch], walking smoothly over the hard bed rock, to a point where the land took a more precipitous dip downward to the bottom of the ravine where Big Beaver flows.

The entire slope is abundantly covered with timber which grows more leafy and luxuriant as we approach the foot. Over the dry trunks of fallen trees, under the rustling shadows, we soon descended below the region of the wind, and experienced a pleasant warmth. Sylvan solitude—recalling pleasantly to mind days long ago when we went to the woods beyond the Deveron to gather blae-berries. Half way down grew bushes of wild grapes, tart to the taste, but of a heavenly blue, while further down we found sweet sarvis berries that taste not unlike the maple.[8] Down still down

8. The "wild grapes" were chokecherries. "Sarvis berries" are serviceberries; the word is pronounced as Chisholm has spelled it.

among the thickening shrubbery, till we hear the hollow gargle of the little stream which is completely hidden by the thick foliage.

Far over-head the wind was roaring and blowing, but here we were in a perfect calm, hidden by the dense wood screen, clambering along the rocky ledges that over-hang the stream, and sitting down betimes to munch sarvis berries. On the other side of the Big Beaver rises the immense slope of which I have already spoken, crowned by a line of high cliffs. The slope is bestrewn with huge boulders detached and hurled down to the ravine from the mighty mass above, while along the foot of the crags are what seem a scattering line of bushes.

Following the course of the brook, we pass through a field of fallen trees, neatly chopped off by the roots apparently, yet the cutting is not exactly like the work of a woodman. In fact it was the work of the cunning Beavers, who gnaw them through just about as neatly. You can see the marks of their teeth. An immense number of these trees had been felled by the marvelous creatures, and we soon had a sight of a deserted Beaver dam.

Now we begin the steep ascent, not attempting to face the hill, but wending slant-wise round the face of it, and insinuating our way toward a gap, far up in which is a mountain spring. We pass into the windy region again as we climb, and experience quite a hurricane. The first curious thing we find is the rock lying on the face of the slope, which looks like some melted mass in which different varieties of stone are run into one lump of rare mosaic. The second curious thing we find, after long and toilsome climbing is that "the scanty line of bushes along the foot of the cliffs", have expanded into a pine forest, while the fallen trees below, over which we had been stumbling, now looked like the small ends of fishing rods. And we had as yet but reached the crest of the slope.

The enormous crags were yet above us, high above the tallest pine tree.

For the sake of diversion we both employed ourselves in detaching the largest boulders we could handle, and inaugurated a second war of the Titans against the trees in the valley. I have frequently indulged in this kind of warfare, but never with such war material, or at such a signal advantage over the enemy. Gods! how the great boulders went thundering down, leaping a hundred feet at a bound, spinning round like a grindstone, clearing the tops of the trees in the ravine, and striking dismay into the banks beyond. It was such a rare satisfaction too, to know that there was no crusty old fellow living down there, who would come out and shake his fist at us, and threaten to carry a complaint to our mothers. Our youthful ambition was not satisfied, however, by this innocent recreation, so we again directed our steps heavenward, and by dint of hard labor, won the loftiest heights.[9]

At this elevation there was little or no wind. We seemed to have left it below. The appearance of these crags held my attention strongly. They are said to be a kind of lime stone, but I should have taken them for masses of lava—hard, solid, heavy and corrugated—almost like coral. We crawled snake fashion to the giddy verge and peered fearfully over, looking down first to the tops of the pine trees beneath, and then away down to the bottom of the ravine.

Two hawks were wheeling and swooping and rising far below us in mid-air. The thither slope down which we had come, now appeared a level plain dotted with low bushes and strewn with small canes. The Big Beaver was indistinguishable. The blue mountain range [Wind River Range] to which I looked up with awe and wonder before, was now

9. Chisholm and Means had climbed the high Beaver Bluffs, to the east of Miner's Delight and across Big Beaver Creek.

"over the way" on a friendly equality, although it could boast its eternal snows. Immediately beneath lay the wide slope facing the South East, down which the gulches run in parallel lines, and the Miner's Delight was a small speck in one of the hollows. A glorious prospect stretched away beyond, of mountains and vales, with here the trace of a road, and there a shining speck in the distance like a standing lake. The back of the cliffs are covered with pineries—some of which consist of dead trees, thunder blasted, or burnt. Others are green and have a pleasing odor. It is wonderful to note how these trees grow out of the clefts of the rock, where not a vestige of earth is visible.

I lay down in the quiet sunshine among the pines and through a vista of green branches looked dreamily down upon the noblest panorama that was ever disclosed to my sight. High mountains were diminished to mole hills, and rivers to small silver threads. The air so pure and fresh was a luxury to breathe, and the wind sung in the pine tree belt below and over the face of the rocks, hardly stirring the tree tops on the height. Numerous game tracks were to be seen, and traces quite recent of Elk and other visitors to this airy solitude, while we found some bleached skulls of mountain sheep.

Proceeding still further along the top of the crags we saw to the Northward the Wind River Valley faintly indicated by a dark green strip—unlimited views of high tablelands, mountains, valleys, and streams—the Little Popogia [10] at no great distance. The bluffs near it show a bright reddish color, and I am told that there are good gold prospects there.

Our ramble occupied the best part of the day. Passing through the woods along the back of the cliffs we descended through a gap and came down to the Beaver only a mile or so

10. The Little Popo Agie River, pronounced *po-po-sh i a*, an Indian word meaning "the beginning of waters."

above the point from which we ascended. A few men were engaged in building a stamp mill for Nichols & Co.[11]

Result of my excursion—a severe attack of neuralgia in the right eye.

11. The only Nichols concerning whom information has been located is David C. Nichols. The *Sweetwater Mines*, April 7, 1869, announced that D. C. Nichols had been named an election inspector at Hamilton City. The U. S. Census of 1870 records David C. Nichols as a miner, living at Willow Creek Gulch, who owned real estate in the amount of $500.

III

LIFE AT MINER'S DELIGHT

September 16

CONFINED TO THE HOUSE all forenoon by neuralgic agonies—all in my eye—my right eye.

The miners here are a quiet industrious class of men, mostly old Californians—very intelligent, and affording more practical information on mining matters than one can derive from mere book students and theorists. There are no idlers in the camp—in fact a professional bummer would very quickly perceive that there was no show for him here. In the evenings when the day's labors are over, the men engage in a quiet game among themselves, more for amusement apparently than gain.

Some unusually rich float rock which has been found from time to time in the vicinity, has created a little excitement and numbers of the men have been out every day prospecting for the "Hidden Hand"—the name of the unknown lead to which the rock is supposed to belong. This morning the prospectors came in after a fruitless search and the Hidden Hand still remains a mystery.

There is a young Grizzly *Bar* in the camp, who is an object of much consideration among the miners. Young "Cuff" was caught last fall, and has been brought up by hand by John Connor in whose family he resides. He is now a good sized round fat ball of a grizzly, a comical, mischievous kind of a devil, whose bump of acquisitiveness is already strongly developed, and just old enough to be a somewhat dangerous pet, to be handled with care. He has within a week signalized himself by biting a man's arm and tearing a few coatsleeves. Cuffy is after the honey pots all the time. He makes straight for the table when he pays a visit to the neighbors, and if there is no sugar he has very little to say.

The other day he went up to a cabin when the mother of the family was out, and seeing nothing in the way but the children he contrived to terrify them by growling like an old bear. The children ran out scared and clambered upon the mud roof, while Cuffy, who had gained his point, went leisurely through the contents of his favorite pots. Once he went into a house, and finding no grub he gave the empty platter such a cuff as sent it ringing to the opposite wall. You cannot hide a pipe from him. He will find it out somehow, and although he is not addicted to the weed it tickles him hugely to handle a pipe. But he is getting altogether too much grizzly, and will have to be converted into dinner by and bye.

Had a piece of Buffalo hump for dinner to-day. Having heard a good deal of the excellencies of this savory morsel my expectations were great. But it proved tough, sir,—very rough and tough—so tough that I was induced to go and take a look at the bull himself, who had been shot a few miles from this spot. He was a very skinny, lean looking old bull, and I suspect the tenderness was taken out of him, hump and all, a long time ago.

The miners came around in full force this evening, playing and drinking to a considerable extent. Perhaps this may afford some explanation of the fact that these men, although earning good wages, are generally moniless. They spend their five dollars a day and very often more by losing the treat three or four times of an evening.

September 17

This is the day of Rest, and the miners observe it after a fashion. If there is any special job to be done they set about it. If there is not, they set about the card table and consume the hours in play. When the drink begins to operate you can see the wild element come into play, manifesting its presence generally in a kind of rough boisterous merriment, which a slight breeze, however, may in a moment blow into a fierce outbreak. "It is the little rift" through which the savings make their escape. Many of the men around this camp seem to be proof against the tempter, and you may rely upon it, such men keep the pot boiling all winter. But a vast amount of the gold dust is ground in the whisky mill.

Today has been one continued scene of dissipation, and full of the most comical quarrels. Dave Manson, usually a steady sensible fellow, but liable to occasional "busts", has been on an elevation all day. Being of Scottish birth we had a cheerful interchange of Scottish anecdotes during the forenoon. This was presently interrupted by the entrance of one Fry, a heavy set, lymphatic individual, who was deplorably drunk.[1] Mr. Fry good naturedly declared for the informa-

---

1. Dave Manson was listed in the U. S. Census of 1870 as aged forty, born in Scotland, owning real estate to the amount of $25,000

tion of the card table company that he would not work for the d——— &c——— &c——— alluding to a certain company.

Now it happened that Dave, being one of that very company, he naturally resented the appellation as applied to him and took Fry to task in a friendly way. Poor Fry who did not mean anything, took it all back, saying it was one of his by words. "Its a very poor by word Mr. Fry and you should drop it". Fry was of opinion that he shouldn't back down for no man, and that if any man didn't like it he could "put to it". Whereupon Dave would like to know what he meant by "put to it"—put to what? did he mean put to this?—baring his bony arm—and Dave, who is a long spare wiry man, jumps from his seat, throws his cap off, and commencing a series of preliminary war dances, expresses his readiness to jump down Mr. Fry's throat and perform a gallop through that gentleman's intestines in the quickest possible space of time. It is plain that his highland blood is up.

Lymphatic Mr. Fry's is not perceptibly stirred. He tries a second apology, but being very drunk he only succeeds in still further aggravating the enemy. Dave's lean form is contorting itself into the most approved fighting attitudes, the most formidable of which is curving his back up like an angry cat's, as if he were preparing himself for the promised jump. But the inebriated Fry will not fight, and even allows Dave to take him by the throat and administer a hostile tap on the cheek, without making a demonstration.

After that there is nothing more to be done, although Dave has a good deal to say by way of goading the lethargic man to madness. "Don't say another word Fry—you're a very good fellow. I wouldn't hurt a hair of your head. You're an old woman Fry. Fry you're a coward, you're no

---

and personal property worth $600. Coutant credits him with being one of the discoverers of Miner's Delight. The 1870 Census lists Charles Fry at Rock Creek Gulch, age forty, a miner born in Kentucky who owned real estate in the amount of $300.

man at all. D—— my high-land heart I could travel through his [anatomy] in half a second." Such is the intensity of Dave's honest emotions that tears come to his eyes, and all day long his wrath works like a sea after storm, his fingers twitching convulsively as if he would fain be after that expedition through the system of Mr. Fry.

More whisky gave his frenzy another turn, and very soon he was enthusiastic on the subject of Robert Burns and the battle of Waterloo, but anon the sight of the drunken Fry staggering past, would revive the original feud. Then Dave's cap was off again, his spine curving up, and d—— his high-land heart he would just give him one lick on the snoot any how. By and bye he gets crazy enough to seize a knife and talk of letting out the heart's blood of some incautious individual who had unwittingly excited his ire, and so amid card playing and foolish quarrelling happily not resulting in anything serious, the Sunday evening passes into Monday morning, and the card table is vacated just about the time I get up to breakfast. They generally keep up their game till about six or seven o'clock.

We have been supplied for the past few days from the Wind River Valley, with some of the delicacies of the season, such as green corn, turnips, and c.[2] Many of the men move over there to camp for the winter. The season is not

2. The *Sweetwater Mines* (June 17, 1868) reported that about twelve men were farming in the Wind River Valley. To that date they had sown 400 pounds of barley and planted 1,000 pounds of potatoes; the peas and corn sown earlier were three to four inches high. Hiram Lusk, in a letter to the *Mines* (June 27, 1868), said there were fifteen men in the valley, specifically mentioning Messrs Kutch, Davidson, and Evans.

The first permanent settlers, according to Captain H. G. Nickerson's "Early History of Fremont County," were William Evans, James Rodgers, Tilford Kutch, U. P. Davidson, and Steve Geni "in 1868 on Little Wind River in what is now the Shoshone reservation. In the same year, Birch, Austin Likely, Saylor and Shafer settled in the valley of the Big Popoagie" (*Quarterly Bulletin*, Wyoming State Historical Society, Vol. 2, No. 1, 1924).

severe, the snow rarely falling over two feet deep and quickly disappearing. It is the great winter quarters of the Snakes who find plenty of game to supply their wants.

Between here and the valley a fine oil spring has been discovered, which flows from the surface yeilding from 8 to 10 barrels a day without any work. [This is probably the oil spring at the present Dallas Field of the W. H. Barber Company, located on the Popo Agie River about eight miles southeast of Lander.] I have seen specimens of the oil in its crude state, it being extensively used here for various purposes. A little valley has been described to me, lying not more than eight miles from this place, in which are oil springs which will yeild a big supply. It has never been located, and in fact few are aware of its existence. Gold, oil, and a rich agricultural country near by—such a combination of treasures should make a howling wilderness for to blossom in the course of time. I propose to go and smell this oil well very soon.

Monday September 18

I hate to become personal, but this neuralgia has given me such exquisite torture for three days that I must expose it.

This morning I visited the gulch diggings, and saw the gallant Major working like a Trojan shovelling in the dirt. Even Mrs. Gallagher was doing a little amateur work with a pan, exhibiting with great glee to her lord the tiny results of her prospecting. Nothing but the want of sufficient water supply prevents the work turning out a handsome yield daily.

Mr. Walsh of Chicago is proposing to erect a twenty stamp mill in connection with the Miner's Delight. It would cost about $30,000, and if the parties come to an understanding, it may be in operation within four weeks.[3] The mill now being put up by Nichols is a small one with wooden stamps shod with iron, which works in connection with an arasta. The quartz will be ground to a certain fineness in the mill, and then put through the Arasta. It was purchased from an individual who came here in the spring with some impracticable theory in his head, of softening the rock, and who as a matter of course made a failure of it.

To return to the subject. The Sunday's dissipation has been prolonged in three or four cases, the most prominent of which (to me) is the case of my friend and countryman, Dave. He found a new enemy to-day and was breathing threatenings and slaughter against him worse than Saul against the Christians. In the evening he went after him and actually fired two shots at him, one of which passed through the rim of his hat—a rather close shave. His friends managed to draw him away after arranging a duel for the next morning, which was to be fought according to either of the three following propositions: 1. Pistols at fifteen paces. 2. Hand to hand with bowie knives, hat in one hand and knife in the other; or 3. Throw away all weapons and come down to the bare knuckles.

This matter having been satisfactorily arranged Dave came over to spend the evening. Partially sobered and merely talkative he afforded me infinite amusement by his rambling reminiscences of his childhood, of his boyhood, of Prince Edward Island and the Dundas's and Morpeths and McKinnons—then of his own father and mother, of his wife, his children, his trade, his ramblings, his losses and his gains.

3. On November 25, 1868, the *Sweetwater Mines* reported that the twenty stamp mill for Miner's Delight had been shipped for the mines and that Mr. John L. Walsh, the owner of the mill, and his family had left for the mines. The U. S. Census of 1870 lists John L. Walsh at Hamilton City as a miner who owned real estate valued at $12,000. The Census also lists his wife and four children.

By and bye he gets upon the subject of his wanderings over the mountains here last fall when they struck this camp, and his account of their sufferings from hunger was most unintentionally humorous—as when he spoke of creeping into a cave with his little black dog in the desperate hope that some wolf would jump out and furnish a meal for them, he looked so like a lean hungry wolf himself and conveyed such a comical impression that it was impossible to keep from laughing—and Dave joined in it most heartily of all. They fell out of provisions among the hills and could strike no game and so about the third day they were about giving out. Dave had a favorite black slut with him—very sleek and fat. Twenty times did he point his gun at the pet and thought what a treat she would make, but he couldn't do it.

They met a grizzly in the valley and the whole three went for him like darnation, but the Bar knew how hungry they were and he *put*. Dave says he himself went along after the others for a whole day and eat grass like a cow—which feat amuses him so intensely that he must need stop and have a good laugh. Most pathetic were some of the incidents notwithstanding the comical recital. Billy Jones, who was very near giving out, comes up and says Billy "Dave if we could find a big wolf now, we would fight him like damnation." "You bet." "Dave, little Mollie there—she's nice and fat arnt she?" Dave looks ruefully at the poor dog again, and shakes his head. "Wait a while longer Billy. I'd just as soon starve."

Here Dave appeals to Billy who is playing cards—"O Bill Jones, d'ye mind the time when you lay down on the rock and I went to turn a somerset?" Billy apparently don't relish the remembrance. They had to climb a high hill, pursues the narrator in his disconnected way, and when they came to the very top Billy lay down on a flat rock and said feebly "Dave, I'm giving out." "Giving out!" says Dave (who is just about in the same fix) "look here Billy, did you ever see me turn a somerset?" "I'm afraid" quoth Billy very faintly "you can't turn any more somesets now Dave".

"Well sir, I left 'em there and went down the hill, and be darned if I didn't shoot two rabbits—pop-whack—killed 'em both—ha! ha! I didn't take the skins off, but just gutted them. Now would you believe that I sat down and ate one of them rabbits heads up raw—chawed it all up raw, and then fell asleep (ha! ha! ha! ha!) Billy and Jonathan came down and found me basking in the sun (ho! ho! ho!) Tell you what it is gentlemen"—in a confidential tone—"people may talk as they like about eating raw meat, but I tell you there ain't any better way to eat it. It's better with a little salt and pepper if you have it, but give me a peice of good raw meat, and I can make as hearty a meal as I want. After that we got a sage hen and I got hold of the neck—pretty long neck you know nearly all bone—Well sir (here Dave explodes again in anticipation of the joke) that whole neck disappeared—d—— me if I didn't chaw it up like a dog".——

All this happened last fall about the time they discovered the Miner's Delight. When at length they reached a friendly cabin they swallowed a morsel of bread and slept. "Next morning" says Dave "I commenced to eat breakfast and I never stopped eating till noon. Lord I was so hollow!—and I thought I would never fill up."

It would be doing injustice to Dave, however, to represent him altogether in the light in which he appears while in his cups. The best of men are liable to occasional *busts* and as for Dave, a more worthy, intelligent and peaceable man is not to be found in the camp.

Another choice spirit from Caledonia, a man of diminutive stature, and with something in his manner remotely suggestive of Mr. Simon Tappertit, has been staying in the camp for a few days.[4] From him as an authority in matters

4. Simon or Sim Tappertit, a character in Dickens' *Barnaby Rudge*, was described as an old-fashioned, thin-faced, sleek-haired, sharp-nosed, small-eyed little fellow about five feet high.

connected with Scottish history, I have gained some astonishing facts touching the venerable iron crown. The following incident has probably been omitted by Victoria in her memoirs and I am happy to be able to supply it.

The ancient iron crown was taken, as everybody knows, by Sir William Wallace from one of the Pharaohs during the Egyptian wars. This may seem a surprising fact to many a student of history, but it is nevertheless true. Moreover Wallace, who was a patriotic individual, guarded this crown sacredly for years and kept it hidden in a well, and afterwards restored to Robert the Bruce at the time he extricated the latter from some bad fix. Probably this may have been after the champion's own head was stuck on London Bridge, but never mind that. According to the ancient legends, this crown was never, never to pass into the hands of the foreigner, and if it should ever press the forehead of an English King, the consequences thereof, in virtue of the treaty, would be—would be something dreadfully calamitous to poor old Scotland. The English King would immediately acquire unlimited sway and Scotland's rights would be forever annihilated.

Well, this crown being now in the possession of the duke of Hamilton, the present Queen Victoria cast an eye upon it, when she paid a visit to the Duke, and in the innocence of her heart, she requested the ancient seneschal to hand it to her that she might put it on her head. The hoary warden complied, and Her Majesty was about to place the crown upon her brow. But the Duke drew his sword and said, "Victoria, Queen, lay down that crown". And the Queen said "My Duke of Hamilton what meaneth this?" But the Duke only repeated "Victoria Queen, lay down that crown". And again the Queen said "My Duke of Hamilton what meaneth this?" and then the warden suddenly remembered the ancient legend, and the treaty, and so he plucked the iron crown from the Queen's hand. And once more the Queen said "My Duke of Hamilton what meaneth this?" To which the Duke replied "Victoria Queen, had you put on that crown your head would have danced upon this pavement in your blood." and the Queen was so terribly scared that she quite forgot to put it down in her diary I suppose.

The new stamp mill is expected here in the course of six weeks and of course the expectation is that it will be an immense benefit to the country. At the Miner's Delight the company are now widening the shaft, while within the last few days the quartz has become richer than ever. The specimens of rock are particularly rich—sticking full of free gold. The owners are jubilant over the prospects which seem to be opening before them. Yet some of the older miners appear to shake their heads as if they were not to be quite deceived by so fair a beginning.

This abundance of gold near the surface is not the best indication of a vein that will hold out well. It certainly dazzles the eye to see a piece of rock covered over [with] little masses of pure gold and these specimens are of course much sought after by those who wish to carry samples to the East. But the experienced eye will not be deceived by all this surface glitter, and will place more reliance in those ledges where the gold is not so perceptible to the naked eye especially near the surface. Where the cooling process has been sudden—after the great convulsion by which the melted rock containing the precious metal (which is the base of all other strata) has been forced upward through the vacuum—the gold will naturally fall into masses through the quartz. Where the process has been slow the gold remains in a fine granulated form diffused throughout the rock.

I saw a specimen just now taken from a new ledge discovered by Mr. Quinn in which the gold is scarcely visible except through the glass.[5] Mr. Quinn is about to commence work upon it, and he seems pretty confident that it will ultimately yield a better prospect than the Miner's Delight. From the Caraboo [later spelled Caribou], quartz has been taken out which shows not a trace of free gold, but which give a much larger result. The gold there is in infinitesimal particles.

In one claim in Spring Gulch to-day two men washed out $65 which may be considered a satisfactory earning for one day. With proper appliances and an adequate supply of water it would be possible to produce perhaps $400 in one day from the same place. Lower down the gulch the men are barely making wages.

What a contrast is there between the quiet life of this mountain camp, and the roaring hells of railroad towns which I have but recently quitted. Cheyenne, Laramie, Benton, Green River—a sketch of these several places would form an interesting study. The very mention of the names calls up a crowd of reminiscences which on the whole are anything but refreshing.

The sight of a gambler from Green River who came up here on a brief visit, recalled vividly to my mind a succession of old familiar horrors—the flaring gambling tents—the dance houses—the eternal strumming of old banjoes—the miserable females who have to dance all night till the broad day light, with about as much hilarity as so many prisoners in the treadmill—the game of Faro—the game of three card Monte—the game of Roulette, Black and White—the hundred and one games too numerous to mention—the perpetual tumult and uproar and din of mingling cries—"all down, all set, make your game—seven of diamonds *an-d* the red wins"—

5. Thomas T. Quinn, a resident of Wyoming from 1868 to 1890, was born in 1816 and died in 1900. He served as a member of the Territorial Council from Sweetwater County in 1873. The U. S. Census of 1870 listed him as living at Willow Creek Gulch, fifty-five years of age, a miner born in Kentucky.

"Come now boys I only want one more couple for the next set"—quarrels, cursing, drinking and the flash and bang of pistols—shameless pimps, shameless women, broken gamblers, thieves—depravity that flaunts its banner in the broad daylight—such are a few of the memories that haunt the vacant chambers of the brain.

I often speculate on what will finally become of all that rolling scum which the locomotive seems to blow onward as it presses westward. Will they get blown clean off the continent at last into the Pacific Ocean? One is gradually surrounded by the same faces in each successive town, the same gamblers, the same musicians playing the same old tunes to the same old dance, the same females getting always a little more dilapidated. As the excitement dies out of one town, and the railroad leaves it behind in a kind of exhausted repose, these old familiar faces die out to reappear in a new state of existence.

Up go the old tents in a new location and round it come all the old bummers. Here is the Empire tent which got busted down at Benton.[6] There goes Billy Martin who kept the big gambling house at Cheyenne. There is Fat Jack who used to have a table at Charlie Greers, now running a game of his own. In they come creeping day by day to the new town. Here comes John, who plays the elephone, and Al who plays the fiddle and Brad who sings comic songs. Here comes Mag & Moll, and gentle Annie, and Moss Agate, and the Schoolmarm, and Mormon Ann, and crazy Jane, and all the pioneers of vice, to keep the dance agoing till the town is danced away again to another point.

6. "In those three short months [of Benton's existence] it reveled in the reputation of 'Hell's Tent Town, where the rails end and the trails begin.' It was a rendezvous for outlaws, a hole-up for killers, a hurdy-gurdy for the madams. And for over one hundred who came to Benton, life ended without benefit of marker in the boothill" (Pence and Homsher, *Ghost Towns of Wyoming,* p. 56).

I happened to be in Green River before the high tide had quite begun to ebb from Benton, so for a time we enjoyed comparatively speaking a sort of immunity from these floating wrecks. But they had just commenced to gather in when I departed and I suppose are now in full blast. The gamblers are, to give the devil his due, of a friendly generous disposition and helpful to one another in a manner which would do honor to a christian. But for this, how many would be "busted" beyond all remedy and left behind in the cold. There are always a crowd of hangers on around the tables who watch when one of the lucky number "makes a raise" and ask him for a "stake". Nor do they often ask in vain. It is their only hope for a meal.

I remember one of this kidney whose acquaintance I accidentally formed at Cheyenne. He had been a hotel clerk, and in the East might have been working at a respectable calling. But the fascination of gambling had seized him, and there he was, broke and a youthful wreck. I had seen him hanging round a gambling house day after day, doing nothing apparently but watching the several games. On asking him what he was after, he told me he had not had a meal for two days and he was watching to see if "Charlie" made a stake, so that he might get a dinner. So again when one town fizzles out these same bummers have to attach themselves to some of the more fortunate of the fraternity and thus get hauled on to the next place. There again they are stranded. They would probably go back gladly to the East if they could, but there is no such hope for them. At each step they drag a lengthening chain, and this is how the question occurs "what will become of them?" It seems to me the whole crowd will find themselves in a difficult fix when they get to Salt Lake, for Brigham is a highly moral prophet and will not permit gambling, nor the presence of any superfluous women—but his own.

Were this a prosperous crowded mining camp, I suppose

all these disreputables would not be long in penetrating here too. But at present we are far removed from them. Compared with that we are living in a kind of Arcadia—an Arcadia with a little whisky to now and then sweeten it. As I said there are no such superfluities as "bummers" here. Every man is occupied, and every man knows what his neighbor is. They are all friendly, neighbourly, hospitable, honest. You might leave your purse in any cabin and be sure that not a man would touch it. This diary of mine—they see me scribbling in it every day, and it would hardly be human nature to suppose that they are not just a little curious to know what I'm saying. Yet I leave it laying around everywhere, and I know that without permission asked and granted, not a leaf has ever been turned. No doors are barred by day or night, and no pistols are disposed under the pillows when they lay down to rest.

The little cabins are mostly deserted during the day—except with those who are blessed with a better half (or its equivalent)—In the evening the men come dropping in with their picks and shovels on their shoulders, and then from every chimney rises a little blue cloud of smoke, while the men are preparing their supper of Elk or Antelope. Then the roaring logs are piled on, and round the spacious ingle they form a cheerful circle and chat or read or think or play the evening away till bedtime.

It was just about this time last fall that they struck this camp, and the men have much to tell each other by way of reminder of these hard times, of their wanderings in the deep snow and the hardships they endured. The excitement soon followed, and the adventurers from the East and from the West came and crowded the camps for a brief season and went away again, and only the few original discoverers now are left. It is pleasant for them on this anniversary to sit down and play a quiet game of cards, but a year ago the same men had to do hard battle with the snows, and prospect every ledge at the risk of their lives; beset by hostile Indians on every hand, and with no hope of protection other than their own rifles which every man had to carry, along with his pick and shovel.

My poor friend Cuff is dead. I saw him hanging ignominiously by the hind legs in the meat stall. *Requiescat in—*that is after I have enjoyed a nice fat tender steak off him. Cuff was getting too bearish to be borne with any longer. He would go off on excursions through the cabins and his zeal in the search after forbidden fruit outran his discretion. I saw him yesterday tied to a stump, and howling dismally; but all his promises of future good conduct could not avail him, and this morning he was compelled to yield up the ghost.

The meat market exhibits at present a variety and abundance of choice food such as would be deemed no small treat in an Eastern city. Elk, deer, antelope, Buffalo, and Bear and all in fine condition. For my part I much prefer Elk to all the others, it is so tender and savory. Besides, we have a herd of cows which furnish a plenteous supply of milk. In short as far as living is concerned, *We Live!*

I do not go much into society. Mrs. Gallagher is my only female acquaintance, and she sometimes pines for home so pinefully that I get quite sympathetic on the subject. It is amazing how frequently I find myself walking along the streets of Chicago, especially about the time my waking senses begin to fade into dreamland.—No, I do not go into "Society."

Society in the city of Miner's Delight consists of three females. The first is a plump, dumpling-faced woman built very much in the shape of a bale of cotton drawn together in the middle, and with a big coal scuttle on the top. She has one white haired little darling and she dotes right onto it. The second is a shadowy secluded kind of a being whose profile I have had a few passing glimpses of while passing her cabin door. I don't know who or what she dotes onto. The third I will call Dalilah. She is an adventuress. She dotes onto Jack Holbrook. Jack is interested in the Miner's Delight and she is interested in Jack.[7]

Dalilah is not beautiful. She is not handsome. Her face is lean and spotty and unhealthy looking, and the upper part of her form is like an old whale bone umbrella not properly folded. She was not a respectable person when she first struck the camp, but she is now studying virtue under Jack. The miners used to address her familiarly as "Candy", but now she puts on airs and they call her Mrs. Holbrook. When any of the old hands call her by her old name and ask impertinent questions, she tosses her head and tells them to go along. So Jack is left in undisturbed possession and she is the mistress of his mud covered cabin.

Therefore I don't mingle in society.

7. Jack (John H.) Holbrook was one of the original owners of Miner's Delight. He is listed in the U. S. Census of 1870 as twenty-six years of age, a miner, born in England, and owning real estate valued at $13,000. C. G. Coutant states that he was a brother of E. D. Holbrook who was elected Delegate to Congress from Idaho Territory in 1865. Dr. Thomas Maghee, who was Acting Surgeon at Fort Stambaugh and Camp Brown, mentions in his diary of 1873 that Jack Holbrook, "who had Jim-jams," had created a false alarm causing the troops to make a fruitless tiresome ride of 136 miles in search of Indian raiders.

IV

SUCH STUFF AS BOOKS ARE MADE OF

THE WONDERS OF WIND RIVER VALLEY have excited my craving and I cannot leave here without making an excursion thitherward. A small party of three have already been organized and we are only waiting to get a third horse for the purpose. As it is getting late in the season we are building upon the expectation that the Siouxs have pretty well forsaken the region. Moreover, as the saying is, we have not lost any Indians, and it is no part of our programme to look for them. But in case of emergency we have quite made up our minds as to our mode of warfare, so the Siouxs had better look out. So had the Bears and the Buffalo and the Elk and the Jack Rabbits and the Sage hens, for we mean to make a clean sweep.

Mention of the Wind River and hunting prospects naturally suggests a number of Bar and Buffalo stories. Everyone can recall some incident, generally of an amusing character, of the times when they were on the chase. One reads so many "adventures with a grizzly" that he is apt to regard at least one half of them as fabulous. But just listen for an evening to the personal reminiscences of these old mountaineers, and you will come to the conclusion that a good many fat volumes might easily be filled yet. I will only record one anecdote among a score or two of a different kind. It is vouched for by Judge Dildine.[1]

A small party of men were out on a hunting excursion when they espied at no great distance from them a black bear, and all lay down flat to watch his movements. The Bear had found a bee's nest in a honey tree and was making an abortive effort to reach it. Several times he clomb a few steps and fell back on the ground in a sitting posture. At length he got round to another point and went through the same performance, but this time he remained motionless after falling back. Once only he raised his head to the tree and then let it fall on his breast.

The hunters were curious to know the meaning of such a quiet meditative attitude, so creeping very softly through the bushes till they were quite near him, one of the party took good aim and fired. The ball was seen to pierce him, but still the Bear made no motion, but sat upright with his head sadly drooping on his breast. They approached a little nearer—still he took no notice. They hollared but he never heeded them. Finally they advanced in a body to the spot, and found to their amazement that the Bar was stone dead.

A post mortem examination showed that it was not the

1. The *Frontier Index* (September 18, 1868) lists A. J. Dildine as a probate judge in Carter County, Dakota Territory. In December he traveled east with James Chisholm, and the minutes of the Commissioners of Carter County of December 19, 1868, record the acceptance of his resignation as probate judge and the appointment of P. A. Gallagher to replace him.

rifle bullet which had killed him. It appeared that a long strong sharp pointed stake, part of some embedded old stump had been sticking up near the tree at that point, and the luckless Bruin, on falling back, had sheathed it up to his heart. And there he sat impaled. Mr. Dildine vouches for the truth of this story. I simply report it.

It isn't safe to meddle with a Buffalo, unless you mean to finish him at one shot. Don't fool with him 'cause he aint on it, and you might find yourself in the same fix as a coura- geous Dutchman did the other day. The Dutchman went out with some of the boys to Wind River and one day he saw a bull running by himself, away from the herd. Think- ing to immortalize himself he made up his mind to go for the bull all alone, and so, being mounted on a good steady mule, he gave chase.

When he got along side of the Buffalo he proceeded to empty the contents of his gun into the animal's hide, but somehow he failed to make an impression, and very soon he found that he had fired away all his ammunition. Just at the same moment the bull made up his mind that he would not be fooled with any longer, and he stopped. So did the mule. The Dutchman began to wish he had not gone quite so far. The Buffalo, who looked mad and bothered at the Dutch- man, just gave the mule one "hyst" with his horn and sent him kiting one way, while his rider found himself at the foot of a tree facing his intended victim, who was squaring at him in the following manner: [see "The Dutchman in a fix," in picture section following page 58]. This kind of pantomime he kept up for fifteen minutes without commit- ting any overt act, and giving utterance to an occasional bellow in which the Dutchman heartily joined. At length the rest of the party came up and put an end to the scene by applying to the bull a quieting dose of lead.

"Hallo, Jacob!" cried the boys, "got scared, didn't you?"

"Not by a darn sight" quoth Jacob stoutly.

"What were you doing on the ground then?"

"Doing? Why I shust got down to tie mine shoe before I finish him".

Sudden change of weather. Hark to the wind upon the hill. The fields are white with snow this morning, and the eye is blinded as it looks abroad in the keen pure air. The feathery splendor lies upon the dead boughs along the slopes, or sifts down like a smoke from the still green branches of the young trees. The low shrubbery in the hollow is mounded over, and the great naked trunks stand out bare and lonely, etching their sharp points against the blue above the ridge. Fragments of pointed slate rock and boulders shine out black and distinct from the white ground. Unsightly stumps have now a perfect architectural finish. In one brief night the face of universal nature has undergone the great change, and one looks out with the old wonder on a new world. Only the slender young cottonwood tree refuses to don the white mantle and still waves her leafy branches of delicate green above the snow.

No sound of pick and shovel to-day. The dams in the gulch are frozen over, and the sluices are glistening, not with golden sands, but icicles. The inside of the cabins look so cheerful that linnets and other little birds venture to hop over the threshold and pick up a friendly crumb. One of these timid strangers, emboldened by the friendly reception, even mounts up to the rafters and remains there. The miners come into the store stamping the snow from their boots and exchanging the old commonplaces on the sudden change— then gather round the fire and prepare to make a day of it.

For my part I can only regard the storm as a personal ca-lamity—one of the unforeseen misfortunes which are forever looming up in the way of my plans. We were all ready to start on our excursion to Wind River. The last horse had just been "scared up" and our equipments completed, when one evening a white ghostlike cloud came stealing over the brow of the cliffs. The miner, with that instinct which belongs to a child of the mountains, foretold a snow storm.

Next day the clouds were tumbling in great masses over the hill, down the ravine and folding us in a drizzling mist. Sometimes they would lift up, and reveal the sun for an hour, shining clear over distant lands, while the hills around us were completely enshrouded. Towards evening the wet clinging mist emitted a few scattering white specks. Then a wind arose. The wind soon grew into a blast. It sighed, and flapped, and whirred and blew, and raved, and drove us to the fireside with closed doors. It whitened the fields, it darkened the skies, it choked up the doors, it blew thin white streaks along the floor, it drifted, it sifted in a fine powder through the chinks in the log wall, it sifted all over the blankets all night long, it bedewed my hair, my brow, and down to the tip of my nose, it blew, it blew!

In the morning all was over. There it was—the snow. There were the hills—white, there were the boys—laughing at us. There were our horses, our blankets, our coffee, our flour, our pistols, our guns, our *all*. But we are not to be beaten yet, and it is some consolation to know that it is not a universal storm, and that there will be fine weather yet. So we are off in the morning in spite of fate. Old Wash-ke and his band are now on the way from Bridger and we shall probably meet them in the valley, so if any Siouxs are there we will have protection.[2]

The boys are roaring good humoredly over their portraits, and Harry swears as soon as he gets over his drunk and is able to lick me, that he will give me ——. Perhaps it is not altogether safe for a child like me to tickle the bear, and

2. Washakie and his Shoshone band usually spent some time in the Bridger Valley each year. On July 3, 1868, at Fort Bridger he signed the Great Treaty which created the Shoshone Indian Reservation in the Wind River Valley. The reservation included the land on which Miner's Delight was located.

poke straws playfully at his nose, but somehow his growls have not a threatening sound. Besides I can sometimes sing a song, tell a story, or break a joke with any of them, and then they purr. One day—it was the day of Dave's memorable drunk—(and I believe I was to some extent instrumental in aggravating Dave's enthusiasm) I raked up all the odd scraps of ballads I could think of—Irish, Scotch, and Yankee—comic and sentimental, and howled away at them like a good 'un to the infinite delight of my audience who encored and applauded to the echo.

I never do sing but when I am in the mountains, and then only for philanthropic motives. It is quite amazing to see how much good it does them; what a deal of brotherly feeling it infuses into the human heart, and what an amount of whisky into the system generally.—But this is only one class of the people in this camp. They are not all of this *enthusiastic* tendency (tempered with whisky). By no means.

There are among "the boys" some grave and temperate men of sedate habits and superior intelligence with whom it is a pleasure to converse; who love to talk on history, politics, science and literature; who are well versed in geological theories, and better in geological experience—old men with grey locks and a life time of hard experience at their backs who are glad to learn of a young man, and equally glad to teach him. I generally find that their knowledge of books is fragmentary and imperfect, as hands long unused to a trade may bungle with some once familiar tool, but their judgement of men and things is none the less sound and accurate. They are such stuff as books are made of. Their wide and varied rambles give them a deep knowledge of men, whom they see, not under one aspect, but many. They take broad and liberal views. They are thinkers, for their information is obtained at first hand and they have to shape their experience into thought for themselves. The tradesmen of the city, the politician, the lawyer, habituates himself to look only at one side of a man, or a question, and becomes subordinate to his craft. But this thinking wanderer of the mountains is better than his craft. Over and above it he remains a man.

He is a reader, because one life is not long enough to collect all the facts he needs. He is a mechanic, if not by early training, then by subsequent necessity, and can build a house, or forge a tool, sink a shaft, run a mill, mend a wagon and doctor a horse with the same readiness that he throws up a spadeful of auriferous dirt. In the course of his searches after the yellow treasure he finds out secrets and wonders richer than the gold he seeks. He is a philosopher, or at least he philosophises. He moralizes too, and has generally laid out for himself one broad rule for guidance through this life to the next, which has no element of faith in it. Usually he is a skeptic. You will rarely find an out-and-out orthodox man among what I would designate as the *thinking* population of the hills. (But real old fashioned orthodoxy is so extremely rare a thing among thinking souls anywhere in these days, that this can hardly be named as a characteristic.)

The other evening I listened to an argument on the existence of God, and the reasonable side of the question—(the denier was only an unreasoning utterer of certain infinitely diluted dogmas handed down to him by tradition and through many sorry confusions, from Thomas Paine)—was upheld with a logical clearness and vigor which showed that the reasoner would construct his credo with as much ingenuity, strength and exactness as he would build an engine.

Withal—despite his occasional eccentricities when whisky takes the reins—he is a peaceable, order-loving being. If an unmistakable wrong is being done he will prevent it, or avenge it with his life regardless of consequences. He will appeal to law if it is handy, but if it is not he will right it on the spot. He does not spend much time in drawing nice distinctions. His instinct and experience combined, lead him by a short cut to the right conclusion, and he acts on that promptly. Thus an accomplished rogue would be far more safe in the claws of organized "justice" than to fall into the hands of these men who only "do by nature the things contained in the law". I will cite an example:

While living in Green River I became acquainted with a rather dignified, airy young personage, distinguished in my recollection chiefly by a pair of dark close brows and a showy white bosom, who was made known to me by the title of Judge Thurmond. He seemed to be aiming at some kind of respectable distinction there, and one was tacitly given to understand that on the whole it was desirable to cultivate his society. He was a lawyer by profession, but, as I soon perceived, a gambler by habit and inclination. At a subsequent period I saw him take a somewhat cowardly part in one shooting affray of which he was the cause.

I was from the first biassed in my impressions regarding this man by reason of a report that he was obliged to flee from Montana rather suddenly by order of the Vigilantes. Now I entertain a sneaking respect for the Vigilantes, and I believed that he had given them good cause. Yet Vigilantes are not infallible and I afterwards learned that the only fault Thurmond had committed was in defending professionally a murderer who had been condemned by them to die. Of course a lawyer has a right to exercise his professional zeal in favor of any client, be he thief or murderer, and the Vigilantes were very foolish as well as unjust in attaching any blame to the advocate. Such was the popular impression at Green River in regard to Thurmond, and after all he really seemed a very good sort of fellow, a martyr to professional zeal.

But since my advent to this camp I have ascertained some facts which give a different color to the case. The honest people of [two-inch blank space in original] Montana had been outraged by a succession of robberies and murders and Judge Thurmond was in every case the counsel for the robbers—a perpetual thorn in the side of honest meaning folks. By means of intimidations and threats and bullyings he managed to free quite a catalogue of gallows birds. By and bye it was ascertained to a "moral" certainty that Thurmond was "in cahoots" with the robbers, that he incited them to these depredations, planned them, and insured his tools their freedom, relying upon his unvarying success as an advocate. The Vigilantes would have been a long time in proving these charges *legally*, but they soon proved it to their own satisfaction. Whereupon they gave him one hour's notice to depart from thence, and the "Judge" did not linger to argue the question. Now this may have been rough and tumble justice, but it hit the right mark.[3]

As there are drones in the beehive, quacks among doctors, rotten boughs in trees, and loafers in all society, so there are useless members in this industrious frontier life. They cannot quite be classified broadly as either formidable whisky drinkers or formidable thinkers. There are undoubtedly a variety of pretenders and adventurers around the camps, who have no knowledge and never will acquire it, who are simply drifting along this particular current because they happened to drift into it. Of such I have nothing to say. Let them drift on. I have seen them ere now carrying their pretensions pretty high in the East, and they may be found blowing their empty horn at the very mouth of a shaft—but they can easily be distinguished.

3. J. M. Thurmond had been in Bannack, Montana, where he and Judge Smith had been counsel for the road agents about the year 1864. The two men were banished from the area, according to Thomas J. Dimsdale's *Vigilantes of Montana.*

During 1868 three items in the *Sweetwater Mines* mention Thurmond. On March 21 his legal card appeared—"J. M. Thurmond, Attorney at Law and agent for buying and selling mine claims, Sweetwater Mines, D. T." On June 3 it is reported that after an address at a Democratic mass meeting, he was appointed to the committee to draft resolutions. The final item on July 3 reads: "Hon. J. M. Thurmond leaves today for Green River for a visit. We hope he will correct some misstatements on this part of the country."

Let me say in conclusion as I am now about to leave this camp, already full of pleasant reminiscences to me, that here I have discovered, among other good things, what I call genuine hospitality. It is not merely that I have been comfortably housed and have lived on the best of fare. It is not an ostentatious kindness which looks for an equivalent. There is a hospitality of the eye and heart. One has not to fight his way into it, if he is frank and honest. The stranger is welcomed as an old friend, and all that they have is his.

In another year, if all goes well—if the mines turn out according to the present expectation—these lonely valleys will be peopled. These immense piles of dead timber which now cumber the ground will be utilized into snug frame cottages and stores, and the noise of busy mills will be heard along the banks of the Beaver. From the top of these high crags the traveller will look down upon the sunny slope covered with garden plots and comfortable dwellings. An industrious community will spread over and cultivate these tufted heights and leafy hollows. Capital will flow in, and the gold will flow out. Content will sit basking on the cheek of toil &c &c—if all goes well.

Not thirty miles from the mines lies one of the richest agricultural districts in the world, a valley of unbounded fertility, with scenery of matchless beauty, where summer lingers all the year. This valley will soon be settled, and teeming with all kinds of produce. All along the intervening space between the Big Wind River and this mining district there are fine pastures, the loveliest green meadows, streams and valleys, in more than one of which the cold oil is seen bubbling up in wells or from the bed of the brooks.

Away still further to the Northward are the Big Horn Mountains where silver prospects have been found that would rival Nevada's choicest ore. It is an undiscovered country as yet, for the Indians are numerous there, but the few travellers who have returned bring tidings of a land prodigal in mineral and agricultural wealth. And all this lies at no great distance from the line of the Union Pacific. From "Point of Rocks" where the railway passes, to South Pass is a distance of not more than fifty miles. In the course of time then, the locomotive will be thundering through these mountain solitudes, bringing along its armies of emigrants, and driving the hostile Red man and his Buffalo and Bears away to get remoter hunting fields.[4]

If it is inevitable that some great inland city must arise midway between San Francisco and the East, I know not where there could be found a likelier location than at the head of this great valley. The wide territory of Wyoming is one vast whitening desert all but these broad lands of milk and honey which lie among the Big Horn and Wind River Mountains, and the government propose to portion them off as Indian Reservations!

The above was intended for a stump speech.

4. Point of Rocks, where the Union Pacific tracks crossed Bitter Creek, lies about seventy miles straight south from South Pass City. It was the closest the railroad came, and for a time stages ran between the two points and mail also was carried by this route. Today there is a filling station at Point of Rocks (twenty-five miles east of Rock Springs on U. S. Highway 30) and the remains of the early stage station. But no locomotive is as yet "thundering through these mountain solitudes." In 1906 the Chicago and North Western built to Lander, about thirty-five miles north of South Pass City, and Lander is still the end of the line.

V

MOUNTAIN BILL RHODES

O UR LITTLE PARTY is diminished to two—George Mc-
Kay and myself, and the hour has at last come for
us to start.[1] The snow is lying on the hills but the air is tolerably mild during the day. This promises to be a delightful
excursion, and we have both an object in our ramble which
is not wholly connected with mere pleasure and the study of
nature. Our outfit consists of a mule and a pony, two rifles,
two revolvers, blankets, flour, coffee, yeast powder, a bit of

1. According to C. G. Coutant, McKay was a California miner who
reached South Pass in March 1868 and helped with the construction
of the ten stamp mill at Miner's Delight. He was the first Superin-
tendent of the mill in 1869. The U. S. Census of 1870 listed him at
Hamilton City, a miner, age forty, born in Scotland, owning real estate
valued at $1,000. In 1898, McKay, who was still in the mining district,
claimed that during the first six months the mill turned out $300,000
in gold, and that up to 1898 Miner's Delight had produced $1,200,000
in gold.

bacon, fishing hooks and lines, two mugs, tobacco, matches, a small *phial* of brandy, and one scalping knife!

Down in Spring gulch this morning I saw a nugget taken out by Jonathan Pugh—the largest yet found in these diggins. It weighs five ounces all but two & a half dollars and is worth $107.00 in greenbacks.

$123 in gold taken out that day. Weekly return $860.

We left Miner's Delight at two o'clock in the afternoon and proceeded at a leisurely pace through the gulches. There was no path, and our way lay, through an intricate maze of timber and rocky ground, toward a point of the hills where we were told we should strike the Wash-ke trail. Neither of us were familiar with the route, and without guide or compass it is not easy for an inexperienced traveller to avoid a certain confusion of ideas as regards the four points. The mountains are like so many mischievous individuals who would maliciously volunteer all kinds of information to a stranger—one pointing this way, another that way, and a third contradicting the other two by disclosing a curving ravine which leads you nowhere.

Such, to a certain extent, was our experience at the outset, yet by a kind of bull head luck we managed to wend and weave our way pretty much in the right direction. Thus when we crossed the Beaver, passing through a deep grassy basin we found ourselves in a dead lock. Here were hills sloping down on every side and we had the choice of various gulches through which to climb to the heights beyond.

We might have adopted the old method of setting up a staff on end and following its lead. But we debated, considered, paused, took counsel of the sun and went up round the face of the hill to a high level covered with long spear grass. A solitary antelope started up two hundred yards ahead and trotted off at a dignified pace, looking round in a kind of mute wonderment at the intruders. Although we had no use for him dead or alive, George was not proof against the temptation so he fired. The creature gave a start and trotted off on three legs. The two bloodthirsty monsters followed him up the hillside round by a cluster of rocks and over the brow of the mountain, tracking his bloody footprints all the way on the snow. He died, and we left him there to the wolves.

We were making poor progress all this while, and the sun was getting toward the hills while our journey was but just begun. The uncertainty as to the road was soon set at rest when we perceived an old Indian trail and followed it down a back bone and round by many a winding slope till it crossed Twin Creek.[2] Here we suddenly recollected a remark made by Van Buren to Harrison,[3] so we stopped and took the oath.

For a pair of travellers out on a pleasure hunt we were as badly mounted as travellers very well could be. My sorrel was nothing to boast of. He was broken winded as I soon discovered—rather gaunt and bony, and so absent minded that without constant nudging he would stop a hundred times a day to meditate over a bunch of grass. George rode a mule, who started out bucking and continued to buck at every ten steps to the last. He had a tolerably grave stubborn face, but he was evidently meant for a comedian, and so long as I rode behind him I could see that his whole game was to annoy his rider and make my horse laugh. He did not so much buck as throw out first one leg and then the other

2. According to James Carpenter, the trail from the Wind River Valley followed up Red Canyon for about a mile, thence up Cherry Creek, crossed Deep Creek and continued on to Twin Creek. It then followed Twin Creek to the headwaters and crossed to Big Beaver, followed up Trail Creek, crossed Rock Creek, Slate Creek, Dunbar Meadows, Willow Creek and angled around the mountains to the Sweetwater River. The main trail went west to near the present site of Daniel, Wyoming. On this first journey to the Wind River Valley Chisholm missed Red Canyon.
3. "Let's have a drink." (Apocryphal)

and shake it. I was making merry over his drolleries once, when he threw a leg at me and nearly split my shin bone in two. After that I didn't laugh, but went on ahead.

The trail—very faint at first and broken, soon broadened into a distant track as it drew over a long stretch of high rolling grounds which gradually dipped to the right and left commanding a magnificent prospect of mountain scenery. The nearer hills were golden with the light of the sun, and the verdure down their slope had a soft velvety gloss. This peculiar effect is heightened at sunset by the dark shadows which steal over the furrows and dimples.

A deep winding gorge or valley lies far below us to the left, seeming to descend to unfathomable depths, and from the thither side of it rises a belt of blood-red cliffs which they say are full of iron. A soft thin haze floats over the valley like a dream and a far off murmur of waters from its unseen recesses strikes upon the attentive ear. Beyond it, range above range of rugged hills swell upward to the heavens, while tracking the course of the ravine the eye wanders back through a lane of golden sunlight, till it rests upon a wondrous pile of blue mountains, over the distant peaks of which the sun is retiring. In what unimaginable shades of beauty and grandeur they lie around us—silent, untameable, brooding over their own great thought as if they would keep it all to themselves forever.

One involuntarily refrains from talking in presence of such a sight when the evening silence is creeping over it, as if he had no business to intrude upon their eternal sleep. The antelope starts up at the approach of the stranger and looks round at him, but more in wonder as it seems than fear—then flees with stately nimble step over the brow of the hill. The wolves and cayotes which are rarely visible by day now begin to gallop abroad and make night hideous with their howlings and yelpings. "They roar after their prey and seek their meat from God". (Psalms XXIV. 9)

I think the best inspired painter that ever drew would fail in attempting to describe these mighty mountains. He may convey correctly enough an impression of their shape, their vast extent and sublime beauty. But there is a something always left out which escapes all his colors and all his skill. Their aspects shift and vary continually. Their very shapes seem to undergo a perpetual transformation like the clouds above them. There is a mystery like the mystery of the sea— a silence not of death but of eternity. Unless the painter can realize to me on his canvas a glimpse of this meaning, I may admire his handiwork, but I cannot believe in "art". I have seen Bierstadt's pictures of the Rocky Mountains and while I recognize their wonderful merits as representations of mountain scenery I think I can appreciate the verdict of the European critics who characterized them as elaborate geographical maps.

One can distinguish a thorough mountaineer by nothing more characteristic than his careful attention to trifles—his faculty of not losing anything, not even a rag or a piece of string. He carries nothing with him on a journey but what he absolutely needs, and the loss of one little trifle may occasion the most serious inconvenience. "Despise not the day of small things" is an aphorism which it is well to keep in mind in the mountains. I know a man who saved his life once by having a few lucifer matches in his pocket. Let an inexperienced man start on a ten days ride without some watchful counsellor at his elbow, and ten to one he will arrive at his destination without the coat on his back.

I am competent to offer good advice on this subject, for I have been a sufferer, nor am I yet cured of my carelessness. We had not proceeded many miles on this very trip before I discovered that my pistol had dropped out of the scabbard. We rode back for an hour or so until it grew quite dark, so we could not find it—and we had just come within sight of a good camping spot when we had to return.

This camping spot lay far down below us—a creek with willow bushes in a valley, walled in by high smooth hills. As we approached nearer to it down the end of the hill we caught sight of a blazing fire. This was not an encouraging sight for we naturally concluded that it was an Indian camp. As it was quite dark, however, we adventured at a stealthy pace through the soft grass in the bottom till we got within the shelter of the willows about a hundred yards from the fire. Then we saw it was a solitary white man, and so risking our lives and fortunes we made a daring charge right through the intervening space and cried "hillo!" We showed no mercy to the enemy but threw a bottle of whisky at his head before he had time to defend himself.

It was "Mountain Bill" [Bill Rhodes, also known as Dutch Bill], one of the oldest hunters in the West; and his dog "Calamity". He had killed a fine fat Elk and we all sat down to a dainty supper after turning the animals loose—broiled meat, bread and coffee—a supper fit for a King if a King were hungry.

Bill Rhodes is a type of the genuine hunter. He is at home in this world of mountains where he has roamed for twenty seven years, and not a spot but is familiar to him as his old fireside. He hunted bears at seventeen and they have remained his favorite game to this day. All through Montana, California, Oregon and many other lands he has been, and now he is living in the Wind River Valley where he has a tract of farming land.

Bill is about forty five but he might pass for five years younger—an active, well built wiry looking man of middle height. The expression of his face is frank and pleasing—his manner usually earnest, indicative of a handy fearlessness of nature, but with a touch of broad, Western humor in it— long straight hair, a face browned by the sun and wind, a large clear eye, keen as a hawk's, and slight trace of the German accent in his speech.

He was not averse to talk, after supper was over and we had gathered round the fire to enjoy our pipes, and his conversation, abounding in personal anecdote and philosophic observation, was full of interest. He had much to say concerning the mines and the men who were working them while he afforded me some interesting information about the oil springs in Wind River and elsewhere, as well as about the productive capacities of the valley generally. He was curious to know what the government's intentions were with regard to Wind River, whether they would give it up as a Reservation and turn adrift those like himself who had braved the dangers and rendered the place a habitable field for the white man.

Without this valley, he said, these mines will be of no account for years to come. Provisions will be too high for poor men to live, and the quartz will be worked at enormous expense. This valley here is the only place in the whole territory worth settling. It is the finest stock raising country in God's world and the best farming land. Old Bridger tried to prevail on the Mormons to come to Wind River when they settled at Salt Lake which was a desert then, but they didn't take his advice. They have tried several times since to settle in it, but the Indians always drove them out. Here the miners can raise all they want. They can raise a family, they can raise stock, they can grow barley and oats, wheat, corn, potatoes, and all kinds of vegetables. If the government won't interfere the Indians could be driven out in one season, and we won't need any of Sherman's cavalry to help us either. If you are writing anything for the papers, he remarked, just put in a word on this subject.

Although Bill is anxious for emigration, however, you could see that he would have been better contented had the whites never come near the valley. "I am sorry a white man ever saw this place", he said. Talking of the Indians—and he is no Indian lover himself, he said

"When I travelled this country twenty years ago there was no trouble with the Indians. I have been all through their camps, the Blackfeet, the Siouxs and the Crows, and I turned my horse out and lay down at night with just as little fear as I would in St. Louis or any big city—and a d——— sight less. When I came across their camps they treated me to the best they had. They gave me the best supper they could set down, and they let me have as many Buffalo skins to sleep on as would smother me. Now these same Indians, if I got near them, would scalp me. Who has brought about all this change? Why, the government itself."

Old Wash-ke he characterized as the best Indian he ever knew. He has a wiser head on his shoulders than any Indian. Washke makes Wind River his headquarters all winter and the Siouxs clear away to the Big Horn when he comes. He wants the white men to settle in the valley, and this fall he offers to go after the Siouxs and clean them out if the white men will raise a hundred good men to assist him. His band is now reduced to ninety lodges or about four hundred warriors. Not many years ago his people numbered as many thousands. But they died or dropped off by the demoralizing influences of civilization. Numbers of them are now hanging around the forts—useless incumbrances. These are what they call the "Sugar and Coffee Indians". They steal and beg, and are disowned by their tribe. The Snakes hereabouts will not steal—Washke won't allow them.

They are tolerably virtuous too—more so indeed than they generally get credit for. If a squaw belonging to a Buck is unchaste with a white man, the Buck drowns her. "They tied one" says Bill "to a horse and run her to death". Widows are exempt; they may follow their inclinations and nothing is said about it. A young unmarried squaw may be punished by the parents, but they don't take her life.

It appears there are a class of squaws corresponding to a certain class of white women in cities. They are not permitted to dwell alongside of the others, but have their tepees outside of the encampment. Yet the Bucks are not generally so particular as most husbands among the palefaces, but they insist on having the remuneration themselves. They will sell a squaw for a good pistol or a round of ammunition. If they are hard up they will lend you a squaw for a whole winter if you find him in grub. The girl, when she is sold to a white man, is generally skeary for a while and will take the first chance to run away. Should you take her again, and whip her well, and perhaps clip a little slice out of her ear, then she will stay.

Of the habits, abodes and characteristics of various nations I heard from Bill a whole history enough to fill a volume, but my interest in the subject is not particularly strong, so I refrain. Some tribe whose name I forget, are strong catholics. "They never sit down to eat" said Bill "without crossing themselves like damnation." On the other hand a certain missionary went over to a tribe in Montana and told them all about the Great Spirit. But the chief came up to him and said "If your Great Spirit is so good as you say, why don't he provide food for his people. Why don't he give them plenty of Buffalo and Elk. You white men have to come to my valleys and kill all my Buffalo, because your Great Spirit won't give them any at home. I don't want your Great Spirit. You go away".

I asked Bill whether the Indians gave him much trouble in the valley now. He said they seldom came near his cabin. Some time ago the Blackfeet cleaned out everything he had.

"I had a squaw then" he said "and she was down at the creek washing some skins. She gave the alarm and I crept up the bluff and saw about forty of them ransacking my cabin. They carried off my gun and my horses, and about two thousand dollars worth of furs and skins. The squaw and me took to the brush and we had to walk along that creek fifteen miles with them after us". However said Bill "I got even with them afterwards, for I went after them and got forty horses".

He had a notion he said to go after the Siouxs lately in company with another man to make a raid, but old Wash-ke advised him against it. "Don't you go Bill" said Wash-ke "for you'll go the same road as —— went" (naming a man) who was scalped by them lately.

He was quite indignant with George and reproved him sharply for killing the antelope when he knew he couldn't pack him. Such wanton murder he considers an infringement on the law scarcely less reprehensible than killing a man without just cause. "I don't want to see many more such boys as you out with a gun".

The Buffalo he said are getting scarcer in the Wind River every year. They are all driving North—up by the Red River. Four years ago in this same valley he had seen as many as ten thousand at once.

I might recite a hundred different Bear stories here, but they are too numerous. Bill is fond of Bears—that is, he is fond of fighting them. He has killed grizzlies often with no other weapon than a butcher knife, but it is dangerous sport. In fact, most old hunters will tell you that the longer you follow grizzlies the more afraid of them you get. "Bad-hand Martin" is the best hunter of bears in the country. He does nothing else but follow bears, and his body is all torn up from head to foot with their claws. "It does me good" says Bill "to hear 'em yowl when they get a shot". He told us of one fight he had with a bear when he had to go home after, as naked as Adam. Every rag of clothes had been torn clean off.

"The first time I ever got into a fight with a Grizzly" he said "I had a close shave. I was nothing but a boy then—not seventeen. I saw a she grizzly with two cubs, and she made for me before I ever fired at her. I was a good deal excited and I didn't more than just wound her a little. Well I made for a willow tree and got up, and the grizzly she made for the tree as savage as blazes. It wasn't thicker than my leg, and she clawed up and got hold of the branch I sat on and drew me down right to her mouth. I could see clear down her throat. She hadn't sense though, to hold on and catch me with the other claw, but always let me swing up again. Darn me if that Bear didn't keep me swingin' in that tree, between her jaws and old God Almighty for eight hours. She went off at last, and I got down and went for some other boys. We went after her again and I killed her myself after all".

He couldn't live in the States again. He has been back several times in the course of his life, but was always glad to get away. Yet he has a notion to go back once more, and that too with a laudable object. Civilized people are gathering round him, and Bill is not above some of the weaknesses of civilized humanity. He wants a wife. He imagines that his beautiful valley, green and productive as it is, might become fairer and perhaps still more productive, if he could find an helpmeet to look after his tea kettle and keep his cabin tidy.

I suggested the probability of his being able to find many a woman who could be prevailed upon to undertake the job.

"Yes, very likely, but the devil of it is could you find the right kind of one? Better be without them at all than get hold of the wrong kind".

"In that case" I remarked "you would have to take the chances as we all do".

"Well" he mused "I suppose if it turned out bad, you could drop her as you do the squaws. There's no divorce laws in this country".

"Suppose she got tired and wanted to drop you".

"Why I could take her over to the other side of the Big Horn Mountains, and then she couldn't get away. If she ever wandered from camp the Sioux would get her".

He did not talk about "Natur'" or the Great Spirit nor expatiate finely, with the untaught philosophy of a child of the desert, upon the works of the Creator. He knows all about cities, although he cannot live in them, and the value of greenbacks, and the state of politics, and in short betrays a shrewd practical worldly wisdom sufficient to overturn all the romantic notions concerning the traditional hunter of fiction. And yet he is as genuine an old hunter as Natty Bumpo himself.

His life is passed in solitude. He had lived among the Indians, and he has fought them. He knows every range and valley and rock and hollow of all this mountain country as well as "the oldest citizen" knows his native town. He can follow a trail with the nicety of a Red Skin, and can tell by the print of a mocassin whether it was on a white foot or a red. He lives alone in a small cabin which stands on a beautiful woody island in the Wind River Valley. And this is all I have been able to find out in one evening about Mountain Bill.[4]

We camped with him that night, and in the morning he treated us to another meal off the fat Elk, and pointed out

4. Several sources, including C. G. Coutant in his *History of Wyoming* and Noyes Baldwin in a manuscript in the Bancroft Library, state that Bill Rhodes was killed in the spring of 1868. Chisholm's chance meeting with Rhodes refutes these stories, which may have confused him with Bill Rose (see page 61). Rhodes did lose his life the following spring. In May 1869, the Indians raided Little Popo Agie, robbed the Stone ranch where Frank Morehouse lived, and then killed Morehouse on the road to Cottonwood, taking some $1,500 from his body. They next met Mountain Bill Rhodes, killed and stripped him, leaving his deady body in his wagon. They cut his four-horse team from the harness and took them. Near the same place on the road to Cottonwood they met and killed Dutch Henry and the mule he was riding.

the right road from which it seems we had wandered a little. He proposed to remain in that valley for sometime and hunt the surrounding hills, so we would probably find him there on our return.

VI

WIND RIVER VALLEY

W E WERE ON THE ROAD soon after sunrise, with my dreaming sorrel more meditative than ever, and George's comic mule shaking out his hind legs like a clog dancer. The air was quite warm now and we had long been free from any trace of the snowstorm. Our first resting place would be the Little Popogia, and from that we could push on to the Big Popogia where the valley properly speaking begins. We soon regained the trail again, and travelled on as merrily as the animals would permit. They were the cause of much profane talk at times. I had entertained a notion of buying the horse as I was offered him cheap, but my experience of him spoiled the bargain effectually.

The mule was valued at a hundred dollars in case he should fall into the hands of the Siouxs. But this was a possibility we had ceased to contemplate. Somehow Bill's talk had familiarized us with the idea of Indians, and familiarity begets contempt. Pooh! the Indians were all out of the valley. We cried holla, but we were not quite out of the wood.

The day was not far advanced, and we were approaching within a few miles of the river. The valley through which it flowed could be distinguished ahead, while we could see far over the rolling land beyond. Any speck in these lonely regions instantly arrests the attention—a distant Elk, or a cabin—and the eye is quick to perceive objects which seem not to belong to the place.

George drew my attention about this time to a black spot far off which seemed to move, disappear, and come into view again. It was some time ere I could detect the thing, and after a variety of idle conjectures we concluded that it was a team. Whatever it was it was moving toward us and gradually enlarging. When sufficiently near we at length made it out beyond all doubt to be a small party of travellers with mules or horses. They were about the same distance from the valley as we were, so we expected to meet them there when we camped.

The valley is a long one though not of great width and is covered along the course of the stream with a dense growth of willows. The river is shallow and noisy, brawling down from an enormous canion above, with an agreeable sound. A sudden dip of the ground left the travellers out of our view for a little time, and just as we emerged upon our slope of the bottom they were coming down the other side. One brief glance was all we took of them then, for that revealed to us that we were within rifle range of a small party of Indians. There were four of them and two horses.

We had never quite tried the paces of our animals till that moment, and I will give them credit for doing one short heat to admiration. We made one dive for the brush— our only chance of safety, and the Indians acted on the same impulse and disappeared among the willows further up the stream. Perhaps they were as much frightened as we were, but I hardly think it. I would not wish to insist on it as an absolute certainty, because one is apt to be mistaken often in things which seem to be palpable facts, but I *think* —I merely put it as a probability—*I think I was a little scared just then*. If anyone can convince me to the contrary I shall be ready to retract.

We plunged across the stream and both dismounted, dragging our horses hastily under shelter, and then creeping ourselves forward through the thick brush till we could peep through the open valley. I might close my account of the fight here, for here it virtually ended, although we were by no means sure of our scalps at that time.

This was our only chance of safety, for Indians will never attack you in the timber. They know that the chances are against them, because the party in ambush is sure to have the first sight. We had been well posted in regard to this, and my "Companion in arms" (if I may use the expression now, having seen some service—h-m.!) was fortunately no unpractised hand. Had we encountered them in the open hills we were gone up. When a man takes to his heels— whether his own or his horse's—he is sure to be overtaken and shaved for a priest, so his only chance anyhow is to offer fight.

Now that it is all over I almost wish that we had made a fight of it and that I had brained three of them and taken their scalps and carried off their horses, and cried out "come on if there's any more of ye!" But I didn't, and after all one has a complacent satisfaction in passing his hand through his top hair.

But as the novelists always say just when they anticipate (and do it on purpose too) I must not anticipate.

Our fight lasted the greater part of the day, and when I mention the fact that we never exchanged a shot, and never saw the enemy all the time, one would say it was rather queer one. But we had not lost any Indians so we had no mind to go and look for them. We had come to the valley about noon and we lay among the willows till dusk. As long as we lay there we were safe.

The principal trouble was to keep the animals quiet, and prevent them from running away. We tied them fast to a tree and they remained tolerably peaceable. Whether the Indians remained in their concealment all the time, or went away through the head of the valley I cannot say. Probably they were as anxious to avoid a fight as we were.

About dusk we ventured cautiously out of the bushes and stole softly into the stream, then followed it down, keeping well under cover all the way, till we were out of view of the original spot. Finally we landed, swallowed a lunch, struck over the hills, and started on a brisk run for the Big Popogia. Soon we came to Willow Creek and there we breathed and got over our scare. Stopped to eat and feed our animals and again proceeded.

For more reasons than one it was well to travel by night. It is safe, and the country over which we passed was so grey and desolate that it would have been no cheerful sight by day. Nothing but a monotonous succession of ridges and long bare flats. The Wind River Mountains were on our left, high, craggy, and sombre looking—lower ranges of hills extending along the right. Before us the long grey hollows, one succeeding another.

The horses were tired, and without constant goading threatened every minute to give out. Would we never come to a creek! The worst of it was we both got a little out of temper. While resting at the last creek I had laid this diary down on the grass, and left it behind. But I would not have turned back then for a bag of gold. George lost a rope too, and we had not enough left to hobble the horses. I was disappointed at the loss of my book but I trusted to luck that I might get it on my return. Travellers were few and far between in these parts.

We had travelled over ten miles according to our calculations and in a very dispirited condition. Another ridge was yet to climb—surely that would be the last. I made a last spasmodic effort and found myself on the other side of the hill.

I was descending a vast spreading declivity. The character of the ground was different and the climate felt more genial. The night was too obscure to enable me to discern anything at a distance, but I felt that we were now among long grass, which waved and whitened in the dim light like fields of wheat. Was that a rush of distant waters? We stopped and listened. The old mule pricked up his ears and gave an ecstatic flourish of his hind legs. Yes, we were not mistaken. Faintly audible was the long wash of a river far below. From that moment I moved through a land of enchantment. Never had I heard a more welcome sound.

Although we could see nothing clearly, imagination was busy filling up the blank, and perhaps my first impression of Wind River Valley (for we were there at last) gained an additional charm by looking on it through those mysterious optics. We made a break for the river thinking soon to find some cabin. How fresh and musical grew the sound of the water as we neared it, and the grassy field was so smooth beneath our feet that I would not have been surprized to light upon some old homestead—some venerable farm with cattle grazing in the meadows.

Presently a cabin glimmered into view, but we found it deserted. Approaching the bottom we saw the dark fringe of trees along the banks, and on the other side a broad expanse of rich bottom land. Down over the bluffs and into the river bottom, and our horses were wading up to the hocks in grass. George had not quite got over his discontent and was peering and groping along in search of a cabin. As for me I felt as if I had reached home, so throwing up the bridle and resting one limb over the horn of my saddle I let old sorrel follow as he pleased. We came to another cabin, deserted as the former one—halloored round it for a minute and passed on.

We wandered down the valley for miles and found no trace of human beings. We passed beautiful wooded islands in the river—bowery paradises dimly seen through the basky shadows—doubled numerous rocky capes, sometimes scaling the bluffs, and anon threaded our way through mazes of cotton wood and willow, and long grass as high as our heads, till at last, finding no trace of a habitation we lay down near the river and slept, the rushing water singing lullaby. The water—yes, and the wolves. Their howl is the most dismal thing to be heard in the mountains. They came so near us that we took the precaution to pack our provision bag close to our heads. They would steal it while you slept and you might never know.

In the early morning I saw them scampering off in every direction as I lifted my head. It was a lovely morning notwithstanding there was a white coating of hoar frost over us, but when the sun rose came warmth. The animals were fairly revelling in the rich pasture, and praising the Lord for his bounty with all their teeth. Great flocks of birds were winging their way overhead—magpies and wild ducks, and numbers of smaller feathered citizens. The shy antelope came peering over the bluffs and disappeared in a flash to inform his fellow creatures of the arrival of new comers.

I kindled a fire with exceeding great caution fearful of setting the bottom in a blaze (what could Bill Rhodes say if that should happen?) and prepared breakfast, while George went to the river with hook and line and returned with a tempting dish of fresh mountain trout, which we broiled over the hot coals. O wasn't it a dainty dish!

If the valley seemed beautiful in the night time, its enchantments were magnified tenfold as I looked abroad in the morning. Here I thought summer surely reigns perpetual—and this is all but literally true. The winter is scarcely felt as soon as you strike the Popogias, and the severest snow storm rarely remains over a few days. The sudden change of scene from the bare mountains to the rich verdure and leafiness of the valley had quite a magical effect. I compared myself to Satan lighting upon the garden of Eden after his rough journey through Chaos. Poor Devil! he must have enjoyed himself hugely that time. I suppose the reason he assumed the form of a snake was that he could roll in the grass so conveniently.

The waters of the Popogia are wonderfully clear, of a dark green color, and its densely wooded banks, where they are not rocky, seem heaving with plenty. It is not an easy task to approach the side of the stream by reason of the thick groves of cotton wood. I spent a pleasant hour in the morning fishing, while my companion was abroad elsewhere with his gun. Swarms of wild ducks came scuttling round the bend every minute, so thick that I could bring them down with stones. Speckled trout, whitefish and suckers abound in the river and they bite readily so that one can soon get up a dinner.

Near our camping place were the ashes of several fires and the bended twigs with both ends stuck in the ground showing the trace of Indians. In the forenoon we started again and proceeded still further down the valley where fresh wonders met us at every step. The incidents of the trip were trivial and I need not continue the details.

The Big Popogia flows down for several miles till it is joined by the Little Wind River, and then again falls into the Big Wind River which flows to the Big Horn which empties into the Missouri.[1] The whole length of the valley is about eighty miles, and the width of the bottom (the farming land) varies from two to seven miles. But beyond the bottoms there are vast expanses of fine grazing ground on which thousands of herds could be raised. Along the course of the rivers there is any quantity of heavy timber while the soil is capable of producing the best of grain, wheat, corn and . . .

[*Pages 119 and 120 missing.*]

. . . anything to surpass this valley. As an adjunct to the mines it is invaluable. It is necessary to their development. The two together will form one of the most prosperous countries on the continent. Without the valley the development of the mines will be retarded for years. And when this is settled up so that it will hold no more there is another valley of equal fertility on the other side of the Big Horn Mountains stretching for over sixty miles in length, where not only agricultural, but mineral wealth abounds.

One of the most picturesque objects to be seen is a natural archway of rock on the Big Popogia, which is formed by the junction of several streams. It is as symmetrical as man could make it and has a natural road across.

I could linger among these scenes forever and a day. To be emancipated from all care, and to wander day by day through ever changing scenes of splendor, down by winding rivers, through spreading valleys—what a life me thinks. But "sounds from home" come stealing through the remotest solitudes. I long to mingle again in the excitements and gaeities of a big city.

Lying broad awake one night I dreamed a dream and in

---

1. The history of the naming of the Wind and Bighorn rivers is not clear. Actually they are one stream: the Wind River, flowing north, enters the Wind River Canyon under the name just given, and emerges from the canyon as the Bighorn River.

the morning I said "George we must get back at once—let us turn". So we turned. We had already proceeded as far as was necessary, and in a little while we might have been among the Blackfeet. Washke and his band had not yet arrived at which I was disappointed for I expected to make his acquaintance being a gentlemanly Indian. Nor did we see any Buffalo on our rambles although their traces were everywhere around us.

We returned by the same road as we came, and just on emerging from the valley we succeeded in killing two antelope. This time we flayed and cut them up and hung the hind quarters on a tree, placing a stake near the place so that Bill might get them when he came that way. When we returned to Willow Creek I found my book lying undisturbed at the foot of a bush.

It was near evening as we got back to the valley of the Little Popogia where we had such a long rest before, and we took an hour again for refreshments. It was all quiet and safe now. At one end of it was a small stone cabin, built by Bill Rhodes in 1857. I found in it a Beaver's head, and a doll which had evidently been left by some small papoose. On many of the creeks we passed there were beaver dams, but the creatures are not to be seen except you lie and watch very still for them at night.

We came to our old valley again late at night and found Mountain Bill still there. We had a long talk that night concerning some business matters and he and George and I went into partnership.

Next morning we all three went out on a hunt, and were gone the best part of a day without finding any game. Bill shot a cayote and laid him dead in his tracks, and this was the only result of our day's sport. "Calamity" was left in the hollow to take charge of our traps. He is a foolish idiotic sort of a dog, but has good points about him no doubt or Bill would not keep him. Bill spoke of going out prospecting this fall to the Big Horn Mountains and it seems there are several miners bent on a similar expedition. The last one this summer was interrupted by the Indians who killed one of the men.

We soon departed from this spot and took our way to Miner's Delight, Bill accompanying us part of the way. As we came to a path wending round the face of a hill the hunter, bidding us a brief adieu, directed his steps toward the top of the mountain and soon was lost to view among the scrub cedar on the heights. Half an hour after we heard the crack of his rifle, and looking back I saw a man dismounting from his horse among the rocks on the hill top. And that was my last view of Mountain Bill.

VII

"IF I CAN MAKE THE RIFFLE . . ."

LATE AT NIGHT we arrived at Miner's Delight where every-thing was just as we had left it. The card table in the corner was in full blast. The parties whom we had left on a drunk were now sobering off and those we had left sober were getting on a drunk.

In mining matters the principal theme of discussion was the result of the last clean out at Toger's Mill.[1] The rock

1. The Tozer and Eddy mill was located in Hermit Gulch and was the first erected in the area. An item in the *Sweetwater Mines* (June 13, 1868) describes the mill: "Messrs. Tozer and Eddy have purchased a six stamp quartz mill of Messrs Jennings, Godbe, Lawrence and others, of Salt Lake, which will cost, when put up and in running order, from $10,000 to $15,000. They will have the mill and two ar-rastas in operation within thirty days from this date. The mill and arrastas will be run by water power, and will be capable of working fifteen tons of ore, in a thorough manner, per day. The mill was made

taken out of the Jim Dyer lead had been pronounced equal to anything in the district, and the owners were building up greatly on what it would turn out. After it was taken to the mill they were offered $40 per ton for the rock as it lay and they calculated on a return of at least $60 per ton. The actual returns were $5.25 per ton. Great dissatisfaction exists through out all the camps and suspicions are pretty openly hinted that there is a screw loose somewhere in Toger's Mill. The Jim Dyer boys are not a whit discouraged and have the same confidence in the ledge as before. The shaft is down thirty feet and the quartz gives richer prospects than ever. Only Col. Tozer will not have the grinding of any more of it. The miners are all distrustful and Tozer is in bad odor. Perhaps the "tailings" could tell a tale.

Nichols' little mill on the Beaver is now running, and grinding about four ton of rock per day. It is but a small affair, only four wooden stamps connected with an arasta, yet it will prove a paying speculation, and Nichols is a trustworthy industrious man who minds his own business and does not play poker.

In the diggings at Spring Gulch two men are taking out about $80 per day. The cleanings out from the Toms the last two days yielded $86.00 and $86.15 in the upper gulch.

The oil springs in Wind River had been much "cracked up" to me by certain parties here who were interested in one of them, but I found the reports to be considerably exaggerated, although there are indications enough to set

---

at the Union Foundry, San Francisco, and although it has got but few stamps is very perfect and complete in all its fittings. The stamps weigh six hundred and fifty pounds each. There is one Wheeler Pan of the new style lately adapted to the use of gold quartz mills; also, one Beldin Settler and a Hendy's Concentrator. This is the kind of news we are most happy to give our readers and we wish these enterprising gentlemen unbounded success in their undertaking."

Tozer and Eddy were reported as owners of the Carissa mine on July 13, 1868.

many a man crazy. A spring owned by Connor yields a fair run daily, oozing steadily out of the ground, and coating the surrounding space with a black tarry substance like shoemakers wax. The claim is disputed with Connor by several parties, and apparently none of the parties are doing anything with the property. Other claims in the vicinity have been located this fall, and I fully expect to hear of an oil excitement here before long.

But by far the most important of them all is a well quite unknown to any of the men hereabout, excepting Bill Rhodes and two others. It is situated about twenty miles from the old emigrant road and lies E. N. E. from South Pass City.[2] This spring *flows*, not oozes, at the rate of at least ten barrels per day. There is a fine sulphur spring close by it, and plenty of timber. The flow is much larger than all the springs in Wind River put together. Bill discovered it a few years ago but never thought of taking steps towards securing it.[3]

---

2. James Carpenter and Phil Brandon of Atlantic City state that this oil spring was probably located on Beaver Creek six miles west of the present Lander-Rawlins highway on the Larson (now the Johnny Ourr) ranch four miles above Haley.

3. Several oil springs were known at an early date in the Wind River Valley and vicinity. Captain B. L. E. Bonneville reported the discovery of the "Great Tar Springs" in Washington Irving's *Adventures of Captain Bonneville*: these are the springs found at the present Dallas field below the mouth of Twin Creek. "From the date of Bonneville's visit up to 1867," Professor W. C. Knight of the University of Wyoming reported in 1897, "the oil springs was unknown except to the hunter and trapper who frequented the locality to secure the oil for medicinal purposes."

North of Lander at the old Plunkett Field there was a seepage of light oil with a good deal of paraffin. It took several days to obtain a vessel of oil from this seep. About three miles northwest of Lander was the spring known for many years as the Washakie oil spring and claimed by Chief Washakie. It was located on the side of a steep bluff facing the west, about one hundred feet above the gulch which cuts its base. According to Professor Knight, several springs existed here at one time. The oil was so light and pure that no beds of asphaltum were formed. Professor Knight also reported an oil spring northeast of present Fort Washakie and on the north side of Little Wind River;

Since my return to the mines I have occupied myself in acquiring a more accurate knowledge of the country before bidding a final adieu. I have spent a good part of the day in diving into the shafts, wandering over the different leads, poring over bits of rock, and taking a survey of the district generally. I may now proceed to note down a few of the results on my observations.

The entire mining district may be designated as a great Talk range extending from the California district to the Oregon about 40 miles in length and from 15 to 20 miles in width.[4] The general formation of the talk range lies North of East and South of West. It is bounded on the North by a granite formation; on the South by granite and sandstone; on the North East by sand and lime, while on the West lies the broad sandy desert through which I passed.

The talk formation is mixed with gneiss and porphyry (showing heavy crystallization) and the wall rocks of the ledges exhibit a mixture of gneiss and Talk. In all the leads the gold so far has been found free from all base metal. This, as I understand, is the general character of the gold found in talk formations. (In the mining districts of Colorado where the quartz is mostly found in granite formations the gold is considerably mixed with base metals, rendering it hard and expensive to work—and this is one of the great drawbacks to Colorado although gold may be found in abundance.) The richest gold, both in placer and quartz, is always found where it approximates to the sandstone—as in Miner's Delight which lies on the North Eastern limit of the Talk range, and is bounded by a high range of sand and lime stone.

The hill in which this celebrated lead exists, forms the

it was said to be surrounded by a bed of asphaltum measuring fifty by one hundred yards and from a few inches to three feet in thickness.

4. Some of the mining districts formed in this area were: Lincoln, Shoshoni, Pacific, Summit, California, Oregon, Mill, Wyoming, Kentucky, Atlantic, Lewiston, and Oregon Gulch Placers.

"divide" between the Wind River and the valley of the Sweetwater. The Beaver on one side cuts through the sand stone range and seeks the waters on the Popogias which ultimately fall into the headwaters of the Missouri; while the Sweetwater on the other runs to the Platte River. This hill declines from a high peak down a broad slope cut into a succession of ridges and gulches, and all more or less penetrated with ledges of rich quartz. The course of the Miner's Delight ledge is tortuous—in some instances taking a direction almost across the face of the hill—but running on the average in accordance with the general formation, and dipping Northward.

Originally the company took up 1600 feet on Discovery Claim, but it is now divided into two companies, each running 800 feet. It extends 1½ miles Easterly and 2 miles Westerly. No work has been done however on the extensions. On each claim is a well defined ledge from 2½ to 3 feet in width. On the Westerly end of Discovery they are now working 500 feet, and taking out good pay rock which averages from 450 to $800 per ton.

In all the specimen ledges the gold is found at the base of sulphate or oxide of iron. The Jim Dyer [located one half mile south-southwest of Atlantic City], the Cariso, and the Miner's Delight are all specimen ledges. The Lone Star, Buckeye, and Caraboo, are considered the best prospecting ledges for granular gold. The whole district, however, is as yet undeveloped, and the general opinion is that the richest ledges have never been struck. The specimens of rich float rock which are being found in many places, give sure indications of a ledge surpassing anything which has yet been discovered.

I looked today at the Bennet Lead, which runs about parallel to that of the Miner's Delight. The shaft is sunk on a spur of the same ridge, a little distance to the North West.

It runs across the head of Yankee Gulch,[5] where good placer diggings could be struck if there was a water supply, and was first discovered by Nichols who traced up the float rock through the gulch till he found the lead. The rock is very similar in character to that of Miner's Delight and shows abundance of free gold, more granular in form, running all through the ledge. Averages from 18 inches to 2 feet and prospects from 4 to 20 cents to the pound. Claim 1400 feet in extent. Shaft down 25 feet.

Another rich ledge in the same vicinity is the San Juan which stretches across the head of Yankee and Meadow Gulch and is supposed to supply them. Both gulches when working have paid from $50 to $200 a day to two hands. Free gold can be seen in the rock which will average $80 to the ton. The ledge averages 2 feet in width, and a shaft has been sunk on it to the depth of 30 feet. Like all the others it is undeveloped as yet, but shows as rich indications as are to be found in the district. Good facilities for working it.

But the most wonderful ledge of all is the *Atlantic* which stretches over some eight miles, and Heaven knows how much further if it were followed up. It is well defined throughout, and ranges in width from eight to forty feet— the most gigantic quartz ledge that was ever discovered. One could trace it for miles by the croppings of quartz on the surface, about as clearly as a turnpike road. The principal shafts have been sunk at Atlantic City, but the first indications of the lead are visible about a mile to the Southward of Miner's Delight where a shaft was sunk some forty feet. From that point it runs almost in a bee line to the Westward. It is a pity there should be any drawback to such a magnificent discovery. But the truth is the rock, so far as they have gone, is barren, or at best, gives such a poor pros-

5. Miner's Delight is located on Spring Gulch. Just north, running into Big Beaver is Yankee Gulch, and north of here is Meadow Gulch.

pect as will not pay to work. The rock may be rich enough after going down a few hundred feet, but who will throw in the money to prove it. If such a ledge were but tolerably rich it would be impossible to calculate the results.

I looked down the shaft where the work was first begun upon it. The quartz is burnt almost to a cinder and the ledge can be traced over several spurs by the black croppings between the wall rocks and the surface. In the quartz, while no trace of gold can be found, one finds large masses of glistening black slag of iron.

It would have been a sight for mortal eyes to be present, if that were possible, at the upheaval of these wondrous masses, to have seen old Pluto coming up with all this load upon his back. Here we can see the very print of his glowing hoof.

I am still wandering round and round the slopes of this vast spreading hill, which seems to branch out on every side in great spurs and gulches. The declination from the peak down to the Beaver is probably 1000 feet [about 800]. From the heights I can oversee the greater part of the principal mining districts. Down on the low rolling land to the South are the line of bluffs marking the course of the Sweetwater. Nearer is the Little Beaver whose headwaters are up in this hill, and which curves round till it flows due East. The smoke from Atlantic City ascends from the hollow yonder over the hill and Rock Creek cuts into the very heart of the mining district. Far to the South West are the sandy deserts with the two great Table Mountains [Oregon Buttes] rising clear and sharply defined high in the air. Westward the view closes by the range of the Rock River Mountains [Wind River Mountains]. Here from the extreme limit of this talk range we can gain a view of the whole as it sweeps round in a curve like a vast amphitheatre. From this point, where it is closed off by the Sandstone range the formation curves away due East.

All over this Southern slope of the hill I note plentiful outcroppings of quartz. Sometimes it is distributed in veins—what are called protrusions—throughout the loose talk, like skeleton leaves imprinted on the rock. Ascending nearer to the top of the hill I come at last to a dividing line, on one side of which is pure porphyry, and on the other grey gneiss. Pick up a piece of rock and you find the two conjoined and yet distinct from each other. Here is a thin reddish streak running through it. That is called Tiff [tuff, an organic rock]. The porphyry is pure black and harder than the hardest steel could penetrate. A little more crystallization would convert it into flint. It breaks off in splinters with sharp edges that would cut a hair. The Indians use this for arrow heads.

Down the back of a ridge which runs parallel to and nearly joining Miner's Delight we find croppings of quartz which gives rich indications. It runs straight in a line with the gulch where the best diggings are. This claim has been taken up and is called the "Last Chance", but no work has been done on it as yet.

This long ramble is rather fatiguing the first thing you know. I am getting into the rudiments of geology without the aid of books and I fear I know exceedingly little. But these rough observations may be of great assistance in future studies. This is a good place to begin in. Meanwhile a glass of beer will be very refreshing as you say.

October is here and I am not yet on my way home, and I have yet to see Salt Lake. I must be stirring now, else my Christmas dinner in Chicago will be getting cold. I have now relinquished the idea of going round by San Francisco.

News of battle! News of battle!

The whole camp is in a state of excitement and warlike preparation. The miners are mustering, and getting together all the rifles and arms that can be had. Some five or six horsemen and about fifteen infantry are ready to start on the war path, and my own rifle is at this moment slung over my back. The minstrel boy to the war has gone, and has left his book behind him. If he never returns, let em send it home, and tell them where to find him.

P. S. Alas, that I should have to record an unmistakable fizzle! And we were all bristling over with courage too. It came to pass in this way. A man of the name of Davis came into the camp and reported that George Owens [6] and another had been in all probability coralled by the Indians about fifteen miles East. He had seen a number of pony tracks and also the smoke from their camps. George Owens and Bill had gone down there to cut hay and as George had promised to be back yesterday, and had not come, it seemed likely that the Indians had got him in a tight place.

In less than half an hour the whole camp was in arms and prepared to start. There was no fuss made over it. One got up a list of names of those who were willing to go, and everyone set about hunting up guns and horses and ammunition. When all mustered we were six on horseback and fourteen on foot. We put blankets and provisions in a light wagon and started over the hill. Jeff Walford was elected Captain.[7] Everybody seemed in high spirits over the prospect of giving the Injuns a thorough clean out. Some had scalping knives and one man put a rope in the wagon. He was bound, he said, to hang some of them if he had a chance.

6. The U. S. Census of 1870 reported George Owens at Atlantic City, a miner, twenty-five years old, born in Ohio, owning real estate valued at $75.00.

7. Jefferson Wofford was listed as living at South Pass City in the U. S. Census of 1870. He was a farmer, thirty-four years old, born in Georgia, and owned personal property worth $300.

The expedition had not proceeded many miles when we saw a man on horseback down in a valley. The man was evidently not under the influence of a scare, for he got off his horse and went up the hill after some black tailed deer. It was in short no other than George Owens himself who had not been molested by the Indians and was on his way home. So we all turned right about face and got back in time for supper.

Of course we were all glad to find that George had not been scalped; but unless I am mistaken a few of us were just a little disappointed at losing our sport. I do not quite know what was my object in going out. Partly for the fun of the thing and partly for an experiment. I don't know whether I am a brave cuss or a coward, and it was a capital chance to find out. I will own up to a kind of sneaking half formed wish that the other man, Bill, whom I don't know, had got some of his hair cut off, so that the party would be sufficiently fired with vengeance to give them a desperate whipping. Sanguinary thoughts for a man of peace. I hope nobody who has any respect for me will believe a word of it. Perhaps 'tis fortunate that the affair has turned out as it did after all. I may now resume my geological lessons. In the morning I was wandering alone upon the hill chipping off bits of rock and making the most profound observations to myself regarding porphyritic, talk and other formations. Before evening I was (figuratively speaking) painted red, and calculating whether I would bring home a scalp to Chicago as a specimen or leave my own somewhere. I quite forgot to mention that I thought of her at the last.[8]

A very ominous growl may be heard from every section of the mines directed against Tozer and his mill. The returns made on the Dyer rock I have already alluded to. On the heels of that disaster comes another. Eighty five tons of

8. Chisholm is alluding to Mary Garrison.

rock from Miner's Delight had been contracted for by Col. Tozer, and the owners, although a little uneasy over it, were still pretty confident of a fair return. The value of the rock was then being crushed in Nichols' mill so that comparisons could be made. The results of the clean up were made known the other day when the rock yielded $23.19 per ton—just enough to defray the expenses of crushing and hauling, or in other words enough to a fraction to clear Tozer's expenses, leaving the owners $800 in debt for the expense of taking out the rock. The nicety of the calculation is something remarkable.

It is not in my province to join with the miners in denouncing Col. Tozer, but it is worth while to inquire into the causes of these discrepancies. Either the machinery is faulty, or there is gross dishonesty on the part of someone. Such returns reported without some explanation would seriously damage the reputation of the country. But the returns are beyond all question incorrect.

In the first place a six stamp mill which crushes at the rate of from 15 to 20 tons a day, is not doing thorough justice to the rock. Even Tozer himself does not pretend to deny this. The battery screen is not fine enough, and he uses too much water in the battery, so that a large quantity of the gold must escape through the tailings. This, however, will hardly suffice to explain the enormous discrepancy. A quantity of refuse rock from the same shaft in M. D. which was not thought worth the expense of hauling, was run through Comstock Arasta, and it has yielded $53 to the ton. Nichols is now crushing the same rock as went through Tozer's mill and the result will soon be known.

A 25 tons of Caraboo rock is at present undergoing the Tozer process, but I am told he has substituted a screen to the battery some six degrees finer than the other, and is taking more pains to pulverize the quartz. Tozer is interested in the Caraboo. I will return to this subject as circumstances develop themselves, and perhaps by placing an array of facts in proper shape, we may be enabled to arrive at a conclusion. I perceive my sojourn is likely to be prolonged for another week, as something has turned up which promises to excite my curiosity.

The Caraboo has turned out [$10] per ton.

"I tell you sir, there is but one theory in this world in regard to mines, and it is this:—that silver runs in ledges, and gold is where you find it".

The speaker is standing in a hole ankle deep in water, and has just thrown up a shovelful of dirt into the sluice. He is a man of fifty perhaps, with strongly marked expressive features, dark thoughtful eyes, firmset mouth, hair sprinkled with grey. A solid looking man of heavy powerful build, slow and deliberate in his movements, in whose meditative aspect and somewhat stern countenance one might read, me thinks, many an untold tale of suffering and wrong.

His attitude toward me is slightly agressive I fancy, and yet his manner is courteous. He seems to question the stranger—"Are you some city feather head, coming round here to put on airs, or a man?" Thinks I, "Old man we will see".

Mentally I threw myself into an attitude of self defense, as is my habit when I encounter something formidable. Physically I sat down on a dump of gravel and peered at him, debating within myself, shall I take the trouble of knowing this old chap, or shall I leave him among the unremembered host. Deciding to cultivate him, I take refuge behind a few inoffensive commonplaces, and wait quietly for an opportunity to assert myself.

"There's one of your gulch feeders" said he throwing up a big quartz boulder and speaking at it familiarly like the grave digger over Yorick's skull, "see if you can find any gold in that"———.

[151]

"Yes sir!" he resumes resting on his shovel "That's what I told Mister Major Lyon when he came round here to teach us old miners ———".

But I need not recite what he said to Major Lyon. I gather from the nature of the talk that when the man of theory and the practical man met, they had had a tussle. Further I infer that they had separated, mutually elevating their noses at each other. The miner thinks the Major an old pedant who would improve himself by taking to the pick and shovel for a year or two, while the Major, rooted to his own notions doubtless looked upon the miner as a wrong headed old California boulder.

The philosopher stations himself in the middle. They are both mistaken. The major is a man of sound judgement, of great scientific acquirements, and varied knowledge—only rather eccentric and opinionative. The miner—I am just getting acquainted with.

Stranger (mildly) "How much are you taking out of this gulch a day?"

Miner (giving a ferocious dig with the pick) "wages, sir, wages—and not very heavy at that".

Stranger—"Oh!"

A pause and the work goes on. A young fellow who is attending to the Toms asks me what I think of the country. He might just as well have asked me what I thought of the weather.

Old man—"Well sir, you'll get some notion of what gulch diggin is out here. Do you think you could take a hand at it? Dr. McGovern [9] told me he knew mighty little about it from all his studies till he came round here".

9. Francis McGovern was one of the original discoverers of Miner's Delight. (See Chapter II, footnote 1.) He was appointed a Justice of the Peace for Carter County by the Dakota Legislative Assembly on December 27, 1867. He was also recorder for the California Mining District in 1868. The U. S. Census of 1870 lists him as twenty-seven, a miner from Illinois, owning real estate valued at $10,000.

Stranger—"I suppose you are pretty well posted in theories as well as in practice".

Old man—"Yes I have studied geology from books and from Nature too, and I guess Nature's the best guide after all. I have a pretty good collection of books at my old home in Missouri".

Viewing his work in a contemplative mood he remarks "That's what you call auriferous dirt".

"That", said I, "is auriferous dirt".

"And here am I, an old fellow, working in it for five dollars a day instead of laying up at home and taking my comfort."

Here I thought I had found an opportunity to say something original at last, and make an impression, so I said "Such is life!"

The profundity of the observation apparently had no effect, so I walked away, and my friend called after me "Come down again young man and have a chat."

So I did. I visited this old man at his cabin where he was cooking his frugal dinner, and had a long chat. We chatted upon science, on books, on men and politics, and foreign lands and I gained a deal of information. He has travelled round a wide circuit and has apparently neglected no opportunity to extend his knowledge by reading. He talks Spanish fluently and has a habit of interspersing Spanish phrases occasionally when he wishes to emphasise.

What I like in him is his perfect candor and open mindedness. I can place implicit reliance upon his opinions as regards the different leads. He has been my daily companion during these latter days of my sojourn here, and he is always pleased to accompany me on a ramble. He does not play poker nor imbibe whisky, but practices a severe economy. "If I can raise enough" he said "to give my boy a thorough education, that is all I care for".

I never asked him to tell me "his story" and he rarely

shows a disposition to obtrude his private affairs upon our talk. But from various allusions to other times I am enabled to discern as through a glass darkly:

A home in old Missouri before the war. Goodly acres of rich farm land with growing crops and wealth of flocks and herds. A family living in affluence, surrounded by Southern luxuries—the "domestic institution" not wanting. The father had been a successful miner, and returning after years of hard experience with a snug little pile, he has settled down happily to enjoy the remaining portion of his three score and ten. The sons are growing up, the eldest, "a noble young fellow" as the old man proudly says, just entering manhood.

The war came flaming round that way, and the dark hour saw all this happiness and wealth, so hardly earned, ascend in rolling smoke to heaven. The Yankee soldiers came swaggering in and told the mother to "get up for a d——— rebel ——— and cook grub for them", and the old man has learned these words by heart. *His* battle had to be fought all over again.

No use crying over spilt milk. His home is in ashes, his household goods are scattered, but life remains. One day he goes out to the wood and cuts a stout piece of hickory, the which he fashions into a pick handle. Say the neighbors, what are you after now? "With that peice of hickory". Says he "I am going to dig up another fortune, please God".

So with a strong heart he wanders back alone to the hills—making no complaint, nursing no blind wrath, but cheerfully accepting the drudgery and hardships he had endured before. The "boys in blue" who helped to burn his home may have done glorious things, and got their names wrong spelt in the papers for doing them, but is there no heroism here?

That old hickory pick handle has been well polished by constant use, and I am able to affirm that it is the best one in the camp. It has made many a hard strike for a "riffle", and the hand that plies it I do believe, has never willingly

wronged anyone. I saw by chance a portion of a letter from
his boy, who is struggling on to fortune and he says "I send
what money I can to my dear mother to keep her from
want". ———"Let the past be forgotten. Father, I do believe
that when you went away you sincerely thought it was all
for the best, but it is hard to see an old man at your time of
life starting out to make a new path in the world. I need not
ask you to be economical upright and energetic, for that I
know you will be, and I pray that God will prosper your
efforts". ———To which I say Amen! For I honor this brave
man and "black hearted rebel". Which is the bravest the
man who can lay down his life, or he who can take it up
and bear it nobly, making it one long sacrifice for others,
enduring in silence "the opressor's wrong, the proud man's
contumely, and the spurns that patient merit of the un-
worthy takes"?

And now this nameless hero of mine who seemed to chal-
lenge me so roughly at first sight, is one of the gentlest and
most unassuming of men—a patient instructor and a willing
listener—a delightful companion on the hills, an agreeable
entertainer by the fireside. But I hope he may never meet
the Yankee soldier who commanded his wife to get up and
make grub for him.

Probably Mr. Quinn would be a good deal surprised were
he to look over my shoulder at this moment and find me
lauding him so grevously, and so no doubt would his friends
in this camp, although he is held in high esteem by all, for
I do not imagine that every one would take the trouble to
analyze him so curiously. I confess I have been singularly
interested in him since our first acquaintance in the gulch,
and I am sure I have not exaggerated my impressions.[10]

He has prospected extensively throughout the country
and is the discoverer of a variety of leads none of which,

10. This is the same Mr. Quinn mentioned in the September 18
entry. See Chapter III, footnote 5.

however, he has retained. Unless one can afford to spend some money in developing them they are of little use. As Mr. Quinn remarks it would be a wiser economy if the men who waste so much labor in discovering new ledges, would concentrate their energy upon one good one, and develop it well. The whole district is dotted with little holes sunk down for a few feet, which labor properly directed, would have sunk a deep shaft in some paying lead.

Two bull teams passed through the camp bearing a large family to Wind River Valley where they intend to winter. If the place suits them they propose to take up some locations. Look out! in another season there will be a stream of emigration thither. A hundred settlers would keep two thousand Indians at a respectful distance.

The following ballad appears to have been dropt out of the popular collections. I have not been able to trace the author, but I suspect he was some unsuccessful prospector under the influence of brain fever induced by long ineffectual effort to "make the riffle":—[11]

> It was an old miner—
> Pick upon his shoulder,
> Sat upon a rock,
> Looking at a boulder.
> Hello! old fellow,
> What's the good cheer?
> "I want to make the Riffle
> And I think I'll make it here".
> Same old miner
> Sat at a table—
> Played Poker all night

11. "Making the riffle" = striking it rich. See note on page 213.

As long as he was able.
Got dead broke,
Drank all the beer.
"I'm Bound to make the riffle
But I can't make it here".

"I've been in good luck
I've been in bad, O
All through from Mexico
Up to Colorado.
Chawed raw dog
When I couldn't chaw deer
'Cause I couldn't make the riffle
And starvation was near.
Old woman far away
Waits for my coming
Doesn't think her old man
Goes around bumming
Wait a while old lass
Its panning out clear
And when I can make the riffle
I will soon quit here

I've got a claim here,
Prospects fair—
I've got a castle gay
High up in air,
Waiting to be furnished
For more than twenty year—
But if I can make the riffle
It'll all come out clear.
If I can make the riffle
I'll buy a new hat.
If I can make the riffle
I'll have a good suit of clothes on my back.

I'll go into business
That'll pay me a hundred percent clear
And I'll walk in the best Society
For other twenty year.

Plans I've laid out for life
Straight as a line—
They've been laying out I guess
Since "Forty nine"
I'm getting in the yellow leaf
I'm an old fellow I fear
But if I can make the riffle
You'll find me all here.
I've got a son at home
Able to stand up and preach.
I've got a grown up daughter
Gay as a peach.
They have not seen their daddy
For many and many a year,
'Cause I couldn't make the riffle
And had to stay out here.

I drink my beer among the boys
I sit down with them to play
And sometimes I go it blind
For a whole night and a day
I look a rough old specimen
And I've had a rough career
Trying to make the riffle
For more than twenty year.
Now I've struck a big thing
And yet—who can tell—
Before another season goes,
It may be all in
So let's be jolly while we may

> And pass round the beer
> There's many a riffle made and lost
> In less than twenty year.

This very ancient and rough shod doggrel is scarcely up
to the standard of our miscellany, but we gave it a place in
the hope that the author may be discovered and punished.
I suspect the thing is a forgery. All the respectable miners
have disowned it, and they gave it over to me in order that
it might be carried out of their camp.

To make amends for this imposition I will now insert a
genuine Mormon Song which I learned from an apostate
saint—Sandy was born in the Cowcaddens and became converted along with the rest of the family, but the good seed
was planted in stony ground. Instead of learning hymns
Sandy picked up all the vilest odds and ends of blackguard
songs. He was too shocking a fellow even for the Mormons
and he left them an apostate: He is the very picture of a vil-
lainous looking Scotch Tinkler—a duddy vagabond, seamed
with small pox and full of all manner of improprieties. We
gave him full license one evening and the rascal abused his
privilege by dragging his memory for the foulest slime of
rhymed obscenity.

The following, however, is one of the popular songs or
hymns of Mormondom sung to the tune of "Missletoe
Bough:"

> Brigham the Prophet he is our head
> He is our Seer since Joseph is dead
> The keys of the Kingdom of God now he holds
> The gospel of Jesus to the nations he rolls
>   For the lion of the Lord
>   Is Brigham, is Brigham, is Brigham Young
>   Hail to the brave!
>   Hail to the brave!

[159]

The mantle of Joseph right straight on him fell
In spite of apostates and devils in hell
How many this mantle have sought for to gain
They have sought it, and sought it, but sought it in vain.
    For the lion of the Lord
        &c.   &c.
When Joseph and Hiram were morted in jail
The devil thought then that he had a fine tail
To boast to the nations of what he had done,
But little he thought of the brave Brigham Young
    For the lion of the Lord—&c.

[*South Pass City*]

    I feel as mean and miserable as the latter end of an ill spent life. I have been waiting to see Bill Rhodes who promised to go with me to our oil well and getting impatient yesterday morning I started for a walk over the hills. Found myself in South Pass before I stopped. My old friend Mr. Tappertit I discovered "stretched out", but the sight of me brought him back to life. He is an indefatigable drinker and I had hard work to keep the poison from my lips. To show the quality of the poison they keep here I may mention that a few tastes brought me to my level and to-day I am more dead than alive—can't get around at all—can't write—can't eat—can't think.

    Don't like this place so well as Miner's Delight. Met a tipsy Bachanal yesterday whose name was Lib—dark eyed—splendid hair but unfortunately drunk. A strange sight in this lonely town. She was reciting Shakespeare and passages from Byron and Moore and would have proceeded to tell me the history of her first drunk, but I cut her short. This morning I found Lib sitting at her cabin door playing with a great black mastiff. I sat down upon a rock in front of the hut, when Lib, still half tipsy, set the dog at me for amusement. The brute nearly tore me to pieces.

The town is full of Indians—portions of the Bannock band on their way to Wind River. They are under the command of a one-eyed fellow who can talk English very well. The Snakes and Bannocks are both portions of the Sho-Shonee tribe. They have all been very peaceable ever since the Bear river fight when Connor whipped them so badly.[12]

Over at Spring Gulch two of the Indians came into the store and were hospitably treated. As they went to join their band they stole Pat Skeine's horse and sold him to Comstock for three dollars.

12. In January 1863 Colonel Patrick E. Connor led a detachment of men from Fort Douglas, Utah, against Bear Hunter and 300 warriors of the Bannock and Shoshone tribes. These Indians had been committing depredations along the Oregon Trail, and were encamped at Bear River. Connor, after careful reconnaissance and investigation, thoroughly defeated the hostiles.

According to Brigham D. Madsen, who has made a detailed study of the Bannock tribe, they are not a part of the Shoshone group as Chisholm states. In *The Bannock of Idaho*, Madsen traces the history of this mistaken identity.

VIII

CORONACH

[*Written after receiving word of the death of his brother Harry, drowned in a sailing accident on Lake Michigan, June 21, 1868. The news was more than three months in reaching Chisholm.*]

SUMMER HAS DEPARTED, and October is ringing his stormy changes on the desolate hills.

Red leaves are drifting through the air—falling among the dead trees and tangled brush on the slope below, where they shine like spots of gold. The skies are cloudless, but the sunlight brings no warmth. Over the face of the landscape sweeps a mournful wind, and as the sere grasses bend beneath it, a white pallid shadow passes over, like the unutterable "change" that comes upon the face of the dying. A sound of lamentation is in the air like one wild wail, as if all things were about to fade away.

Listening to these sad dirges and facing the bleak skies, a strange dreary chill creeps involuntarily over the heart. On such evenings as these the glittering cloud castles which all men build, fall crumbling into ruins; the golden dreams, the rosy hopes, and plans and prospects seem all to vanish in the cold glare of a dreary reality. For weeks past my brain has been busy working out certain feasible projects for the future, but just now they are hopelessly blotted out of my mind. I am thinking of old times—with sorrow and pain of a lifetime, and how it has led through many changes on to this very October evening on this wild rocky hill. And there my course of thinking ceases. I have no wings to carry me even so far as Christmas.

Let me try to track up, as the sublime Mr. Tupper would say, "my truant thoughts". This book is my own, and I believe I may write what I please in it. Look a melancholy thought in the face, and maybe, like the devil, it will flee from you. I was thinking—no, my memory was wandering.

I was looking just now at two lonely trees in a hollow where a flock of magpies had alighted, and there came vividly across my mind the two old elm trees that grew beside the corn yard on the old farm. I remember how the magpies used to chatter on the branches when we were little children. Our grandmamma told us they were birds of bad omen, and even at this day I can never feel quite easy at the sight of a magpie.

Whither now?—There seems to be a flood of tears rising up from my heart and choking me, as I think of early summer mornings when we set forth, we two together, on a weekly journey of twelve miles—I acting as convoy half of the way. The village is fast asleep and the dust on the quiet street is yet damp with dew, as we trudge cheerily over the hilltop and past the well known farms which are not yet stirring. Norah, our family pet, who is always with us, chases the hares and rabbits in the fields, and so we come to the brig o' Castleton, the half way point where we always stop to roll over great stones into the water before we part. Once I remember, lured on by the desire to see the great world, I ventured the whole length of the way, and from a hill beheld for the first time the wonder of the sea, and the "bonny town of Banff."

When I recall it now, what a deep unconscious love it was that knit me there. That was the early blossom of a long friendship which is ended now. It seems like a wild dream to me that I should be here to-day, and that when I return it is but to look upon a grave. I think of all our earnest talks about the one great mystery—how we would often sit through a long night and think aloud to each other. He has gone to seek it, and we may wait and hearken, but he can send no tidings back. There is a deep unfathomable silence yonder which is forever sealed but one key. You may weep and wail, you may pray to it, but the answer never comes. There is no healing there. There is no true comfort but to turn back into life, away from these desolate lonely heavens where souls are lost to us, and mingle in the glad festival. Dream out the dream.

Sometimes I can hear his voice so distinct and clear, asking some familiar question, that it startles me, and then a whole train of recollections come wandering through my memory. There were many happy times since we came to Chicago, but I oftenest think of him in earlier days—our obscure, hard but happy life in Edinburgh, before he had found his way into print, and was writing poems and tragedies by the ream that were to astonish the world. These were the days, too, of glorious evening parties of which he was the accepted lion—when fair haired Jeannie, (who squinted a trifle), was the queen of my soul, and Maggie with her mincing refinement and sentimentalism, was adored by him. Days, too, of the Robin Hood and the Noctes, when we praised or censured the actors with the audacity of finished critics, when Byron and Shelley were the watchwords of "our set", and Bulwer was our guide, philosopher and friend. The spasmodic school and Alexander Smith had then come into vogue, and we sneered at it with all our might, and roared over Firmilian.[1] How little we both knew, for the world was all before us, and Carlyle was as yet unknown to our little bookshelf, to dispel illusions and teach us how to think.

This was probably the happiest period of his life. He was rapt in a glorious dream of literary fame. Every production was submitted to me, but as a critic I was useless for I applauded everything he did. And when the opening verses of a new poem, or the first scene of a new play was duly approved, and the plan brought under consideration, what rambles into the country, and building of castles we had on the strength of it. It was fun for us both in after days when the drama was on the decline and common sense began to rule, to travel over critically the fragments of these early effusions. So irreverently we dealt with the most venerable heroes that I wonder they did not start from their graves. Indeed their ghosts have often haunted us since, and some of them haunt me to this day.

I recal in particular one very doleful tragedy whose hero was a Jew. His name was Shadrack originally, but in case he should be improperly identified with the companion of Mesech and Abednego, we altered it to Shadock. But that did not sound sufficiently oriental so in the next act we docked him of two letters and reduced him to a Shado. In this unsubstantial condition he was condemned to death by

---

1. Alexander Smith (1830-1867) was a Scottish poet and author of a book of essays, *Dreamthorp* (1863). In *Firmilian*, "a spasmodic" tragedy by Professor W. E. Aytoun, the "spasmodic school" of poets was parodied.

the Barons of York. But that was not the last of him. He became a standing joke between us, and "old Shad" was long a familiar household word. And yet he was a highly respectable old Jew in his best days and could talk in the most carefully measured blank verse.

His daughter was lost in the opening scene—stolen in fact by the Baron—and the dialogue commenced by three ancient Isaacs informing the parent that "not a leaf had been left unturned in the forest," to which the father responded that haply the cold lake did hide the peerless maid in his dark unfathomable caves. The Baron, when you came to know him, talked precisely like the Jew. So did Rebecca, and so did the young man who was slain by the Baron in the second act. We had a world of trouble over this accident, for the valiant youth had fallen in love with the fair Jewess, and what was to be done? There was nothing for it but to bring him to life again, so we applied restoratives till in the end of the fourth act he was in a position to kill the Baron. And he did it too, and would have married the lovely Rebecca had it not been for the untimely death of that hapless maiden.

I could give the genesis of every poem, song and story that was written in these old days. They almost seemed my own creation as much as his, and if I shall ever reach the age of seventy I suppose I will come to believe that I had a share in their manufacture. But my position was merely that of corrector and refiner. I altered, added, and substituted phrases. If I had any hidden talent for verse making then, my genius was rebuked by his.

If I cherished my secret aspirations toward the laurel crown, they were buried deep down in my inmost consciousness, never to be breathed to mortal ear. Many a time and oft he tried to coax me into authorship, but in vain. I was either too conscious of my own incapacity, or had too deep a veneration for the immortal nine to intrude. To his very perseverance and success in that direction I think I may attribute the circumstance (a rather curious one for a lad of my inclinations) that I never once attempted literary composition till I came to do so for a living.

I take a melancholy pleasure in running over these old reminiscences, and writing them down. It offers at least a kind of solace as if I had found some one to talk to.

Next, after an interval, comes Glasgow city, and my own woeful experiences there. I remember the ignominious slavery to which I had bound myself—the hostile tummult and jar—the petty oprcssions of base men—the dreadful indifference of the world—the unutterable sense of loneliness which over-whelms the young heart in the midst of multitudes. I remember the serious difficulties in the way of my endeavors to make ends meet—the barracks I was condemned to live in, rendered barely endurable by the partiality of an old housekeeper. I remember, too, the fast little girl who took a fancy to me, and dropt kisses at me from an upper floor. But I was such a serious fool then that I repelled her attacks until we had a scene one day and she danced away with another the next.

There was only one thing which lightened my burden during that dismal year. Our old companionship was renewed from time to time. He had dropped temporarily from his high pedestal to the practical level of a Commercial Traveller and he was often in the city. That was the era, with us, of Carlyle, and all the influences which flowed therefrom. From Byron we had ascended to Wordsworth, and we had forsaken Bulwer for purer teachers. The amount of solid reading I went through at that time was indeed commendable.

On Sundays we usually wandered away to the suburbs together, gladly escaping from the black coal smoke to seek for green fields and forests. There we would roam for half a summer day discussing the new Evangel. Ah, what a tower of strength he was to me then—a "strong star-bright companion".

He was possessed of that restless active energy which was sure to win. He was never lazy. His indefatigable labors with the pen through so many years, if they failed to lift him to the top of Parnassus, had developed in him a power of rapid thinking and writing which is rarely surpassed, and fitted him to be a brilliant journalist. An opportunity soon presented itself. The pamphlet on Burns which he published in Glasgow was the means of bringing him into the sphere of newspaper life, and from that day his path in life was fixed.

We all know the tendency which that life has to destroy the romance and purity of a fine ambition. It fared with him as with all others. "Shades of the prison house began to close", or in other words he became prosaic, practical and useful. He was never more the aspiring poet, or the diligent student, but a brilliant versatile writer. Therein he proved his wisdom and good sense most people would say. I do not quite agree. Perhaps it is a pity that any of us should ever lose sight altogether of that high mark which was the object of our boyish dreams.

In one of his impulsive temperment which needed severe restraint and wise guidance, it was a misfortune. Had he been enabled to retain that earlier and better dream, he would have led a higher and nobler life. Yet he never wholly lost sight of it. All through his later career I could see him struggling to regain those early aspirations which had been his solace and exceeding great reward. His letters to me from Rock Island seemed to breath the original healthy spirit.[2] I may have been deceived, but they carried hope and comfort to my heart.

2. Henry Chisholm had resigned as city editor of the Chicago *Evening Post* "to assume the management of a newspaper at Rock Island," Illinois (Chicago *Tribune*, June 22, 1868, 4:5).

Where now, I wonder, are all those young enthusiasts—
that glorious brotherhood "who made this world the feast
it was" six years ago? Scattered far and wide? Guest is in
Chicago, and I shall see him soon again. David Smith is married alas!—No more will he "arouse the spirit of melody"
at Earwakers or the Baillies's. But Hodson—the great hearted
genial Hodson where is he? Where is Donald? Sand? Russell? Gossip? Where, O, where is R. P. Scott? Have they
too degenerated into common clay, pursuing vulgar aims?
Have they heard of mournful tidings from over the sea, or
do their hearts sadden at the loss of a once dear comrade
and friend? These were happy days. O for one hour together as we used to be! Would not Hod take his old place
in the chair and speak like one inspired? Would not David
forget his bondage and give forth his choicest melodies?
Would not Donald throw up his heels with a wild shriek of
freedom?

Sandeman, Donald, Russell and I, once stood by the Well-
ington Statue where we were wont to assemble on a Saturday evening, and we made a serious compact, which was
never likely to be fulfilled, that if it were ever possible in
the years to come, when we might all be scattered over the
world, we would have one more meeting together. That
compact I have often remembered and I still cherish a
thought that it may yet be realized. I would not for the
richest lode in this hill be deprived of the belief that these
old friendships remain as green as of yore. I would not believe—although a wicked whisper tells me it might be so—
that all that youthful enthusiasm has died out of their hearts
long ago, and that they would meet this pious feeling of
mine with a sneer. Why should it be so? New pursuits have
intervened with me, and many new friends have I known
and loved since then. Yet I have kept loyal to these days of
auld lang syne. Will not hearts be kept as green in Merry
England? Yes, dear old cronies, "Though seas between us

braid hae roared"—though other ties may have been formed by all of us—though we may all be grey old fogies—though we may never more see or hear of one another—let us cherish the faith that if we *do* meet once again we shall prove that friendship is more than a name.

I have pursued my reverie whither it would lead me. I commenced to write it down last evening and now that white day-light is peeping through the chinks of the old log cabin. Think what a happiness it would have been, if instead of making him the subject of so many sad notes, I could have carried home my rough pencillings for his inspection—Not so, but otherwise was it decreed. We parted in kindness and with full hearts, at the Rock Island depot. I saw him go into the cars—and I was never to see him any more.

What a memorable year to me. When I look back upon it, life seems a drama all written and conceived by the author long ago, and we have nothing in our power but to obey the directions of the stage manager, Destiny. We have our exits and our entrances, and one man in his time plays many ungrateful parts. What brought me here? It seemed of my own free will no doubt. Yet in this weird hour of morning, this melancholy state of mind I have fallen into, it seems as if my will had no share in it, and it is merely a part of that mysterious programme which has been laid out for us that I am wandering on the mountains, while he is sleeping yonder, inheriting that "secure and measureless contentment" which life cannot yield.

But that is an unsatisfying thought at best, and the heart rejects it in spite of reason. I cannot think of him as having utterly faded away into a sleep. Why should I go and look at the grave? There should be no such wounded sorrows left to chill our hearts. We abolished the deaths head that was wont to grace the festival. We hide the poor dust. We should hide too, the sad memorials—forgetting the earthly part which perishes, and looking beyond that, to the spirit which is still around us and within us. Let us look at the bright side of death even. He is not sleeping under that green sod. He is one—of that innumerable company who in broad circle, lovelier than the rainbow, girdle this round earth in a dizzy motion with noise too vast and constant to be heard.

I can recal a day as if it were yesterday when I copied these lines and the sublime passage which follows, into a laborious letter which I wrote to him in Glasgow. They occur in Coleridge. The words come stealing over my memory now like a strain of organ music in some old cathedral. To me there is even a kind of vague consolation in such ideas, for they help to lift the soul beyond the prison of Time to the freedom of immortal Being. We, too, are of that innumerable army. If we believe in the immortality of the Spirit, death being but a change of garments, why should we grieve and make moan, since there is no real separation?

The heart lies warm in the sunshine of such a thought. It is better than lingering by the dreary churchyard.—Jean Paul [Richter] says "I passed through sleeping villages and close by the outer churchyards where crumbled up-cast coffin boards were glimmering, while the once bright eyes were mouldering into grey ashes. Cold thought! Clutch not like a cold spectre at my heart. I look up to the starry sky, and all is life, and warmth, and love—all is Godlike or God".

IX

RETURN TO WIND RIVER VALLEY

I AM ON MY WAY to Wind River Valley again. My last trip was not satisfactory. I did not see enough, the Siouxs were not quite cleared out, and there was some danger of becoming prematurely bald. I was poorly mounted, having to work my passage all the way, and in short I returned with the disappointed feeling of one who has failed to carry out his intentions.

Now I have got an excellent horse, and I am out for a fortnight's ride. I am going to locate some land in the valley. I am going to hunt. I am going to prospect. I am in no hurry, and I will see all I want to see before I return. I will go and visit old Washke and go out with his young men to chase the Buffalo. I will know all about this wonderful valley which has completely fascinated me, and then I will go *home*.

My companion this time is John Means of Miner's Delight. He has a countenance which so shines with good nature as to deceive people into the notion that he is bald on the top. An Indian could never take an aim at that head when the sun shines. To see him trotting along as he pulls off his cap to wipe the perspiration from his brow, you would say here is one of the old cannonized saints come back to the earth with the glory round his head. Only no saint in the Calendar ever carried such a needle gun as that over his shoulder.

But I wish someone could take my own portrait at the present moment for I am got up regardless of appearances. Having no ambition to captivate (or purchase) any of the fair Snakes in the valley, my apparel is arranged with an eye to convenience rather than ornament.

These useful articles called buttons have all disappeared to [but?] one, and the requisite connections are made by means of a belt studded with cartridges which encircles the waist. A small hatchet and a butcher knife slung to my side; a Starr breach loader hanging from the horn of the saddle; a sack of flour, tea, coffee and bacon tied behind; a coil of rope; a tin cup, and old peach can to boil water in; a very Irish looking white hat with a hole burnt in the crown; conspicuous boots and panteloons rolled up to the knee; cloth undergarment nothing to boast of, and innocent of buttons; beard, something to boast of. Such is a rough pen sketch of this formidable object which rattled out of Spring Gulch yesterday morning on all fours.

Rather than follow the trail as I had done before, we struck over a hill and lost our way. We preferred to lose our way. Some people I know would say that we couldn't help it, but I know better. It was just what we were both wishing for, to get lost in the mountains. It is so delightfully romantic you know. Didn't John say so, when after leading confidently across the creek, and over the hill, and down a valley, and through a ravine and over another hill and into the jaws of a tremendous gorge, I finally confessed that we had gone just a little—just a little bit astray! Didn't John good-naturedly say, "I couldn't wish for anything better"? Of course he did. Didn't he remind me that we wanted to see the country, and that we could camp anywhere? Of course we could! And yet it *would* have been desirable to reach Bill Rhodes' cabin that night if possible.

However we were out upon a ramble and so we did not lose temper. As regards John indeed the idea of such a thing was preposterous. Had he fallen down a precipice and broke his back, I am sure he would have smiled cheerily and said he had just come out to get some sport. When we came to the verge of that abysmal gorge it was not easy to see how we could get round it or through it without wings, and really, some people might have been inclined to invoke unnecessary Gods on the occasion. But *we* didn't. No, we admired the beauty of the place and assured one another that we wouldn't have missed seeing that gorge for the world.

Our eyes caught something far down on the opposite slope, that looked like mules. They must be lost mules, we thought, in such a place, and we thought they might very easily be found. A hundred dollars apiece at the very least! Didn't we say it was better to come out this way than to follow the trail? We left our ponies and began to edge our way down to them, rifle in hand. Very soon a creature on two legs began to creep very softly up to the mules, and drew them gently down to the bottom of the canon, disappearing among the bushes.

Without a word we both returned and mounted our horses. Said John, "*I* didn't want these mules. I wouldn't have 'em anyhow."

I suppose the owner, whether he was an Indian or a white man, got a bit of a scare just then.

Clambering along the side of this canon we are led into a long valley running N. N. W. & S. S. E. (I ascertain this by my pocket compass which also gives the time of day). The northern side of the valley is lined by a belt of high cliffs of a dusky red color—a deep blood red—scolloped out and corniced, tier above tier, from base to summit with architectural symmetry.[1] On the southern side a sloping wall of smooth grassy hill, a good half days journey from the base to the summit. A creek runs through the bottom which would seem to be a favorite haunt of the Beavers to judge from the multitude of Beaver dams. As the sunlight falls upon these red cliffs they reflect a portentous dusky hue. It is enough to make one sanguinary just to look at them. If one were to hang a white shirt out to dry in this valley it would dye crimson in two hours.

I am curious to know what these rocks are made of. I have seen this bloodred belt before. The truth is I passed on the other side of that range when I went to Wind River last. I see now how far we have wandered from the right trail. John passes on with the horses while I start for the opposite side of the valley to look into the rocks.

The creek is overgrown with thorny bushes and I got caught in the thicket as fast as Abraham's ram. I am all torn with the bushes. Had it not been for a Beaver dam where a good bridge was built across the creek I could never have emerged upon that other slope. However I succeed in chipping off a few specimens of the red rock, and look round for John.

"Hello-ho!" (from a distance) "why don't you come over that creek?"

The villain has taken a bottle of whisky out of my pocket and is evidently enjoying himself. I always took John to be a tee totaller till now. Good heavens! suppose he should get tight and let loose these ponies. And I wanted to carry that

---

1. Red Canyon. The present Lander-Farson highway circles the upper eastern edge of the Canyon.

bottle down to Bill Rhodes. See how he points the broad end of it at the sky as if he were an astronomer.

———"Say, if you feel dry why don't you go down to that creek and drink?"

"John! lay down that bottle or I'll fire at you."

"Take a good aim—here's luck!"

I soon found another Beaver dam and crossed. I would not tell—because nobody would believe it—what condition I found that bottle in. It was labeled "choice old Bourbon". The label was still there and part of the cork———.

In this valley we camped for the night, close by the side of a flourishing Beaver dam—haubled one of the horses and tied the other one to him by a long rope. The night was as warm as summer and the stars were shining. John, returning to the subject of astronomy, raised a dispute concerning a certain constellation which he called the Dipper. I do not say that this had any connection in his own mind with his frequent applications to the stream below us. But I wish he had let that bottle alone, or as he politely called it, the salt ham. Before he lay down he filled up every available mug with water and placed them at his head. When these were emptied he would get up and run to the creek again, and every time he had something new to tell concerning that infernal Dipper. It was no wonder I couldn't sleep all night, with a thirsty astronomer at my side.

The moon rose and set—the great constellations moved in silent procession over the heaven, and before dawn I saw the bright morning star blaze like a beacon on the hill top. It was about this unearthly hour that Bob, my pony, having broke loose from the other, came down to take a drink. When we got up we discovered to our sorrow that he had made a straight shoot for home. John goes in pursuit, and he is gone all day.

I did not flatter myself into the belief that he would soon be back, but made up my mind to pass one day and perhaps a night alone. I have seen the day (not far off) when I would have been a little skeared at such a prospect, but it is surprizing how soon one gets at home in the hills. I breakfasted and then went over the hills to look for game. There was none, not even a sage hen. The Indians were through here a few days ago and I suppose they drove everything before them. I returned disappointed to the old camp and for amusement to pass away time, examine the architecture of the Beavers, try to sketch the red bluffs and fail, thinking all the time with a kind of humorous compassion of John's long run after the pony. It is not far from sundown when he returns—wearied but smiling as cheerfully as ever.

A fire is soon kindled and the kettle on when we both perceive that the long grass near is in flames. Then a scene followed. I jumped at it with a long stick and endeavored to beat it out but it was too late. In a moment we were all but surrounded. John seized all he could lift in his arms and would have rushed up the bluff while I took to the creek with an armsful. We had a pile of cartridges and a large flask of powder lying somewhere, and in the excitement of the moment they could not be found. It was a question whether we would have to flee and lose everything or risk an explosion. Each was calling frantically to the other to look for the powder and at last I found it right in the fire and fled with it to the creek. Most of the cartridges we got in a blanket and carried them off. We saved nearly everything.

The whole scene did not occupy over a minute. Then we had half an hour or so of hard labor beating back the fire from that spot till we could get our horses saddled. John's hair and whiskers were singed all over and my hands were blistered while the sudden exertion and excitement almost laid me prostrate. When everything was packed we swept out of the valley at one end while the fire went roaring through it and away over the hills followed by a moving cloud of smoke in the sky.

[177]

We did not proceed far that night. Darkness overtook us just as we found ourselves in a kind of a trap formed by the junction of several streams, none of which were approachable. [Junction of Red Canyon Creek, Cherry Creek, and Bear Creek.] Twice where we would [have gone] our progress was interrupted by swampy jungles, saving at one side where we came to a steep precipice overlooking the Popogia. Thinking it safest to wait for daylight we camped and prepared supper.

Here I learned the art of making bread without an oven. It is a very simple process. Knead up the dough in the usual way, then twist it round a willow stock and hold it over the coals and you have a delicious little loaf like a doughnut.

We saw the fire we had kindled spreading on for miles and committing unknown devastation, while it was slowly working its way round the hollows to the very point where we lay. I did not sleep easy all night in consequence, and was up before daylight.

I had only about three miles to walk this time after the horses, and then we struck into the old Indian trail which led us on to the stone cabin where I had been before. From this our road was easy enough to the valley of the Big Popogia and we met with no accidents or incidents by the way. The game was very scarce. We saw nothing but a grizzly and he was in the act of disappearing into a canon as we caught sight of him so we had not a chance to fire.

We crossed the Popogia near the place where I had camped on my former excursion and proceeded down the valley in quest of Bill Rhodes.

Nothing but the fear of Indians could prevent the settlement of all these valleys. There are no finer ranges of grazing land in all the West, and the bottoms are capable of raising the best wheat, vegetables and fruit. Very little labor is required to irrigate the great expanses of land now covered with bunch grass and sagebrush. The water of the stream could be brought to the foot hills almost at any point, while upon the higher ranges stock can fatten all the winter. Last December a man passed through the mines with some cattle nearly starved and as lean as Pharaoh's lean kine. In February one of them was killed at the camp—a good fat ox. Two months in the valley had fattened him.[2]

But even those people who best know the value of the land, have hitherto been afraid to venture a summer in the Wind River. I am satisfied that a hundred or even fifty settlers would keep the Indians at bay. And if only a few white people would take the risk then the Snakes would muster courage to remain. For this reason Washke is very anxious to see white people come and settle, and he would do everything to afford them support and protection against the Siouxs.

At the head of the Popogia valley I found several ranches —one a family of the name of Shafer who have a considerable herd of cows.[3] Major Baldwin, a trader at South Pass, has also built a store for trading purposes.[4] Beyond these I saw

2. "The story is told that a government trader, on his way to Camp Douglas in Utah Territory in 1864, was caught in a severe snowstorm on the Laramie Plains. He went into winter quarters and turned his cattle adrift. Curiously, they stayed around camp all winter, pawed the snow off the ground and ate the cured hay. In the spring they were in better condition than when they had reached the region." By 1870, stories of Wyoming's "grass bonanza" had been generally circulated, and drovers "planned to reach the Sweetwater, Laramie, Platte, Pope Agie, or Powder Rivers in the fall and make the most of winter pasture." See Linford, *Wyoming: Frontier State*, pp. 230-232. The grass is called wheat grass.

3. Identified as among the first permanent settlers. See Chapter III, footnote 2.

4. Major Noyes Baldwin, one of the earliest settlers in the Wind River Valley, was commander at Fort Bridger in the summer of 1865 and spring of 1866. In the late summer of 1865, with a group of forty picked men he explored the South Pass area and as far north as Wind River. After he was mustered out of the service he located at the mouth of the Popo Agie and set up as an Indian trader. When the Indians forced him to leave in the spring of 1867, he took his family to Salt Lake City for a short interval. In 1868 he returned to South Pass City and from that time on lived there and in the Wind River

no evidence of farming for many miles. Here and there an empty cabin stood in some luxurious nook on the river bank showing where some enterprizing individual had intended to lay the foundation of a fortune, but the actual work was postponed and in some cases entirely abandoned. Nowhere that I can think of at present could a moderate capital be laid out more profitably than in the purchase of some stock and agricultural implements to turn up a furrow in this valley.

This was a long ride. We had been in the saddle with scarcely half an hour's intermission since sunrise and now the sun was going down behind the rocky Mountains while we were still wending along the banks of the Popogia. An old trail and sometimes the trace of a wagon wheel was all that indicated the presence of human beings below, and the actual whereabouts of Bill Rhodes was an uncertainty. By and bye we described something far off. A horse. Then some Indian horses. Then a herd of cows—all feeding on a noble rich pasture that extended for miles along the bottom.

At first we fancied we had come among the Indians, and even that was a grateful thought, but soon we saw some hay fresh cut, and sweeping around a point of the bluffs a long low cabin glimmered into view through the trees. Bill, who was cutting wood, threw up his hands with a halloo of welcome as we galloped up from the river and in a few minutes I was "in clover"—drinking butter milk *ad lib*, and eyeing with unconcealed satisfaction some choice slices of Buffalo meat that were frying for our supper.

Bill was not alone. Another hunter by the name of Wilson

Valley, where he returned to trade with the Indians again. In 1870 Camp Stambaugh was established near Atlantic City, and he secured the position of post trader. In 1876 he established a merchandise store in Lander which is still being operated by the Baldwin family.

The U. S. Census of 1870 listed Baldwin as living at South Pass City, a brick mason, forty-one years of age, owning real estate valued at $6,000 and personal property at $1,000. His wife, Josephine, and his six children aged one to fourteen were also listed in the enumeration.

See also Supplementary Notes, pages 216 and 219.

was living with him and old Dad Davis had brought his cows down there to winter. So with "Calamity" and a young calf we found altogether a pleasant society on the farm. Bill was occupied in dressing skins. Wilson was cleaning and salting fish, and Dad was making butter.

I have always had very vague notions of Paradise, but it seems essential for one thing that we have unlimited supplies of fresh buttermilk. It took away all the fatigue of the days journey like a charm, and Bill had just killed a fat Buffalo cow so we had a royal supper. The wolves made music to us all night long. Not that I particularly relish the howling of wolves. I think it is one of the most dismal sounds in nature —but Bill says they sing to him and he likes to hear them.

This was altogether too sweet a spot to hurry away from. I could not very well cite it as a specimen of Wind River farming because Bill has devoted but little attention to agricultural [affairs] and he intends to move over to Little Wind River next year. Yet the natural fertility of the place could not escape the most casual observation.

Bill's dwelling is a curiosity in itself. One part of it was built by him twenty-two years ago when he remained one winter, (how far it seemed from civilization then!) and he has added bits from time to time till it has grown to be a little range of log cabins very little higher than the tall grass which shelters it on every side. The river sweeps round from a point of the bluffs, between groves of cotton wood and willow brush, with a broad shingly beach fringing a strip of flat grassy land. The cottage stands in a sequestered corner, the back of it facing the river and the valley, while it fronts an even line of high bluffs. The magpies hover in flocks among the branches all morning. The river swarms with trout and whitefish. The air is pure and warm even while you can see the storms gathering over the surrounding hills. Let it storm where it may, winter seems to forget this valley.

Across the shallow a fish trap has been constructed by the

hunter and they draw out as much as would fill an ordinary flour sack three or four times a day. Bill caught a strange monster the other morning which I would fain carry home were he not too large. He measures 18 inches in length. He has no scales and is of a dark color, spotted like a leopard. The head is rounded and flat on the top, the eyes protruding, while a sharp horn protrudes from his under jaw. One enormous fin runs along the back and round the tail—altogether he has more the appearance of a snake than a fish. Bill keeps him alive in a cage and feeds him with flesh. The Indians say they have never seen anything like it before.[5]

Apropos of the Indians. The great body of them have gone down on the first Buffalo hunt about sixty miles below, while a number of lodges are scattered here and there over the valley. One of them came round with a horse which he requested Bill to take care of till he returned. He would be back, he said, in one moon and a half. The horse evidently was in need of some care. His back from the neck to the tail was one horrible festering sore—the most pitiful figure of a horse I ever saw. How the Indian managed to drag him so far was a wonder. The magpies, getting wind of the sore back, came down by twos and threes and began to peck him. He endured the torture for a time and then lay down and died. Two hours after dark scarcely a bone was left—the wolves devoured him every inch and picked the ribs clean.

Washke is so far away that I am afraid I must forego the pleasure of his acquaintance for a season. If I were not anx-

5. According to Dr. Harold W. Manter and Dr. T. B. Thorson: "There can be no doubt that the fish described was the eel pout, or ling, or American burbot, *Lota lota maculosa*. This fish ranges from New England and the Great Lakes to the headwaters of the Missouri. It occurs in the Big Horn River and some of its tributaries and is abundant in the Big Wind River of Wyoming. [Chisholm] gave a rather good description of this fish. The 'sharp horn' protruding from the under jaw is actually a fleshy barbel. The size, the color, the elongate shape, and the long dorsal and ventral fins, and the absence of scales (microscopic scales are present) all fit the eel pout. This fish is a freshwater relative of the cod." See James R. Simon, *Wyoming Fishes*, Wyoming Game and Fish Department, 1946.

ious to get home soon I might wait and go down with Bill who is going to hunt and trap there in ten days or so. After all I don't want much to see Indians. I don't like them. They are unlovely, intractable, useless, strutting, ridiculous, pompous humbugs—lying, faithless, stealing, begging, cruel, hungry, howling vagabonds—cowardly, treacherous red devils. That is my opinion of Lo the poor Indian.

The Snakes are mighty friendly with the whites, because the whites whipped them soundly at Bear River and taught them to fear and tremble. If the Government would set to work and whip them all, instead of bribing them there would soon be an end of all trouble.

Washke is entitled to respect as a consistent and unwavering friend to the white people. He had sense enough to perceive the advantages of a union, and it is his boast that he never shed a white mans blood, nor ever encourage his people to do it. He refused to join the others at Bear River and withdrew a large number of his band. Even among his followers Washke is disliked on account of his friendliness to the white man, but then they fear him more than they dislike him.[6]

Bill having promised to take us out with him on a hunt, we started on the second morning after our arrival taking an extra horse to pack our provisions and carry back the spoils. Leaving the valley we struck westward across the hills, traversing a bare undulating tract of country which lay between the Popogia and Little Wind River. For the first few hours the ride was a pleasant one, but it soon became monotonous, and our expectations of finding lots of game were disappointed. Once we discerned some Buffalo far to the right, but they were beyond range.

In the course of the day Bill frequently reverted to the subject of his matrimonial project and reminded me of my promise to look out for a girl for him in the States. "You

6. Chief Washakie died on February 21, 1900, and was buried with full military honors at Fort Washakie.

must bring one out Jim" he said "or you must forfeit your own". This is the alternative he has finally brought me to. As to her qualifications, she must be fat, hearty and goodnatured. It is not essential that she be *nailin'* good looking, but she must be cleanly and tidy—a good housewife. She will not have much work to do, and she will have plenty to eat and lots of furs to wear. If she is prudent, she may soon be rich.

In discussing the probabilities of the valley being speedily settled Bill can hardly conceal a shade of dissatisfaction. "I want to see people come in" he says "but if they come too thick I guess I'll have to move further down. I don't want too many round me. I want to be where I can hunt all the time".

After riding fifteen miles we came in sight of the Wind River at the head of the valley which is here about six miles wide. As we descended the easy slope from the wild hills it lay before us, broad, green and beautiful, watered by numerous mountain streams which flowed into the river. On the opposite side rose the vast range, the main chain of the Rocky Mountains presenting a smooth green slope for a considerable distance, seamed into a succession of monstrous canons, and above, towering into jagged peaks and long lines of splintered rock.

To the North East where you look across miles of level ground past the hot springs, the valley closes in abruptly to a narrow pass, beyond which it broadens out again to another green expanse. Timber is not so plentiful in this part of the valley, but up in the canons there is abundance of pine which can be hauled in half a day.

We accepted of the hospitality of Mr. Krutch one of the few settlers who are cultivating this part of the valley.[7] His

7. The spelling should be Kutch. Tilford Kutch was one of the first permanent settlers on the Little Wind River in 1868. An announcement in the *Sweetwater Mines* (April 7, 1869) listed him as one of the election inspectors in the Wind River Valley at the polls at Baldwin's store.

cabin stands on the bank of a small creek about the centre of the area, and his domestic affairs are presided over by a lovely and accomplished daughter of the ancient family of Bannocks. Mary is the name of this dusky maid. For an Indian she is tolerably good looking although her figure is not a model of symmetry.

She has one strong recommendation as a wife—she rarely opens her lips. We remained there all night and the only articulate expression I heard her give utterance to, was the word "Baby". Bill Rhodes had lots to tell her concerning some of her people on Snake River, how this one was married and that one scalped, yet she betrayed no surprise, nor once gave any response. Bill told me she was full of chat when there were no strangers present, and that she is a good affectionate creature who works hard.

As her eye fell upon my belt, with the tomahawk and row of cartridges her face lighted up with a lively expression of pleasure. She came and examined it all over, while I unbuckled it, and then held it up in her hands admiringly. Her baby about two years old is the prettiest little cherub I ever saw. Such fat chubby cheeks, olive skin, and glittering black eyes.

While Mary was getting ready supper (she is a good cook and got up a capital meal) we went out to look around us. There was a patch of turnips sweet and juicy, and a field of potatoes, and that was about all the signs of farming I saw on *his* farm. He had not got so far as a plow.

Nearer the mountains we found the emigrants whom I had seen pass through Spring Gulch. They are so pleased with the valley that they intend to remain and farm. They are from Lancashire and have "coom a greet waas to coom cop here"—namely from Montana. The woman is a garrulous old lady and has an infant three years old at her breast, and quite a troop of blowsy faced boys and girls. They were all happy and full of glee at the prospects they seemed to have in the valley. It costs them little to live, and the climate was so healthy and mild. In the course of another season I have no doubt matters would look so prosperous that the old woman might venture to wean that burly infant.

A party of Indians are camped not far from here. One of them paid a visit to the dame the other day and she treated him to a hearty old fashioned meal. Indians are proverbially bashful on such occasions. Mr. Lo smote his heart with emphasis, shook hands with her, and ate "heep"! Mr. Lo was so energetic in making everything disappear, and thumped his big heart so fervently that the old woman was quite delighted. Mr. Lo's appetite was wonderful. "He crossed his knife and fork on the plate"—so madam told us with delight—and shook hands several times to testify his gratitude. Not only that but he called again and brought his friends with him. The good natured lady would not be sorry now if they all went down the valley—or up the flume for that matter.

By the time we returned to Krutch's cabin Mary had a most inviting supper prepared—fish and beaver tail, potatoes, turnips and bullberry pies. The Squaw did not sit down with us, but waited dutifully till we had eaten, then made ready a supper for herself and the papoose.

In this country it is better I believe, to marry a Squaw than a white woman. They are more profitable. They have no expensive luxuries, and they can dress skins, catch your horses and do all kinds of work. They are docile and industrious, and their conversational powers are limited. The great drawback is that you have generally to marry a host of relations along with them. A squaw who gets a white man usually discovers two or three papas, a couple of mamas and scores of uncles and cousins: and these must be fed.

Krutch had a tough fight with the Siouxs here this summer and lost all his horses. It was at the time Jeff Standifer and his party, who started on a prospecting tour, were surrounded. One was killed, and the others escaped. The Indians pursued one man as far as Krutch's place, but when they came within sight they dodged among the hills, when Krutch took his gun and went after them. His horses were feeding at some distance and Krutch's partner, Davis, went to protect them. The Indians made a manoeuvre, and attempted to surround Krutch, but he baffled them by retreating back toward his cabin. Davis, thinking his partner was in danger, left the horses and ran to his rescue, when the Indians went and drove off the whole stock. Krutch pursued them for a short distance. Whenever the Indians stopped he levelled his rifle and they went on again. The most remarkable part of the adventure was that when Krutch afterwards tried to fire off his rifle it would not go.

I relate this story just to show how easy it is to keep the Indians at a distance.

["On June 29th a prospecting party consisting of seven men, whose names were Jeff Standifer, Andrew Newman, Robert Kenneday, C. T. Macaulay of Rochester, N. Y.; John Moore, of Canada; Henry Lehman, of Ohio; John H. Duncan, of Nye County, Nevada, were attacked by a band of Sioux Indians numbering over a hundred warriors, on Big Wind River, about a hundred miles north west of this place. The party were surprised while at dinner, their horses being turned out, and as far as known, only three escaped, vis: Standifer, Newman and Kenneday. Lehman was killed in the early part of the fight, and the other three were pursued and killed, or supposed to be, near Bull Lake. Mr. Newman came across their trail the same afternoon of the attack and crossed it several times, and when he left it, was about four miles from the Lake; leaving it at this point he crossed the Lake, and when upon this side, heard firing, and saw the smoke from their guns, and shortly afterward he saw three fires; this was on Monday morning, and he supposed the fires were signals to the rest of the Indians who were hunting for the unfortunate whites in other directions, that they had secured their prey. Two of the survivors, Standifer and Kenneday, arrived here on the 5th. All had suffered more or less from hunger and fatigue . . ." (*Sweetwater Mines,* July 11, 1868)].

In the morning I rode down the valley toward the hot spring.[8] A cloud of steam rises up from it in the morning. Two miles from the cabin I crossed the river. On the other side of the stream are high white cliffs which look like the finest marble. But the stone is soft so that one can pare it with a knife. Krutch has put it to good use and proved it to be a more valuable acquisition, perhaps, than marble. It makes the finest plaster of paris, and when burned would be useful as cement for building purposes. He is just now building a new cabin, and has plastered the outside walls with this material, while he intends to use it likewise for roofing.

Near the white cliffs is a range of red sand stone rock. Chipping off a piece I found it saturated with oil, while at the foot of the cliff near the waters edge the oil may be seen oozing out in small quantities. Ascending to the top of the bluff I rode on a few rods in a northward direction and came to a large oil spring.[9] It is situated on the higher land which is covered with grass and sagebrush.

A kind of mound has been formed by the deposit which is a thick tarry substance hardened into a crust. Tons of this sediment might be gathered in the vicinity. The people use it for fuel. A panful will make a hot blazing fire which lasts a whole evening. They tell me that the Indians chew it as we do tabacco. At the centre of the spring the oil bubbles up in quantities upon the surface of the water.

Baldwin has put a fence around this oil spring and calls it his property.

About a mile and a half from this spot is the hot spring.

8. Washakie hot springs, located about three miles east of present Fort Washakie. This was a spot favored by Chief Washakie.

9. See Chapter VII, footnote 3.

Baldwin has put up a few sticks near the margin, in the shape of a cabin and calls it too his property. The question occurs to me—can Baldwin erect a line of shanties all along the Wind River, and so convert the entire valley to his own use?

This hot spring is one of the largest to be found in the country. I should judge it to be over 200 feet in diameter, and is as round as one could draw it with a compass. The pool is deep and the waters have a milky appearance. The spring is evidently in the centre and the water there is hot enough to boil meat. At the margin one can just hold your hands in it comfortably. The sides and bottom are covered with a soft glutinous looking substance that looks like rock.

A creek of considerable size flows from the spring. The wind was blowing rather chilly or I should have bathed in the pool. But I was afraid of catching cold, so I contented myself with bathing my feet. Further down the valley there are other hot springs but this is the most considerable.

Another wonder of the valley is a soap spring near the foot of the mountains. It is a curious deposit of a yellowish color and answers all the purposes of ordinary soap.[10]

It was yet early in the day when we mounted the bronchos and resumed our journey. Crossing the valley we approached nearer to the foot of the mountains, winding our way at leisure through green pastures and mountain passes of surpassing grandeur. By striking into the chain of mountains at a venture through one of the vast Canons, one leaves, almost at a step, the quiet scenery of the valley, and enters upon the matchless glories of the hills. The heart of the mountains—mother of a thousand streams—the home of the Martin, the Beaver and the Bear. What awful heights and depths—walls of rock rising sheer up a thousand feet and more above your head, throwing the gloom of an eternal twilight among the pine forests, black and solemn, that

10. Old-timers of this area who have been questioned regarding this soap spring can give no information about it.

crown the ridges below. Under the influence of such scenes as these the heart of the wildest mountaineer is hushed into a kind of mute worship.

Here is the cradle of great rivers borne ages since, when this vast mountain side was riven asunder. If one could strike into the tune which this wild infant sings, what an idyll might be sung—to follow one of these mountain streams from its infancy among the remote Beaver haunts, through the gloom of these rocky recesses, onward to smiling valleys where it swells and grows and joins other streams and becomes a river and earns a name—flowing through desolate wastes where the Buffalo and the Indian roams, by solitary cabins where the hunter dwells, by small frontier towns, and farms and mighty cities till it becomes a giant Mississippi.

What a romantic chapter, for instance in its early history, might be found here. Tracing the course of one of these torrents through the ravine, we came to a point where it takes a sudden curve back when it seems to run up the channel for a distance. All at once it disappears into a tremendous cavern, blacker than midnight into which we had not the courage to venture. About a mile further down it reappears in a boiling eddy and bickers down the mountain till it forms the Popogia.[11]

The way through the canon is rough and narrow, and occasionally we come to a belt of timber so dense that the horses cannot follow. As the view widens upward to the heights we can see them mirrored in lakes that lie among the hollows one above another, all fringed with living green. They have the appearance of artificial ponds for the Beavers have built their dams across the outlet. A huge grizzly made his appearance at some distance from us among the

11. What Chisholm refers to as "a tremendous cavern" is known as "The Sinks" on the Popo Agie River just south of Lander. Here the river plunges into an underground channel in which it drops a vertical distance of 200 feet before emerging again a half mile below.

pine trees and a few shots were aimed at him, but he would not show fight, and we were not in a position to track him easily.

The great snowy ranges were now above us—"a palace lifting to eternal winter". We preferred eternal summer and retraced our steps to the valley once more.

I am growing wearied of watching these great cold staring planets all night. Out of the valley the nights are freezing cold, and when the camp fire goes out, and the winds blow down from the hills, the cold always wakens me up. Sometimes I lie whole hours, sometimes a whole night long, looking at them, because there is nothing else to look at. "From yonder wied casement" it may be a very agreeable occupation to "look on great Orion", with Cousin Amy at your side, but when you are lying on a rough gunnisack with a California saddle for your pillow, among the wild sagebrush, your boots freezing beside you, your blanket white with frost—it is quite a different thing.

Under these circumstances I watch Orion "sloping slowly to the West", but I am only calculating how long it will be till daylight. Long after he goes to rest, the morning star begins to shine above the hill, and then there is another interval of uncertainty as to whether it is actually dawn or not. While I am debating the question in my own mind I drop into a short slumber from which I am awakened by Bill who wants to know if we mean to locate here. He is up and doing tearing up dry willows and setting the fire agoing.

Still our small hunting party jogs cheerfully along, though alas! our pack horse is yet waiting for a load: We have not been lucky in finding game. Bill says he never was out so long before and saw so little—possibly for the reason that he is cumbered with company.

We arrived betimes at a small creek in a valley, and it being dinner time we threw off our saddles and kindled a fire.

The wind was blowing and the self same thing happened which had happened before. The grass took fire and all our efforts could not extinguish it. This time the situation was really alarming, for there was a prospect that the entire Wind River Valley might go up in a flame. Bill was annoyed beyond measure at the mischance and would not for the world let it be known how the fire got abroad. He would never hear the last of it. The flame went over the nearest hill with amazing velocity and away, Heaven knows how far.

There was one chance yet for the valley. If the fire would not cross the creek. But it did cross the creek and was surely travelling round toward a narrow pass beyond which it would quickly spread back in the direction of Krutch's ranch. Who were the three valiant men who defended the pass at Thermopylae? I forget their names. It was Bill, James, and John. John remained by the horses while Bill and I armed with saplings, went forth to do battle.

I wished with all my heart it was burning in its own native home. We fired the grass a few rods nearer the bluff and then with the saplings, beat it into bounds. Now it was almost down, and now it flushed out again with a fresh gust of wind, until we nearly despaired. Half an hours severe labor had reduced it to proper limits at that particular pass and the country was saved.

The mountains were black and bare over which we travelled for the rest of that day, and we saw the fire pursuing its way far ahead in several directions, but fortunately keeping away from the valleys.

Our camping ground was beneath a clump of timber upon the bend of a creek in a hollow surrounded by lofty hills. The fire had not passed that way. We hauled logs and made a blaze that illuminated all the valley round. O, the pleasant warmth! The cold bright moon shone down upon us through the branches, but a warmer light shot upward, while we gathered round and thawed into conversation for an hour or so.

Bill is a gossipy fellow and his talk is always entertaining. The future Mrs. Rhodes had got to be a standing joke between us. I have now got her dimensions, qualities and so forth so accurately noted in my mind that I don't think I can fail to discover her.

It is natural enough that we should have a good deal to say concerning our red brethren and neighbors here. A great deal more indeed than I care to note down. No one will accuse me, I think, of cherishing too warm a sympathy with them, but if I had any to spare I think I could bestow it upon some of the impoverished tribes who are wandering here.

How rapidly the red people are vanishing from the earth. Several years ago the Sho-Shonees held the sway over all the country from the North fork of the Platte to Nevada. They were a powerful nation in the time of Washke's predecessor. The Siouxs and all other tribes fled before them. Now they are reduced to a few scattered hundreds here and there. Doubtless their reflections must be of a mournful character as they look upon their fallen condition, and see this persistent irrepressible pale face always crowding him out of every desirable corner.

"I saw the Snakes crossing Green River once" says Bill "and it was a pretty sight too, when they had thousands of head of stock—cattle and horses—and it took them more than three days to cross the stream".—

Ah these must have been palmy days. Now, look at them. The light of other days had faded and the Siouxs can whip them out of their own valley. Many of the bands are at Snake River and cannot join their nation because they are too poor to travel. Thus a great nation disperses and melts away.

I am sorry for you Mr. Lo, but I can't help it. I am afraid you are not the kind of person calculated to take hold of this country. You are not sharp enough. You don't know a good thing when you get it. You leave things no better, but rather worse than you find them, and that, you know, is not the proper way to treat property in this particular planet. The very horses that you steal you cannot treat wisely. You give 'em sore backs and let the magpies eat them. You are not wise enough, my noble red brethren, to understand that labor is the price of life. You are a kind of red bummer who wants to eat all the time and never pay for it.

Now the law of pre-emption and homestead, which, if you only knew it, is just like the law of nature, provides that if you make no improvements your claim may be jumped. We would like to do the best we can with you. We would like to know that you were all enjoying yourselves away in the happy hunting grounds, where you can smoke big pipes, and eat heep for nothing. But, strange as it may seem to you, my poor dusky friend, this world is not wide enough to hold you unless you mean to set to work in it. You will positively have to earn your living somehow or it won't keep you. You don't know what science and progress is, and you don't want to know, because they would set you to work. They are big chiefs, Mr. Lo, and they will never stop till they hunt you out of every fine spot they take a fancy to.

Although the old romantic illusions about Indians have been pretty thoroughly dispelled, there are many, I think, who still believe in a certain picturesqueness in their way of life. Being removed from the commonplace routine of civilized life, people imagine a something of enchantment in it, as if the Indians were some high souled being returning into a proud isolation and the enjoyment of nature. I have been unable to discover anything romantic in their habits or character. To me he appears a lazy, sullen, most uninteresting personage. He is not courageous, but he is enormously self-conceited. When he gets semi-civilized the first evidence he gives of the fact, is to beg. So much for his pride, which is said to be a prominent characteristic.

They live generally in a state of filth and squalor worse than could be seen in the hold of our Irish emigrant ship. I don't think the hungriest white man could partake of the foul messes which they boil in willow baskets by throwing red hot stones into it. They will pick the vermin off their bodies and eat them. That small dappled animal which Shakespeare says "is a familiar beast to man and signifies love" they cultivate. When they catch one—if he happens to be undeveloped they put him carefully back on the pasture till he reaches maturity.

Their women are the most degraded slaves in the earth. It is no wonder the squaws are homely. They do all the rough work while noble Buck struts proudly about like an inflated turkey cock. If he travels she walks behind and carries the burden. He goes out to kill the Buffalo, but the squaw has to dress the hide. The operation is a most laborious one. A hunter has told me that when he saw the amount of labor they bestowed upon it before it was ready for sale, he would sooner pay the price of three Buffalo skins than undertake it.

One looks in vain into their dull impassive countenances for any trace of human emotion—of gladness or sorrow. You may talk to them, but as soon expect to get a response from a cow grazing in the meadow.

As we left camp in the morning and struck across the face of the mountain we perceived two fat black tailed deer feeding in the bottom. In the course of an hour one of them was strapped on the back of our pack animal while the other went over the hill with a broken limb. We came to the north fork of the Popogia and travelled down the valley all day.

Here we met Ten-Doa the chief of the Bannocks accompanied by his two wives and a small party of warriors.[12] He

12. Tendoy, also spelled Ten-doi, was chief of a band of mixed Bannock and Tukarika Indians who made their headquarters in the Lemhi Valley, Idaho. Known for his friendly attitude toward the

was dressed in all respects like an ordinary western man with the exception of the moccasions. In order to show my knowledge of the Indian language I said "How", but I did not find it necessary to go deeper into the mysteries of that dialect for Ten-Doa talks tolerably fair English. He treated us very politely, lifting off his hat while he addressed us in his peculiar gesticulative manner and answered our various enqueries relative to the valley and the hunting prospects there.

He is a really fine looking Indian, over six feet in height, and about thirty two years of age. His bearing is dignified and graceful. He has a light complexion for an Indian, a well shaped brow, Roman nose and large dark eyes. His people he said were all down on the Buffalo hunt and he was on his way to join them.

As Bill was anxious to get home with his load by this time we did not stay long to converse, but passed on.

Being desirous to record impartially my impressions of Indians as well as of everything else, I will say that Ten-Doa appeared to me to be a very fine fellow. Knowing but little about him personally, however, I prefer to give Ive Caldwell's experience of him, and I will do so as far as I can remember them in Ive's own words.

"Ten-Doa" said he one evening when we were talking on Indian matters, "is a particular friend of mine. He is one of the best Indians in the mountains. I will tell you how I got acquainted with him. It was up near the head of Snake River. I had travelled a long ways when I struck his camp and my horse was completely rode down. His back was all covered with sores so that he was no use. As I was looking about for a place to camp, Ten-Doa stopped me and said, 'You camp right here' at his own tent. 'Send your horse out and my

whites, he frequently visited the settlers in the mining camps of Montana with whom he traded. He was a leader on the reservation later established at Lemhi Valley, and held the Indians there in check during the Nez Perce war. Tendoy died on the reservation May 9, 1907.

men will look after him for you. You stay here'. He told his squaws to get supper ready. He sent some of the boys to the river and they brought back a mess of fresh salmon. When I had supper they spread down skins for me to lie on and made everything comfortable. Next morning Ten-Doa says to me 'Do you stay here or are you going on?' I told him I had to travel. 'Look here' says he pointing to my horse 'your horse isn't fit to use any more. You leave him here with me and take a fresh one.' They drove about three hundred horses into the corral and gave me my choice. I selected a fine gentle horse and I went on my way.

"I met Ten-Doa a year after that and stayed with him over night. He was pretty poor by that time and had lost most of his stock. He told me he was poor just then but he would soon be rich again. He was in want of a coat so I gave him mine. Well in a few minutes in came one of his squaws—I had seen him pow-wowing to her but didn't know what he was saying—and brought me a pair of elegant buckskin pants.

"I tell you, sir, you can't out-clever that man. If you make him one present he will make you two for it.

"Another time I met Ten-Doa" continued Ive "we were in the mountains, a pretty large company with me, and we fell out of tobacco. Says I 'Ten-Doa, my men have got out of tobacco, and Americans can't live without it.' He mounted a kind of a stump and called all his men round him and make a short harrangue to them. He said 'these men are my friends. They are Americans and they have not tobacco. They cannot live without tobacco and you can. I want you to give them your tobacco.' So the men came round and we got all they had—seven pounds of it."

If all Indians were like the chief of the Bannocks there might be some ground for the wonderful affection which is entertained for them by the Far-Easters. But I am afraid such men are rare exceptions among the red people.

It seems to me, however, that their intelligence has been often undervalued. In peace or in war they have been, and are, a difficult race to dispose of, and it has been the great misfortune that those who undertook to prescribe the remedy, did not take the trouble to understand the case. The history of the Indian question is a story of mismanagement, injustice and dishonesty from the beginning. Whether in distributing blankets and grub to the friendly tribes, or bullets to the hostile, we have never done justice to the Indians. The responsible agents of the government have invariably been corrupt men—

But this is a subject which would lead me over more paper than I have to spare. I have an itching to commit my ideas to paper, and some day I may do it, but new excitements are springing upon me here every day, and I prefer in the meantime to confine my pencillings to my travels.

I am at Bill's cabin once more. We have had a Buffalo hunt. About three miles below this place a herd of seven Buffalo were feeding—one of them a grey old bull of immense size. Bill brought him to his knees at one shot when the others started off at a heavy thundering gallop, the hunters after them. The pursuit lasted a whole day and all the killing was done by Bill. I am afraid his friends were very little assistance to him. I gave out very soon and returned, but Bill did not re-appear till late in the night, by which time he had killed three Buffalo. The old bull was no use being too tough, and grey with age.

An Indian came to our cabin and stayed with us all night. He asked Bill to give him some Buffalo meat in the morning. Said Bill "go and kill 'em yourself g—— d—— you". The Indian took this gentle rebuke mildly like a man and a brother, and shifting his ground a little, made a proposition to Bill to come and hunt Buffalo for the Snakes, which was not accepted.

The fact is, Bill, or any experienced white hunter could kill three to their one. In trapping Beaver or any other kind of game Bill could teach them all. Says he "I can show them trails that they never dreamed of."

After an interval of repose and buttermilk we again started over the hills in another direction. By this time the storms had been gathering all round and as we ascended we found ourselves in deep and deeper snow. I shall not attempt to describe my feelings on this trip. Sometimes I did not know very well whether I was alive or dead. Every now and again after night came on, we had to jump from our saddles and run for it. The great white billows of snow which sparkled around us were awful to behold. The worst of it was I had no under clothes with me—not even stockings and how my feet escaped freezing was a wonder. One of us—Wilson—got his toe frozen and he had to mend it with coal oil.

I am glad to find on my return home that some of my prospecting friends have been as good as their word. I, too, have some stake in this country. They are about to run a tunnel under the . . .

[Thus abruptly James Chisholm's journal ends. A page and a half in an inserted section at the end of the notebook remain blank. Penciled memoranda on a few inserted pages —jottings incomprehensible to the reader today—suggest that from the South Pass area he intended to go to Salt Lake City. His oldest brother, John, a miner, was there. One note reads: "Mem. Salt Lake send a pair of spectacles for Mr. Quinn age 45 good eyes."

In any event, whether or not he visited Salt Lake City, he left Wyoming for the east on December 11, 1868. On that date the following notice appeared in the Cheyenne *Daily Leader:*

Personal. Jim Chisholm, of the *Chicago Tribune*, David Manson, one of the original discoverers of the renowned Miners Delight ledge, Sweetwater, and Judge Dildine, of the Carter County Probate Court, arrived here from Sweetwater to-day, on their way east. Mr. Chisholm has notes embracing a complete history of the mineral resources of Wyoming, having spent the entire summer in this territory, and upon his arrival in Chicago, will give the benefit of his experience to the public through the columns of the *Tribune*. The other two gentlemen have sold some valuable mines, and go east to enjoy the fruits of their good fortune and hard work.]

It must remain a matter for conjecture whether James Chisholm ever wrote the articles which were to be based on the notes in his journal. Quite possibly when they learned that the Sweetwater mines had failed to live up to the early reports of their richness, the *Tribune* editors scrapped the project. At any rate, so far as can be ascertained, the story that Jim went to South Pass to write never appeared in the *Tribune* or any other paper.

But he got the girl.

SUPPLEMENTARY NOTES

WYOMING

Although the Lewis and Clark Expedition of 1804-1806 opened the first overland route to the west, theirs was not destined to become the main route to California and the Oregon country. The discovery of South Pass opened a more direct and practical way, over which it has been estimated that more than 300,000 persons trekked westward. The pass is broad, measuring more than twenty miles in width, and the ascent to the Continental Divide here is so gradual from either side that Lieutenant John Charles Fremont, crossing this point on his 1842 expedition, found it difficult to realize he had reached the summit.

1812   Robert Stuart and his party of returning Astorians cross through South Pass on October 22, probably along its southern extremity. It is doubtful if they were aware of their important discovery.

1824   Trappers of the American Fur Company under the leadership of Thomas Fitzpatrick (later known to the Indians as Broken Hand) locate South Pass, following directions given by the Crow Indians. Having crossed to the valley of the Green River, they begin extending their operations westward. The discovery was publicized by General William H. Ashley, head of the American Fur Company.

1827   First wheeled vehicle, a rude carriage on which a cannon had been mounted, is said to have been taken through South Pass.

1832   Captain B. L. E. de Bonneville directs the first wagon train through the pass. His exploring party was a well-organized, military group of trappers and explorers numbering 110 men accompanied by twenty wagons.

[203]

1835   Reverend Samuel Parker and Dr. Marcus Whitman are the first missionaries to travel overland to the west coast, accompanying a fur brigade under the direction of Lucien Fontenelle through the pass.

1836   Narcissa Whitman and Eliza Spalding, brides of Dr. Whitman and Reverend H. H. Spalding, are the first white women to cross South Pass, traveling west by buggy. In the years 1838-1840 other groups of missionaries, all small parties, follow the Whitman-Spalding party to the west coast.

1841   Emigration to Oregon begins with a small party making its way westward through South Pass.

1842   Gold first reported in South Pass.

Eliza White leads a group of 123 settlers to Oregon. Lieutenant Fremont with his guide Kit Carson lead a trail-exploration expedition through the pass and into the valley of the Green River.

1843   The great western tide of emigration begins.

The first party of dudes follows the trail of the emigrants through the pass to the valley of the Green River, traveling merely for the sport of riding hundreds of miles to the Wind River Mountains and for the excitement of buffalo hunting. This lighthearted journey was led by Sir William Drummond Stewart, accompanied by twenty gentlemen and thirty hunters, muleteers, and camp servants.

1847   The Mormons, seeking asylum, follow the trail through South Pass to the valley of the Great Salt Lake. Each year thereafter increasing numbers of their faith followed this way to the new Zion.

1850   The first U.S. mail contractors begin mail service from the Eastern states through Salt Lake City to South Pass. Operation was to have been monthly but it was always irregular.

1855   The freighting firm of Alexander Majors and William H. Russell begin freighting operations across the plains along the Oregon Trail.

1857   Colonel Frederick W. Lander and his corps of engineers explore the South Pass area under government order to survey and improve a wagon road along the Central Overland Route.

A military force under Colonel E. B. Alexander and, later, a force under Colonel Albert Sidney Johnston cross South Pass on their route to Utah, with orders to put down the rebellious Mormons.

1860   Russell, Majors and Waddell obtain a contract for mail service from St. Joseph to San Francisco. They also inaugurate the first regular overland stage line along the central overland route through South Pass. The Pony Express begins to operate on April 3, carrying mail from St. Joseph to Sacramento in ten days. Stations for the express and the stage line were built in the vicinity of South Pass, Pacific Springs to the west and Upper Sweetwater to the east.

1861   First transcontinental telegraph line completed in October, heralding the end of the Pony Express. The line followed the Oregon Trail through South Pass.

1862   The Overland Stage Line is forced to abandon the central route through South Pass because of the Indian menace.

1865   The telegraph line is said to have been abandoned along the Oregon Trail and moved south along the Overland Trail. (I have never been able to verify this.—*Editor*)

WYOMING CHRONOLOGY, 1803-1869

1803   Louisiana Purchase includes three-fourths of present Wyoming.

1804–1806 Lewis and Clark Expedition opens an overland route west through present Montana.

1807   John Colter, first known white man to enter Wyoming, spends the winter of 1807 in the Cody and Jackson Hole area. His exploration trip marked the beginning of the fur trade period in Wyoming.

1809   White trappers of the Missouri Fur Company along the eastern edge of the Rocky Mountains.

1811'   The Wilson Price Hunt party en route to Oregon crosses the state from the north central to the western area, the first organized expedition through Wyoming.

1812   The returning Astorians under Robert Stuart cross Wyoming from west to east. This was the first known white party to cross South Pass.

1822   Rocky Mountain Fur Company organized by William Ashley of St. Louis. He revolutionized the fur trade by employing none but expert riders and rifle shots, and instead of establishing permanent trading posts he instituted the annual fur rendezvous where the trappers and Indians met the traders to barter furs to the company for ammunition, whisky, and supplies. These rendezvous, which with few exceptions were held annually in central and western Wyoming on the Popo Agie and Green rivers between the years 1824 and 1840, were carnival scenes noted for their mixture of business, gambling, and brawls. Missionaries, scientists, and adventurers often accompanied the traders to the rendezvous.

1824   Discovery of South Pass, making a central route across the continent practical.

1832   Captain B. L. E. de Bonneville, with 110 men and a train of twenty wagons (the first through South Pass), builds "Fort Nonsense"—Fort Bonneville—so called because of its poor location in the upper Green River region.

1834   Fort Laramie established, the first permanent settlement in what became Wyoming. Founded by Robert Campbell and William Sublette, it was intended as a post for barter and for protection against hostile Indians.

1840   Last rendezvous as trade shifted from beaver to buffalo, from rendezvous to fort.

1843   Fort Bridger established by Jim Bridger and Louis Vasquez, the second permanent post in Wyoming. This marked the beginning of a new phase of history, that of the great migration to the West Coast—to Oregon, to Utah, and to the gold fields of California during the 1840's, '50's, and '60's.

1845   Texas Annexation brings a segment of the future state of Wyoming. The settlement of the Oregon boundary dispute in 1846 and the Mexican Cession in 1848 completed the acquisition of the territory comprising the state.

1849   Gold rush to California.

Fort Laramie becomes a military post on the Overland Trail. Fort Bridger and Platte Bridge Station (Fort Casper) were also to become military posts in 1858 and 1859, to provide protection for the emigrants and to keep open the lines of communication.

1851   Great Treaty at Fort Laramie providing annual payments to Indian tribes in return for various privileges. But the Indians remained a constant menace along the trails, and battles were to be fought for more than a quarter of a century.

1854   Indians kill Lieutenant John Grattan and his men near Fort Laramie.

1860–1861 Pony Express between St. Joseph, Mo., and Sacramento.

1861   The transcontinental telegraph completed.

1862   Repeated attacks on stagecoaches and stations force Ben Holladay's Overland Stage Company to move his route south from the Oregon Trail to the Overland Trail.

1863   The Shoshone sign a peace treaty at Fort Bridger.

1865   The "Bloody Year on the Plains"—the Custard Wagon Train massacre; the Battle of Platte Bridge in which Caspar Collins was killed; and the Powder River Expedition under General P. E. Connor.

Construction on the Union Pacific starts from Omaha.

1866   The Fetterman Massacre near Fort Phil Kearny.

1867   The Wagon Box Fight.

Establishment of Cheyenne and Fort D. A. Russell.

Carissa Lode opened at South Pass in June.

The Union Pacific reaches Cheyenne in November.

1868   Second treaty signed at Fort Laramie with the Sioux, Arapaho, and Crow tribes prohibiting white men from entering the Powder River region north of the Platte River and reserving it for the Indians.

The Fort Bridger treaty with the Shoshones creates the Wind River Reservation in central Wyoming.

Wyoming Territory created July 25.

End-of-track reaches the western boundary of Wyoming.

1869   Wyoming Territory organized. Formally inaugurated under Territorial Governor John A. Campbell in May.

Union Pacific completed across the territory; meeting with Central Pacific at Promontory Point, Utah, May 10.

"VIGILANTEES AGAIN—TWO MEN HUNG"

(The text of the story in the Cheyenne *Daily Evening Leader, March 23, 1868.)*

This morning rumors of Vigilantee doings were in circulation at an early hour, and about eight o'clock, the bodies of two men were brought to the City Hall, just as they had been cut down, with the ropes still on their necks. They were soon after taken in charge by Dr. Johnson, County Coroner, and an inquest held. Various parties testified and the following facts were elicited:

Chas. Martin who was recently acquitted of the charge of murder, by a jury of his countrymen, was last night about one o'clock, called to the door, of the Keystone dance house, where he was dancing and told that a friend wished to see him. Martin went to the door, others being prevented from going out, by a display of several revolvers. The last that was seen of Martin, he was making some desperate struggles, and marks on his head show, that he had been beaten with a pistol, or some other instrument. He was found this morning just east of the city, hanging upon a temporary scaffold, consisting of three poles. Martin we learn, said last night, that he would soon furnish another man for breakfast, for the citizens of Cheyenne, little thinking however, he, himself would so soon be the victim. His body was cut down by policeman Shaw and Scott, who delivered it to the Coroner.

Morgan, the other unfortunate victim, was found hanging in the rear of the Elephant Corral. It appears that some mules had been stolen and the owner had suspected some parties, and, on the road between here and Denver, found Morgan and a man named Kelly, who after being taken into custody, confessed being in with other parties, from whom they bought stolen mules, knowing them to be stolen. W. G. Smith, one of the owners of the mules, was bringing Morgan and Kelly to this city, for the purpose of giving them up to the officers of the law, when they were met, last night, about nine o'clock, near Crow Creek, by about a dozen men, who took the two men from him, which was the last he saw of them. Kelly is yet missing, and it is suspected that he has met the same fate as his companion; but up to this time he has not been heard of.

It seems to be the general opinion that the hanging last night was not done by the old Vigilance Commitee, but by a new and temporary organization gotten up for this occasion.

The following are the verdicts given by the juries in the respective cases:

We the undersigned, summoned as jurors to investigate the cause of Chas. Martin's death, find that he came to his death by strangulation, he having been found hanging by his neck on a rude gallows, at the extreme end of 16th St., in the suburbs of Cheyenne. Perpetrators unknown.

> F. W. Wilkinson,
> E. M. Tower,
> John H. Follett,
> Harry Powers,
> Fred Clifford,
> Bud Sternburger,
> Dr. F. W. Johnson, Coroner.
> Cheyenne, March 21st, 1868.

––––––

We the undersigned Jury, summoned by the Coroner to inquire into the cause of the death of Chas. or J. Morgan, find by the evidence that his death was occasioned by strangulation, he having been found hanging by the neck on three poles in the rear of the Elephant Corral, in Cheyenne, D. T. Perpetrators unknown.

Same Jurors as above.

Dr. F. W. Johnson, Coroner.
Cheyenne, March 21, 1868.

MINING

Arrastra

An arrastra was a rude dragstone mill for pulverizing ores. In this method of mining the ore was ground in a shallow circular pit paved with stone (an arrastra). Large blocks of stone attached by beams to a central rotating post were dragged around the arrastra by mule-power, reducing the ore to particles. If the gold particles freed by the arrastra were coarse, they were agitated in water to separate them from the sand and other materials; the gold sank to the bottom and the other materials were washed off. If the gold was fine, it was extracted by amalgamation—a process involving the use of mercury.

Arrastra (also spelled arrasta) is a term borrowed from the Mexican miner's word *arrastre;* and this method was long used by Mexican miners to reduce silver ore. Where it was feasible, a water-wheel might be used instead of mules for motive power.

Stamp mills

A gold stamp mill operates on the principle of the pestle and mortar. Ore, water, and mercury are fed continuously into a long narrow iron box called the battery, in which, ranged in a row, are heavy steel stampers. These are raised and let fall in succession, crushing the lumps of ore and driving the pulp through screens set in one side of the battery. As it comes from the screens into tubs called amalgamating pans, the pulp is further reduced by grinding in tube mills—rotating cylinders half filled with large pebbles or lumps of unbroken ore. On early stamp mills just outside the screen there were copper plates which had been amalgamated with mercury. As the pulp flowed over them, the gold particles would adhere to the plates.

A description of a stamp mill in operation is given at the end of this glossary.

[211]

"Cleaning up"

In order to retrieve the mercury with its imprisoned gold and silver, at intervals—perhaps of a day or a week—the stamp mill's machinery was stopped and the pans and batteries washed out. The recovered mass of metal was placed in an iron retort from which a pipe led to a pail of water. When roasting heat was applied to the retort, the mercury turned to vapor and was trapped in the water, as it cooled becoming liquid once again. The gold, silver, and other metals obtained from the ore remained in the retort.

Float rock

is mineral or ore found as a loose fragment some distance from the vein outcrop or bed. Erosion or the action of water causes it to be detached and carried away. Float rock is usually finely divided, flakey particles of ore.

Wall rock

is the rock through which a fault or vein runs. It is often called *country rock*.

Lode

A lode is a mineral deposit filling a fissure that has occurred in country rock. The mineral deposit is a later formation than the enclosing rocks and was produced either by the filling of a fissure or by the alteration, impregnation, or replacement of the original rock near a fissure or system of fissures. In United States miners' usage, and under the statutes, a lode is an ore deposit occurring in a place within definite boundaries, separating it from the adjoining rocks. *Lode, ledge, vein, lead,* and *reef* are practically synonymous.

Tailings

are the refuse materials resulting from the milling or treatment of ground ore. The crude methods of milling used in 1868 usually left a good deal of precious metal in this refuse.

Toms

A tom is an inclined trough in which gold-bearing earth or gravel is crudely washed. The bottom of the trough is fitted with riffles (see below) to catch the heavier gold particles which fall to the bottom as the lighter gravel and earthen particles are washed out of the trough.

Riffle

In gold washing, this is a contrivance placed across the bottom of a sluice and forming a series of grooves which will break the current and catch and retain the gold. Mercury is sometimes put in the grooves to assist in the process. A riffle may be made of blocks, rails, poles, iron bars, sacking, matting, or hides with hair up.

For ore sampling, a riffle is also a device for dividing ground ore or other material into two equal parts. It consists of an even number of narrow sloping chutes of equal width, either adjacent chutes discharging in opposite directions or parallel troughs separated by gaps of the same width as the troughs.

While no authority can be cited, the expression "making the riffle" apparently was the equivalent of "striking it rich"—catching the gold, scooping up rich pickings.

A STAMP MILL IN OPERATION

In the Sweetwater mines, the stamp mill method was the principal means of reducing the ore. Mark Twain, who prospected in the Nevada gold fields in the 1860's, gives the following description of a stamp mill in operation in *Roughing It* (Hartford: American Publishing Company, 1873), pp. 252-253. Although he is writing about silver mining, it is the best description I know of a stamp mill of that period.

> I had already learned how hard and long and dismal a task it is to burrow down into the bowels of the earth and get out the coveted ore; and now I learned that the burrowing was only half the work; and that to get the silver out of the ore was the dreary and laborious other half of it. We had to turn out at six in the morning

and keep at it till dark. This mill was a six-stamp affair, driven by steam. Six tall, upright rods of iron, as
large as a man's ankle, and heavily shod with a mass of
iron and steel at their lower ends, were framed together
like a gate, and these rose and fell, one after the other,
in a ponderous dance, in an iron box called a "battery."
Each of these rods or stamps weighed six hundred
pounds. One of us stood by the battery all day long,
breaking up masses of silver-bearing rock with a sledge
and shoveling it into the battery. The ceaseless dance
of the stamps pulverized the rock to powder, and a
stream of water that trickled into the battery turned it
to a creamy paste. The minutest particles were driven
through a fine wire screen which fitted close around
the battery, and were washed into great tubs warmed
by super-heated steam—amalgamating pans, they are
called. The mass of pulp in the pans was kept constantly stirred up by revolving "mullers." A quantity
of quicksilver was kept always in the battery, and this
seized some of the liberated gold and silver particles and
held on to them; quicksilver was shaken in a fine shower
into the pans, also, about every half hour, through a
buckskin sack. Quantities of coarse salt and sulphate of
copper were added, from time to time to assist the
amalgamation by destroying base metals which coated
the gold and silver and would not let it unite with the
quicksilver. All these tiresome things we had to attend
to constantly. Streams of dirty water flowed always
from the pans and were carried off in broad wooden
troughs to the ravine. One would not suppose that
atoms of gold and silver would float on top of six
inches of water, but they did; and in order to catch
them, coarse blankets were laid in the troughs, and
little obstructing "riffles" charged with quicksilver were
placed here and there across the troughs also. These
riffles had to be cleaned and the blankets washed out
every evening, to get their precious accumulations—
and after all this eternity of trouble one third of the
silver and gold in a ton of rock would find its way to
the end of the troughs in the ravine at last and have to
be worked over again some day. . . .

AMERICAN GOLD RUSHES

The earliest gold discoveries in the United States—in North Carolina in the 1790's and in Georgia in the 1830's—failed to cause any particular excitement and in neither case was there a gold rush. But in 1848 word of the first great gold strike in California at Sutter's Mill aroused a more settled East, and from then on rushing to the gold fields of the West symbolized high adventure.

During the years 1849-1851, California fever assumed epidemic proportions: men streamed west by land and sea. By 1855, however, the easy gold had been taken and mining in California had become a corporate business. It is estimated that the California gold yield was approximately a half billion dollars in the decade following the Sutter's Mill strike.

Throughout this period there was at least a rush a year to some part of the West. Pikes Peak in Colorado and the Virginia City (Nevada) area were the scenes of the next large strikes and the biggest rushes, both in 1859. When the king of lodes, the Comstock, was discovered that year, it touched off a population boom which enabled Nevada to achieve territorial status in 1861. Similarly, the Pikes Peak rush created Colorado Territory, also in 1861.

Soon after gold was found in 1860 in the Clearwater country of Idaho, there were rich strikes made in other nearby areas. Gold-hungry men swarmed in, and three years later Idaho was organized as a territory.

What began as a minor rush following a strike on Benetsee Creek, Montana, in 1862, developed into a stampede in 1863 and Virginia City was born. Then came discoveries at Last Chance Gulch and the founding of Helena, and in 1864 Montana Territory came into being. Between 1862 and 1882 gold from the Montana mines totaled more than $175,000,000.

The same pattern of mining was repeated after each gold discovery. The easy gold was quickly removed by the hordes who rushed to the new locations. Within a short time the lodes would be worked beyond the stage where they could be exploited by a lone hand or by small groups of miners with primitive equipment. At this point companies would be formed to take over mining operations, leaving the "old pros," the lone hands, and the "ten-day miners" free to try their luck again when the next big strike was rumored.

The rush to the South Pass gold fields—or as they were generally called, the Sweetwater Mines—followed the usual pattern, another in that series of rushes which took men into every nook and cranny of the western mountains. After the discovery of the Carissa Lode and Miner's Delight in 1867, the rush lasted for several years; then, as elsewhere, companies took over to exploit the mines with better equipment.

SOUTH PASS GOLD FIELDS

Gold was first reported in the South Pass area in 1842. According to a story in the *Sweetwater Mines* (March 24, 1869), the discovery was made by an employee of the American Fur Company, a Georgian who was killed by Indians before he could leave the country. Ironically enough, he had come west for his health.

Very little is known of the early history of the mines. There was some mining activity in 1855, 1858, and 1860-1862. The remains of rotten sluices, rockers, and toms believed to have been built in 1860 were still in evidence in 1869. The Indians, whose ancient hunting trails crossed the Pass, had much to do with the delay in developing the mines. In 1862, after the outbreak of the Civil War, when seasoned troops were withdrawn to serve at the front, hostiles forced the Overland Stage Company to move the Overland Trail farther south, and all the miners in the South Pass country were driven out. The only known mining activity in the region until the war's end was conducted by troops stationed there to guard the telegraph lines.

Despite continued harassment by the Indians, prospecting was resumed in October 1865. Grubstaked by Major Noyes Baldwin of Fort Bridger and John F. Skelton, John A. James and D. C. Moreland made a six months' exploration of the South

Pass area and found promising ledges. (See pages 219-224.) With other miners who had entered the region, they organized the first mining district, the Lincoln, on November 11, 1865. According to the original minutes, the meeting was held on "one of the tributarys of Beaver creek," and laws concerning location and representation of quartz leads or lodes of silver-bearing rock were adopted. W. H. Shoemaker was elected president of the district and John A. James secretary.

Mining activity continued in 1866, and in June 1867 came the discovery of the famous Carissa mine. The rock in this lode was rich beyond anything heretofore located in the South Pass fields, and news of the find, greatly exaggerated, soon brought in a large number of miners and adventurers. A second great discovery, the Miner's Delight mine, was made in September of the same year. During 1868 and 1869 a number of additional mines were located, among them the Young American, King Solomon, Mary Ellen, Caribou, Buckeye, and the Bennet Line. By 1870 it was estimated that fifteen hundred lodes had been discovered, some valuable, many worthless.

As the rush developed, towns were founded at locations convenient to the mines. The first to be laid out was South Pass City on Willow Creek, a half mile below the Carissa mine, where a number of substantial cabins had been built by October 1867. On December 27 it was designated by the Dakota Legislature as the county seat of Carter County, Dakota Territory. The second town in the district, founded in April 1868, was Atlantic City, located about four and a half miles from South Pass City on Rock Creek. A third town was on Spring Gulch, three and a half miles northeast of Atlantic City. It lay seven hundred feet below the Miner's Delight mine and was first called by that name, but shortly thereafter was rechristened Hamilton City. The two names have been used interchangeably over the years.

Following the organization of the Wyoming territorial government in 1869, South Pass City became the county seat of Sweetwater County, Wyoming. As mining activity declined in the early 1870's, the population center shifted to the southern end of the county, and in 1873 the Wyoming Legislature moved the county seat to Green River.

Claims of a 5,000 to 10,000 population for the gold fields seem to have no basis in fact. Because of the ebb and flow of population during the years 1867-1870, it would have been almost impossible to obtain a census which would hold good for any period of time. Reports of new finds drew crowds into the area; Indian disturbances, rumors of richer strikes elsewhere, better pay on railroad construction crews, and disgust with their luck took men away. In April 1868, the editor of the *Sweetwater Mines* reported that South Pass City had been almost depopulated as a result of rumored new gold discoveries in the Big Horn mountains. In July, he claimed there were 1,030 men in the country, and made a plea for military protection against the Indians. In August the *Frontier Index* announced that almost the whole of South Pass City had moved to Green River: men were in demand on construction crews there as end-of-track was nearing the town. The claims of a large population also are refuted by the Census of 1869 (made by the U.S. Marshal for newly created Territory of Wyoming) which gave the total population of the mining area as 1,517. In the official U.S. Census of 1870 this number had dropped to 1,166. By 1872 it was reported that the population of the three South Pass mining towns probably numbered less than one hundred each.

The period of greatest mining activity in both lode and placer properties of the South Pass District lasted until near the close of 1872. By then the rich pay streaks in the placer claims had been worked out, leaving only lower-grade material which could not be handled at a profit when worked on a small scale. The oxidized ores found in the leads from the surface down to a depth of about 150 feet had been extracted and milled. Lower than the 150-foot level the ore was of lower grade and more refractory in character, so that the operators with their rather crude equipment were no longer able to mine it at a profit. Lack of good transportation also hampered the entire mining operation.

Gold mining has never entirely ceased in the South Pass region, and from time to time activity has revived with new discoveries or new enterprises. In 1876 a man named Lewis, placering in Strawberry Creek, discovered the Bullion Lode. That winter he sunk a shaft, ran a drift out under the creek, and took out a small fortune. The next spring a town was organized and named after him. In the summer of 1879, placering in what was later named Burr Gulch, A. T. Burr discovered the Burr mine. Emile Granier, in 1884, initiated an ill-fated attempt to install

[218]

hydraulic mining along Rock Creek. During the years various other companies acquired this property, and in the 1930's the E. T. Fisher Company successfully dredged the area for gold.

No exact accounting of the gold taken from the South Pass fields can be given, but it has been estimated that since the first discovery the output has been nearly $6,000,000.

South Pass and Atlantic City, those romantic monuments to gold-rush days, have never been completely deserted, and the faith of the remaining residents may yet be vindicated, for once again mining is to be revived in South Pass. But this time there will be no great rush of prospectors, no newspaper correspondents, no dreams of "making a riffle." Iron, not gold, is the magnet. As this book goes to press, the Columbia-Geneva Division of the United States Steel Corporation has ordered construction begun on a multi-million-dollar flotation processing mill, which will use the vast resources of Iron Mountain near Atlantic City. A spur line from the Union Pacific will soon enter the South Pass country to serve the mill.

THE JAMES-MORELAND PROSPECTING TOUR, 1865-1866

(From the Grace R. Hebard Collection)

Fort Bridger, Oct. 31st 1865

We the undersigned acknowledge to have gone into the following agreement. That is as we have been outfited by Noyes Baldwin and Jno. F. Skelton in provision and mining tools suficiant for a six months prospecting tour, do hereby agree to represent and look to the interest of the above named Gentlemen the same as our own. We four are to be equally interested in all locations of Gold or silver bearing quartz leads, and all other mineral locations, whatever that are made by us.

Jno. A. James
D. C.

⎰ *South Pass*
⎱ *March 18th 1866*
             Major Noys Baldwin
                Fort Bridger

Well Major, as spring is near at hand, and there is some hopes of getting a letter out to you. I think it a good plan to drop you a fiew lines in the way of report of what we have done. We went over and prospected the proposie courtrey. to our purfect satisfaction. we can raise the color any place in that courtrey but nothing more. and after you cross beaver you find no more slate or granit Bedrock. what slate and granite wash you see there. we have found to be entirely surface. the bedrock being sand & Lime stone. I have been from oposite St. Marys on beaver, to near the head of the same stream, and find that this is the dividing point between the slate and Sand stone, consequently the gold streak must be on this side of that stream, at least that part of it that lies east of wind river. Well *About the Ledges.* I am not yet prepared to give you a definite report concerning the Quartz on willow creek. we spent about one month there, but the weather was so intensely cold and so much snow. that we did not have a chance of thouroly trying any of the ledges that are visable, while we were there we burnt & washed out in a horn spoon croppings from several of the ledges, but have not found any thing in them as yet, in fact Major we think the most of the leades here are basterd, from thier striking similarity. to the basterd quartz of Montana & Idaho Camps, but that there is one good ledge in that immediate vicinity, we have not a doubt. for we have tested those digings that old Cambell had out there enough to satisfy us. of that fact. tho what prospecting we done in that gulch was limited. from the fact that we had to shovel about ten feet of snow drift off. before we could reach the ground, but what little we have done, satisfies us that there is near by a good lead of gold bearing rock, we have two good reasons for this opinion. first because the gold that we get is entirely unwashed, being of rough irregular shape bearing the appearance of having just tumbled out of decomposed rock in the immediate vicinity. why we think it is a good lead is because we find all sizes from course to fine flour gold. and that of a verry fine quality. in fact Major, it is the finest quality of gold I ever saw, except that obtained in the Countaney digings. and that coined $21 per oz. I think this equaly as good. from what we have seen there. togather with the prospects obtained on rock creek & strawberry. which places are on a paralell with the run of the leades. on slate. er are satisfied that the above (which we are trying to find) is a blind lead. we have made a survey and find that we can get watter on them digings sufficiant to grounsluce with for a month or six weeks, without much trouble, we think that with the aid of watter we can strike it in that time, I think we can go to work on the ditch in the course of 10 days from now, we will use all diligence, to advance the certainty of the fact. at as early a period as posible. for two reasons. first that if we are luckey enough to strike it and find it to be really good. you know that the sooner machinery is got the better, and we would have to make preperations earley to get the machinery started this season, secondly because if there is nothing here to keep us. we want to go on to the head of wind rive & yellow stone. where some of our boys were two years ago and obtained good prospects of both quartz & placer digings. but were run out by the Indians, even should the enterprise fail that we are now engaged in, (which my best judgement tells me will not be the case) should it be congenial with your and the captin's feelings we should like to share with you still in the search, and profits of a part of the hiden treasures of the mountains, which we are determined to pursevere in the pursuit of until we find it, knowing that there are plenty of good fortunes in these mountains, in the shape of quartz. and having some confidence in our ability and judgement. our mottow is never give it up so, but try try again, and feeling yet deeply indebted to you and the captin for your generous acts towards us while we were mere strangers. we feel it our duty to exercise every means at our hands to bring about what we all have sanguinely hoped for, and to still pursue it untill we find it, we have plenty of grub to to last us out the ballance of the six months. by that time we will have satisfied our selves concerning this region, we have had such good luck this winter killing buffalo, that we will have becan enough to last us all summer, consequently our outfit will not be so expensive as it was last fall. the great ledge that Mr. Eddy made such an excitement about. we do not think worth any notice, I think that from the way the same rock cuts a hammer in beating it up. that he has mistaken hammer dust for silver, at least that is all that we can get out of it, and from the fine quality of gold that we find here satisfies me that there is no silver rock here of any richness, for in places where there exists both gold & silver bearing rock, you always find the gold of a dull silver color. varying in value from $4 to $12 per ounce. while this is pure & bright, and worth at least $20, Mr. Sinclair the operater here tells me that Mr. Basset the assistant superintendant of the pacific telegraph company, who is located at Salt Lake City had some of the rock of that Eddy lead sent to Virginia City Nevada and there assayed by one of the best assayers on the pacific cost, and his report was $0.85/100 in silver per ton, and nothing else in it. to amount to anything. I know that you do not want us to bother with such as that, I am satisfied that with a little time and good weather, we can strike $50 per ton quartz, this or anything above will suit us. and I think will meet with your aprobation, for altho $20 rock will pay a small dividend. I think $50 as low as our company should stop on. when we have sanguine hopes that there is plenty of that kind & better, the boys are all well. Moreland & Burch have gone to kill some meat, to pack in to willow creek, I heard that Mr. Sinclair was to be moved from here is what brought me over alone. for we left the most of our grub with him in the winter. I came over yesterday found him here and everything right. he expects soon to go to the rive to be mustered out. we will then move all our things over to willow creek. as soon as we can accertain any thing definite concerning willow creek. I will come in and report to you in person,

Yours Fraternally
Jno A. James

Ps   we still have the mule that the boys left with us. he is some better of his lameness. he has been of great survice to us I do not see how we could have got along without him, in packing our meat to camp, and packing our grub over here he is the best pack animal I ever seen. I forgot to mention above that Mountain Jack was killed a few days ago, by a man named Johnson, who used to stay about grangers, Jack was a desperet character, had on several occasions thretend Johnson's life. in fact all the crowd with him were afraid of him. I have talked with several who were known to the circumstance, and they all agree. the Johnson was justifiable. it happened about twenty miles below where we camped on proposie.

Jno A. James

JAMES CHISHOLM

LETTER TO MRS. GARRISON

(Opening passages of the March 27, 1868, letter
quoted in the text, pages 28-34.)

To the happy family at 65 Park Avenue
A Rambler in the Far West sends friendly greeting.

I would commence this letter with the good old time honored
formula, but really I could not find an adjective comprehensive
enough to embrace you all, without, perhaps, infringing on the
rules of good taste—and one must respect the proprieties even
in the wilderness.

The truth is, I have just conceived a rather bold undertaking
in which I shall have to ask your kind indulgence. I said to myself "some fine day I will write a letter to the girls"—and, I hope
Mrs. Garrison will forgive me, but I included her in that cate-
gory. (Now this might be characterised in vulgar phraseology
as "Cheek", and truly if I offend, I will prove myself a true
christian and turn to you the other also.) Perhaps the motives
that urged me to this were not unmixed with some alloy of
selfishness—a certain jealous apprehensiveness lest a straggler
from the fold might be forgotten did he not seek to preserve
his own memory by some token.

And here a difficulty at once presented itself in the selection
of an appropriate "token". The first idea was to send a tiny bit
of blue ribbon to Julie,* but that was too suggestive of a love-
sick sailor, and "all round my heart", so I dismissed it as *sentimental*. A strain of flute melody by telegraph would have been
deeply affecting, but the operators at this end of the line are
not so expert as they ought to be. Next I thought a bar of gold
from Sweetwater might be appreciated, but unfortunately my

---

* Julia and Anna Coursen, half sisters of Mrs. Garrison, were members of the Garrison household. The four "girls" of the letter are Mrs.
Garrison, Mary Garrison, and the Misses Coursen.

specimens are all so heavy that the expense of freightage would be overwhelming. Finally I decided on simply endorsing my autograph—prefaced by a few lines of explanation.—And here ends my prologue.

And so up goes the curtain, and I make my bow before a select audience of four ladies, who are doubtless anticipating an entertainment. What shall it be? A Diorama of the Unholy Land? The Pilgrim's Progress to the New Pandemonium? The Rovers of the Far West, or the Last of the Red Cents? To be very candid with you I am dreadfully embarrassed at the outset, considering the requirements of the occasion, the shabbiness of my equipments, and the qualities of my auditors; for in order to enlist your various sympathies my discourse would needs be witty, lively, sentimental, fanciful, airy, poetical, practical and all combined. But alas, my fair hearers, you are to know that I bestride no soaring Pegasus, but a plain old mule—docile and trustworthy, sure-footed, yet unaccustomed to "tot the air". And thus do I perceive my ambitious designs already dwindling down into a mere prosaic gossip about common everyday events—in other words, as I remarked to begin with—"a letter to the girls".

Tis pleasant, believe me, in the midst of the riot and excitement which prevails around me, to escape for an hour or two in this manner, and fly off on the wings of a goose quill, (literally, a steel pen, Mrs. James) back to your hospitable fireside again. I am sensible here of a rising tendency to quote verses and become lack a daisical, but I sternly refrain. I may observe incidentally that the far West is not favorable to the cultivation of the muses—not at least in the higher branches. During my residence in Omaha a young poetess there, I remember, gave to the world a lyrical rhapsody on Mud; and it was painfully apparent she could soar no higher.

I myself had an experience scarcely less deplorable. Musing one dreamy afternoon upon a group of barnyard fowls I was suddenly seized with an inspiration and the contagion caught a friend who was with me. So we laid our heads together and produced the following Ode to a Hen.

> The hen it is an useful beast
> And struts about the door also.
> There's ne'er a wife in all the West
> But keeps one, or two, or more, or so!

That's what I call an odd ode. It hath not the odor of poetry, is in odious rhyme, and is not at all melodious. It was my first ode and my best, for I will never write *anoder*.

While in Omaha I frequently saw General Auger, without however knowing it was he until the day I left. I am sorry I did not make his acquaintance.

LETTERS TO HIS DAUGHTER
(Neither letter is dated, but they probably were written in the late 1890's.)

I

I am sorry that I cannot say that I ever saw Abraham Lincoln, *but once*, and he was dead. [On May 1-2, 1865, Lincoln's body lay in state in the Chicago Courthouse en route to burial in Springfield, Illinois.] I suppose Mama will have lots to tell you of her fathers rememberances of him, if she can recal them. Mr. Garrison knew Lincoln well. They were very much akin in spirit and political principles, and were lawyers together, all working in the same groove, so to say, and they had many confabs and conferences both here and in Springfield. Mr. Garrison never went deeply into politics, but clung to law, while Lincoln was distinctly a politician as well as a statesman. I have heard Joseph Medill tell many old reminiscences of Lincoln in a casual way. [Lincoln] had a habit of wandering into the Tribune office, and sitting down to "gas" with Scripps, Dr. Charles Rae,[1] and Medill, with a lunch bag perhaps in his hand, and putting one of his long legs athwart the table, would begin and tell a good thing. When getting on his feet he would say "Well I must be going."

1. Dr. Charles H. Ray, former owner of the Galena *Jeffersonian*, purchased a one-fourth interest in the *Tribune* in 1855 at the same time that Joseph Medill purchased one-third interest. John L. Scripps, Ray's assistant, was appointed Chicago Postmaster by President Lincoln in 1861.

"Hold on Abe", Rae or Scrips would say. "I want you to stop and hear this." Then would follow some good story of the day. Whereupon Abe would resume his seat, put up his leg again and say: "That reminds me of a good thing" &c and so they would keep along chatting for hours.

Lincoln was a man of the people in a supreme and peculiar sense. He was endowed with rare sagacity, what we know as common sense, and a loving heart. He loved his fellow men, not as an intellectual recreation, but from his soul. He said once: "God must love the common people, the poor—he makes so many of them".

[Chisholm then refers to meeting President Grant at Galena, Illinois (see Letter II below), and mentions that at that time he was a representative of the Grant newspaper, the *Inter-Ocean*, the *Tribune* having gone into the Greeley movement.]

I have a strong love and admiration for Grant. He hated war. He was a man of peace. He did his duty as an American citizen, bravely, manfully, modestly, grandly. He died the death of a brave man. It takes sometimes many years to properly focus men of the stamp of Lincoln and Grant.

[Mary Garrison Chisholm here continues the letter.]

Father & Lincoln were great friends and once, before Lincoln had even thought of running for Senator father went down to Springfield & getting into town late could not get a bed. So he & Lincoln sat up all night by a stove & told stories. When father was in Washington for two months he was the guest of Hon. Isaac N. Arnold Senator from Ill.[2]—Then he saw a great deal of Lincoln—never a man loved another as father did him. Now let me tell you a little Episode. At the time of the Democratic convention [August 1864] Gen. Augur came to our house which was filled with Albion & Holley people. George Pullman & many others [3]—Among the men who were proposed for President was

2. Isaac Newton Arnold was elected as Representative, not Senator, to the Thirty-seventh and Thirty-eighth Congresses (March 14, 1861–March 3, 1865). He was a Republican.

3. Albion and Holley are adjacent towns in Orleans County, New York State. Andrew Garrison had come to Chicago from Holley in 1852. George N. Pullman (who designed the Pullman car and organized the Pullman Palace Car Company) had been a cabinet-maker in Albion; and General Augur (see note on page 26) was born in the town of Kendall, also in Orleans County. It was natural that all these "home-town folks" should foregather at Garrisons' while in Chicago.

Sandford Church of Albion. Mrs. Church & Mother were old friends. . . . Well, as I said we lived down town & all Albion was at our house—& that was the day Church hoped for the nomination [4]. . . . Gen. Augur about lunch time came with . . . General Sherman.[5] The people present were rabid democrats— but father was true to his principles & Gen. Augur & Sherman laughed to hear father give vent. As at the time of the war a democrat was considered almost against the Union I didn't think much of Shermans call, until years after. I was introduced twice to Grant, went to a reception of his with Orville Grant, then Mother & I went with Gen. Augur. What a snicking mean thing that baptist minister [*name deleted*] did when . . . [he] borrowed the letters that passed between father & Gen. Grant. We asked for them in person & father wrote for them. He, the dominie, said he lost them. Mrs. Augur lives in Georgetown, D. C.

II

You want to know if I ever knew Grant or Sherman. Yes, when Grant was presented by the people of Galena with his house on the hill I was commissioned by the Inter Ocean to go to Galena and meet him.[6] I had the pleasure of helping Nellie Grant (plain Nellie Grant then)[7] to decorate the walls with evergreen &c the night before he arrived, and we had a good time over it. Of course I was introduced to the president, but had no talk with him then, although I had some trouble about getting back to Chicago on his special train (due to General Babcock.)[8]

4. On 29 August, 1864, the Democrats nominated General George McClellan for President and George H. Pendleton for Vice President.

5. General William Tecumseh Sherman (1820-1891), of Civil War fame, who succeeded Grant as general and commander of the army in 1869.

6. Chisholm's memory appears to be at fault here. The *Inter-Ocean* was not founded until 1872, and the house was presented to General Grant in the summer of 1865. See William B. Hesseltine, *Ulysses S. Grant, Politician* (New York: Frederick Ungar Publishing Company, 1957), p. 57. Grant did not become President until 1868.

7. Nellie Grant married Algernon Sartoris in May 1874 (*ibid.*, p. 299).

8. Colonel, later General, Orville E. Babcock was Grant's private secretary. He was indicted in the Whisky Ring scandal of 1875, but was saved from conviction through the President's intervention. See Richard B. Morris, ed., *Encyclopedia of American History* (New York: Harper & Brothers, 1953), pp. 251-252.

Another time I met Gen. Grant was on his first public visit to Chicago after his election, when I was sent by the Tribune out as far as Willow Springs to board the train.

[Chisholm remarks that he knew and liked Fred Grant
—Frederick Dent Grant, the President's younger son.]

I also know Robert Lincoln, the son of Abraham, but I cannot account for him. I cannot explain him. He is simply a product. There is space enough above the eyebrows for any quantity of brain, but one cannot tell from the outside what vacant chambers there are "to let." [9]

BIOGRAPHICAL SKETCH

The story of James Chisholm's first thirty years has been sketched in the text, pages 8-14. On his return to Chicago in 1869, Chisholm continued his connection with the *Tribune*. His particular forte was dramatic criticism, and in the years to come he was to make a nation-wide reputation as a dramatic critic. His homecoming, as we know, was shadowed by his brother Harry's tragic death.[1]

9. Frederick Dent Grant, Robert Todd Lincoln, and General Philip Sheridan—to whom Chisholm also refers in this letter—were all figures in post-Civil War Chicago society, and all attended an exclusive dancing class organized by Mrs. George N. Pullman (Dedmon, *op. cit.*, pp. 120-121).

1. On Saturday, June 21, 1868, Harry Chisholm was one of several guests aboard the "Little Western," a new type of sail lifeboat, designed by one Captain Garrett. With his partner, Professor LeGendre, Garrett planned to sail to Europe in the boat, starting from Chicago. "The announcement of this perilous enterprise in a boat so small (only twenty feet in length and about six feet beam) caused an excitement . . . equal to that created by the venturesome trip of the life-raft Nonpareil, from New York to Liverpool . . . ." A trial run in the morning was successful and Harry went along again on a second trip in the afternoon. When they were about three miles offshore and preparing to turn back, he went into the cabin to take a nap. Shortly thereafter the boat was struck by a squall of wind and overturned. Harry, trapped in the cabin, was drowned. All the others, except for Captain Garrett, managed to hang on until they were rescued. (Chicago *Tribune*, June 22, 1868. 4:4)

Chisholm's courtship of Mary Evelyn Garrison culminated in their marriage on January 25, 1871, at the Garrison home. (Mrs. Garrison, who had so stoutly opposed the marriage, later became one of her son-in-law's most ardent admirers.) They left that evening on a honeymoon trip to St. Louis, and an encounter on the train with Joseph Medill revealed their status as newlyweds, much to the groom's embarrassment. Medill was very hard of hearing, so the vital statistics about the wedding and Medill's congratulations were clearly audible from one end of the parlor car to the other.

The Chisholms' marriage was a congenial one. In her own right, Mary was an able and witty columnist, writing under the name of "Evelyn." At that time it was the custom for artists of the theatre and concert stage who were playing in Chicago to meet on Sunday afternoons at the Sherman House, and James and Mary often would join them. They entertained many famous personalities of the day in their home, and enjoyed close friendships with such celebrities as Maurice Barrymore, the Drews, John McCullough, Lillian Russell, and Isadora Duncan. Attesting the regard in which Chisholm was held, his friends in the theatre commissioned a portrait of him, which was duly presented to James and Mary. His picture also hung in the foyer of Daly's Theatre in New York City until that house went dark for the last time.

No biography of Chicagoans of this period would be complete without a mention of the great fire of October 1871. Judge Garrison suffered the loss of all his valuable property, including his law library.[2] When Jim learned that some of the *Tribune* presses had been saved, he rushed down and helped get out an edition. As the first copies came off the press, Jim sold them over the counter in a small shop nearby as long as the supply lasted. He told his daughter years later that all his pockets were bulged out and overflowing with pennies, and finally he took off his coat and made a sack of it. The approaching flames soon compelled them to withdraw, but Jim and the others rejoiced in the knowledge that they had gotten out the *Tribune* under fire.

Chisholm's work on the *Tribune* apparently was not confined to drama criticism. In a letter to his daughter dated December

2. Andrew Garrison was always called "Judge," but he never held this office.

15, 1901, he refers to accompanying George S. Boutwell, Grant's Secretary of the Treasury (1869-1873), on "some inspection of the outer harbor." As told in an earlier letter (see page 227), he was a strong supporter of President Grant, and when the *Tribune* declared for Horace Greeley in the 1872 presidential campaign, Chisholm left its staff to join that of the pro-Grant *Inter-Ocean*.[3] While on the *Inter-Ocean*, he wrote a regular column of wit and satire under the byline "John Barleycorn," as well as serving as city editor. It is uncertain when he returned to the *Tribune*—Joseph Medill regained control of the paper in 1874 and Sam Medill became managing editor—but he was connected with it nearly twelve years in all.

Four days before his forty-second birthday, Chisholm realized a long-cherished ambition to publish a paper of his own. On February 14, 1880, *The Free Lance*, "James Chisholm Sole and Responsible Editor," made its debut on the newsstands. Chisholm's without-fear-or-favor journalistic policy and the boldness of his criticisms in the spheres of politics and the arts created a furor, but the paper soon failed for want of business management and lack of financial backing.[4] Following this disastrous venture, Jim was city editor of the Chicago *Evening Journal* for a time before becoming a free-lance writer. His newspaper career ended in 1900, when he took a position in the office of the county treasurer.

James Chisholm died on May 5, 1903, after a brief illness. The immediate cause of his death was pneumonia, but his illness began with what was called bacterial poisoning resulting from unsanitary conditions. The Chicago papers alleged that eight other employees in the treasurer's office had died within a short period of time, and they labelled his death "municipal murder."

Mary Garrison Chisholm survived her husband by seven years. She died at the home of her daughter in Cranford, New Jersey, on October 14, 1910.

3. The *Inter-Ocean* was founded in 1872 by a banker and real estate operator, Jonathan Young Scammon. History also credits Mr. Scammon with introducing in Chicago the boutonniere as an acceptable masculine accessory. See Emmett Dedmon, *Fabulous Chicago* (New York: Random House, 1953), p. 20.

4. *The Free Lance* appeared weekly on Saturdays; the issues averaged six to twelve pages. Files running from February 14, 1880 to September 11, 1880 have been checked; I have not been able to ascertain how long it continued thereafter.

SOURCES

THE CHISHOLM JOURNAL

James Chisholm was not by nature a man who sought a rough life, but it is fortunate for history that circumstances allowed him to come west and record his experiences. Although there are many stories about the South Pass gold rush, only a few documents remain to tell the real story. The Chisholm journal is an important contribution to the history of the period.

The journal has been treasured for many years by members of James Chisholm's family, first by his daughter Myra—Mrs. George Carson Moon of New York City—and later by his grandson, James S. Moon of Detroit, Michigan. In 1953 Mr. Moon presented the journal to the Wyoming State Archives and Historical Department, feeling that the chronicle should be preserved in the archives of the State in which and about which it was written.

The journal consists of a hardbacked, lined notebook six by eight inches in size. The entries are written in pencil. When he had filled the book, Chisholm enlarged it by adding pages of various sizes, sewing in the extra leaves. The book appears to have been carelessly treated by Chisholm—as we know, on his first Wind River trip it was left behind at one camping place and not retrieved for several days—and the back cover is broken. As a result, some of the pages are loose and a few are missing. Age and handling have caused some smearing of the penciled notes, but the entries have remained quite legible.

There is a possibility that Chisholm may have started a new notebook which has not been preserved. Mrs. George C. Moon relates that after her father's death his papers were destroyed without the knowledge of the immediate family, and all that remained was this journal, which she had in her possession.

Until his return from his first trip to Wind River Valley, Chisholm consistently supplied titles or "running heads" for each page. A list of these headings, with page references to the text, appears on pages 241-242. Besides writing up happenings for his personal reference, Chisholm enjoyed illustrating his notes with sketches. All but four of these sketches are reproduced in the text. Omitted are "The Table Mountain" (probably the Oregon Buttes) described on pages 69 and 146; "The spacious ingle" mentioned on page 103; and "A Glass of Beer is Refreshing," see page 147. The fourth sketch is captioned "Dick Rice"; this name does not occur in the text, but he probably was one of the men at Miner's Delight.

As shown by the one instance in which it can be checked, the date of the entries is incorrect. Writing on a Sunday at Miner's Delight, Chisholm set down the date as September 17 (page 91); but in 1868 September 17 fell on a Thursday. Assuming that the date of his first entry is correct, there is no way to tell when and for what reason he lost count of the days. But it is easy to understand how this could come about in a remote frontier community where the daily activity was self-regulated and depended on weather and season, and where there was no continuous or consistent contact with the world ordered by clocks and calendars. Although his only comment is a tacit one, eventually, of course, Chisholm did realize he had lost track of the exact date, for he gave up dating his entries.

While every effort has been made to identify the persons mentioned in the journal, the transient character of the population at that period, the absence or loss of reliable contemporary records, and—in some cases—the sketchiness of the references have made the task impossible to fulfil completely. Where there is no footnote on an individual, I was unable to find anything about him.

BIOGRAPHICAL SOURCES

Except for what is told in his journal and letters, nearly all the information about James Chisholm has been supplied by his daughter. Truly exhaustive biographical research would entail an examination of every issue of every newspaper published in Chicago from 1864 to 1903—to say nothing of all the contemporary periodicals to which James Chisholm might have been a free-lance contributor during these years. Since this book is primarily concerned with a particular episode in Wyoming's history as seen through James Chisholm's eyes, and is not intended to be a biography, such an undertaking was not even contemplated.

Where a germane biographical datum could be determined by hours or days—rather than weeks or months—of research, this has been done. In cases where information could not be verified, it is so stated in the text or in the accompanying note; but in most cases undocumented information and dates which could not be checked definitively were omitted. (For example, there was a Soldiers' Fair, corresponding to the one on which Mary Garrison worked, which began the night of November 13, 1867, and ran for a week. However, a check of *Tribune* accounts of the Fair's progress revealed no mention of her.) Although a number of events cannot be tied to a precise date and there are several gaps in the chronology, the sequence of happenings is, to the best of my knowledge, the correct one.

THE PERIPATETIC PRESS

The *Sweetwater Mines*, the first paper in the South Pass region, was established by Warren and Hazard at Fort Bridger, Utah Territory, in 1868. (Charles J. Hazard subsequently was the sole editor.) The *Mines* was published twice weekly until late in May 1868, when the office was moved to South Pass City.

All known existing copies are at the Bancroft Library, University of California at Berkeley. Dates and location of the publishing office of the known copies are as follows:

Fort Bridger, Utah Territory, starting with Vol. 1, No. 11
    March 21, 25, 28, April 1, 4, 8, 11, 15, 1868.
South Pass City, Dakota Territory
    May 27 (Vol. 1, No. 23), May 30
    June 3, 6, 10, 13, 17, 20, 27
    July 3, 11, 18 (not all included on film), 25

Aug. 1, 8
Bryan City, Wyo.
Nov. 25, 1868; Dec. 2, 5, 23, 26, 30, 1868
Jan. 9, 23, 1869
South Pass City, Wyo.
Apr. 7, June 19, 1869
I have not discovered when this paper stopped publishing.

The *Frontier Index* came into being at Fort Kearney, Nebraska. It originally had been the *Herald* there. The Freeman brothers, Leigh R. and Fred K., acquired the press and started the *Index* in 1865 (no date given exactly within that year). The paper, published in tent, railroad car, hotel, or shack, came west with the Union Pacific. It carried on until November 20, 1868, when the presses were destroyed by a crowd of the rough element, joined by some construction workers, at Bear Town, Wyoming, near present Evanston.

According to my best authority, "Press on Wheels" by Burton DeLoney, in the *Annals of Wyoming*, Volume XIV, Number 4 (October 1942), pp. 299-314, I find the following:

One copy of the *Frontier Index* published July 1867 at Julesburg, Colorado, is in the Union Pacific Historical Museum at Omaha, Nebraska.
The Bancroft files contain the following numbers:
   March 6 and 24, 1868 published at Fort Sanders, D. T.
      (just three miles south of present Laramie, Wyoming).
   April 21 to July 7, 1868, published at Laramie City, D. T.
   Aug. 11 to 21, 1868, published at Green River City, D. T.
   Aug. 25 to Oct. 13, 1868, published at Green River City, Wyo.
   Oct. 30 to Nov. 17, 1868, published at Bear River City, Wyo.
One copy published at Laramie, July 21, 1868 is located at the University of Wyoming Library.
According to Douglas C. McMurtrie, the *Index* was also published at Fort Kearney, Plum Creek, and North Platte in Nebraska.

BIBLIOGRAPHY

Unpublished Materials

Wyoming State Archives and Historical Department:

Governor John A. Campbell, original letterpress copy book, 1869-1871.

Minutes of the Linco[l]n Mining District, Dacotah Ter. Nov. 11, 1865, W. H. Shoemaker, President and Jno. A. James Secratery [sic].

Manuscript, "Indians in Sweetwater County," by H. G. Nickerson.

United States Census Records of 1870 (photostat copy of original).

University of Wyoming Library, Archives and Western History Division:

Agreement, Major Noyes Baldwin with Jno. A. James and D. C. Moreland, dated Ft. Bridger, October 31, 1865.

Houghton and Cotter Ledger, South Pass City, 1868-69.

Letter, Jno. A. James to Major Noy[e]s Baldwin, dated March 18, 1866, South Pass.

Letter, P. S. Quinn, to Grace Raymond Hebard, dated October 13, 1926, Columbia, Missouri.

Manuscript, "Noyes Baldwin," from the Bancroft Library, on microfilm.

Manuscript, "An Ill-fated Expedition to Wind River, Wyoming, June 1868," from the notes of C. G. Coutant.

"Minutes of the County Commissioners of Carter County, Dakota Territory, 1868." On loan from Sweetwater County.

Articles

Andrews, Frederick B., "Gold Is Where You Find It," Casper, Wyoming, *Daily Tribune*, February 15, 1925.

Fourt, E. H., "Lander Region Among First in Diversified Resources," Casper *Tribune*, January 22, 1922.

Lindsey, Charles, "Diary of Thomas G. Maghee," *Nebraska Magazine of History*, Vol. XII, No. 3 (July 1931), pp. 249-304.

Nickerson, H. G., "Early History of Fremont County." *Quarterly Bulletin*, Wyoming State Historical Dept., Vol. 2, No. 1 (July 1924), pp. 1-13.

Sherlock, Peter, "Active Mining Operations at Atlantic and South Pass Recall the Gold Rush Days when Men Made Millions," *Wyoming State Journal*, Lander, April 11, 1935.

"Interesting History from Mining Country," *Wyoming State Journal*, Lander, September 21, 1927.

Documents

Beeler, Henry C., *A Brief Review of the South Pass Gold District Fremont County, Wyoming*. n.p., 1908. [Report of the State Geologist.]

Jamison, C. E., *Geology and Mineral Resources of a Portion of Fremont County, Wyoming*. Cheyenne: S. A. Bristol Co. 1911. Bulletin 2, Series B. [Report of the State Geologist.]

Knight, W. C., *The Sweetwater Mining District, Fremont County, Wyoming*. Bulletin of the University Geological Survey of Wyoming. June 1901. n.p.

Marzel, John G., *Fifteenth Biennial Report of the State Geologist*, October 1, 1928 to September 30, 1930. Chapter X, "The Petroleum Industry. Early History of Petroleum in Wyoming."

Raymond, R. W., "Mines and Mining West of the Rocky Mountains." Executive Documents Printed by Order of the House of Representatives, Sec. Sess. 41st Cong., 1869-70. Washington, 1870. Government Serial Doc. 1424, Section VII, Wyoming Territory. Pp. 325-338.

Trumbull, L. W., *Atlantic City Gold Mining District, Fremont County*. Bulletin 7, Series B, The State of Wyoming Geologist's Office. Cheyenne, S. A. Bristol Co., 1914.

Books

Alter, J. Cecil, *James Bridger*. Salt Lake City: Shephard Book Co., 1925.

Beard, Francis Birkhead, *Wyoming from Territorial Days to the Present*, Vol. I. Chicago: American Historical Society, 1933.

Clark, Thomas D., *Frontier America*. New York: Charles Scribner's Sons, 1959.

Coutant, C. G., *History of Wyoming*. Laramie, Wyoming: Chaplin, Spafford & Mathison, 1899.

Crofutt, George A., *Crofutt's New Overland Tourist and Pacific Coast Guide*. Omaha, Nebraska: Crofutt Publ. Co., 1872 and 1884.

Dimsdale, Thomas J., *Vigilantes of Montana* (4th ed.). Helena: State Publishing Co., n.d.

Erwin, Marie H., *Wyoming Historical Blue Book*. Denver: Bradford-Robinson Printing Co., 1946.

Field, Matthew C., *Prairie and Mountain Sketches*. Norman: University of Oklahoma Press, 1957.

Fremont, John Charles, *Report of the Exploring Expedition to the Rocky Mountains in the Year 1842*. Washington: Blair and Rives, Printers, 1845.

Ghent, W. J., *The Road to Oregon*. New York: Longmans, Green & Co., 1929.

Hafen, LeRoy R., *The Overland Mail, 1849-1869*. Cleveland: Arthur H. Clark Company, 1926.

Hafen, LeRoy R., and W. J. Ghent, *Broken Hand*. Denver: The Old West Publishing Company, 1931.

Hodge, Frederick Webb, *Handbook of American Indians*. Washington, D. C.: Government Printing Office, 1910.

Jackson, W. Turrentine, *Wagon Roads West*. Los Angeles: University of California Press, 1952.

Linford, Velma, *Wyoming: Frontier State*. Denver: The Old West Publishing Co., 1947.

Mokler, A. J., *Fort Caspar*. Casper, Wyo.: Prairie Publishing Co., 1939.

Pence, Mary Lou, and Lola M. Homsher, *Ghost Towns of Wyoming*. New York: Hastings House, 1956.

Progressive Men of the State of Wyoming. Chicago: A. W. Bowen & Co., 1903.

Sabin, Edwin L., *Building the Pacific Railway.* Philadelphia: Lippincott Co., 1919.

W. P. A., *Wyoming: A Guide to Its ·History, Highways and People.* New York: Oxford University Press, 1941.

Newspapers

Cheyenne *Daily Evening Leader*
Chicago *Tribune*
Chicago *Times*
Sweetwater Mines
Frontier Index

LIST OF ORIGINAL HEADINGS

Trip to Sweetwater . . . Green River Scenery—R. R. Progress, 59; Camp Life Again . . . Indian Affairs, 61; Baptism . . . Over the Moors, 61; Indian Scares . . . Eldorado, 62; Sweetwater No Humbug . . . Big Sandy, 63; Night and Storm . . . And Darkness, 65; Hail Horrors . . . A Few Leaps in the Dark, 66; Lost . . . Struck by Lightning (?), 66; A Moonrise . . . Left Alone, 67; A Wet Blanket . . . An Early Start, 68; Morning Glory . . . Big Sandy, Little Sandy, 68; Dry Sandy . . . The Sublime and Beautiful, 69; Crossing the Sweetwater . . . Storm Signals, 70; Another Night . . . Torrents, 71; Lost Again . . . A Watery Bed, 71; Snakes . . . Supreme Wretchedness, 72; Paradise Regained . . . My Cold, 72; South Pass City . . . And Surroundings, 73; Western Life, 74; Generalities, 75; Indisposition . . . Mining Talk, 75; New Acquaintances . . . Off to Miner's Delight, 76; The Wrong Road . . . The Right Road, 77; A Mountain Ramble . . . Scenic, 77; Atlantic City . . . Solitude, 78; A Race with Sol . . . Miner's Delight, 78; Golden Dirt . . . Gallagher's Home, 79; O! Woman . . . Woman!, 80; A Rose in the . . . Wilderness, 80; Chat . . . Luxuries, 81; Descriptive, 82; The Shafts . . . Hunters, 82; The Gulches, 83; Water . . . Opening My Eyes, 83; A Ramble . . . Berrying, 84; The Beavers, 85; Ascension . . . A Boy Again, 85; On the Heights . . . The Prospect, 86; Descriptive Again, 86; Still Descriptive, 87; The Miners . . . The Hidden Hand, 89; A Grizzly Bar . . . Characteristics, 90; Buffalo Hump, 90; Life in the Camp . . . Sunday, 91; How it was Spent . . . Comical Quarrels, 91; Dave on His Muscle . . . Getting His Back Up, 92; Getting Crazy, 93; Vegetables . . . Ile [Oil], 93; Panning Out . . . Stamp Mills, 94; More Dissipation . . . A Duel, 95; Dave's Reminiscences . . . Starving, 95; Dog, 96; Raw Head, 97; A Long Fast and . . . A Breakfast, 97; Historical . . . The

ACKNOWLEDGMENTS

This book could not have been compiled without the generous assistance of many people. To James S. Moon, grandson of James Chisholm, I wish to express my gratitude for calling this journal to my attention a number of years ago and for his generosity in allowing its publication. The personality of James Chisholm has emerged from the information supplied by his daughter, Mrs. George Carson Moon, who has searched her memory for snatches of his earlier life which she heard as a child, and who has shared the letters from him which she received after her marriage. James Carpenter of Atlantic City, Wyoming, who knows the gold fields of the South Pass country and who has lived in that area since 1890, has guided me through the mining fields, pointing out the mining sites and landmarks. He also has given his time to review portions of this book for accuracy. L. C. Bishop of Cheyenne, former State Engineer of Wyoming, assisted me with geographical information on the Green River to South Pass route.

Thanks also are due Mrs. Stuart H. Danovitch, Assistant Reference Librarian, Chicago Historical Society, and her associate Mr. Ralph A. DePratt for their assistance in verifying details of James Chisholm's early days in Chicago and in locating news stories on the South Pass gold rush; and to Professor Harold W. Manter, Chairman of the Department of Zoology and Anatomy, University of Nebraska, and Professor Thomas B. Thorson of the same department for identifying the fish described in the journal.

[243]

Finally, I especially wish to thank the University of Nebraska Press for suggesting the plan of this book, which was developed from their experience with other volumes of the Pioneer Heritage Series.

LOLA M. HOMSHER

"An absolutely beautiful, hear...
I felt this giant balloon of love ...
again that love and imagination are life's biggest magic."
—**Rebecca Stead, Newbery Award–winning author of** *When You Reach Me*

"Both a beautiful book and an honest book; it is, in fact, beautiful because
it is honest. We see the pain of loss, and the glory of community. We see love in
its many forms, and we witness the truth that love goes on despite all barriers."
—**Gary D. Schmidt, Newbery Honor–winning author of** *The Wednesday Wars*

"Some books change the way you see the world. Some change the way you
breathe. This book will leave you breathless. This is Paul Griffin's
best book yet—and that's really saying something."
—**Patricia McCormick, author of National Book Award Finalist** *Sold*

"Full of pace and laughter, bruises and heart. Paul Griffin is
the sort of writer you're torn between telling the whole world
about and keeping all to yourself."
—**Markus Zusak, #1** *New York Times* **bestselling author of** *The Book Thief*

"[T]his bittersweet, well-paced book . . . left me with faith that people
can feel discarded, as though everything they love will be taken from them,
and still end up whole, if they are touched by love and friendship."
—*The New York Times Book Review*

Impossible to keep a dry eye.
—*BookPage*

"This is a multi-tissue read . . . Griffin's characters are unique and charmingly
multidimensional. Readers looking for a deep read will take to this story as
quickly as Flip takes to Ben."
—*Booklist*

★ "Although this middle grade book covers some tough topics . . .
it never loses hope."
—*School Library Connection*, **starred review**

OTHER BOOKS YOU MAY ENJOY

Almost Home	Joan Bauer
The Best Man	Richard Peck
Counting by 7s	Holly Goldberg Sloan
Feathers	Jacqueline Woodson
Fish in a Tree	Lynda Mullaly Hunt
Hope Was Here	Joan Bauer
Lost in the Sun	Lisa Graff
One for the Murphys	Lynda Mullaly Hunt
Saving Marty	Paul Griffin
A Tangle of Knots	Lisa Graff
Three Times Lucky	Sheila Turnage
Under the Egg	Laura Marx Fitzgerald

WHEN FRIENDSHIP FOLLOWED ME HOME

PAUL GRIFFIN

PUFFIN BOOKS

PUFFIN BOOKS
An imprint of Penguin Random House LLC
375 Hudson Street
New York, New York 10014

First published in the United States of America by Dial Books for Young Readers,
an imprint of Penguin Random House LLC, 2016
Published by Puffin Books, an imprint of Penguin Random House LLC, 2017

THE LIBRARY OF CONGRESS HAS CATALOGED THE DIAL BOOKS FOR YOUNG READERS EDITION AS FOLLOWS:
Names: Griffin, Paul, 1966– author.
Title: When friendship followed me home / by Paul Griffin.
Description: New York, NY : Dial Books for Young Readers, [2016] | Summary:
Seventh-grader Ben, always an outsider, is led into a deep friendship with
Halley, who is being treated for cancer, by the special dog he and his
adoptive mother take in.
Identifiers: LCCN 2015032638 | ISBN 9780803738164 (hardcover)
Subjects: | CYAC: Friendship—Fiction. | Dogs—Fiction. | Cancer—Fiction. |
Adoption—Fiction. | Middle schools—Fiction. | Schools—Fiction.
Classification: LCC PZ7.G8813594 Whe 2016 |
DDC [Fic]—dc23 LC record available at http://lccn.loc.gov/2015032638

Puffin Books 9780147510068

Pages 8 and 149: Quotes from *Feathers* by Jacqueline Woodson, copyright 2007
by Jacqueline Woodson. Used by permission of G. P. Putnam's Sons Books for Young Readers,
an imprint of Penguin Young Readers Group, a division of Penguin Random House LLC.
Photo on page vii courtesy of Library of Congress, Prints & Photographs Division,
Detroit Publishing Company Collection [LC-DIG-det-4a12420]
Photos on pages 36 and 47 by Risa Morimoto

Printed in the United States of America

Design by Jasmin Rubero

1 3 5 7 9 10 8 6 4 2

For Risa, with all my love and thanks for letting me travel time with you.

AND

For John, kid brother, superhero.

⚡

LUKE SKYWALKER: What's in there?

YODA: Only what you take with you.

Star Wars, Episode V: The Empire Strikes Back

1
CHUNKY MOLD

You'd have to be nuts to trust a magician. I learned that lesson the hard way. And then, if you can believe it, I actually became a magician's assistant. That part was the Rainbow Girl's fault, but the rest of it I blame on a little dog named Flip.

The trouble started the second Friday of seventh grade. Damon Rayburn shoved me out of the lunch line. "Thanks, Coffin," he said.

"For what?" I said.

"Offering to buy me a slice."

If you think a little threat like that could get me to surrender my pizza money to an idiot like Damon Rayburn, you know me pretty well. He slapped the back of my head and cut to the front of the line.

"You're half a foot taller than him, Coffin," this kid half a foot shorter than Rayburn said. His name was Chucky Mull, but everybody called him Chunky Mold. "You should have belted him. Now he knows he can push you around."

"Allow me to quote Yoda, from *The Empire Strikes Back*," I said. "'A Jedi uses the Force for knowledge and defense, never for attack.'"

"You were being called upon to defend your inalienable right to eat meatball pizza," Mold said. "Yoda also says don't be a wimp."

"Yoda never uses the word *wimp*."

"He says, 'Fear is the path to the dark side.' Dude, hello, *The Phantom Menace?*"

There was no debating Mold on this stuff. He had the T-shirts—the sheets too. I shoved him toward our spot far, far away in the dark corner where they kept the garbage dumpster nobody ever dumped. Mold's mom had stuck a note on the waxed paper that barely covered his foot-long hero. It said, LOVE YOU. ☺ He tossed the note and crammed a hunk of sandwich into his mouth. "Any chance you would consider splitting that with me?" I said. "Come on, Mold, you'll never be able to finish the whole thing."

"Watch me," Chucky said. "Holy crud, here she comes."

Mrs. Pinto worked her way toward us. She was really pretty for a principal or even a normal human being. "Hi guys," she said.

"Good, how are you?" Mold said.

"If you ever need anything, stop by my office, okay?"

"You too," Mold said.

Mrs. Pinto patted my shoulder as she left.

"She totally just touched you," Chucky said. "You, a loser,

caressed on your loser shoulder by Mrs. P. I sent her the wink almost like four hours ago now. Nothing. Why are you staring at me like that? Dude, the emoticon? Are you visiting from The Stone Age?"

"I know what the wink is. I just can't believe you sent her one."

"So?"

"She's old. Mold, she's like *thirty*."

"It's not what you think. On Facebook the wink is a sign of supreme respect. It's like when somebody inspires you, you wink at them. It's true. It's an ancient custom that goes all the way back to classical times, the Greeks and Romanians. It's like you're bowing to her to acknowledge her awesomeness."

"Then why not just send her a bow?"

"Because there's no emoticon for that, you moron. Just because she has a totally amazing butt doesn't mean she can't be my hero too, for her, you know, incredible wisdom and everything."

"*That's* why you winked at her—her *wis*dom."

"What do you know anyway? You're not even on Facebook. It's a real thing, I swear. In many cultures it's considered rude *not* to send the wink." He batted away a fly from where the peanut butter slimed his lip like a gluey booger.

I had to believe him, firstly because you can tell when somebody's lying, and he truly didn't think he was, and most of all because he was right about me not being on Facebook. The whole *friends* thing: It wasn't really happening. Even Mold was more aggravation than ally. I moved to the neighborhood less than two years before. In a year me and my mom were heading to Florida, right after she retired. We could live great down there for cheap, she said. I figured why bother making friends when I was out of here pretty soon?

"Chucky, not even a bite? Really?" I said.

"Dream on," he said, or something like that. I couldn't tell with the sandwich all gunked up in his braces.

2

HEIR TO THE EMPIRE

My stomach was growling by the time the last bell rang and they set us free for the weekend. I headed down the boardwalk toward the library. Mrs. Lorentz always kept a plate of Chips Ahoy! at the front desk.

I was feeling pretty terrific for somebody who got robbed of his pizza money. You can't be sad in Coney Island on a clear September day. The ocean was glittery. The air smelled salty and sweet. My audiobook was nearing the climax. I couldn't get caught walking around with a *book* book, of course. That's like begging for a wedgie. I cranked up my headphones and *Heir to the Empire,* by Timothy Zahn. Things were looking crummy for Han Solo. Thrawn's fighters swarmed the *Millennium Falcon.* The sound cut out when somebody came up behind me and ripped the headphones off my head.

"Who buys yellow headphones?" this girl Angelina Caramello said. She was really pretty even though she was friends with Damon Rayburn. "It's like lemons growing out of your ears."

"Plus you missed a belt loop," Angelina's best friend Ronda Glomski said. She yanked on the loop I missed. "I truly don't understand how you got skipped a grade. How can you be so lame yet so totally adorbs?"

"Ew," Angelina said. She chucked my headphones at me. Then Ronda shoved me so hard she knocked the gum out of my mouth.

I had to think about this. Ronda Glomski, ranked eleventh prettiest in our grade, said that I, Ben Coffin, was not totally revolting. Even though she practically decked me right after she said it and her name was a little gross sounding. I know, like I should talk when my name reminds you of where a zombie escaped from. We were kind of perfect for each other if you took out the part about Ronda being really mean.

In my side vision I saw Damon Rayburn coming, which meant I had to be going, and fast.

I was wheezing a little by the time I got to the library. It wasn't that far a sprint, but my asthma was kicking in, and I had forgotten my inhaler. Fortunately Mrs. Lorentz had it. "You left it on the windowsill again," she said. She pushed a book at me. "I need you to read this. My daughter can't stop talking about it. I'm looking for a second opinion before I put it on top of my stack."

It was *Feathers*, by Jacqueline Woodson. "This doesn't look like sci-fi," I said.

"You won't spontaneously combust," Mrs. Lorentz said. "Ben, you'll love it, trust me."

"After you just said you haven't read it?"

"Why are you standing here talking to me when you should be reading?"

"It's written by a girl," I said.

"So?"

"Like, I'm a dude."

"Take some cookies with you, *dude*. And yes, you can keep the fire escape door open a crack."

She let me do that on asthma days. The breeze felt nice. I didn't know it just then, but getting stopped by Angelina and Ronda, which led to me getting chased by Rayburn, which got my asthma going, which made me crack the alley door, was about to flip my life upside down.

I propped open the door with one of the grimy old encyclopedias Mrs. Lorentz was always trying to dump on everybody—Volume 10, Gargantuan to Halitosis—and settled in at my table hidden away in the back. There were all these giant pictures silkscreened onto the walls, photographs from the old days when Coney Island was the most famous beach in America. My favorite was called *Dreamland at Night*. It was the way Luna Park, this amusement park right on the ocean, looked in 1905. The tower shined like a softer sun. Think of honey lit up with the kind of electricity inside an angel's mind when she's wishing only the most beautiful things for you.

I took a breath from my inhaler and eyed *Feathers*. The cover was a picture of, guess what, a feather. No spaceships, no exploding Death Star, not even a freaking laser sword. The story went like this: There's this new kid in school. Some call him the Jesus Boy, others think he's a freak and they bully him bad. I related to him. I'm not talking about the bullying but about how I always felt like a stranger, even to myself sometimes. I just didn't know where I fit in or what I was supposed to do or be in life, like maybe I was a mistake.

Pretty soon I was on the last page of the book. The story was the kind that ends too quick and leaves you worrying about what's going to happen to the characters, almost like they're your friends, except not annoying. Frannie, the narrator, wants to be a writer. Her teacher is telling her that each day comes with its own special moments and that Frannie had better keep an eye out for them and write them down for later. I was okay with that part. I'm sure Timothy Zahn did that kind of stuff when he was writing *Heir to the Empire*. But I had to stop when I read the next thing Frannie's teacher said about these so-called special moments. "Some of them might be perfect, filled with light and hope and laughter. Moments that stay with us forever and ever."

This was a lie. Nothing lasts forever. It's a scientific fact. Things happen and they're over and you can't get them back.

Einstein said we can travel to the future, and the astronauts proved it. They synchronized twenty clocks and took ten into space. They spent six months up there, whipping around at 17,000 miles an hour, almost five miles per *second*. When they landed, *all* the clocks in Mission Control were .007 seconds ahead of *all* the ones that went into space. You see what happened? They traveled a fraction of a second into the future. Look it up if you don't believe me. This means if you travel *really* fast, like at light speed, when you land back on Earth the clocks will be *years and years* ahead, and you've escaped far into the future. Here's the problem: Einstein used the same math to prove we can never go back to the past.

I stared into the picture of Luna Park in 1905. I would never get to be there. I'd never feel safe with all those gold and silver lights on my face. I'd never see the world from the top of the tower. I'd never believe magic was real.

A cat hissed outside the fire escape door. It charged something down the alley. Then came that creepy sound a cat makes when it's mad, like a demon possessed it.

3
THE DEMON, THE DOG AND THE DIVA

I stepped into the alley. The cat was beating the heck out of this other, much smaller one, except the little guy was a dog.

I shooed away the cat. The dog was a shivering mess. His fur was all tarred up. His tongue stuck out the side of his mouth. His eyes were gunky and pointed out toward the sides. His tail was chomped up and bent, what I could see of it. He had it between his legs. What a shrimp he was. He weighed maybe eight pounds. He wasn't young either, with the gray in his muzzle. I went to pet him. He ducked and scampered out of the alley. I tried to find him, but he was gone.

I brought *Feathers* back to Mrs. Lorentz. "So?" she said.

"It makes me upset."

"That's great," she said.

"*Great?*"

"Why does it upset you, Ben?"

"I'm not sure. Can you hold it for me?"

"You don't want to take it home?" she said.

"I forgot my backpack today."

"It weighs four point five ounces, not to mention its title is *Feathers*. You can't *carry* it?"

I looked out the window. A bunch of guys were hanging out by the free newspaper boxes everybody throws garbage in. They'd take *Feathers* and rip it up, and then Frannie and the Jesus Boy would be in pieces, getting kicked around in the wind. "How do you know it weighs four point five ounces?" I said.

"I'm guessing." She dropped the book onto a postage scale: 4.5 exactly.

"You're not human," I said.

She nodded and leaned in and whispered, "I'm a librarian." She wrote on a sticky paper and stuck it to the book. Then the weirdest thing happened. Her lips trembled and I swear she was about to cry. "Don't forget your inhaler," she said as she put the book aside to help this other kid check out a stack of video games. I leaned over the counter to see what she wrote. The note said: HOLD FOR MY BEN.

I was going to miss her next year, when Mom and I moved to Miami. It almost made me want to join Facebook, the idea that if I didn't, I'd never see her again. I would send her the biggest wink, Mrs. Lorentz, to acknowledge all the kindness she showed me the past two years, not to mention her totally amazing wisdom. I'd send her the wink every freaking day.

I was heading out when this girl was coming in. I held the door for her. She wore a lime-green beret, oversized sunglasses, a glittery scarf, and a red suit jacket with gold buttons buttoned up to her neck, even though it was like seventy-five degrees out. She wore purple gloves with the fingers cut off. Her high-tops were pink sparkles. She pretty much had every color of the rainbow covered. Her backpack was one of those mesh ones so she could show you how totally brilliant she was with all the books she had in there.

The big bad tough guys outside didn't mess with her—no sir. She was the kind of girl who, if you cracked some lame comment about her books or *gloves* or whatever, she'd come back with something that made you feel even stupider than you are, and in front of all your buddies too. Even the dumbest guy knows not to mess with a diva.

And boy, was she one. She stopped to check a text. Here I am, holding the freaking door for her, and the whole time she's texting back. And then she brushed right past me without even tossing me a thanks.

"You're *wel*come," I said. No I didn't. I just left.

It was five thirty. Mom liked me home by six to help with dinner. The tide was coming in. The salt smell was strong enough to make you cough. Papers blew around the street. I had a feeling I was being followed.

I turned around. Mermaid Avenue was packed with everybody coming home from work, but nobody seemed interested in me. I headed up to Neptune, which was a little less crowded, and now I was sure somebody was stalking me. I spun around, and there he was.

4
THE STALKER

That little dog from the alley stopped maybe fifty feet away and sat and watched me.

"C'mere then," I said, but he wouldn't. I walked toward him and he ran off. I shrugged and went on. I looked over my shoulder, and he was following me again.

I went into the supermarket to where the lady in the hairnet was always trying to push the free cheese samples on you. "Can I have some?" I said.

"What else am I here for?" she said.

I scooped four fistfuls into my pockets.

"At least tell your mom the cheese was good," the lady said. "You know, so maybe she *buys* some next time?"

"Oh, I will."

"*Right*," she said. I felt bad for her. Selling fancy cheese in a mediocre supermarket is a hard job.

When I came back out, the dog was waiting for me. He was

closer now, and boy was he shaking. I put a piece of cheese on the sidewalk and stepped back twenty feet. He approached real slow, and then he gobbled it. I put another one down and stepped back ten feet this time, and it was the same thing. Then five feet, then he was eating out of my hand. I swear he wolfed down a quarter pound of cheddar. He let out a burp louder than any I ever made. His breath was not particularly fantastic. Then he leaned into my leg and shook so hard he shook me.

I scooped him up and took a quiet side street home. No way was I getting caught carrying around a girly little dog like that. It would have been worse than being caught with a book.

5

MOM

"The answer is yes," my mother said. I didn't even get a chance to ask her. She just saw the little varmint in my arms and said okay. "Now let's get this dog into the tub."

"Thanks, Mom." I'd wanted a dog for as long as I could remember, but we were going to wait until we got to Florida. Luckily, Mom liked to go with the flow.

"He picked you for a reason," she said.

"Right, I'm the first sucker who fed him."

She messed up my hair. "Life's a journey, Traveler."

"And we're all in for one heck of a ride."

"Hiking uphill is the best part of the trip, never forget," she said.

"How could I when you remind me twice a day?"

She was sixty-seven years old. She didn't dye her hair, which she kept short, no fuss, no muss. You might be doing the math, her age minus mine, a seventh grader's. She'd have to be in her mid-fifties when she had me, right? Except she didn't. I was ten when she took me in.

"Get the towel," Mom said.

We dried him off, and wouldn't you know that little mutt was sort of cute. His coat was spiky. With the gunk gone his eyes were gold brown. I tucked his tongue into his mouth, but it fell out.

"Let's fatten him up," Mom said.

Her saying yes to the dog so quick got me thinking. "Mom, all those kids in the group home. You could have adopted any of them. I've always been afraid to ask, but why me?"

"Why were you afraid to ask?" She started frying up some hamburger.

"Sometimes I think if I talk about it, it'll disappear. Living here, in the apartment. My own room. Dinner while we watch TV. You and me."

"Traveler?" she said. "You and I will never disappear. We're forever. You know that, don't you?"

"Of course."

"You're a terrible liar, son."

"How do you know I'm lying?"

"Because you do this adorable little thing with your eyes. They open a bit too wide, and you look off to the right. Ben? It's like this: When Laura died so suddenly I was at a crossroads. We'd always talked about becoming foster caregivers, and I thought, well, if I find the right kid, the one who really needs me, I'm going to do it." She stopped cooking to look at me full on. "I just knew you were meant to be my son."

"How'd you know, though?"

"Magic." She wasn't talking to me now. She looked past me, at the picture on the wall above the kitchen table. Mom's partner Laura watched over us every night as we ate. She had a true smile, like she wasn't forcing it for the picture. She got cancer, the kind that hijacks your blood. "She would have loved you," Mom said. Then she snapped out of it and got back to cooking. "There's not much here. You'll be hungry. You'd better go pick up some Chinese food." Now *she* was lying. There was plenty of hamburger, even with the dog there, but I saw she wanted to be alone for a bit. She didn't like to be sad in front of me.

"Mom? They have this new cheddar at the supermarket. It's really terrific."

"Good to know. Hey, our new friend here, what are you going to call him?"

"Not sure yet."

"You'll know when you hear it."

I made a leash from my bathrobe belt, but I didn't need it. That little dog trotted right alongside me, all the way to the Palace of Enchantment and back, and he never once took his eyes off me. Even when he was eating he wouldn't stop staring at me. After dinner when we watched *Star Trek II: Wrath of Khan*, it was the same way, eyes on me the whole time. He had a thing about him that was hard to describe. Like this very golden stillness. His name had to show that.

"Why are you smiling?" Mom said.

"I don't know," I said, but I knew. It was so perfect, just plain old hanging out, Mom, me and the dog. It was so safe. "Maybe we could call him Woody."

"As in Woody Coffin?"

"Right, scratch that."

"Coffin's a tricky name," she said.

"It's awesome. Remember how you said I could stay a Smith if I thought Coffin was too creepy?" There were lots of Smiths in the foster homes, and Joneses and Washingtons. "That was the best, the day you let me share your name."

"That was a beautiful day. Yes, it was."

"I just felt different, like finally I was getting a little closer to becoming the person I was supposed to be, even if I didn't know exactly who that person was yet."

"I like that you tell me these things. Oh, don't be embarrassed now. Ben, your friend is trying to get your attention."

The little guy had slid out of my lap and trotted to the door. He put up his paw and yipped, just once. I took him out and he peed right at the curb. When bedtime came he wriggled under my shirt, into my armpit. I woke up to check on him, and his head was resting on my chest. He was looking at me with those gold-brown eyes. It occurred to me that I hadn't taken a breath from my inhaler since the library, and I was breathing fine. I ran my fingers through his coat, back and forth, and like no hair came off him. My lungs were cool around dogs who didn't shed a lot. "You're awesome," I said. He dove at my mouth and licked my lips. "Except for that breath. Whoa."

When I woke up the next morning he was checking out the Chewbacca poster I'd tacked up by my bookcase. It was life-size—seven feet of Wookie staring right at you. The little mutt cocked his head, like, Dude, you are the weirdest dog I've ever seen.

6

THE MICROCHIP

"His teeth are in decent shape, which means he was well cared for," the veterinarian said.

"Then how'd he end up on the street?" I said.

The vet shrugged. "Maybe he was a companion animal for an elderly person. She dies, the family drops him at a shelter. From there, let's say he's adopted by people who had good intentions but no time to care for him. The dog gets dumped again. Or . . ."

"Or?"

"Maybe he's just lost. He has a microchip embedded in his skin. Look." The doctor passed a scanner over the dog's shoulder. A phone number came up on the iPad screen. "That's his owner. There's an email address too."

"Maybe he ran away," I said. "She was probably treating him really rotten."

"Traveler?" Mom said. "Think how you would feel if you lost your dog. Think about the dog most of all. It's in your power to reunite him with the person who cared for him all these years."

My power, huh? I wasn't feeling very powerful. I was feeling like I wanted to barf all over the vet's office.

We plunked down on the bench outside the veterinarian's and waited for Mom's sister, Jeanie. We were hitching a ride with her to the Bay Ridge mall. The website said you could bring your dog inside the pet supply store, except he wasn't really my dog now. I took out my phone, hit speaker and dialed.

Mom chucked her arm over my shoulder. "I'm proud of you," she said.

The dog was snoring in my lap. Then came the voice. *The number you are trying to reach has been disconnected.*

Mom nudged me. "We're halfway home. There's still that email address, Traveler."

"Mom—"

"Send it off, and we have a clear conscience we did everything we could."

I tapped the email into my phone with a message to call our home number. I forced myself to hit send right as Aunt Jeanie pulled up. Her boyfriend Leo leaned out the window. "First a kid and now a dog, huh Tess? Better you than me." He laughed like it was the best joke ever. He got out with Aunt Jeanie to help Mom into the car. She had a touch of the arthritis. "I'm *fine*," she said. "You're such a gent, Leo, but I'm not an invalid—yet."

"You'll outlast all of us, sweetheart," Leo said.

"I certainly hope not. Ben, give your aunt a hug."

Jeanie was nice and all, but when she hugged you, she pushed you away the slightest bit, like you'd better not mess up her makeup. She worked as a manager at Macy's, and she got a huge discount at the cosmetics counter. She was younger than Mom but looked older. The skin around her eyes wrinkled out like spiderwebs, probably because she was always squinting and scrunching up her forehead the way you do when you get worried. She came over to the apartment now and then. "Tell me about school, are you doing any sports, are boys really wearing their hair that long now?" She wasn't nasty or anything. More like she was just, I don't know, a little *nervous* being around me. Leo I didn't know so well. I'd see him holidays, for dinner or whatever. He was a little over-friendly, like he'd shake your hand all exaggerated and slap your shoulder and practically yell, "Hey, how the heck are ya?" Except he didn't wait for you to answer, and then he was running back to the TV to watch the game. I'd watch with him and I swear he'd say it fifty times, "Have some chips, champ. Put a little meat on those bones." I always wanted to tell him that chips weren't made of meat. They were made of freaking *kale,* if Aunt Jeanie had her way. She was kind of a health food freak. I don't know. Leo was okay, I guess.

We got into the backseat of Aunt Jeanie's Mercedes. There was a sheet over it. "Will he stay back there, the dog?" Jeanie said. "I can't have all that fur everywhere, Tess."

"And good morning to you on this gorgeous Saturday, sister darling," Mom said. She kissed Jeanie's cheek, then Leo's.

"Sorry," Jeanie said. "It's just that I had the car vacuumed yesterday."

"Babe, relax," Leo said. He winked at me. "Right champ?"

The dog nudged my hand and put up his paw.

"He wants you to give him a high five," Mom said.

I gave him a knuckle bump and he dove at my face and licked my lips.

"Whoever had him before trained him well," Mom said.

"Totally. I really hope she's dead," I said.

"Well, Traveler, I'm not particularly thrilled by that sentiment."

At the mall we picked out a leash and collar and this pet carrier backpack so you could take him with you on the train. It was like that diva girl's mesh backpack except sturdy. The little guy didn't mind the pack at all. The cashier dropped a chew stick in there and the dog hopped right in after it. The pack was half off, but it was still expensive. "Should we wait until we're sure he's ours?" I said.

"We'll give it to his owner, if it comes to that," Mom said. "And if she doesn't want it, we'll have it for when we get another dog."

"Another dog," I said. "Sure."

7

THE MOLD HORDE

"He's totally part Ewok," Mold said.

"Teebo, right?" I said.

"More like Wicket. That's what you should call him."

"How about Spidey?" I said. "Flash?"

"Wicket's cooler. Or Gandalf."

"No way."

"Potter?"

"No magicians," I said.

"Dude, chill, no need to be racist about it. C'mere, little guy. Coffin, he is *awe*some. My sisters are going to flip."

We climbed the stairs to his porch. I'd never been to his house but knew it from half a block away by the bent light saber in the driveway and the kiddie pool filled with green-brown water. The peekaboo window alongside the front door was patched with cardboard from a Dr Pepper box. Inside, barefoot kids ran all over the place.

"Mom, this is Coffin," Chucky said. "He's my friend, sort of."

"Hello Coffin." She hugged me. She smelled like cookies, and she was a good hugger all right. I couldn't breathe.

"I *love* him," this like four-year-old girl said. She had a peanut butter beard and jelly splotches on her nightgown. The dog went straight to licking the peanut butter off her lips. A horde of other girls in nightgowns joined in. Not in licking off the peanut butter. In cuddling the dog, I mean. One of them was crawling around with a loaded diaper. The dog found that terrifically interesting.

An old golden retriever limped into the swarm. The dogs sniffed each other's butts. The retriever lay down, and my dog—maybe—settled in next to her. Their tails beat the dust from the carpet. All of a sudden my dog jumped and begged me to pick him up.

A scrawny old cat came into the room, sat and licked its butt hole in front of everybody. Now I knew why I was having trouble breathing. The cat hair was all over Mrs. Mold's nightgown and everyone else's. Only certain kinds of dogs made my throat itch, but cats got me wheezing every time. And why was everybody in nightgowns at three in the afternoon?

"Ginger *loves* dogs," Mrs. Mold said. "Ears, GinGin. Ears."

The cat licked the wax out of the retriever's ears and the dog sighed happily.

"Ginger can clean Fuzzball's ears too, if you want," Mrs. Mold said.

"I think his ears are totally okay," I said. I left out the part about wasn't the cat's tongue just up its butt? Mrs. Mold took the dog out of my arms. The cat went straight at my dog's ear with her slimy tongue, and my dog stopped shivering and started thumping.

"That means he *loves* it," one of the littler kids said. "The other way you know they're happy is they hump you."

"It's true," Chucky said.

"Stay for pizza, Coffin," Mrs. Mold said.

"Do we have enough?" Chucky said.

"*Yes*, Charles, we only have about a billion boxes in the cellar freezer."

"Sorry, bud," Chucky said, "it's just that living around here, I have resource allocation concerns. I acknowledge that I have a problem, and I'm dealing with it."

I couldn't breathe but I was famished. Air or food?

We had burnt frozen pizza, and it was awesome.

8
THE UNDERWEAR THIEF

Monday morning I took the dog with me on my coupon delivery route. A lady in a housedress came out of nowhere and hit me with a broom when I left a pennysaver at her door in front of a sign that said DO NOT LEAVE SALES MATERIALS OF ANY KIND. My boss told me to ignore those signs especially. "Sorry ma'am, just following orders," I said.

"See if you can follow them after I beat your brains in." She swung the broom at my rear end.

That little dog rolled over at the lady's feet and wagged his crooked tail. The lady forgot about me and scratched the dog's belly. She was a whole different person now, like actually *nice*. She invited us in for a bagel, but I had to get to Health and Safety class, where Rayburn nailed me with spitballs. Avoiding him the rest of the day was no problem because, well, let's just put it this way: He wasn't in Honors. I ate lunch under the stairs.

After school I ran home. I'd set up my phone with the

camera on time lapse to see what the dog got up to. Here's what he did all day after Mom went to work: Nothing, except he got into my laundry basket and grabbed hold of my underpants. He made a pillow of them in the hallway and sighed, eyes on the door the whole time, until—and this was crazy—he went insane scratching at the door five minutes before I even put the key in, like he had ESP that I was on my way home.

I checked my email. Still no word from the dog's previous owner. She was dead for sure. I was feeling really, really terrific about everything.

"You got a dog, right?" Mrs. Lorentz said.

"How do you know these things?" I said. I turned around so she could see the dog through the mesh panel of the backpack.

"You don't swamp the online reservation system with requests for dog training books when you adopt a ferret. Come around back here and let me see."

I went behind the main desk, put the backpack on the floor, and unzipped it.

"I want to eat him," Mrs. Lorentz said.

"*Why?*"

She scooped him up. "Hel*lo*, you little wombat." The dog attacked her with a kiss. I mean he like totally Frenched her. "His eyes," she said. "They remind me of our little guy

Harry. We lost him in June. He was old. Died in his sleep in my daughter's arms. You can't wish for a better good-bye-for-a-while than that, right?"

"Good-bye-for-a-while," I said. "Sure."

An old man came to the counter to return a laptop. His book bag said: READING MAKES YOU LIVE LONGER. JUST LOOK AT ME.

Mrs. Lorentz put the dog into my backpack. She nodded to a stack on the counter. "Those are yours, Ben." On top of the dog training books was *Feathers*. When I turned to put the books into the backpack, the dog was gone.

9
RETURN OF THE RAINBOW GIRL

The little mutt trotted to the back of the library where the diva was camped out. She wore a yellow beret, fluorescent pink nail polish and a tangerine scarf. The only thing not popping bright about her was her skin, which was really pale. She had bags under her eyes too, like she stayed up the whole night reading all those books I saw in her backpack last time. The dog climbed into her lap. "It's criminal, his adorableness," she said. "What's his name?"

"Not sure yet," I said. "I've only had him three days."

She'd spread her books out all over the table that was previously mine until she took over the entire freaking thing. One was a copy of *Feathers.* Crazy-colored sticky notes marked off the pages.

"You're her," I said. "Mrs. Lorentz's daughter." The book was in my hand, *Feathers,* the library copy. "I'm almost done reading it."

"Some books change the way you see the world, and then there's the one that changes the way you breathe. How are you loving it?"

"You know, totally."

"Then you may sit," she said. She gave the dog a belly scratch. "I love how his tongue sticks out the side of his mouth."

"How come I've never seen you around here before?" I said.

"I just started homeschooling. I work in my apartment until lunch, but after that I get totally stir-crazy. Besides, you have seen me before."

"You mean on Friday when you made me hold the door for you the whole time you texted your friend back?"

"Before that, and sorry for being preoccupied. I was in the middle of a pretty important exchange. You really don't remember me?"

It took me a little while to remember that I actually had met her. The oversized beret covering her head threw me off, but she was the girl with the loopy light brown hair from last winter break. "You helped me check out my books while Mrs. Lorentz was on the phone," I said.

"Who admits to having read *I, Robot* and then *renews* it?"

"You look—"

"Different," she said. "Look closer. See?" She had practically no eyebrows. "The chemotherapy is actually working.

My latest bloods and scans are looking pretty decent. Bad numbers down, good ones up. I'm totally going to kick this thing's butt, you know?"

"I know," I said, like an idiot, like I knew anything about her except she made me feel the way I did when I saw the dog following me but afraid to follow me. It was like when Darth Vader chops off Luke Skywalker's hand. Vader will let Luke live if he joins the dark side, but Luke doesn't. He doesn't submit to Vader's light saber either. He freaking jumps into a reactor. The Force is with him, though, and he falls into a garbage chute, and after that Leia rescues him, and he gets a totally cool bionic hand. Yeah, this girl was tough like that.

"That was the email I got when you were starring in the role of aggrieved doorman," she said. "The old thumbs-up from the doc. Yeah. I'm one of the lucky ones. The side effects from the chemo aren't totally awful, other than I get tired for a few days after. And of course the, like, hair thing." She nodded, and that got me nodding, despite the fact I was totally confused. It just made zero sense. You don't take medicine that makes your hair fall out unless you're *really* sick, and she was my age.

"Anyway, it's just hair," she said. "And it grows back, just so you know."

"You still look totally beautiful, though," I said. Sometimes I want to punch myself in the mouth, except it would hurt and just make me look even stupider. "Sorry, I have this problem sometimes where I forget not to say what I'm thinking."

"How is that a problem, and why would you ever apologize for saying I'm totally hot?"

"Excuse me, *beautiful* I said."

"That's twice now." She reached across the table and squeezed my hand, just for a second. "Thanks," she said. Her fingers were cold and covered in sparkly gel ink. So was the top page of her spiral notebook, with the prettiest script, starbursts instead of dots over her *j*'s and *i*'s. "I'm writing a novella," she said.

"Seriously?"

She made her face overly serious. "I'm afraid so. You're not a writer?"

"I'm twelve."

"Then what are you waiting for? My mom thinks you're really cool, by the way."

"She's totally wink-worthy," I said.

"Ex*cuse* me?"

"No, like on Facebook, you know? The wink? I'd totally send her the hugest one."

"Ew." She packed up her books.

"I'm getting the feeling the wink doesn't mean what I think it means," I said.

She tapped up this blog about Facebook etiquette and appropriate use of emoticons. Here's what it said:

;o) also known as "the wink," is totally okay from your
boyfriend, totally *not* in most other cases, and totally *ick*
from the creep who thinks you're hot when he's so not.

"Wow," I said.

"Yah." She wasn't too tired that day, the way she was
marching for the exit.

I leashed the dog and scooped up the books Mrs. Lorentz
left at the main desk for me and shoved them into the backpack.

"Why'd she storm out like that?" Mrs. Lorentz said.

"*No* idea." I couldn't even look at her.

The dog and I caught up with the Rainbow Girl on the
side street. She was heading for the boardwalk. "You'll never
guess what I thought the wink meant," I said.

"I don't want to know," she said.

"Anyway, I didn't think it meant what it *means.*"

"I know," she said. "I overreacted. I do that. It's just one
of the many facets that make up the intricate gem that is my
persona." She picked up the pace and huffed and puffed as
she walked ahead.

"So homeschool, huh?" I said, trying to keep up. The dog
nipped at our heels. "Sounds awesome."

"I can't wait to get back to *school* school," she said. "Ever
hear of Beekman 26?"

"That's the arts school, right?"

"It's paradise. I'm there just as soon as I'm back to a hundred and eleven percent. That'll be the start of next quarter, definitely. Till then it's me and Dad at the kitchen table. A hundred and eleven's my favorite number, by the way. It's the atomic number of roentgenium. You can't find it in nature. You have to conjure it up in the lab, but it has the same properties as silver and gold. You probably knew that, being a sci-fi geek."

"A hundred and eleven's also the magic constant for the smallest magic square using the number one and prime numbers. Here, check it out." I grabbed her gel pen from behind her ear and wrote on my palm like this:

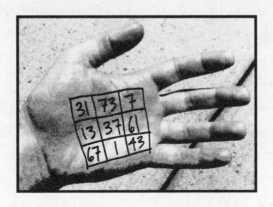

"Add those numbers vertically, horizontally or diagonally, and they equal a hundred and eleven," I said.

She grabbed my hand and added and nodded. "How do you know this?" she said. "You're like genius-level smart, aren't you? Like smart enough where I'll have to hate you for being smarter than me—than I am?"

"*No,*" I said. "You're totally smarter."

"All right then. In general, anyway. But clearly not in math. So annoying. I hate being a stereotype. You know, girl equals math dummy. Except I'm not. I was better than all the boys at school, if only to make them mad."

"I'm not mad."

"Why would you be? You don't go to my school."

"Huh?"

"Never mind, go on. I'm feeling better about you now, about our comparative intelligences. Please, continue."

"I got this book for Christmas once," I said. "It was like a math puzzle book." I held up my palm. "It's not like I thought this up myself or anything."

"Who said you did? Anyway, I'll need a copy of it." She pressed her palm on mine and the ink transferred to hers.

"It's backward," I said.

"It's perfect," she said. "My mom. She was right. You're cool. You've redeemed yourself, and from a *very* deep hole."

"Your dad. He's taking off work to be your tutor?"

"He works nights mostly. You're really twelve? You look older."

"Seriously? Thanks."

"You're hilarious."

"How much older?"

"Twelve and a half," she said.

"You're like thirteen, right?"

"Am. You're freaking hysterical."

"Why?"

"Oh my gosh, stop making me laugh."

"But you're not laughing."

"Do you have any money on you?" she said. "Buy me a Reese's and I'll forget that whole thing back at the library entirely."

"What, that I wanted to send your mom the wink?"

"Why are you reminding me?"

I bought a three-pack and we sat on a boardwalk bench. She nibbled the candy. "Sweet Cheez Whiz, that's good," she said. "This dog's very existence is preposterous. He's sho goofy I want to shmoosh him and munch him up into a biwwion widdiw peeshes of fwuff. Gonna eachou! How do you not have a name for this little freak? I love the way he looks at you."

"And how's that?"

"Constantly," she said. "You should get him certified as a therapy dog. That way he could come into the library, and nobody can give us dirty looks."

"You mean like a Seeing Eye dog?"

"Exactly not. Are you blind? There's this thing where kids who have a hard time reading, read to dogs. The dog doesn't judge the kid when he mispronounces a word or whatever. The dog's just completely psyched the kid is giving him all this attention. The kid feels like, whoa, this dog is totally listening to me, I must be reading pretty great. The more confident the kid gets, the better he reads. I swear, it's a real program. They do it in schools and libraries and jails and stuff. I think your little guy here could do it. Look at him listening to us. To me anyway. I talk a lot."

"Really?"

"Do you mean 'really' as in, do I think your guy could do it, or really I talk a lot?"

"That he could do it."

"Liar. Your eyes are open too wide and you're looking away." Any guy who thinks he's smarter than a girl is an idiot. But this girl was as smart as my mom, which was *totally* scary. "Read to Rufus, it's called, where the dog listens to the kid," she said. "I read about it in the education section of the paper. I'm going to be an English teacher by day and a novelist by night. You?"

I shrugged. "Waterslide tester?"

"That's the last thing I would've expected you or anybody to say. Okay, I am now officially falling in like with you. That is so freaking awesome. You are my hero." I think that's what she said. Things got fuzzy after *falling in like with you.* "Stop jackhammering your leg," she said. "It's spectacularly annoying."

"Sorry."

"Stop apologizing. Don't feel compelled to say anything at all. I know, I'm bossy."

"I'm not saying anything at all."

"Flip," she said. "That's what you should call him."

"Why?"

"Because that's his name. Watch. Flip. See? He cocked his head."

"He cocks it no matter what you say to him," I said.

"Flip Flip Flip Flip Flip."

The little dog licked the Rainbow Girl's lips and she smiled the most awesome smile, like in the picture of Mom's partner Laura. Not pushing it, just real. Then she pushed up from the bench and headed off. "Gotta go study. Dad's dropping an algebra test on me first thing tomorrow morning."

"Beats what I have, a quiz on chapters one through five of *To Kill a* freaking *Mockingbird.*"

"What, you expect them to let you analyze *Starship Troopers* in English? At least you love *Feathers,* which means there's hope for you. Look into the therapy dog certification. Maybe I'll help you get that Read to Rufus thing going at the library. My mom would be totally into it."

We were backpedaling away from each other, and we had to shout now. "Hey, I'm sorry about your dog," I said.

"We're adopting a new one as soon as I'm a hundred and eleven percent."

"What's your name anyway?"

"Halley, like the comet."

"Wow."

"Yup."

"I'm, like, Ben, just so you know."

"I, like, know. Mom told me, plus it's on your library card, duh."

"What's it about, your novella?"

She spun around once and skipped and smiled. "I don't know you well enough to tell you yet!"

"Does that mean you'll be at the library tomorrow after school?"

"I have a doctor's appointment! We look like idiots, hollering as we're backing away from each other! You're about to backpedal into an old man in a wheelchair! Ben?"

"Yeah?"

"A hundred and eleven! That's how many books I'm going to write! That's how many years I'm going to live! Bye Flip!"

I texted Chucky.

> BC: Who told you the wink means profound admiration and respect?
>
> CM: Rayburn, why?

10
DESTINED FOR AMAZINGNESS

"He's going to be amazing with the kids," the lady at the Read to Rufus office said.

Mom elbowed me and got back to signing the paper that said she would sponsor my training to become a Read to Rufus facilitator because I was underage.

"This girl, my friend, we'd like to start a program at my library," I said.

"Sounds fantastic," the lady said. "You and Flip will need to attend some classes to get him certified. There's a bunch of homework too. Can you commit to that?"

"A hundred and eleven percent," I said.

"He's absolutely devoted to you, Ben," the lady said. "Go ahead, do it again. I'd like to take a picture and post it on the website, if you're cool with that."

I read to Flip from *The Memory Door*, by N. T. Castillo-Cormier. His little ears perked up and he cocked his head, his big gold eyes on me. When I winked at him he dove at my mouth and stuck his peanut-butter-stinking tongue in there.

"Check your training books about how to teach him not to fly at the reader's face," the lady said. Her phone camera clicked. "Keep going, Ben."

The book was about this guy who finds a doorway that'll let him travel a hundred and forty million years into the future. "'He opened the door and the whole Earth was ice. The sky was black even though the sun was shining. The sun itself was ten times bigger, but the future was all cold wind. He turned around to go back home, but the door had disappeared, and now it and everything and everyone he'd ever known and loved existed only in his memory.'"

The subway car was crowded on the way home. I left the backpack open, and Flip stuck his little head out to look around. This girl in the next seat said, "I want to cuddle him till I crush him." I held the backpack a little closer to me. The train stopped and the girl got off and actually said bye to me.

"Wield your newfound power gently, Traveler," Mom said. "Who's this friend you were talking about? The one who's going to help you set up a Read to Rufus clinic at the library?"

"You know, just this girl I met."

"Okay," Mom said. "How long have you known her?"

"Like, since last winter? Mom, she's a *library* girl, for cripe's sake. Relax."

She put me into a sort of headlock and kissed my forehead and then she went back to her book, some nonfiction thing about getting traumatized kids to talk again. That's what she did for work. That was how we met.

I didn't want to think about it anymore, the time before I went to live with Mom.

I put on my headphones and listened to the *Transformers* soundtrack and dreamed about the future, about all of us hanging out at the library: Flip and me and the Read to Rufus kids and Halley Like the Comet.

11
I WRITE,
THEREFORE I AM

Wednesday was Rayburn-free. Word was getting around school that he cut out to do something illegal, not to mention profitable. Angelina started the rumor, and the way she said it, I was pretty sure she thought Rayburn was the most fascinating humanoid on the planet. "He's gonna be so rich someday!" Big deal. A rich moron, some prize.

Chucky and I were going to eat in the cafeteria, but the urge for half-decent slices overwhelmed us and we went out to Nice Guy Eddie's. "Does she have a nice butt at least, the library chick?"

"Mold?"

"*Coffin?*"

"Do I need to smack the snot out of you?"

"Sure, pick on the short kid. *Now* you're a tough guy. My hero. Are you going to eat the rest of that?"

"What, you want to lick the plate?" I said. He did, too.

After school I picked up Flip and we went to the library. I looked through the window and saw the place was packed. Somebody was bound to hiss, "No dogs allowed!" I rapped on the glass until Mrs. Lorentz came out.

"I did what Halley said. I started getting Flip certified as a therapy dog."

"Totally awesome," Mrs. Lorentz said. "Coincidentally, she started looking into setting up the reading clinic here. She was just talking about you, in fact. She said, 'I bet sci-fi boy shows up in ten minutes.' That was—"

"Ten minutes ago," Halley said as she came outside. She wore a red beret and a black hoodie with white writing on the front that said: I WRITE, THEREFORE I AM. She scooped up Flip and slung her backpack over her shoulder. "Let's go."

"Where?"

"You know on the back wall inside, the picture *Dreamland at Night*?" she said.

"It's my favorite."

"It's everybody's." She grabbed my hand and led me toward the water.

I'd never held hands with anybody before, especially in front of their mom.

"I'm not crushing on you," she said.

"No, I know," I said. "Just friends, totally."

"*Just?* What's better than friends? Sorry my hands are freezing."

"I don't mind," I said.

She double squeezed my hand and we didn't say anything for a while and just walked sort of fast. We both breathed hard. Then she said, "So?"

"So."

"What's your dad do?"

"Who knows?" I said.

"Oh," she said. "Sorry."

I shrugged. "My mom's a speech pathologist, though."

"That's awesome."

"What's your dad do?" I said.

"He's a magician. What's with the face?"

"No, that's cool."

"It *is*, at least that's what everybody says except you."

"They're sneaky," I said. "Their purpose in life is to trick you."

"To make you *believe*," she said.

"In what?"

"A hundred and eleven." She showed me her palm. She'd retraced the backward imprint from Monday with a sparkly purple marker.

"The magic box," she said.

The magic box. I blinked it away. "It's actually called a magic square," I said. "Besides, that's math, not magic."

"They're the same thing," she said.

"I kind of had a bad experience with a magician this one time." I blinked harder to push it back.

"Tell me," she said.

"What's your book about?" I said.

She rolled her eyes. "Okay, I'll show you."

We went to the new Luna Park. It was closed that day, but we looked through the fence. The golden tower from 1905 was gone. Flip begged me to pick him up. This seagull was giving him bad eyes, like he'd make a nice snack. The roller-coaster track was one of those high-tech ones, just one long mean rail slicing up the gray sky. "I like the old one better," I said.

"I love 'em both," Halley said.

"The 1905 one was all silvery and soft gold."

"Because it's a black-and-white *picture*, hello? The new one's *bright*. Look at all that pink paint. Anyway, you'd be able to go back and visit the old one if I let you read my novella. Which of course I totally won't, not ever, which is a shame since the most pivotal scene in the whole entire story is set in Luna Park, 1905."

"I understand. I won't push you—"

"Okay, *okay* already, if you insist. But for all my bravado

I'm actually spectacularly fragile when it comes to my art, so even if you hate it, tell me you love it. I'm perfectly okay with being lied to on that score."

"Deal."

She huffed. "So there's this girl."

"There always is," I said.

"She runs away to Luna Park."

"The new one or the old one?"

"Both."

"Interesting," I said. "Why's she run away? Crummy parents?"

"They died instantly in a car crash."

"They always do."

"Well, you have to get rid of them somehow, and that seemed the most merciful yet expeditious way. Otherwise how do you turn her into an orphan? This is a middle grade story, like for ages ten to fourteen, and the rule is you need an orphan."

"I hear you."

"The girl, she has these flying dreams all the time. She thinks they mean she's supposed to be a trapeze artist, so she starts training to do that. You know the ride where you can do the trapeze, and you're connected to safety cables in case you fall? Well, she's the one who hooks you up to the wires."

"The ride attendant."

"At night, when the park closes, she practices. Problem is,

she's not very good. She doesn't have the confidence, you know? She needs somebody to cheer her on."

"This is where the boy comes in. Let me guess: He's the guy who keeps the lights on for her after the park shuts down. The park electrician or whatever, right?"

"No, but I like that. I may steal it."

"All yours. Everybody's always stealing from me anyway."

"What do they steal?" she said. "Are you rich? I'm both suspicious of and fascinated by rich people."

"For a twelve-year-old I do okay. I have probably like the third-biggest coupon delivery route in my whole district."

"Golly."

"Thanks. Yeah. So how do they meet in the first place, the girl and the boy?"

"Through the girl's friend, this magician who works at the park," she said, "and I'm going to stop right there for now. You'll have to meet my dad before I can continue."

"Why?"

"Because you have to believe in magic for this story to work, and Mercurious Raines is the best person to get you there."

"Mercurious *Raines?*"

"Yup. Okay, so from what you've heard so far, the setup, what do you think?"

"I love it."

"You're lying again." She pecked my cheek and grabbed Flip and they went down to the water. She cheered Flip on as he chased the wave froth. The sun came through here and there and it was like spotlights. One of them passed over Halley and she was gold for around ten or eleven seconds.

All I could think about on the way home was that I didn't want to move to Florida now. Flip started whimpering as we came to my apartment building, probably because the rain was starting, I figured. Nope.

I stepped into the apartment and saw an old lady sitting at the kitchen table with Mom. Flip jumped into the woman's lap. She smothered him with kisses and said, "Darling, how Mommy missed you!"

12
THE TRAVELER
FROM THE PAST

Flip licked the tears out of the old lady's eyes. Her clothes were dirty, her sneakers worn thin. She showed me a grimy picture, her and Flip all cuddled up in front of a pine tree lit silver and red. In the picture the woman looked nice, pretty clothes, sweet smile. The dog's tail wasn't bent and chomped. It was all fluffed up like somebody went at it with a blow dryer for an hour and a half. "Spencer's first Christmas," she said.

"We've been calling him Flip," I said. When the dog heard the name Halley gave him he squirmed out of the woman's arms and hopped up into my lap. He was shivering.

"Where do you live?" Mom said. She poured the woman coffee.

The woman called out, "*Spen*cer. Here now, my angel."

I set him down. He hesitated. He went to her, licked her hand once and came right back to me.

The woman nodded. "I see," she said. She looked around our nice comfy kitchen. She stopped on the picture of Laura. She looked at Flip in my arms. "Spencer seems to have found a fine, safe home here," the woman said. "Flip, I mean. He seems to have found himself a family."

I wasn't going to say anything to that, but Mom was halfway into "Well, now, let's talk about this," when the woman just up and ran out of our apartment.

"Ben, get the umbrella and come with me," Mom said. "Leave Flip here."

The elevator doors closed just as we got to them. By the time the next one came and we got to the lobby, the woman was gone. We went outside. Here it was September, and the air was cold with all the rain. It tore the leaves from the trees. Then I saw her at the end of the street, sitting on the curb.

"Come back inside," Mom said. "We'll have some nice hot soup."

"Forty dollars," the woman said. "I got sick and had to go into the hospital. I couldn't pay my doctor's bills. I lost my apartment. They don't let animals into the homeless shelters. We slept in the waiting rooms at the airport terminals, traipsing from one to the other when the security guards made us move. When I fell asleep, a man tried to take Spencer. After that we slept in the ATM lobbies. I was begging out in front of the bank one night, holding the door for people on their way to the cash machine. A woman said she would give me forty dollars for Spencer. She seemed like a nice woman. I thought Spencer would be safer with her."

"You were going to sell him again, if we gave him to you just now, right?" I said.

"Ben," Mom said. "I won't have you talking that way to our fellow traveler."

"She's not my fellow anything."

"I could never do that to him again," the old woman said. "I still can't believe I did it. I couldn't feed him anymore. I couldn't feed *me*. I was starving."

"Do you see how messed up his tail is?"

"Not another word, son," Mom said. "Come with us," she said to the lady. "I can help you find the help you need."

"What I need is money."

Mom took all the money out of her wallet and gave it to the woman. "Ben, give our friend here whatever you have."

I reached into my pocket. "I only have a dollar," I lied. All year round I delivered those coupons before school, rain, sleet, heat, snow. In winter I shoveled sidewalks and driveways on the block where the people owned one-family houses. In summer I washed their cars and weeded their gardens. First Rayburn and now this lady. Why should I hand over my money to somebody who sold Flip to a stranger? I was so mad I didn't even want to let her have the crumpled dollar.

"Give it to her," Mom said.

I put the bill into the woman's hand, and she took off.

Mom nudged me to follow her. "Here, go, give her the umbrella."

The lady wouldn't take it. She kept going.

"Thank you, Ben," Mom said.

"It was just a stupid dollar."

"It was everything."

That night Flip did great at his training session for the therapy dog certification. He already knew lots of tricks, roll over and play dead and even this one called the fighter. The guy running the class said, "Flip, box." That little dog stood on his hind legs and jabbed the air with his front paws. I couldn't stop thinking about the old lady and how many hours she must have spent teaching him that one.

It took a long time to get home. The rain made the trains run slow. Mom nudged me. "Cheer up."

I took Flip out of the backpack and he snored in my lap and I cheered up.

13

THE UNEXPECTED
SOLUTION TO THE
FLORIDA PROBLEM

Thursday was good all through school because Rayburn was "out sick" again. On the way home Mold wanted me to come over and chill for a round or two of *Infinite Crisis,* but Flip and I had a date with Halley, except it wasn't a date. "She's a *friend,*" I said.

"That's not what I asked," Chucky said. He'd asked if she was a babe.

"She's beautiful," I said.

Chucky rolled his eyes. "Compared to Mystique from X-Men, *beautiful* like that?"

"There's no comparison. Mystique is completely blue and this girl's a rainbow."

"Mystique is also completely naked," Chucky said. "A

rainbow, huh? Dude, the way you talk sometimes? You're a riddle wrapped inside an enchilada."

"Enigma."

"See, like right there. Quit looking so bummed out." We were at the corner where we usually split up, but I guess Chucky could tell I needed to talk, because he went with me up the block, toward my building. Turns out he should've just gone home.

"I'm setting up this whole Read to Rufus thing, and in nine months I'm out of here."

"So you set up another one in Florida," Chucky said. "Of course the *rainbow* babe won't be in Florida, but there's still tons of chicks down there." He slugged my shoulder. "Ow," he said. "Bony shoulder you got there. Ow," he said again.

Rayburn had just slapped him in the back of the head. "Pockets," he said. Angelina giggled and Ronda just looked mean.

Chucky turned his pockets inside out: nothing but an empty Skittles wrapper.

"Let's go, Coffin," Rayburn said.

"No," I said.

"What?" Rayburn said.

"What?" Chucky said.

"*What?*" Angelina said.

"Coffin, don't be mental," Ronda said.

Rayburn shoved me, but I stayed on my feet. "No," I said.

"Good for you, Ben," Chucky said.

"Shut up, Mold." Rayburn cracked him across the mouth. I shoved Rayburn and then everybody went nuts. Rayburn was belting me and Angelina was kicking Chucky and Ronda was yelling for everybody to stop being mental and shoving everybody in sight. Half a minute later they were gone and my pockets were empty. The idiot took my headphones too.

I don't know how long it was before I could breathe anywhere near normal. I was on my back, looking up. The pigeons were looking down at me from where they hung out under the elevated train tracks and pooped on everybody. Chucky kept asking me if I was okay, I think. I had a hard time understanding him because his lip was stuck to his braces. We huddled behind the dumpster—always dumpsters for us—and got ourselves together. "Do I need stitches?" Chucky said.

"No, it's just a fat lip. Quit crying," I said. "Quit it!"

I wiped the blood from my nose and turned my sweatshirt inside out to hide the rest of it. No way was I telling Mom. She'd be on the phone with Mrs. Pinto before the words were out of my mouth, and things would be ten times worse in school. I'd explain away the fat eye with the old gym excuse, "I got nailed in dodge ball."

When I got home Flip wasn't at the door waiting for me. "Flip? C'mon bud, let's go see Halley."

He crawled out of Mom's room real fast to my feet. I picked him up and boy was he trembling.

This old lady was in my mother's room, facedown on the floor. It took me a few seconds before I figured out who it was, even though she wasn't supposed to be home from work for another two hours. "Mom?"

She was cold the way you can't be when you're alive. It looked like she died in the middle of putting on her sneakers. That was the other reason we were moving to Florida—her health. Her heart acted a little fluttery in the New York winter, she said.

The weirdest thing? I was kind of mad at her. What the heck was I supposed to do now?

14
ITCHY SOCKS

The next four days passed in a blur. I didn't sleep, didn't have one asthma attack, didn't cry one tear. I was actually kind of mellow. It's not like any of this was a surprise. Here was the proof: Nothing perfect lasts forever.

I do remember one thing very clearly, breakfast the first day of the wake. I was making myself some Cap'n Crunch when Aunt Jeanie came in and said, "That's not a proper breakfast, Ben. That's not even food. Let me make you something that's—oh!" She clutched her chest, like she was about to follow in Mom's footsteps. "Your slacks!"

They were a little short. I must have grown another inch in the last year, since the last time I wore them to my interview for my coupon delivery job, which everybody laughed at me for—but hey, I got the job. "You can see your socks!"

"Only a little," I said, lowering my pants some, except they were already below where my butt crack started.

"They're white!"

"So?" That's what Mom would have said. "So they see your socks, Ben? Is the world going to stop spinning? You look cool. In fact, I might wear my slacks like that too." And she would have hiked them right up and laughed. Aunt Jeanie, on the other hand, turned into a freakazoid. "Let's go," she said. "In the car. Now." The whole way over to Macy's she kept saying, "This is a disaster. You poor dear. If Tess could see us now, she'd have my head on a platter."

Really, she would have said, *Jeanie? Take a pill.*

"We'll get you fixed right up, don't you worry at all."

"I'm really not worried, though," I said.

"You poor thing." She called ahead for them to have a pair of slacks ready for us. She was like the queen when we walked in there. The sales assistant practically bowed to her. She waved him off and said, "Abso*lute*ly not," when the guy suggested a pair of pants that were only half lame, sort of comfy-looking like jeans but with dress pants material, very shiny. "We're not going out to a *night*club, Angelo. We're going to my big sister's . . ." She got all teary.

"Jeanie, I'm so sorry," Angelo said, or would have said if Aunt Jeanie didn't cut him off.

"This young man has a classic look. No no, here." She grabbed a pair of the thoroughly lamest pants in all of Macy's, the kind you see in the catalog where the models are all old men who would have like these tufts of frizzly gray hair growing out of their ears if they didn't trim it.

"Perfect," she said. "Hurry, Ben, go put them on while I get you some proper socks." I swear she picked the itchiest pair in the store.

By Sunday night all the people I never met till now but who hugged me like they knew me forever were gone, and it was just Aunt Jeanie, Leo, me and Flip at the kitchen table. Aunt Jeanie kept at it with the face cream but she couldn't hide the fact she'd been crying pretty much the whole way through the past four days. I heard her at night, through the wall. She and Leo were camped out in Mom's room. "Don't let the dog sit in your lap like that, Ben," Jeanie said. "Not in those nice slacks. The fur. You'll never get it out."

"Babe, easy," Leo said. "You want to end up like your sister?"

"Nice, Leo," she said.

"Ah honey, I'm sorry," he said.

"*Nice.*"

"You know what I mean."

I put Flip on the floor between my feet. He sat like he'd learned at the training place, front paws up, like give me high ten, and that's when I realized I missed his last certification class. I had one chance to make it up, or else we had to start all over and pay the whole fee again too.

"So we have to talk about how things will go from here," Aunt Jeanie said. "Clearly you'll come live with us. Tess left directions, and that's what she wanted. She put away some money for you too, enough to get you through the first two years of college, maybe. She left me in charge of the money until you turn eighteen."

I already knew this stuff. Mom told me and asked if I'd be okay with what she had in mind for me in case she died. I was like, "Sure." What choice did I have?

"Look, champ, it's all going to be okay," Leo said. "I'm even excited about this in a weird way. Not in a weird way. You know what I mean. I can be your coach in Little League or something."

Leo was huge, but a lot of that was fat. I couldn't see him throwing a ball without having a stroke. He was probably sixty-something but looked older. "I don't want to be a problem," I said.

"Stop talking like that," Aunt Jeanie said. "We're happy to have you."

"Happy to have you," Leo said too, almost, but Aunt Jeanie cut him off.

"The first order of business is to take whatever you want from the apartment. I have to return the keys to the landlord by the end of the month, and I'm having somebody come in to sell the furniture and such. Whatever you don't want, goes."

"Champ, there's not a lot of room at the house. All those books. You might want to consider thinning out the collection there. I'm gonna get you the e-book versions, much more efficient."

"It's okay," I said.

"No no, I want to do it," Leo said. "I want to buy you a present, okay? I feel bad for you, being orphaned again and all that."

"Leo, really?" Aunt Jeanie said.

"No, I'm just saying," Leo said.

"I can sell them back to Strand," I said. "The used bookstore. That's where a lot of them came from anyway."

"There you go," Leo said. "Put a few dollars in your pocket. Very enterprising, my kind of guy."

I looked around the apartment. My eyes settled on the picture of Laura. "Can I bring her?"

"Well, now, that will be fine, Ben," Aunt Jeanie said. She patted my shoulder from a distance, leaning away as she reached in. "Yes, I suspect Tess would want that."

Tess. Not Mom. Two years I knew her. I got kind of mad all of a sudden. It hit me: That was the longest I ever knew anybody. I excused myself, and Flip and I went to my room, which was about to be somebody else's soon. I pulled down my Chewbacca poster, rolled it up and slipped it into a tube of gift-wrapping paper that said CONGRATULATIONS! again and again.

I checked my phone. I had like a dozen texts from Halley. They started Thursday afternoon with *Where are you?* and ended Saturday morning with *I have no idea what I did to make you blow me off, but whatever it is I'm sorry.*

I just didn't know how to get back to her. What, I'm going to tell her my mom died when I barely know her? I don't know, I just didn't want her feeling bad for me or bad at all, even though I knew I was making her feel bad not getting back to her.

"Ben?"

I practically jumped off the bed when Aunt Jeanie came in. Mom always knocked, even if the door was open, which it wasn't.

"Your principal left messages for Tess. Three. Apparently you've been fighting?"

I knew freaking Chucky would cave.

15

NO SMOKING IN
MRS. PINTO'S

The next day after school we had a big meeting in Mrs. Pinto's office: Rayburn and his mom, Angelina and Ronda and theirs, Chucky and Mrs. Mold, and me and Leo, because Aunt Jeanie had to work. Turns out it wasn't Chucky who ratted out Rayburn. It was Ronda.

Rayburn's mom put one of those electronic cigarette things to her lips.

"Uh, excuse me, *no*," Mrs. Pinto said.

"It's not real smoke," Rayburn's mom said. "It's *water*."

"It's not happening anywhere near school property," Mrs. Pinto said. "Okay, so Damon, you have something for Ben."

He gave me the headphones. I didn't even want them now that he'd worn them.

"And?"

Rayburn rolled his eyes. His mom yelled, "Damon, you want to get locked up? Shake those boys' hands. *Mean* it too."

He was shaking as he shook our hands. He was this close to killing somebody or crying. Angelina was huffing and Ronda rolled her eyes.

"Now *sign* that contract," his mom said. It said he promised to meet with the guidance counselor twice a week. He signed.

"That's it?" Chucky said. "He's not going to jail? Not even a freaking *suspension?* He punched me in the mouth!"

"Charles," Mrs. Mold said.

"I kind of have to agree with Chuck here," Leo said. "Look, I'm not saying we gotta hook Dennis to the ball and chain— boys will be boys and all—but don't you think he's getting off a little light? I mean, going to the *guidance* counselor? Do we really think that's going to work?"

"And what do you want *Damon* to do instead?" Rayburn's mom said, like she was ready to stick her non-smoky cigarette into Leo's eye.

"Let Chuck smack him back?" Leo said. "Hey, relax, I was just *kidding.*"

Everybody stared at Leo.

Mrs. Pinto sent us kids out while she talked to the parents and Leo. Rayburn and Angelina stormed off, glaring at me like everything was my fault.

"Thanks," I said to Ronda.

"I only did it because your mom died," she said. "You're still not allowed to say hi to me in the hall." She gave me a halfhearted shove and went off the other way. I plunked down on the bench outside Mrs. Pinto's office. Chucky plunked next to me. "Me too, Coffin," he said. "Sorry about your mom." He put his arm over my shoulder, but I shrugged it off. "I'm *fine*, Mold, okay? Seriously."

"Okay," he said. Chucky's fingertip traced what somebody scratched into the bench: THE OTHER WAY TO SPELL FAILURE? Y-O-U.

When we got home, or what used to be home, Flip was already by the door with one of my dirty socks and my collector's edition Wolverine action figure. Leo almost tripped over Flip. "We might have to start making him wear a blinking light," he said. "I've seen rats bigger than him. I guess we better get you packed up now, champ."

"I'm ready." I nodded to where I'd put a bag of clothes and a box of books with the picture of Laura and my Chewie poster.

"That's it?" Leo said.

I'd already packed the other books and brought the boxes down to the mailroom that morning.

Leo clapped my shoulder. "Jeanie won't be back from work till eight. Let's play a video game or something. I'll order a couple of pizzas."

"I have to walk Flip," I said.

"When you get back."

"Actually, I have to meet a friend."

"Gotcha," he said.

"What time do you want me home for dinner?"

"I mean, whenever Tess used to say, I guess, right?"

16
THE EXPLODED RAINBOW

Mrs. Lorentz wasn't at the front desk, so that was good at least. Halley's notebooks and sparkle pens were spread all over the table like an exploded rainbow. Black beret today. Glaring green eyes for just a second and then no time for me. "This is me not talking to you," she said.

"I'm sorry."

"You're an idiot."

"I know."

"You don't know anything. My mother and I were like, did he die or something? Gimme your freaking backpack." She scooped Flip into her lap. "Here I'm doing all this research about the Read to Rufus stuff. Me and Mom are on a video conference with this school where the kids have a hard time reading. Everybody's completely psyched, and we're telling them we're ready as soon as you and Flip are, and you like vanish? What the freak? What did I do? Where were you? And what happened to your face?"

I told her, and then I told her everything else. You know how you can tell when somebody's really listening to you? Like you can almost see the words traveling through the air, into her eyes, and then they sink into her heart? Like she wants to take in the way you feel, even if you're sad, because she wants to be there with you? For you? She hugged me and whispered, "It's okay, it's okay, you can cry."

"I'm really okay," I whispered back.

"No, really, you can. I want you to."

"But I don't want to."

She leaned back a little to look at me. She looked at me for a while, and then she tilted her head to the side. I swear it was like I went from hardly knowing her to knowing her better than I ever knew anybody, maybe even Mom. No, the other way around. She knew me. She could read my mind. "You feel like you can't breathe, right?" she said. "Let's get out of here."

That afternoon was crazy warm for September, and the boardwalk was busy. Somehow her hand was even colder today. "Cypress Hills, by the cemeteries?" she said. That's where Jeanie and Leo lived. "Are you changing schools?"

"No, I'm not being the new kid again." Everybody kept stopping to pet Flip, and he loved it.

"How long were you in there?" she said.

"Where?"

"Foster care."

"Until like two years ago."

She stopped walking. "Why'd it take so long?"

"I was a drop-off," I said. "At the police station, you know? A few days old, my file says. They do blood tests on you, to see if you're healthy. My blood had drugs in it."

"From your mom."

"That scares people away." I shrugged. "The only thing I'm addicted to is those chocolate chip cookies your mom leaves out on her desk."

"Ben? I'm sorry."

"Why? The caretakers were cool, most always." I held back on the fact that everything was always changing. People coming and going. You'd make a friend one day and she'd be gone the next or maybe you would be. After a while you stopped trying to remember names. "One Christmas we had a grab bag. I ended up with this Chewbacca poster. I never hung it. I figured I'd only have to take it down again." I was doing it again, saying what I was thinking. "Hey, did you tell your dad I hate magic?"

"He said he'd like to show you a trick or two."

"I don't think so," I said.

"You can tell me, you know? About your mom?"

"I did."

"You told me she died. You didn't tell me about *her*."

"She's in a better place and all that, right?" I said. "Nothing to be sad about, Traveler."

"Traveler?"

"Life's a journey. The best part is going uphill. Things come all at once, bad brings good, one door closes, two open, go through both."

"She used to say that to you, right?"

"Really, Halley, I'm okay. Yeah. It's windy." I said that in case I started to cry, which I didn't.

"It *is* windy."

"I wish we had sunglasses," I said.

"Yeah." She squeezed my hand really hard and didn't let go and we kept walking fast and didn't look at each other or say anything for a while.

"Like, how are *you* feeling?" I said.

"Shut up, Ben."

"I'm sorry."

"No, it's just, I don't know, your mom dies, and you're worried about me?"

"No, not worried—totally not. Just seeing if, like, you're feeling good. You know."

"Don't worry about me. I don't like to lose."

"I know."

"You better. My good numbers are up, the bad numbers are down. I'm awesome. So are you. Flip's more awesome than both of us. We are a trio of terrificness. Yeah." Suddenly she pulled me off the boardwalk toward the street. "Frick it," she said. "It's time for you to meet the one and only Mercurious Raines. C'mon Flip!"

17
THE LABORATORY OF MERCURIOUS RAINES

He rented office space in a church basement. The entrance was a red door with black metal hinges. Gothic letters spelled out:

THE LABORATORY OF MERCURIOUS RAINES
ENTER AT YOUR OWN RISK . . .
(MAGIC LESSONS BY APPOINTMENT)

"You've really never heard of him?" Halley said. "He's like the king of the bar mitzvah circuit. He does stuff in Manhattan too." She pushed on the door and it *creeeeaked*. Flip pawed at my leg to be picked up.

The music was blaring, *Fantasia*, *The Sorcerer's Apprentice*. The walls were like the ones at the library, silkscreened with giant pictures. There were Saturn and the moon, and then the Halo Galaxy, and burning bright across the ceiling, Halley's Comet.

A few parents watched from the back. Three little kids

sat in folding chairs and watched a fourth learn a trick from a man in a sparkly purple sweat suit and a white cape. He looked maybe forty. He wore a silver sombrero. His hair was long and pulled back in a ponytail. His goatee was a little long too. Mercurious Raines wore gold basketball sneakers that were so shiny I felt like I was looking into the sun. He knelt on one knee next to the kid onstage and patted the kid's back.

"Go ahead," he said.

The kid frowned. He snapped his fingers, and a world globe the size of a basketball materialized, spinning on his fingertip. "No way," the kid said. "I did that?"

"*You* did," Mercurious Raines said.

"I *did* it, Mom," the kid said.

Halley elbowed me.

"You have sharp elbows," I whispered.

"You have fantastically sensitive ribs," she said.

After the class Halley introduced me and Flip to her dad. "Not a big magic fan, I hear, Ben?"

"How'd you do that thing with the globe?" I said. "Or is this one of those 'A great magician never reveals his secrets'?"

"Oh, I think a true magician shares all the magic he can," he said. "Give me a minute to make a phone call, and then I'll show you the globe illusion." He stepped into a smaller room where he had his desk and closed the door most of the way.

"See?" Halley said. "He's not some evil warlock, right?"

"He's nice."

"Halley, Ben, can you guys help me for a sec?" Mr. Lorentz called from behind his office door. "I can't find my phone. I swear, if my head wasn't attached to my shoulders, I'd lose that too."

I pushed through the door. Mr. Lorentz was standing on the far side of the room, or most of him was. His head was gone.

It was on the other side of the room, on his desk. It said, "Oh wait, there it is." And then back on the far side of the room, his headless body pulled the phone from his back pocket. The headless body crossed to the desk and held the phone to Mr. Lorentz's bodiless head. The head said to the body, "Would you mind dialing for me?"

Halley was cracking up and Flip sprinted circles around the headless body. I pulled out my inhaler and sucked in a double shot.

The headless body stepped toward me, and Mr. Lorentz's head was back on his shoulders. "Ben, it's just mirrors and video projection, son," he said.

"No, I know, it's just I have to get home for dinner." I scooped up Flip and got out of there. I didn't get more than a block away before I had to sit on the steps of an apartment building. Flip nudged my hand to pet him.

Halley showed up out of breath. "Okay, need I remind you I finished a round of chemotherapy not long ago? A little getting out and about and moving around is good for me, but I'm not ready for an all-out sprint. You're actually not as slow as I thought you'd be."

"I truly appreciate that."

She rubbed my back and after a while we'd caught our breath. "Let's have it," she said. "Where's the magician trauma come from?"

"Tell me about your novella. What happens next?"

"I'll tell you after you tell me. Clearly this is something awesome we have shaping up here, this friendship. We click." She winked at me. "So?"

So I told it to her, the story of the magic box.

18
THE MAGIC BOX

Kayla was her name. She was five, I was almost ten. She was my shadow. I was the oldest in the group home and I read to the little kids a lot. She had asthma too. We'd be in the kitchen together, on the nebulizers. They're these machines that help you breathe better. Lots of kids had asthma in that neighborhood. We were just downwind of the power plant.

Anyway, this one time, between puffs of medicine, Kayla and I were gabbing away, which you're not supposed to do when you're hooked up to the machine, but Kayla was all psyched because Christmas was coming. Santa appeared to her in a dream and said he was bringing her a box filled with magic. I was like, "What kind of magic?"

"The real kind," she said. "He told me it's the greatest treasure."

So I already had the box, this old wooden jewelry case I found on the street on garbage night, which is where I found a lot of my books too. This box was perfect, Halley,

I swear—dark blue velvet inside. So what if the top was a little cracked? I could glue it back together, right? But I was like totally freaked for the next two weeks, trying to figure out what I was going to put in that box. I mean, what can be the greatest treasure? The only thing you'll ever need to be happy? It doesn't exist.

Then, two days before Christmas, I figured it out, and of course it was a book. *The Little Prince*. That was the book that got me into sci-fi, this kid flying around the solar system, trying to find out what makes life so beautiful, right? And you learn that your eyes aren't really the things that let you see. That you can only truly see with your heart. Anyway, I figured it was as close as I could get to real magic, reading that book to Kayla. So my foster caregiver took me to the bookstore. I had just enough allowance saved up to get the book, and it fit perfectly in the box.

Christmas Eve came. Every year we had a Santa, and this time it was a Santa magician, and he was flat-out terrific. I mean he turned candle smoke into a goblin head. He made coins spark and vanish and reappear in the kids' hands. I was beginning to think this guy was for real, that magic was real. I was beginning to believe. Then he made a book flap its covers and flutter like a dove, and that's when I got the idea that maybe he could do the same thing with *The Little Prince*, so Kayla really would think it was the greatest treasure.

All the kids were oohing and ahhing, except I was beginning to get the idea Magic Santa kind of didn't want to be with us, a bunch of rejects, because he kept looking at his watch. Pretty soon he was rushing through the show, one trick into the next, no break for applause. He made me his assistant, simple stuff, hold this, get me that. I was standing next to him the whole time, and his phone kept buzzing. Finally he said he had to step out for a sec, Mrs. Claus was calling, he'd be right back.

Our caretaker could tell the guy was stressed, and she told me to bring him a cup of hot cider. So I did, and he's in this huge fight with his girlfriend, practically yelling into the phone, "What do you want me to do? It's a hundred bucks. I just have to give them the stupid presents, then I'm out of here." Then it was, "Fine, good, spend Christmas by yourself." He stuffed the phone into his pocket and noticed me. He sighed. "Sorry you heard that. Let's get back in there and finish up."

"Can I ask you a favor?" I said, and then I asked him if he could make *The Little Prince* fly.

"No way," he said. He told me the other book wasn't really a book at all but a bunch of cardboard rigged special with super-thin wires.

I was a little heartbroken, I have to admit. It made me realize everything else he did was fake too. I mean, that awesome trick with the coins? Who doesn't want to believe things can vanish and then come back? "It all looked so real," I said.

He rolled his eyes. "Why do you need the book to fly?" he said.

So I told him about Kayla and the magic box and how she's expecting this thing inside it to be a surprise that takes your breath away. Those were the exact words I used too. He repeated them, "A surprise that takes your breath away. Okay," he said. "I'll make it a big deal. She'll flip."

"What are you going to do?" I said.

"Just trust me," he said. "It'll leave her breathless."

So I went back in and rounded up the kids for the grab bag. Everybody got something they loved, except Kayla. You could tell she was about to cry, until Magic Santa said, "Now wait, I almost forgot, I have one last present here, a most special present, a magic box for Kayla." He reached under his big red cape and presented it like with a flourish, you know? Kayla was so flipped out her eyes went from almonds to circles. He held the box in front of her and told her to lift the lid, and before she did, she said, "See Ben? Magic is real."

She lifted the lid and this burst of crackly red smoke shot out, all the way up to the ceiling, in like half a second. Everybody jumped back, but then we're clapping, because it was such a cool surprise, right? And we're all covered in this red glitter. And then everybody stopped clapping.

Kayla was on the floor. She rolled up like a pill bug, and she was breathless all right. She couldn't breathe. Everybody was yelling call the ambulance, she has asthma, and the magician was like, "But it's not real smoke. It's just glitter. It's harmless."

But it was the fright that triggered the attack, and it was a really bad one. She was so shocked and panicked her throat started to close up. I was trying to make her breathe off of my inhaler, but she couldn't do it. The nebulizer was no good either. By the time the paramedics got there her chest was all puffed up because she couldn't get the air out of her lungs, and she's passing out and there's this shriek. Her wheezing. Like somebody's screaming, far away. Like you can't see them but you know they're being murdered.

19
FIRE ALARMS AND
FIRE ESCAPES

"She died?" Halley said.

"No, I did," I said. "To her anyway. They took her to the hospital. They let me visit her once, and then the next day she was moved to this special unit, and you had to be family to get in, except nobody believed me when I said I was her family. She was in there for a week, and then of course a new kid came to take her spot in the house, and they moved her to a new home, they said. They couldn't tell me where, of course, her being a minor and all. They keep all that stuff private until you're sixteen. I wrote her letters. My caretaker promised she sent them, but I never heard back."

Halley traced the backward numbers written into her palm. The ink was fading, and pretty soon none of it would add up to a hundred and eleven. She frowned and nodded. "I'm doing the time line in my head. You were almost ten, you said, when Kayla—when this happened. You must have been adopted pretty much right after."

"I couldn't talk from the minute I found out Kayla wasn't coming back to the house. I don't know why. I mean, I was always really quiet, but after that I just forgot how to do it. To make the sounds. I knew what I wanted to say, but I couldn't get the words from my brain to my mouth. They sent Mom in to help me."

"How'd she do it?" Halley said. "How'd she get you speaking again?"

"She visited me three times a week. She'd ask me how I was doing today, and I'd try to talk, and nothing would happen, so I'd just nod my head. She didn't push me. She told me to tap it into her laptop, what I wanted to say. She asked me, 'What do you like?' and I typed *books*. 'Which ones?' *Science fiction mostly.* 'Have you ever read *Dune*?' *That's one of my favorites.* 'Mine too,' and we'd go back and forth like that. She'd bring in the books and read to me for a little bit. She had this awesome voice, like totally calm. There was a fire alarm drill, and everybody was all like, line up, hurry, eyes front, no talking, *march*, and meanwhile Mom whispers to me, 'This is a good time for you and me to sneak out to Dunkin' Donuts.'

"So maybe about the third week, I tapped into her iPad that I couldn't figure out where the words were getting stuck. I had this feeling that if she could show me where in my brain they were gunking up, like maybe show me on a picture or something, I could push them through. I just didn't know where to push. And then she does this thing. It was *true* magic, no offense to your dad. She puts her hand on my head and says, 'I'm so glad you told me this, Ben. We're home free. The words aren't stuck here.' She taps my forehead. 'They're stuck *here*.' Now she rests her hand on my heart. 'Oh,' I said. That was it. She didn't go crazy or anything, like screaming about the fact she got me to talk. She just messed up my hair a little and said, 'So why don't you tell me about Kayla?' And I did. Look, I know it wasn't totally my fault, okay?"

"Who, Kayla? It wasn't at all. *The Little Prince.* That was so awesome. It wasn't the Santa dude's fault either. I know you know that too."

"I guess," I said. "No, I know. He was flipping out."

"I bet," Halley said. "Poor guy."

Flip nudged Halley's hand and then did his boxer trick. Halley smiled and kissed him but she wasn't ready to stop being sad yet, which is why I didn't want to tell her the story in the first place.

"Thanks," I said. "There's only one other person I can talk to like this. Could talk to."

"She's still with you," Halley said.

"Sure."

"She is. She'll always be with you. Kayla too."

"Tell me the rest of your book."

"Not now," she said.

"When?"

"Soon."

"I've really been wanting to ask you about it. What kind it is. I just don't know how."

"You just did," she said.

"No, your, you know."

"Cancer? It isn't mine."

I nodded, feeling like a jerk.

"I want to tell you about it," she said. "I will, okay? I know it's not fair, you telling me about Kayla, about your mom, and me not telling you about *it*, but it has to be noisy."

"Like how?"

"Like in traffic, so it gets eaten up by the horns or the squeaks the train brakes make. You can't talk about it here, by the water. It's too nice here. I just want to say I think you're awesome. Don't say anything. I always have to get the last word." She put her head on my shoulder and turned her face up to the sun and closed her eyes and pet Flip blind.

When I got home, nobody was at the dinner table. Tonight was delivery food from the Palace of Enchantment, except it was all laid out real neat on platters. Mom and I usually ate right from the cartons. Leo was eating in front of the TV, some ESPN show. Aunt Jeanie was in the other room, at Mom's desk, eating in front of her iPad. "Sorry I'm late," I said.

"C'mon, champ," Leo said, "you don't have to worry about that with me." I fed Flip and then myself, and then we loaded the car with boxes and bags. I turned back for a last look at the apartment building, my bedroom window, the fire escape where the pigeons used to bunch up in the early morning. The old man upstairs threw out crumbs at sunrise. I closed my eyes and pretended really hard that I heard the cooing, that I heard Mom's voice. *You and I will never disappear. We are forever.* I opened my eyes and she wasn't there of course.

Aunt Jeanie fussed with my hair. She wasn't a musser. More of a fixer. "You forget something up there, Ben?"

"Nothing."

"Don't cry," she said, crying.

"Don't worry," I said. "I won't." And I didn't. We got into the car and left.

20
THE HOUSE BY THE CEMETERY

"You think you'll be all right in here, champ?"

It used to be Aunt Jeanie's workout room. We moved her treadmill and exercise balls down to the cellar. "I don't want to push you out of here," I said. "I'd feel better in the basement."

"Absolutely not," Aunt Jeanie said. "Your asthma. There's no air down there. I mean, of course it's fine for when I run for a few minutes."

"I don't know why you don't run outside, babe," Leo said.

"This is a total pain for you," I said. "Flip and me barging in on you like this."

"Nah, c'mon, now," Leo said.

"I just want to say thanks. Seriously. I'll pay for Flip's food, mine too."

"Champ, relax."

"I make around fifty bucks a week from my coupon deliveries."

"Now, now," Aunt Jeanie said. She looked like she wanted

to say more but didn't know what to say. She chewed her lip. She patted my back, leaning away. "Well, if you need us, we're right down the hall."

Leo yawned and stretched on his way out. "So happy to be home," he said.

The room was a lot smaller than my old one. The window looked over the cemetery. It sounds crummy, but it was okay, lots of pine trees. I couldn't see them so great in the night, but their shadows were sparkly in the moonlight. Mom got cremated, so now I wouldn't be able to visit her. They take the body after the funeral, and you don't see it again. Then later they send you her ashes, except how can you be sure they're hers? They were supposed to come back any day now.

Aunt Jeanie had made the bed so it was tucked really tight. I remembered the day we had the big talk, Mom, Jeanie and me. I can't remember why Leo wasn't there. The talk where Mom asked Jeanie if she would take care of me if she died. Jeanie clutched her heart—always clutching her heart—and her eyes got wet. "I'm so touched, really," she said. "That you think I would be a good, you know, that I could take care of Ben. Leo and I, kids, we just never had the time. Well, you know." "I know, sweetheart," Mom said to her. "But you make the time, and they give you more time than they take. Good time, they give you. You have a huge heart, Jeanie. Bigger than you know." "It's such an honor to be asked," Jeanie said. "So I'm gonna put you down for a yes then," Mom said. "Not that I'm planning on going any time soon. Just in case. Right, Ben?" She mussed my hair, and then Jeanie fixed it, but they both winked at me, and the same way too, like only sisters can. It was nice, except, just like Mom said, none of us really imagined it would happen. Not before I grew up anyway. Before I went out on my own.

I stared at the empty wall of my new room and wondered where I ought to hang my Chewbacca poster. Flip looked from me to the wall, trying to figure out what I was staring at. I set the big picture of Laura on the desk. I had a small one of me and Mom with the beach in the background on a sunny day. I pushed the pictures together. Laura was like twenty times bigger than me and Mom. I looked away and started to get mad at myself for getting teary. *Never let the hill slow you down, Traveler,* Mom used to say, except she wouldn't have minded me being sad. Then again, she would have cheered me up. I just didn't want to get started on that whole thing. You know, feeling sorry for myself. Once you start up on that, it's harder and harder to stop, and then before you know it you're a zombie.

I went to the kitchen to get Flip a bowl of water. Leo was eating over the sink. "There's crumb cake but no milk," he said with his mouth full.

"Thanks, I'm okay," I said.

Flip sat behind me and stared through my legs at Leo.

"He's pretty goofy-looking," Leo said. "He know any tricks?"

"Flip, box," I said, and Flip got into a match with his invisible opponent.

"That's hilarious." Leo got down on the floor and feinted jabs with Flip. And then he connected with a soft but quick slap across Flip's muzzle.

Flip ran behind me and kept sneezing. Leo crawled like a lizard toward Flip and Flip whimpered.

"I don't think he likes that too much," I said.

"We were just playing." He mussed Flip's head and stood up a little out of breath. "It's weird, you not calling me anything, you know? Dad would be weirder though, right? Unc? No? How's about just call me Leo then, okay? You want to watch TV or something?"

"School tomorrow."

"Hey, I can take of care of him for you. Trip, I mean. While you're at school."

"Thanks, but you don't have to." What, like I'm going to leave Flip with him after he just slapped him? Was he out of his mind? "I walk him for a long time in the morning and then when I get home. Um, I don't mean to say anything, but his name's, like, Flip."

"I never had a dog before," Leo said. "C'mere, pup." Flip didn't.

"He'll just sleep on the bed till I get back here," I said. "You don't have to worry about him at all. Really, Leo. I appreciate it though."

"I guess you have it all figured out then." He shrugged. "Sleep good." He went into his office, which was packed with boxes. He sold golf stuff on eBay, mostly those loser hats with the flap that covers your neck, shirts with humorous sayings, except I didn't get why they were funny. Like the one he was wearing that night was:

PH

GO~~LF~~ER

His specialty was gently used clubs, he said.

Flip and I settled down on top of the covers. No way was I going to be able to make that bed as perfectly as Aunt Jeanie did. I texted Halley the address of the therapy dog certification place. Leo was watching TV on the other side of the wall, and he laughed really loud. Flip shivered and hid in my armpit.

I called Chucky. "Is your mom there?"

"This isn't some wink thing, is it?"

"Chucky, be realistic for like a third of a second."

"You saying my mom's ugly?"

"Of course not. Your mom's really pretty."

"Watch it, Coffin."

While I was talking to him, my phone blipped with a text back from Halley: ♥

I didn't sleep. I watched my phone alarm tick down toward 4:30. Somebody was opening and closing cabinets in the kitchen. After that stopped I got up and made Flip breakfast.

Aunt Jeanie had left one of those padded cooler bags in the fridge. The note said,

Ben,

Not sure if Tess used to make you lunch.

If you'd rather get lunch at school, I won't be offended.

Sincerely,

Aunt Jeanie

It was a turkey and tomato sandwich on like seventy-grain bread or whatever and loaded down with avocado and sprouts and these things that looked like mutant mouse turds but were actually seeds, I hope. The whole thing was wrapped in waxed paper as tight as the sheets on the bed. I was starving and ate it right then. It was good even though it was healthy. I grabbed the pet carrier backpack, and Flip and I hustled to the subway.

There were no seats on the train. Half the people wore fast-food uniforms and slept standing up. The train ran slow because people kept holding the doors. I missed my transfer. When it came, that train was packed. I practically had to shove people to get out when my stop came. I knew I was going to need it, so I took a hit off my inhaler, and then I ran with Flip lockstep next to me to pick up my coupons, and then we *really* ran to get them delivered in time. Flip's tail wouldn't stop wagging, like all of this rushing around was terrific fun.

By the time I finished the coupons I was totally sweaty, and by the time I got to Chucky's I was ready for a nap, and it wasn't even seven in the morning.

21
DOGGY DAYCARE

"Mrs. Mold, I want to pay you for this," I said.

"Don't be ridiculous, Coffin," she said. "Molly and Ginger will love the company—especially GinGin. Now, you and Charles get your fannies to school." She took Flip into her arms.

"I'm coming back, Flip," I said. "I promise."

He licked my face and whimpered and then Mrs. Mold closed the door. I wasn't in that house for even a minute and already I was a little wheezy.

I fell asleep in second period and then again in seventh. My face slipped through my hands and smacked the desk. Rayburn wasn't in school that day either, though. I was pretty sure he wasn't coming back. I was used to it, seeing people disappear. Except you never got used to it. And then you had the ones who were always in your face.

I was at the water fountain when Angelina came up behind me and knocked me into the stream a little, so the water went down my sweatshirt. She'd stuck gum in the hole too, to make the water shoot into your eye. Why do people think that stuff is funny? Ronda wasn't laughing, though. She rolled her eyes. Come to think of it, Ronda never laughed. Never smiled either.

After school I ditched Chucky with the chess club geeks and hurried toward the Mold house. I stopped to pick up some donuts for the girls. One of them opened the door with Flip in her arms. She said, "Ooh, chocolate," grabbed the donuts, gave me Flip and shut the door. I headed off. The door swung open and Mrs. Mold called me back. "Coffin, check this out." She showed me a bunch of videos on her phone. Here was Flip's day:

First, he got an ear treatment from Ginger.

Then he wrestled around with the three-year-old girl. "That's Charlene," Mrs. Mold said. "No, wait, Charlotte."

Then Flip cuddled into the golden retriever's armpit for a nap.

Next, Flip found the garbage bin, and he spent a good five minutes investigating a diaper. Mrs. Mold giggled the whole time she videoed him.

Later the dogs went out into the small weedy patch of cement that was the Mold yard and played chase, sort of. Flip ran up to old Molly and nipped her neck and took off. The retriever wagged her tail and limped a few steps after Flip, who tore around the yard in circles.

The next video was Flip at the window in a staring contest with a pigeon.

Then at noon one of the girls came home from kindergarten and dressed Flip in a doll nightgown and put a bunch of ribbons in his hair, and he didn't mind at all.

In the last video, Flip, Molly, and Ginger the cat are sprawled out on the couch. They're snoring, and Flip is on his back with all four legs out like an upside-down flying squirrel. He wakes up and yawns and shakes himself off and goes to the front door and sits. He cocks his head. Then three minutes later his crooked little tail starts wagging, and a minute after that I show up with the donuts.

"Flip!" Halley said. Pink beret today. The button was a strawberry. She scooped him up and we went into the therapy dog certification place.

My teacher gave Flip a chew stick, and then she said, "Not yours." Flip cocked his head, but he didn't drop the stick. The teacher told me to try. The way I learned it from the library book was to say, "Leave it." Flip dropped the stick. The teacher put down a cookie. Flip went for it. "Leave it," I said, and he turned away from it and trotted to me and sat and gave me his paw.

Halley hooted and clapped and said, "Woohoo Flip!"

Next was to make sure Flip didn't freak when he heard a loud noise, like if a kid shrieked. My teacher had me read to Flip. Behind his back she dropped an aluminum pan. Flip spun toward the clatter.

"Flip, I got it," I said. He turned right back to me and sat and listened to me read. Next time the pan clattered, Flip's ears went up, but he didn't spin around. "I got it," I said, and he lay down.

Next was the most fun. My teacher's daughter, seven years old, sat on the floor and read to Flip. He cocked his head every time the girl said, "Right Flip?"

I got him to do this little trick I taught him. I said, "Flip, who wants a belly scratch?"

Flip tucked himself into the girl's lap and rolled over into the upside-down flying squirrel pose. His tail swept the floor probably a hundred times a minute.

"This guy has the gift," my teacher said.

"He's a traveler," I said.

"She was talking about *you*, moron," Halley said.

Flip licked the girl's cheeks, then her lips.

"I can get him to stop that," I told my teacher, but truth told, I was having a hard time getting him to not make out with every person he ever met.

22

THE MAGICIAN
WHO RIDES THE MOON

Halley and I got tacos and went to the plaza near the dog training place and watched this skateboarder girl in baggy army clothes do crazy awesome tricks. Halley fed Flip chicken bits. "I swear he's trying to tell me something," she said. "Look, you can see yourself in his eyes. Flip, what is it, boy?"

"You should call her Halley," I said. "The novella, the girl on the trapeze? Your name's the most awesome ever."

"It really is, isn't it? Still, it'll be too confusing. We'll call her Helen, as in Helen of Troy. You know, from the *Iliad*?"

"I skimmed the SparkNotes."

"She was the woman who was so beautiful that all the Greeks and Trojans went psycho killing each other over her. Perfect, yes? I'm not really asking you. Just nod. Good. Now, the electrician dude. Gimme a hero's name than begins with *B*."

"Bruce," I said. "As in Wayne? Hello, Batman?"

"I'm looking for classical Greco-Roman tragedy, and you give me comic books. You want to be Bruce, fine. Either way, he's you."

"Wow."

"What now?"

"I'm flattered I made it into your story."

"*Our* story," she said. "I've decided we're writing this together."

"No way. I suck at stories."

"You read like a vampire who feeds on ink. I need your help on this. Even if I write a book a year, I have a lot of catching up to do if I'm going to pump out a hundred and eleven before I die. You and me, twice as fast, twice as fun. And if you suck I'll fire you, if that will make you feel better. Look, Flip's doing the UDFSP for me." That's what she called the upside-down flying squirrel pose. "What, Flip? What are you trying to tell me, you freaky little banana?"

"The Helen and Bruce in the book," I said. "Just friends, right?"

"*Best* friends. Okay, so here's what I have so far. It's night. Luna Park is closed. Bruce the electrician kid is hanging out on the platform with all the lights that light up the trapeze ride. The magician's with him."

"We're totally calling him Mercurious, right?" I said.

"You have to ask? Mercurious and Bruce are watching the trapeze girl."

"Helen."

"Yup. She's at the top of the pole, getting ready to swing. Bruce has her lit up with a spotlight that's as bright as the moon. He's worried. So's Mercurious. It looks like the gorgeous Helen is unclipping her safety cables."

"Why?" I said.

"That's what Bruce the superhero electrician wants to know too. Helen calls out from her platform, 'The problem with the safety wires is you can only swing so far before the wires rein you in. I need to see how high I can go. I'll never be great if I don't know what it's like to soar free.' She swings away from the platform, and up, up until she's as high as the stars. The world is so beautiful from up there, Ben. Everything is sparkly, the moon on the waves, the city itself, lit silver and gold. Suddenly Helen realizes she's flown higher than she ever could have imagined, and she gets scared. Her hands sweat and slip away from the bar."

"Bruce runs as fast as he can off the end of the spotlight platform," I said. "He catches Helen."

"My hero! Except, duh, now they're *both* falling—until time stops."

"Hold on a second," I said. "Time can't stop. It's mathematically impossible."

"Math shmath; in our story, time can stop, and it does," Halley said. "Bruce and Helen stop falling. The ocean freezes. It's like a snapshot. Luna Park fades to gold."

"Luna Park 1905?"

"Exactly. They're not *out* of time at all. They've slipped through one of the little cracks in it, the ones between each moment. The golden tower rises up to meet them. They're in the top of it now, and the sky warms up with silky blond light. The stars spin out of place, into the pattern of the shooting stars on Mercurious's cape. He's sitting on the moon. 'Well now,' he says to Helen and Bruce, 'look at the mess you've gotten yourselves into.'"

"And?" I said. "What happens next?"

"Only the greatest adventure ever." Halley shrugged. "We'll figure it out as we go."

"This is cool, you bouncing ideas off me like this," I said.

"I totally have to talk it all into my phone before we forget." And she did. When she was done, she put a chicken nugget on her lips and leaned down so she was eye to eye with Flip. Of course he ate the chicken right off her lips.

"Feeding him from your mouth like that isn't helping me to get him to stop kissing people."

"Why would you ever want him to stop?" she said.

The skateboarder girl did a backflip and the crowd cheered. The rush hour trains rumbled under the street. The bus brakes sounded like elephant calls. "So, it's definitely noisy here," I said.

She nodded. "I still don't want to talk about it."

"Okay. I just want to make sure you're, like, okay."

"Ben, I'm kicking this thing's butt. Seriously, I am. I feel it. I'm going to get myself to the point I have zero cancer in my body. Then all I have to do is stay clear for five years, and they're going to tell me they're almost positive it's never coming back. Now hold my freezing cold hand, no more talking."

We held hands and watched this boat-like cloud fly past the sun.

"Are you thinking what I'm thinking?" she said.

"You want to put a cloud ship into the story," I said.

"Mind reader."

"How about a spaceship?"

"I *knew* you were going to turn this into a sci-fi," she said. "Okay, spaceship, but then I get to put in another magician."

"We'll call her the Contessa of Starlight," I said. "Tess for short."

"Yes, and her wand is made of roentgenium."

"Except maybe it's more like a magic staff," I said. "Yeah, she has the littlest limp, a pinch of arthritis maybe, but you'll never catch her complaining about it—or anything else either. That's why everybody loves her. She takes the tough stuff that comes her way, and instead of letting it push her down, she picks herself up. She picks up everybody around her and carries them up the mountain."

"She's sounds amazing, Ben Coffin. She sounds awesome. She's my kind of hero, the perfect character for our story. I knew there was a reason I hired you."

23
LEO MEANS LION

"Hi," I said.

Aunt Jeanie was on the phone. Leo was on the couch. He didn't say hi. He pouted and went into his office. Aunt Jeanie hung up the phone.

"Did I do something wrong?" I said.

"He was . . . *sad* that you didn't trust him with the dog."

"It's not that," I said.

Leo leaned out of his office. "It's *exactly* that," he said. "I may look stupider than I am, champ, but I'm not, okay? When did they start letting people bring dogs into school anyway?"

I told them about the Mold situation. "It's just easier for everybody," I said. "I exercise him while I deliver my coupons, and then there's another dog and all these kids for him to play with."

"*Easier*," Leo said. "Right, *that's* the reason, Jeanie. It's *easier*." He huffed back into his office and closed the door.

Aunt Jeanie patted the barstool next to hers and I sat. She took out one of those lint roller things and rolled it over my shirt to get the dog hair off. "I want to tell you a secret," she said. "You have to keep this just between you and me. The word *Leo* means lion. He has a lion's heart. Big. Sensitive, you know? He wounds easily. Ben, I want you to be as comfortable as you can be here. We all need to work on our trust, right?"

"I do trust you."

"I'm not so sure you do. It's horrifying, losing Tess so suddenly. Life is just awful sometimes, even most times. We have to be realistic about that and avoid the rough patches as best we can, you know? Even if you don't need Leo, pretend you do a little, okay?"

"Actually, I do need him," I said.

I knocked on Leo's office door. It opened fast. He nodded at me, like what did I want now?

"I need a sponsor for my therapy dog certification test," I said.

He frowned, then he shrugged. "Okay." He put out his huge hand. I shook it. "You want to play a video game?" he said. It was this racecar thing on his computer, totally from a million years ago. He was the type who *really* liked to win. Flip hunkered under my arm, on the opposite side of Leo. His shirt said: KEEP CALM, CADDY ON. *Wha?* He caught me looking at it. "Hilarious, right?" he said. "Here, I'll get you one."

"That's okay."

"It's no problem, really. I have boxes full of them."

"Cool," I said.

"Champ, speaking of boxes, maybe you want to go through those books and figure out which ones you want to sell. I don't mind, but Jeanie's a little nutty about stuff lying around the basement. She's kind of a control freak. *Neat* freak, I mean. Don't tell her I called her a control freak, whatever you do."

"Never."

"Us bonding like this, two guys keeping secrets? It's fun, right?"

24
THE TEST

Flip and I trained all that night and then the next day after school at the park. Halley had to do some last-minute paperwork stuff with her mom to get the final okay from the Read to Rufus people that we could set up the program at the library, but she was definitely going to be with Flip and me for the test the next day, which was Rosh Hashanah, so no school. The test was at ten thirty, the last appointment available until November. I couldn't wait that long. The Read to Rufus people said the kids were psyched and ready to go, as soon as Flip passed the test.

I woke early that morning of Rosh Hashanah, of the test. I probably didn't sleep the night before either. I wore the shirt Leo gave me to make him happy. I brushed Flip so he'd look sharp for the test. Aunt Jeanie got her lint roller out and picked up the like two hairs that fell on the carpet before she went to work. I took Flip for a good long walk and fed him some cheddar bits. It was nine forty-five, and there was no sign of Leo.

I went to the bedroom door and knocked, and then I knocked louder. Nothing. I went in. Flip hung back in the hallway. "Thanks pal," I said.

Leo looked dead, except dead people don't snore so loud you feel like Darth Maul's jabbing your eardrums with a serraknife. I shook his foot, hard. "Leo? Leo!"

I sat on the edge of the bed. I guess I wasn't surprised. Expecting to be let down didn't make it hurt any less. Just when you think things are maybe going to be okay, why does everything have to get messed up?

I called Halley to tell her the bad news. She was pretty mad. She wanted me to take a pair of cymbals and smash them together right by Leo's ear, except who ever has any cymbals lying around? *"Okay, look, we're not going to be defeated,"* she said. *"Just get on the train and get over there. I have an idea."*

Halley was waiting for us out front. So was Mercurious. He must have come from teaching a magic class, because he was still in his sparkly purple sweat suit. He wore a glittery Brooklyn Cyclones baseball cap. Halley wore no cap. Instead she wore a bright pink wig, a short one, with the hair spiked up. She looked totally freaking awesome. "Um, that shirt," she said.

"I know," I said.

"'Caddy on'?"

"I have no idea either."

"Never mind. Let's do this."

We went in. "Huddle up," Halley said. The three humans held hands, and Flip stuck his paw in there too. "Coffin? You rock. Flip? You rule. Take no prisoners. I have no idea what that means. Whatever. Dad, any words for the boys?"

He mussed my hair. "Just remember this one thing," he said. "Okay?"

"You're magic."

The testing guy called out, "Ben Coffin?" His name tag said Mr. Thompkins. I said, "Thanks Mr. Thompkins," and stuck out my hand to shake his.

"For what?" he said, and he didn't shake my hand. "The examination shall commence in five seconds, four, three, two, one."

We had to pass nine things. Here's what they were.

1. GREET THE TESTER. Flip gave the guy his paw. Check.

2. STAY. I told him to, and then I walked away. He looked sort of totally suicidal and slumped to the floor, but he stayed. Bingo.

3. COME. Like he wouldn't?

4. IGNORE THE STRANGER. Some really mad-looking guy came in yelling about how somebody stole his bicycle. Flip checked him out until I said, "Flip, I got it." Flip kept his eyes on me. Halley mouthed "Nice!" and Mr.

Lorentz clapped until Thompkins said, "No encouragement allowed. *Thank* you." He did a double take on Mr. Lorentz's sparkly purple clothes.

5. VISIT A SICK PERSON. Thompkins sat in a wheelchair. "Go say hi, Flip." He went to the chair and leaned into the tester's leg.

6. STARTLE. Thompkins tried the old drop-the-aluminum pan trick. Flip yawned.

7. LEAVE IT. Puh-lease.

8. MEETING ANOTHER DOG. A German shepherd came into the room. Flip trotted up to her, sniffed her butt and then rolled over at her feet into the upside-down flying squirrel pose.

9. APPROPRIATE AFFECTION. Here it was, the one place we could fail. Thompkins sat on the floor and called Flip over. Flip sat at Thompkins's feet. "Flip, cuddle," I said. He nestled into the grump's lap. Just when I thought we were home free, Flip reached up to Thompkins's face and stuck his tongue in the old man's mouth. Thompkins made a *yuck* face. Halley and Mr. Lorentz looked like they were watching a ship sink.

Thompkins went to his desk and frowned while he wrote all over his stupid test sheet. He stamped it really hard and called me over. "I suppose the gentleman in the lavender exercise apparel is your sponsor?" he said.

"Yup."

He waved over Mercurious. "Sign here, please." Then he passed the paper to me and told me to sign it. This is what it looked like.

THIS LICENSE CONFERS TO HANDLER THE LEGAL RIGHT TO BRING THE THERAPY ANIMAL NAMED HERE INTO HOSPITALS, SCHOOLS AND ANY SUCH ESTABLISHMENTS WHERE THE ANIMAL'S GIFTS ARE NEEDED OR DESIRED.

HANDLER: BEN COFFIN

SPONSOR: MICHAEL LORENTZ

THERAPY ANIMAL: FLIP COFFIN

There was another page, a SPECIAL COMMENDATION. Thompkins wrote, *Mr. Coffin exhibits true grace with Flip. Rarely have I seen such genuine trust between man and dog. I expect this exceptional dog and his equally exceptional handler will go on to mend many hearts. The world is about to become a lovelier place.*

Halley put up her fist for a pound. I bumped her knuckles. "You *so* slay," she said. When I bumped Mercurious's knuckles, sparks shot up from his fist, but not like the Santa magician's sparks, the ones that came out of the magic box. Those were blood-colored, and Halley's dad's were pink and blue and softer, quieter, like a whisper instead of a scream.

Halley scooped up Flip and we went outside and then the craziest thing happened.

A pigeon's shadow raced up the side of a building and met the pigeon on the ledge, and *that's* when I cried, and so hard I thought my eyes might drip out of my head. I know, it was just some totally random thing that set me off, but it was really beautiful. Like even when the bird was darting about here and there so fast, all up in the air, her shadow was always with her, even though she couldn't see it. But when she landed, there it was, touching her again. This would have been the best day of my life if my mom was here to see it. I didn't say that to Halley and Mercurious, though, and I didn't need to. They hugged me and patted my back and didn't say "It's okay," and I really appreciated that.

25
THE LAUNCHPAD

The Lorentzes invited me and Flip over for Rosh Hashanah. "You'll eat so much you'll totally be puking all over yourself," Halley said.

"Sounds great," I said. I called Aunt Jeanie and she said no problem, because she was working late anyway. I didn't tell her Leo overslept, and I guess he didn't either, because she didn't say anything about it. I thought she forgot about the test, until right after I said bye, she said, *"Wait, how'd the dog do?"*

"He passed."

"Oh, that's wonderful, Ben. I was worried."

"Why?"

"Well, I just was. You know." I really didn't know. *"I'm sure Tess is proud of you, watching us from above. Right?"*

"Uh-huh."

"Very proud. Yes, you go and enjoy yourself now. Be polite and thankful."

"I will."

"Good. Good. Okay, good-bye."

The Lorentzes' apartment was nice, tons of books. The paintings were Halley's from when she was in pre-K until now. My favorite was this one of the planet Mercury. Her dad was standing on it. His arms pointed to the sky, and he waved a baton like he was conducting the stars.

Halley's room was wall-to-wall novels. She had every freaking edition of *Jane Eyre* ever printed, like one wasn't more than enough. Flip jumped onto her bed, and she jumped onto it after him while I checked out her books. "I read *Iron Man,* like you told me to," she said. "How is it that I, a sophisticated young woman with near paranormal intelligence, am totally crushing on a cheesy comic book character? You're having a spectacularly negative effect on my reading life."

"You're welcome," I said. "Let's keep working on the novella. What's the title, by the way?"

"I've been thinking really hard about this. Don't freak out. I want to call it *The Magic Box.*"

"Hm," I said.

"Ben, we're going to take the most negative thing in your life and turn it into the treasure you meant it to be."

"How?"

"Okay, it's like this: Bruce and Helen have slipped through

a crack in time, and now they're back in the old Luna Park, right? The one from 1905."

"*Dreamland at Night.*"

"Yupper. Mercurious tells Bruce and Helen there's only one way to survive their fall. They have to get to the exact moment before Helen decided to swing without the safety wires, and instead, she and Bruce will go to McDonald's and stuff themselves with Oreo cookie McFlurries and talk about their favorite books."

"Like, they get a do-over?" I said.

"Exactly."

"So how do they get from 1905 back to the minute before Helen jumped from the platform?"

"It turns out that the golden tower of light from 1905 is actually a spaceship."

"Love it," I said.

"Knew you would!"

"The spaceship is going to take Bruce and Helen to the Contessa of Starlight."

"Go on?"

"Yeah, see, she's the only one who knows how to get Helen and Bruce back to the right place in time, to where they can skip the whole trapeze thing and go for McFlurries instead. Problem is, she's really far away, the Contessa, on a different planet, doing the speech therapy thing."

"Of course. Which planet?" Halley said.

"It's not even in our solar system," I said. "It's hidden in a whole other star cluster. The secret to its location is in the library, of course. They'll need to head to the Branch for Interstellar Travel, which is the main attraction on Libris, a newly discovered moon of Neptune."

"I love Neptune. It's the most awesome shade of blue."

"Which is totally why I picked it," I said. "There they'll seek the guidance of—"

"Penny, Keeper of the Star Maps."

"Your mom's name is Penny? The women in your family have seriously good names."

"I know."

"Penny the librarian. Cool."

"Technically they're called media specialists."

"Technically I need applesauce if we don't want the latkes to taste like I burned them a little," Interstellar Media Specialist Penny Lorentz called to us from the kitchen. We went out and got the sauce and hurried back for the feast.

26
HALLEY'S RAP

The latkes were the size of waffles. We all snuck Flip pieces of brisket, which made no sense since everybody knew everybody else was sneaking. After dessert we played Scrabble for Cheez-Its and blue M&M'S. Mr. Lorentz started whistling a song from the musical *Man of La Mancha*, Halley told me. It was Mercurious's favorite apparently, and then Mrs. Lorentz started singing the words, and before you knew it we all were singing about this old man who never gives up, who keeps on keeping on no matter how bad things get, and then Halley said, "I feel a song coming on, a Halley Lorentz original if you please, oh yes I do."

"Then sing it," Mercurious said.

"Poppers, bass beat please," she said. He laid it down, like really getting into it with some serious head bopping, and then she said, "Okay that's actually totally adorably lame, but it will suffice." Then she rapped:

Got me a bestie, his name's Ben.

He can't see it, but he kills with the pen.

Poet don't know it, you've heard that before,

My boy's got stories, paste you to the floor.

He saved a dog, see, a friend to the end.

He saves me daily, Halley Lorentz.

How you heal me, you and mighty mutt Flip?

All's I can say is you make me feel hip.

Bad comes to worse, and you don't give in.

You don't mope or lose hope, you honor your kin.

You hustle those coupons come rain or shine.

You keep on keeping on in the toughest of times.

Rosh Hashanah means New Year, new wonder—
you'll see.

Mom and Mercurious, Flip, you and me.

She raised her glass of sparkling cider. "Shanah Tovah, everybody. Happy New Year. I'm so grateful that we're all here together."

Her mom patted my back and said quietly, "Yes, we're *all* here. We're *here*." She touched her fingertip to my heart. Then she messed up my hair the way Mom used to and kissed my forehead and hugged me and didn't let go.

Mercurious pointed to the window. A gold laser beam pulsed from his finger and hit the glass, and a silent explosion of fireworks lit up the sky over Brighton Beach and in the distance Luna Park. *Dreamland at Night.* I knew it was only video projection, but it was shiny and beautiful and I wanted it to be real. The rides were spinning and the lights whirled.

27

THE RINGSIDE SEAT

They drove me home in Mr. Lorentz's sparkly purple SUV, and the whole way there we sang *Man of La Mancha*, and then that turned into pop songs, then somehow Christmas carols—in September—and then Halley's song. Flip tried to sing along too. "He's halfway between howling and that warbling sound Gizmo makes in *Gremlins*," Halley said. The more we laughed at him, the more he did it.

The Mercurious-mobile pulled up to the house, and I pretended I wasn't the third saddest I'd ever been, having to get out of that car. The house lights were off, and the Lorentz family waited for me to get inside before they drove away. I clicked on the light and Flip whimpered. Leo was sitting on the couch—just sitting there, no TV, no iPad or music. I said hi and he shook his head. His eyes were glassy. "Jeanie's pretty mad."

"Why? What'd I do?" I said.

"At *me*. Why didn't you wake me up?"

"I tried, I swear."

"Then you didn't try hard enough," he said. He was talking funny, quiet, slow-motion. "I thought I hit snooze, but I hit off instead."

"It worked out anyway."

"For *you* it worked out," he said. "I look like the bad guy now. To her anyhow. Speak of the devil."

Aunt Jeanie came in with red wet eyes. "Hi," she said. She had a pretty wooden box under her arm, a little bigger than the one that triggered Kayla's asthma attack.

"What's in the box?" Leo said.

She did a double take on him. "How could you, Leo?" she said. "I can smell it from here. I'm *not* going through this again."

"For cripe's sake Jeanie, relax, it was one freaking beer."

"It *wasn't* one."

"You have to embarrass me in front of the kid?"

"You embarrass yourself."

"A guy can't even have a couple of drinks in his own house once every five years?" He got up and went to his office and shut the door and turned up the TV loud enough so we could hear it through the wall. Two wrestlers yelled about how they were going to mangle each other once they got into the ring. Aunt Jeanie sat on the couch and tried not to cry. "I'm sorry you had to see that."

"It's okay," I said.

"It's not," she said. "It's not."

I sat next to her. Flip shivered at my feet. I wanted to pick him up, but Aunt Jeanie had a rule of no dogs on the couch. She put the box on the coffee table. "Tess," she said.

"Oh," I said. "That's like . . ."

"Like what?"

"I don't know."

"I don't either," she said. "I really don't." She breathed in slowly and then breathed out fast and choppy and cried. I put my hand on her shoulder. "Thank you," she said. She held my hand for a second, squeezed it, and then put it on my lap and patted it and took her hand away. "It's late," she said. "You don't want to fall asleep in school tomorrow."

We were off for Rosh Hashanah again but I said, "Definitely not. Good night." I couldn't get away from those ashes fast enough. I forced myself not to run to my room. Flip stuck so close to my feet I was tripping over him.

"Ben?" she said. "I'm glad it went well today. With the dog, I mean."

"Thank you." I closed the door and then my eyes and I counted. I figured maybe I'd get to ten before it started, but it kicked in at six. I couldn't hear exactly what Leo and Aunt Jeanie were screaming at each other, but it was louder than the wrestlers.

Less than four years. That's how long we had to last before I'd be allowed to go live on my own, legally. I was a year ahead in school, and if I kept working really hard I could make up another one and graduate at sixteen. Flip and I would get the heck out of the city and tag along with Halley to the same college, and she and I would take the same English classes and become writing partners—except they probably didn't let you bring dogs into the dorm rooms.

28
ROCKS AND BOOKS

The next day was like the night before never happened. Leo and I went to Home Depot and bought bags of rocks and spread them out in the tiny yard. "It's a rock garden," he said. "I guess you figured that out. You're a good worker, running those coupon deliveries at the crack of dawn, helping me now."

"You too."

"I been at it a long time," he said. "I'll die working. You though, always studying the way you do, I think you just might make it."

"Make what?"

"Champ, you like golf?"

"Mini."

"That's not a crime. Yet. *Ha.* I can teach you how to play real golf, you know? Maybe we'll go to the driving range sometime." He farted and covered his mouth for some reason. "'Scuse me. I'll be back." He went in.

Jeanie came out with lemonade. "He's sick from the beer. Serves him right." She was looking at me like she wanted me to say something. I shrugged. She sat and patted the porch step for me to sit next to her. "I ordered an angel figurine online. It looks like marble but it's actually highly durable polyurethane. They make bowling balls out of this stuff. It'll be here tomorrow."

"That's, like, great," I said.

"Yes. Well, I'd like to bury her under it. Tess. Back here. I should have asked you first."

"Asked me what?"

"If you were okay with that. You know, burying her ashes."

"I never really thought about it," I said. "I guess we have to put them somewhere. Are you allowed, though? Like isn't there a law or something, that maybe she's supposed to go into a, you know, cemetery?"

"I don't think so. I just feel like she'll be closer to us this way."

"Right."

"You don't think so?"

"No, no, I do. It's nice, your plan."

"Good then?"

"Good, yeah."

"Great." She patted my back, and I could tell she was working hard not to lean away. "I can help you sort through those book boxes, if you want."

"I'll finish up today."

"Oh Ben, the dog looks like he's going to pee in the rocks. No, dog. Shoo. *Shoo*."

Halley came over to help me go through my books. Jeanie was at work and more importantly Leo was in Manhattan to see his foot doctor. Chucky kept texting me to send him a picture of Halley. "I keep seeing the word *butt* in that text stream," she said.

"You never told me why we're going to call the story *The Magic Box*," I said.

"It's like this: Tess is gonna help Bruce and Helen, but *she* needs their help too. The planet she's on? It's called Mundum Nostrum, and it's total war there. Tess is trying to get the Nostrumians to settle their differences by, hello, learning how to talk to each other again. See what I did there, working in the speech therapy?" She patted herself on the back. "This requires some serious magic, the kind Tess keeps in her totally gorgeous penthouse apartment back on Earth, in the top of the golden tower from Luna Park 1905, in this beautiful wooden box."

"So what's in the box?"

"Only the greatest treasure that has ever existed."

"An antigravity belt that lets you fly? A wearable technology that lets you be invisible?"

"You're such a *boy*. It's *so* much more awesome than

those." She dropped a pile of books on top of the To Go pile.

"Seriously, you're making me get rid of my *X-Men: First Class*?"

"Let somebody else enjoy it," she said. "Hey? You nervous?"

"About what?"

"Monday." She lit up that dingy basement with the biggest lopsided smile. Monday was our first Read to Rufus session with the little kids. "Flip, Flip, Flip, Flip, Flip!" She picked him up and spun around with him.

"Champ, that you down there?" Leo said. He limped into the basement.

"Hi, I'm Halley."

"Hi. Yeah, I thought that voice was a little high for Ben," Leo said. He stared a little too long at her pink wig.

"Well, I better get going," she said. "Gotta get home to help my dad with a show."

"What kind of *show*?" Leo said

"Magic act for a birthday party."

"Ah," Leo said.

"Very nice to meet you," she said. Her hand was tiny in his, but she gave a good shake.

Flip and I walked her to the train. When we got back, Leo said, "Tess didn't mind you hanging out with chicks like that?"

"Mom would have loved her," I said. "Besides, like what?"

"Forget about the pink dye job for now, in my day girls didn't cut their hair to look like boys. It's like she's trying to be in your face about it, you know what I mean?"

"No, I don't."

"She's purposely shocking people. She's drawing attention to herself. I'm doing it again, aren't I? Messing up. I'm only trying to look out for you here, champ. The people you let yourself be around? They're a reflection on *you*."

"Leo?"

"Yeah?"

Even his stupid shirt made me sick, not to mention totally confused me. It said: THREE! [I'M ALWAYS COMING UP A LITTLE SHORT.] All the synonyms for the word *idiot* lunged up from my stomach toward my throat, and they weren't about to get stuck in my heart this time. If I had anyplace else to live—anyplace at all—I would have called him every one of them too. "How's your foot?" I said.

29
READ TO RUFUS

Now I was glad to have my headphones back, even if Rayburn had worn them. I needed them to drown out Leo and Jeanie. They argued nonstop. That whole weekend they were going back and forth about Christmas vacation, Mexico again or Maine? I wondered if they were like this before Flip and I came into the picture. I didn't know what to do except stay in my room and study and tell myself that for every test I aced Flip and I were one step closer to getting out of Leo and Jeanie's. "Four years, Flip. Less than four. Three years, nine months and twenty days until I turn sixteen. We can hang in that long, right?"

He cocked his head and licked my lips. He was the best study partner. He really did love when you read to him. Monday morning I dropped him off at the Mold house. He looked a little sad as I left. "Come on now, Flip bud. You know I'll be back soon. I promise." As soon as he heard that, his tail started wagging again.

〜〜

Monday after school Chucky and I hustled over to the Mold house to pick up Flip. "Ronda Glomski told me Rayburn isn't holding up his end of that contract they made him sign," Chucky said.

"He's not going to the guidance counselor?" I said.

"Nobody knows where he is. My mouth hurts every time I think about him."

"Then don't think about him." That's what Mom would've said.

"I seriously hope he dropped out. Dude, for real, how lame is this Read to Rufus thing going to be? Worse than chess club?"

"Halley's gonna be there."

"Okay, I'll come."

We trotted into the library and right upstairs to where they were waiting: the Read to Rufus lady, Mrs. Lorentz, three kids, a bunch of parents, a teacher, and Halley.

"Cheez Whiz crust," Chucky whispered to me. "Nice butt. Not bad in the chestal area either, Coffin. I mean, they could be bigger, but well done just the same."

"Any thoughts about her *face*?"

"Huh? Yeah, that too." Only then did he notice her wig, which she'd dyed in spiky stripes of color. "Okay, you were right: She's seriously as cool as a rainbow."

Flip jumped into her arms. "Ben, this is Brian," she said.

"I'm seven," the kid said, like he'd fight me if I said otherwise, except he didn't look me in the eye. He was small for seven, and the book he had was *The Dog Who Wanted to Become a Boy*. "I picked it because I figured he'd like it better than *The Velveteen Rabbit*, which maybe he'd want to eat." He nodded to Flip, who cocked his head. "It isn't mine though, the book. It's from the liberry. They made me carry it." He held it away from himself as far as he could, like it was a bag of dog turds.

"I'll hold it for you," I said, "if you hold Flip for me for a sec."

Halley put Flip into his arms, and Flip licked half a smile into the kid's lips. "His breath smells okay," he said. "It's not like rotten milk that much."

We sat on the couch. "Who told you *The Dog Who Wanted to Become a Boy* is one of Flip's all-time favorites?" I said.

"Serious?"

"You know what he also loves, Brian? When you say his name. After you read a little, just say, 'Right, Flip?' Read him your favorite part."

The kid looked me in the eye, but just for a second. "Thing is, it's at the end. It's not a happy ending, but it kind of is too."

"Those are the kind Flip likes the most. Read it if you don't believe me."

The kid read, and Flip was all eyes on him. "'I wanted to

be hum . . . hummm . . . '" He whispered, "What's this word again?"

"Human," I said.

"'I wanted to be human, because then the girl co . . . co-uh-luh-d . . .' Tell me."

"Could. That one's tricky. You're doing so awesome."

"'I wanted to be human, because then the girl could understand me. She was my best fri . . .'"

"You're doing great, Brian," I said. "Just sound it out letter by letter."

"'Fri-een-d—friend'?"

"You're totally amazing. Flip wants to give you a knuckle bump. Right, Flip?"

The kid put out his fist and Flip bumped him. His voice got louder. "'She was my best friend, and I had to tell her that.' Right, Flip?" Flip cocked his head almost ninety degrees. "I think he really is listening to me," the kid said. "'I was getting older and would not be around much longer,' Flip." Flip bumped him again and licked the kid's nose. They forgot I was there. The kid read and read, and Flip was fascinated. "'She told me so many times, in so many ways, that she loved me, and I tried to say it back with cuddles and kisses. I tried so hard. But it was not the same. I wanted to say the words, just once, to say I love you, so she would know.'"

Flip did a wiggle worm into the kid's lap and rolled over for a belly scratch.

Everybody clapped, and the kid got embarrassed and hid his face in Flip's neck. I looked out and Chucky nodded and Halley winked at me. Mercurious was there. He was holding Mrs. Lorentz's hand, and he gave me the thumbs-up. A rainbow-colored flame grew from the tip of his thumb.

Brian closed the book, and Flip put his head in the kid's lap. "The dog never becomes a boy," Brian said. "He never gets to say the words."

"But you said it was a happy ending too," I said.

"Yeah. It's happy because the girl knows anyway. You can just tell. She knows how he feels about her."

30
THE NEXT INSTALLMENT
OF *THE MAGIC BOX*

We got takeout slices with Chucky, and then Halley said Mold had to scram. "Why?" Chucky said.

"Because you need to go rest your eyes after staring at my, ahem, *chestal* area nonstop for the last two hours."

"It wasn't the *whole* two hours."

"Go. Ben and I have to work anyway."

"On what?"

"Our story of *The Magic Box*."

"Why's it magic?" Chucky said. "What's inside? C'mon, tell me."

Halley elbowed me. "That's one copy sold anyway." We went to our bench by Luna Park. "When last we saw our time-traveling alter egos, Bruce and Helen were trapped in a snapshot of 1905 with Mercurious, in the top of the golden tower," she said.

"Except the tower is actually a golden spaceship," I said.

"Maybe it rises off the ground and floats onto its side like a blimp."

"Okay, we're totally doing it. One little problem: Tess and the people of Mundum Nostrum need the magic box ASAP. How do we get a blimp to travel faster than the speed of light?"

"Easy. You use a quantum vector slingshot made of a dark matter neutrino alloy. Add a roentgenium booster, and you're moving a hundred and eleven thousand times the speed of light."

"You have my full attention now. Please proceed."

"Mercurious has buckets of the stuff, and he helps Helen and Bruce fuel up the golden blimp. 'As much as I want to go with you,' he says, 'I can't leave the people of Coney Island stranded—way too many bar mitzvahs this month. Tess is sending me mind waves that put the location of Mundum Nostrum somewhere in the constellation of Canis Major, in the orbit of Sirius.'"

"The Dog Star!" Halley said, scooping up Flip. "Helen and Bruce will need a seriously awesome pilot to get them there. Who better to guide them to Sirius than the mightiest therapy dog in existence? Flip, smooshy face." He gave her one and got his tongue all the way up into her mouth. "Mercurious gives Bruce the magic box. 'Okay, Travelers,' he says."

"'Travelers,'" I said. "Nice."

"'I know you really, really want to know what's inside,' Mercurious says, 'but promise me you won't open it.'"

"Why?" I said. "Shouldn't Helen and Bruce know their cargo?"

"Not in this case. This treasure is so spectacularly unique that Bruce and Helen can't possibly understand its true worth—not until Tess shows them how to wield it. Just to be sure they don't peek, Mercurious locks the box with a key made from sparks, the kind that shine in people's eyes after they witness a good deed. There's only one other copy of the key in existence."

"And Tess has it. Drats." It was really fun watching Halley get into it. She paced and talked everything into her phone and kind of hopped around. Truth told, that was more fun than the story part, which was kind of lame. I mean, transporting a magic box from one planet to another? It was like in every other comic I read. But seeing the Rainbow Girl get all smiley as we thought it up together? That was seriously fresh.

"Ben Coffin, are you ready for the journey to begin? I warn you, it's uphill all the way."

"Like I'd go with you on a downhill one? Flip, set a course for the moon Libris and the map room of Penny the sooth-saying media specialist."

"Speaking of which, my phone's buzzing and, yes, it's totally Mom texting me to get my butt home to go to yoga with her. It's actually not that ew. There's a lot to be said for all this alternative medicine garbage. Namely that she takes me out for Strawberry Dream Donuts after."

"You have a seriously sweet tooth."

"Sweet tooth, sweet heart." She hugged me and pushed me away and went off laughing.

31
GINGER

Flip started shaking when we were two blocks away, and then I heard them—Jeanie and Leo—from two houses up the block. I didn't even go inside. I sat on the stoop. Flip burrowed into my hoodie pocket.

"You think the poor kid wants to be here either?" Aunt Jeanie said. "Nobody wanted it to be this way. He's my sister's kid."

"Ex*actly*," Leo said. "He was Tess's, not yours."

"He is, though. He's my responsibility. I promised."

"He thinks I'm a loser. He looks down on me. It's enough to make me want to start drinking again."

"No way, Leo. Uh-uh. You're not going to get away with that."

"With what?"

"Blaming Ben for your lack of self-control."

"It's *not* a lack of self-control. I can't help myself. It's a disease."

"Whatever it is, it isn't Ben's fault."

"The dog too. It's all too much. Too many moving parts. I like it simple."

"Everybody does, Leo. It just isn't, okay? When are you going to grow up?"

"We never used to be like this, babe. We never used to fight."

"Sure we did."

"Not like this, honey. Not like this."

I texted Aunt Jeanie.

> BC: My friend and I have a huge science project due tomorrow. Can I stay over at his house tonight to finish it up?

A second later Aunt Jeanie and Leo stopped arguing. She told him about my text. "Do you think Tess would let him sleep over at a friend's on a school night?"

"Are you kidding?" Leo said. "A night off. This is a gift."

Flip stopped shaking the second we turned the corner. My phone pinged with a text from Aunt Jeanie.

> JC: No problem. Good luck.

"I lost my key," I said.

"Where's your aunt?" Mrs. Mold said, pulling me inside the house. Flip trotted up to Ginger the cat and let her lick his ears. One of the girls fed him ice cream from her spoon.

"Mexico," I said. "They're on vacation."

"Coffin, I'm the mother of seven children. I can tell when

I'm not getting the truth. Eight children. When are they coming back from Mexico?"

"They'll be home late tonight, Mrs. Mold, I swear."

Chucky and I settled in to watch *Spider-Man*. One of the older girls ran in with a laptop and showed me a deodorant commercial from probably twenty years ago. The pretty woman sniffs her pits and dances around the kitchen and rose petals fall and birds sing. "It's Mommy," the girl said. "Wasn't she an awesome actress? You totally believe she smells terrific, right?"

"Charice, get out," Chucky said.

"I'm Charmaine."

"Whatever. Coffin, did you hear the latest about Rayburn?"

"Do I want to?"

"His mom threw him out. He's living at his cousin's, and the cousin's in the Mafia and he's killed like a thousand people and he's been to jail. You know that completely trashed house by the train station? That's where his cousin is. I give Rayburn a week before he gets locked up too."

"How do you know these things?"

"I like gossip and Angelina likes people to feel sorry for her, like woe is me, my idiot boyfriend's in trouble again, isn't life so unfair? Dude, I can't believe you feel bad for him."

"I didn't say that."

"You didn't have to."

"I better get to bed."

"We're not even halfway into the movie," Chucky said.

"I already saw it like ten times."

"So?"

Mrs. Mold gave me a Benadryl—a second one—and set me up on the couch in the basement. It was nice and quiet down there. I wondered if I could make myself like Leo. He wasn't that bad. Yes, I could do it. I would. I just needed to catch my breath first, to get a good stress-free night's sleep, to dream about an awesome future: Halley and me and Flip and Read to Rufus and *The Magic Box* and how even if it was only in a made-up story I was on my way to see my mom again, the Contessa of Starlight, and it all started to feel so real.

This really loud wheezy sound woke me just before sunrise. Both dogs were with me on the couch now. So was the cat. Good old Ginger was curled up practically on top of my head. The wheezy sound was me. I fumbled through the dark to find my jeans and my inhaler. It was empty.

32
HOW WAS MEXICO?

The emergency room wasn't too crowded. I heard Aunt Jeanie before I saw her. The clicks from her high heels echoed in the hallway. "I can't possibly thank you enough," she said.

Mrs. Mold waved her off. "Coffin's an angel. How was Mexico?"

Aunt Jeanie cocked her head, and I read her mind: Why are you asking me about a trip I took a year ago? "Bliss," she said. "Have you been?"

"Can't say I have." Mrs. Mold gave me a hard look, then she pecked my forehead. "Well, I'd better get a move on. The Nightgown Nightmares run roughshod over Charles. That's the name of their karaoke band."

Aunt Jeanie filled out the paperwork while I finished inhaling the medicine from the nebulizer. "Stay home and rest," the doctor said. That's the last thing I wanted to do. The medicine made me jumpy. Half an hour later we were in the car. "Can we swing by Chucky's to pick up Flip?"

"I'm prepared," Aunt Jeanie said. The backseat was wrapped in a gray blanket. "Ben, how are you feeling?"

"Better. The medicine always helps."

"No, I mean about everything. You know, living with Leo and me."

"Good."

She looked at me and then back at the road. "I think that was the most unconvincing 'good' imaginable. Come on now. It's just us here. How are you feeling?"

"Like I'm messing you guys up," I said.

She pulled the car over and held my hand for a little bit. "I can't have you feel that way, okay?"

"Okay."

"It's going to take some time."

"I know."

"I feel awful for you."

"I don't want you to, though."

"I want to help you. Leo does too. We're all adjusting. It's a learning curve, right? I'm completely thrown, Ben. Tess was so easy about everything. The worst things could happen, and she smiled right through them. I miss her so much, you know?"

"I know."

"I looked up to her. I wanted to be her. But I couldn't. She was always so pie in the sky, and for me it was always, I better have the raincoat handy. I don't want that to be true, but it is. *I'm* messing *you* up."

"No. You got stuck with me."

"Will you stop *saying* that? Please, all right? I'm going to be better. I promise. We'll keep each other's spirits up, okay? You and me. And Leo too. We're all still reeling, right? Things will get better. We just need time to pass. It'll work out fine. I really think it will."

"Okay," I said. "Okay. It'll work out."

"Yes." She wiped her eyes and got herself together. "We'll get the dog now, and then I'll make you some homemade soup. I'd very much like to do that for you. Now, connect your phone to the stereo and play me your favorite music."

I played her this rap ballad Mom loved, full of banjos and trumpets that got her singing along and up out of her chair and dancing, and she'd get me going too, and we swung each other around. The chorus went:

> What's your worry, what's your hurry,
> where you running off to?
> Stay a while, dance up a smile,
> remember we're free to be true.
> We're free. We're always. We're you and me.

I was so happy remembering her, the way Mom laughed loud when she danced like that, and then I looked over to Jeanie and she was crying again.

33
THE MYSTICAL MANHATTAN
BOOKSTORE TOUR

Leo was still asleep when Aunt Jeanie and I got back to Cypress Hills. "Poor guy was up all night packing boxes for an early UPS pickup," Aunt Jeanie said.

"Mine are ready to go too," I said. "My books, I mean."

"Fabulous. We'll drive them to Strand as soon as you're feeling better."

"I feel terrific, really," I said.

"No, rest. Soup's on the way."

I sat out on the back porch with Flip. The fake marble angel had arrived. Its face was—shocker alert—weepy. I called Halley. *Why are you home on a school day?* she said.

I told her, and she wanted to bring me chocolate-covered pretzels. "I can't sit still," I said. "Let's go into the city."

The Mercurious-mobile pulled up to the house. We loaded the book boxes into it. "Ben, are you sure you're up for all this activity?" Aunt Jeanie said.

I felt like dancing. Halley's wig that day was gold with pink leopard spots. Leo came outside with some serious bed head. Mercurious put out his hand. "Mike Lorentz."

"Right, right. Leo Petit." He wiped his hand on his sweat shorts and shook. "I would have done this. Driven Ben, I mean, to the bookstore. I feel bad now. Can I get you a beer? Actually, I, we're out of beer. We have plenty of coffee, though."

"I think the sellback desk closes at one," I said. I had no idea when the sellback desk closed.

"I see," Leo said. "I see. Well, thanks, Mark. Thanks for helping out champ here, I guess."

"I'd love to take you up on that drink another time, Leo," Mercurious said. "We all should get together for dinner."

"That sounds nice," Aunt Jeanie said.

Mercurious helped us load the books into Strand, and then he was off to the Museum of Natural History to talk with the parents of this kid who was having his bar mitzvah party there the next week. The clerk opened the boxes. "You took good care of these," he said. "We'll have an estimate for you by five or so."

We went to Mickey D's and got shakes and a burger for Flip. Halley only had two sips and gave me the rest of her shake, and I was completely messed up with a sugar rush. "Okay, so how's this for the next installment of *The Magic Box*?" I said. "Flip pilots the golden blimp toward the moon Libris without incident."

"He's an expert guide dog, duh." She took back her milk shake and gave some to Flip. His head disappeared into the cup.

"Flip docks the blimp to the antenna on top of the Branch for Interstellar Travel, where Penny is waiting with a dish of Chips Ahoy! of course."

"How much do you love my mom? She's the total Queen of Cookies."

"She whisks Helen, Bruce, and Flip into the star map room and rolls out a chart that goes from one end of the library to the other. Flip trots over it, sniffing one route and then another, until he finds the one he wants and marks it off with two scratches that make an X. Penny looks really worried. 'Flip has chosen the fastest route, but also the most dangerous,' Penny says. Turns out the route goes smack-dab through the Rayburn Belt."

"It has to be done," Halley said. "'However,' Penny says, 'I'm less worried about the nefarious warlock zombie overlord Rayburn than I am the danger you present to yourselves. Promise me you won't peek into the magic box until you get to Mundum Nostrum.'"

"It's that scary, what's inside?" I said.

"That *powerful*."

"Wow."

"Totally."

The manager came over. "Excuse me, kids, but you can't have the dog in here."

"He's a therapy dog," Halley said.

"It's okay," I said. "We'll go."

We went out. "You need to stand up for your rights," Halley said, "not to mention Flip's."

"Let's do a bookstore tour," I said. "Book people love dogs."

"We're selling back all your books and now you want to buy new ones. This makes perfect sense."

"Me and my mom used to do like four a Saturday."

"Let's start at McNally Jackson," Halley said. "It's mystical in there."

"Mystical?"

"The air's buzzy, like when you're watching a lightning storm that's far away and can't hurt you but it lights up the whole sky pink with violet curls." We went to the sci-fi section and sat on the floor, back-to-back, and read while this little boy pet Flip.

"Ha, I got you to like *I, Robot*," I said.

"It's purely research for *The Magic Box*," Halley said. "This is the price I pay for having a writing partner with spectacularly undeveloped reading tastes."

Next we went to Broadway, to the Scholastic bookstore. There was a huge painting of Clifford the Big Red Dog. Flip whined to climb out of the backpack. At Books of Wonder, Peter, the guy who ran it, knew both of us. "And I often thought you should know each other," he said. "When it comes to book lovers, destiny is reality." He treated us to snacks at the Birdbath Bakery. Halley had two bites of chocolate muffin and gave me the rest. At Barnes & Noble Union Square she bought her dad sparkly purple reading glasses. The last stop was Housing Works. "Everybody who works here's a volunteer," Halley said. "They give all the money to people who are HIV positive or have AIDS, and especially to those who're homeless. Ben, we're so lucky."

"That's what Mom used to say. This was her favorite." We went to the checkout desk. "Coffin for a pickup," I said to the clerk. I'd called it in the week before.

"Let me guess," Halley said. "*Star Wars IV, A New Hope*, to replace the *three* copies we just dropped off at Strand."

The clerk handed me *Feathers*. I handed it to Halley. Her eyes widened on the yellow sticker on the cover: SIGNED COPY.

Halley Lorentz screamed so loud the store went quiet. "OMG! *She* held this book. *I'm* holding this book. It's like I'm holding Jacqueline Woodson's hand! Flip, total knuckle bump! Ben Coffin, you are the most seriously amazing human being ever!" We went to the café and took turns reading parts we liked, and then she got to the line about the special moments. "'Moments that stay with us forever and ever.' And there's that face again," she said.

"That's the one line I don't like," I said.

"Of course you do."

"It's a lie. You can't go back."

"But *The Magic Box*, the time travel to the past—"

"Is a story, fantasy. I'm talking about science now. Everything vanishes. It has to. That's how time works. My mom's gone, okay? The sooner I accept that, the fact I'll never see her again, the sooner I can move on."

"You can see her every time you close your eyes and think about her."

"But she's not *there*. Not *here*. She's ashes under a fake marble angel in a little yard in Cyprus Hills. That's it. That's all that's left of her."

"No. Please. I can't think that way. I can't have *you* think that way. I really, *really* need you to believe that we're forever." Her face was scrunched and red and wet.

She was freaking me out. One minute she's laughing and the next she's crying like somebody died. That's when it hit me. You don't tell a friend who's between chemotherapy treatments that you don't believe life goes on forever somehow, some impossible, non-scientific way. No, you be a good friend, and you lie. "Look, I wasn't thinking right," I said. "I was feeling sorry for myself and got messed up there for a second. Truth told, I *do* believe. Halley, seriously, I do."

"You don't, though. You don't." She held Flip close, and he licked her eyes. She put him in my lap and got up. "I better head on home."

"Sure, no problem. Let's go."

"Alone, Ben. I need to think, okay?"

"Halley—"

"No." She put her hands on my chest to stop me from following her. An old guy said to her, "Is he bothering you?"

She got on the bus and pushed into the crowd and I couldn't see her anymore.

34

THE DUMBEST THING
I EVER DID

I called but she wouldn't answer. I texted her and got nothing back. Now I really understood how she felt when I didn't reply to the texts she sent those days leading up to my mom's funeral. Then my phone did beep. It was Strand.

The store was crowded now, and I felt a little dizzy waiting on line to pick up the money. Flip yipped at me and put up his paw and cocked his head. He did a little dance that made everybody laugh, except me. When it was my turn at the counter, the man handed me six hundred dollars. "We gave you top price, I promise," the guy said. "The books were in excellent shape overall. You averaged around a dollar fifty each. You had just about four hundred volumes there. What, you think they were worth more?"

"No, the money's great," I said. "Thanks. It's a lot more than I thought I'd get."

"Then why do you look so . . . ?"

"So what?"

"Like somebody just socked you in the face?"

I was so messed up, I took the wrong train, my old one, to where I used to live. I didn't realize my mistake until the last stop when everybody got off. I got off too. I needed to walk around outside where there was more light.

Flip and I went to the boardwalk. His tail wasn't up and wagging the way it usually would be on a nice day, when we were walking by the beach. My sadness was getting into him. This man in a wheelchair was coming from the other direction. He had two beggars cups and no legs. He was telling me some story about why he needed money, but I wasn't really listening. I was too busy staring into his eyes. He looked really familiar, but I just couldn't figure out from where. I gave him fifty bucks. That was how the guy at Strand paid me, all fifty-dollar bills.

The man in the wheelchair looked at the bill, then he looked at me, and then he looked up to the sky and howled and said, "Woohoo!" He did a wheelie and spun around and said to anybody who'd listen, "Now *this* kid is an angel! Seriously. This kid has true power. This young man *understands*, okay? He has wisdom. Man, you're a gift, okay? You and that beautiful dog. You made my day, little brother. You made my day. It's not the money, I swear. It's your heart. Bless you.

This is everything, man. This is everything." That's when I knew who he reminded me of. Mom. Same eyes, filled with laughing, even during sad times, when she made me give that crummy old dollar to the woman who had sold Flip. I'd said it was nothing, just a lousy buck, but she made me look into her eyes and hear her when she said it was everything.

This man in the wheelchair was a magician for sure. He made me feel like maybe my mom's spirit was still around, traces of her. He made me feel good. Flip too. His tail was up and whipping around. I needed to keep feeling this way, that maybe the beautiful moments in your life, the people you love really can live forever. All you have to do is remember them, like Halley said.

I found somebody else on Neptune Avenue, an old woman pushing a shopping cart full of blankets and a ripped plastic bag filled with clothes. She didn't flip out like the man in the wheelchair when I gave her fifty dollars, but she was just as happy, I'm pretty sure. She was missing teeth, but she smiled like she didn't care. Her laugh was pretty, like a song you can dance to.

A woman in the deli was going to have to put some food back because she didn't have enough money, until I gave her fifty dollars.

The hot dog vendor in front of the aquarium didn't have any business and looked pretty hopeless until I bought franks for me and Flip and told him to keep the change.

I'd given away all but one of the fifty-dollar bills. I figured I'd keep the last one and put it with the money I was saving up from my coupon deliveries, for when I turned sixteen and I could live on my own.

Except I wouldn't be following Halley up to college anymore. All that lightness I'd felt that last half hour, giving away the money, was gone now.

I was about to get back onto the train when I remembered what Chucky told me, that Rayburn was living just down the street with his cousin. I turned around to look back to the end of the block. "What do you think, Flip?"

Flip cocked his head.

The house was even worse than Chucky said. It was more than beat-up. Half the windows were broken. The little front yard was weeds and garbage. Flip looked at me like, Are you sure you want to do this?

I went to the door and knocked. This guy with slicked hair and no shirt answered, even though it wasn't warm that day. There weren't any lights on in the house, and sheets over the window blocked out the sun. The house smelled like rotten food. The guy nodded, like, What do *you* want?

"Damon around?"

"Damon!"

Rayburn was squinting when he came to the door. The

sun was low and bright in his eyes. He rubbed them, like he couldn't believe it was me. "Coffin?"

He looked bad. Really bad. He looked smaller than I remembered, shorter, thinner—and dirty. His hair was all greasy. I gave him that last fifty-dollar bill, knowing the second the money left my hand that it wouldn't feel anything like it did when I gave away the other bills.

He looked at the bill, then at me. "What's your problem, man?" he said. "What are you doing here?"

When I was walking up the steps to the house, I was thinking that if there was a heaven, and my mom was looking down, she would be proud of me. But now she just felt so far away. It all felt bad now, even when I gave away the other fifty-dollar bills, like I'd bought people into being happy, into making me feel good. Still, I gave it a shot with Rayburn. "I heard you were having a hard time," I said. I headed down the steps.

His cousin came out and said, "What's up? Problem out here?"

"Dude just gave me fifty bucks," Rayburn said.

"Why?"

"That's what I said."

"Maybe he's got a crush on you. That little dog, man. That's a girl's dog. Hey, why'd you give my boy Damon fifty bucks?"

I was moving faster now, heading for the front gate. It

was lopsided and dragged on the concrete and hard to open. Another guy was out there now, also no shirt, lots of tattoos. They started calling me names, I probably don't have to say which ones. One of the guys threw half a sandwich at me. Flip and I ran, and they were laughing really loud now. I looked back over my shoulder, and Rayburn was laughing too. He couldn't look weak in front of his boys. He cursed me, but his heart wasn't in it, I could tell. His eyes were wet, like he was going to cry. He looked mad, then sad for a second, then mad again, like he remembered he wasn't allowed to be nice. I was mad too. Mad at myself. How could I be so stupid? I really was losing it. Losing everything, my mind, my money. Losing everyone.

35

THE FAKE MARBLE ANGEL

I saw Leo from outside the house. He was on the phone, pacing in the kitchen. I didn't bother to go in. I took the alleyway into the backyard and sat on the rock next to the fake marble angel. Her eyes had no pupils, I noticed now. Leo came out. His shirt and shorts were all sweaty. "Went for a run," he said.

I nodded.

"Jeanie's still out there," he said. "Yeah. So how'd you do? You make out okay with the books? You didn't let them rip you off, did you?"

"They paid me fine."

"Good. A man makes money, right? Attaboy." He slapped my back as he walked past me. He bent to pull a weed from a crack in the patio. Flip slinked away from him, toward me. Leo stood up and turned toward the weed bucket right when Flip was sneaking behind him. Leo stepped on Flip's foot, Flip yelped. Leo hopped to get off Flip's paw and tripped over a crack in the concrete. He put out his hands to break his fall, but like I said, Leo was a big guy. He landed hard and cursed. "I think he broke my wrist," he said. I tried to help him up but he pulled away. "Get off me," he said. He looked at his wrist. "If it's broken, I'm gonna be mad."

"I'm sorry, Leo," I said.

"Really mad." His eyes landed on Flip. "Stupid dog!" Then he kicked Flip—hard too. Very hard. Hard enough that Flip flew from where Leo kicked him, into the fence. Flip yelped and then staggered and sat and panted and whimpered. He was shivering when I picked him up.

"I can't believe you just did that."

"Stupid little rat!"

"He didn't mean it," I said.

"You can't train him not to be in the way all the time?"

"He weighs like ten pounds," I said. "You could have killed him."

"Stop with the drama, will ya? He's *fine*. Look at him. Freakin' dog." He rotated his wrist. "Ah that kills. Yeah, I think it's broken."

"You wouldn't be able to move it around like that if it was," I said.

"Excuse me, what'd you say?"

"Freaking idiot."

"*What?*"

"Nothing."

"Where do you get it into your head that you can speak to

me that way? I open my house to you, and this is how you talk to me?"

"I said I was sorry, okay?"

"No, not okay. What'd you just call me?"

"It slipped."

"Let it slip again. I need to hear it, just to be sure I heard what I think I heard. Hey, I'm talking to you!"

Him being so mad, well, it got me even madder. I practically yelled it. "I said you're an *idiot.*"

And that's when it happened. Leo swung out at me with a big, meaty, open hand, the one connected to his supposedly broken wrist. He slapped me across my face hard enough to make my head whip to the side. My cheek stung and then went numb. Everything got really still, really quiet. The only thing I heard was the birds. A crow, I think, across the street in the park, and then maybe a sparrow or whatever it was, tweeting high-pitched.

I guess his wrist really wasn't broken. He wasn't rubbing it anymore. He ran his hands through his hair, pulling at it a little. He looked scared. Maybe as scared as I was. All I had to do was call the cops, and they'd pull me out of there fast. Yup, I'd be on my way to foster care. That was the problem: They didn't let you bring pets into the foster homes. Flip would be taken to the dog pound. He buried his head in my armpit and trembled so bad I thought he was having a seizure.

I scooped up the dog carrier backpack and went into the

house, into my room, and got my money sock, which had nine dollars in it because I gave the rest to Aunt Jeanie to put in the bank for me. I grabbed the little picture of me and Mom from the beach that day. I was trying to stuff the bigger one of Laura into the backpack when Leo came in.

"Champ," he said.

I grabbed Flip and the backpack and pushed past Leo and ran, but I had to go back to get my stupid inhaler. Leo was following me around, desperate. He kept saying, "Champ, please, we have to talk about this. Hang on just a minute now," and you bet I didn't. Flip and I were *gone*.

36
THE MOBILE MOTEL

The texts started coming in from Aunt Jeanie. Please come back *to the house*. We're waiting for you *at the house*. We'll be *in the house* expecting your call. She never used the word *home*. I checked for a text from Halley. Nope. I disabled my location tracking. This hacker kid in one of the foster homes taught us how to do it. He was always running away, and he was good at staying hidden until he ran out of money or got sick. The cops were definitely going to try to trace me when Aunt Jeanie called them, which eventually she would have to. That's when Leo would have to tell her he hit me. I didn't want him to go to jail or anything, but no way was I going back there. No way. What a mess.

The sun set, and the air up by the park got cold fast. Flip and I got on the bus, and I held him too close, even though he didn't try to squirm away. I was shaking really bad, and that got him shaking worse. I tried to stop thinking about how I couldn't do anything right, that maybe it was good

Mom wasn't around anymore. This way she wouldn't see how bad I messed everything up—and everyone, Jeanie and Leo, Halley most of all.

I was so freaked, I started to wheeze. I had to take three shots off my inhaler. It was hard to hold the medicine in my lungs, like you're supposed to for a few seconds, before you breathe it out, because I was crying, like the kind of crying where you're so panicked that your heart is beating faster than when you're sprinting. Except you're not sprinting. You're just sitting there, realizing, seeing your life for what it really is, a mistake. It had to be, feeling so bad like this. That's when it all started to hit me, that Mom was dead. I mean, I knew she was gone, but now I *really* knew. She was in fact totally and absolutely nowhere, Tess Coffin. Because if she was *some*where, she wouldn't let me and Flip be in such a bad way. Somewhere like an intersecting dimension, where maybe she could whisper the right words into my mind and tell me what to do. I'd felt lost at some of the foster homes I was in, but never like this. Now I had zero protection, and worse than that, how the heck was I supposed to keep Flip safe? I just didn't know where to go.

I clicked up a video of Mom. She was in the supermarket, trying all the cheese samples, acting all fancy with a fake British accent. "*Now this one has a* weighty *flavor. Do try one, luvvy.*" And she got that sad old lady in the hairnet to crack half a smile. Then I clicked through pictures of Halley and me, selfies she took and texted to me, and our foreheads are touching, and Flip's in every one of them. And then I stopped looking. I shut my eyelids so tight they hurt. I tucked Flip inside my hoodie, and pretty quickly he stopped shivering and poked his head out from the hood and licked my neck.

Somebody shook my shoulder. The bus driver. The bus was pulled over and empty. "It's midnight," she said. She was holding Flip. "He had to pee. I took him out."

"Sorry," I said.

"Lucky it was me and not somebody else. They would have taken him out and kept right on going with him. He know any tricks?"

"Flip, surf."

He surfed her lap and kissed her. "I want you to sit up close, by me," she said. "It's very late. I'm supposed to call the police, but I won't."

"I'm—"

"I know," she said. "I know." She gave me half of a foot-long hero from Subway. I shared the turkey with Flip. She had a bottle of water for me too, and Flip lapped it up from my palm. She put her hand on my forehead and said, "I know," and then she got back to driving. The city passed by the windows. All the lights. The people in the windows of the apartment buildings just doing normal stuff, watching TV, cooking. The people in cars. They all seemed to be leaning forward a little too much. Time slowed down until I thought it just might stop for real. If I didn't have Flip to take care of, I wouldn't have cared if I lived or died, and I was sure nobody else would have either, not really, not anymore.

At one a.m. another driver came on board. The nice driver talked softly to him. She pointed to the left side of her face, the same side where Leo slapped me. The other driver kept shaking his head. He took out his phone, and that's when I got off the bus, and Flip and I ran. When we were clear of the bus I stopped to look at my face in a car window. It wasn't that bad. My lip was a little puffy, and you could see red where his hand went across my cheek—nothing too crazy. In a day or so it'd all be gone. Except it would never be gone, not for Leo either probably.

We went to the Long Island Rail Road waiting room. It was big and I remembered from the times when me and Mom took the train back to Brooklyn from the mall that lots of people slept there. I figured Flip and I would be safe enough until I could figure out what to do, but I couldn't and we weren't. Some creep sat next to me. "You hungry?"

"No."

"I see. Sure. Then maybe you need a place to stay tonight?"

"No." I looked for a cop, and then I remembered I couldn't let one see me.

The creep smiled and nodded. "I like your dog. May I pet it?"

I tucked Flip under my arm and got out of there, and the guy followed and kept saying, "Wait. Hey, wait," and I ran. Yup, Mom was dead for sure.

37
FLIP'S EYES
AND THE LAST GOOD-BYE

I went up the Molds' porch steps and sat on the top one and put Flip in my lap so we could see into each other's eyes. I saw my reflection in his, and I was all warped. "You'll be safe here, boy. That's all I want, even if I can't be with you. You'll be happy." It was cold and he was trembling so bad now. I hugged him one last time and tied him to the door. He cocked his head, and I know he was waiting for me to say it. The thing I said every time I dropped him off at the Molds'. That I was coming back. That I promised. I turned away fast, and he barked, and I ran to the corner and called Chucky.

"*Coffin, what the freak? You know what time it is?*"

"Chucky, you hear Flip, right? He's downstairs. Let him in. Bye."

"*Ben, wait—*"

I did wait too, until he came down and picked up my dog.

He looked around the street, but I was hidden pretty good between the cars. Flip saw me, though. His eyes were on me and he was barking like crazy as Mold brought him in.

I went around the corner and puked and sank down against the side of a building behind a stupid dumpster again. My head ached. I just needed to close my eyes for a minute and catch my breath, except I fell asleep.

38

THE WORST TIME
TO GET THE FLU

It was hot when I woke up, way too hot for fall. It was like in the middle of summer. The street stank from all the garbage bags out at the curb. The sun wasn't too high yet, but the air was like it got late in the afternoon, no breeze. The sunlight was way too bright. Everything glowed mean. I pushed myself up from behind the dumpster and went to the corner. I peeked around it to see the Mold house. The curtains were pulled back, but nothing was happening in the windows. The avenue was busy with school buses and delivery trucks rushing around—the traffic was loud, lots of horns and sirens.

I waited until Mrs. Mold came out with one of the girls. She put her on the bus. Flip came out and slumped down on the porch. Mrs. Mold limped up the porch steps and sat and pet Flip. His tail flicked a little. He'd be okay in a few days, I was pretty sure. That made me feel good, and good and lonely too. Mrs. Mold scooped him up and kissed him and took him in.

My stomach twisted up again. I didn't puke this time. I had to eat. I went up the avenue to Dunkin' Donuts and got a sandwich and iced tea, and after that I only had four dollars left. The lady at the counter was looking at me weird. "You okay?"

"Yeah, why?"

She gave me a hot tea with lemon and a bunch of napkins. "Clean yourself up. Your nose is running."

How could I have a cold on such a hot day? But she was right. My nose was a mess. I was shivering a little too, and the air conditioner made it worse. I went out to the street and looked for a quiet place to eat. It must have been a hundred degrees out there. I caught sight of myself in a store window. I looked rough, like I'd slept outside, which of course I did. My hair was greasy and plastered to my head, and my clothes were grimy and wrinkled and soaked with sweat. One of my eyes was pink and puffy the way it can get when you have a fever. It would pass. I didn't get sick often, and if I did, it was never that bad, or this bad. I stopped to take a bite of sandwich but, even though I was starving, the thought of eating made me want to hurl. I walked for a while, and I kept bumping into people. I was having a hard time keeping my head up. I made my way to the boardwalk, to our spot—mine and Halley's and Flip's—except it wasn't our spot anymore. An old man was sleeping on the bench. Luna Park was stock-still, empty. The beach was empty too, with everybody at work and school, I figured.

I went down to the sand and sat in the shade under the boardwalk. Boy, I was really shivering now I couldn't even get myself to nibble the sandwich crust. The smell of it made me retch. Yup, I was sick for sure—the kind of sick you can't cure on your own. The kind you need to go to a doctor for. I fed the sandwich to the seagulls, and then I curled into myself and hoped nobody found me before I died, because then they would call the cops, and they would take me to the hospital and I'd get better, and then what would I do? Where would I go? I didn't want to be anywhere anymore. Not without Flip. Without Halley.

Except suddenly I wasn't without Halley. She was shaking my shoulder. "Get up, Coffin." She looked awesome, like she did the first time I met her, way back nine months ago, over winter break. Her wig this morning looked like her real hair, long and loopy, light brown. She was kind of tanned too. She held my hand and her fingers were nice and warm.

"How'd you find me?" I said.

"I'm always keeping an eye out for you. Hey? You can't give up. We have to finish our novella."

"We're friends again?"

"Like we ever weren't? I have to make sure you get to see what's inside the magic box, right? The Greatest Treasure. You're so close to figuring it out, Ben. You just have to keep going. It's right around the corner. We have to get you all better. The Read to Rufus kids are depending on us. We can't leave Brian hanging. Right, Mom?"

"You'll break his heart, Ben," Mrs. Lorentz said, hurrying up to us. "Mine too. You poor baby. Come here, sweetheart. Let me check your temperature." She brushed back my hair and kissed my forehead and said, "You're burning up. Here, let me hold you." She hugged me and held me the way she did at Rosh Hashanah, when she didn't let go. She rocked me a little and hummed some lullaby or other, the way Mom did that one time when I got sick last winter. Halley joined in too, hugging and humming. There we were, the three of us, in the shadow of the boardwalk, holding each other really tight, and we were safe. The vibrations from their humming went into me, and I felt buzzy and better, and I would have smiled if I didn't feel so bad about Flip. "He'll be mad I gave him up," I said.

"Oh, he could never be mad at you, Ben," Mrs. Lorentz said. "He loves you no matter what. Look."

Flip was pawing at my leg, begging me to scoop him up. "I've never seen his tail wag so fast," I said. "I don't even think that's humanly possible, right? Not humanly. You know what I mean."

But they didn't. They couldn't. Halley and Mrs. Lorentz were gone. The waves were frozen still. There wasn't any movement anywhere—the seagulls hung midair, and their wings weren't flapping. They weren't squawking. There was no sound. Nothing. Everything was fading away, the heat, the light, and I was alone, and it was cold and dark and silent, except for one thing, Flip's whimpering. And it wasn't fading either. It was getting louder. So loud I could have sworn that little mutt was crying right in my ear.

I woke up where I'd passed out, behind the dumpster. Flip crawled into my armpit, and he was licking my face like I was ice cream. I opened my eyes wide, and it was still night. My phone was buzzing with half a dozen texts from Chucky.

CM: Flip got out. Get back here and help me find him.

I looked around the corner. Flip had dug through that cardboard Dr Pepper box taped to the hole in the peekaboo window that ran alongside the Molds' front door.

I texted Chucky not to worry, that Flip was here with me, and he was. He really was.

39

COUPONS, MOVIES AND PROMISES

Flip and I went to the all-night McDonald's and split a burger. Then I bought a toothbrush and some water from the all-night drugstore. The people who were out at this hour all looked like me and Flip. They looked suspicious, like they were expecting something bad to happen any old minute now.

I went to where I picked up my coupons and brushed my teeth in the alley. The sun started to come up and Flip and I huddled and waited. My boss showed up in his van. "Earlier than usual today, Coffin. You don't look so good."

"Thanks boss."

"You all right?"

"Could I borrow ten dollars?"

We delivered the coupons, and Flip was his old self, trotting right alongside me, head high. Every time I looked at him, he did a little spin and nipped at my sneaker. Then it was more

McDonald's until the movie theater opened. "Shouldn't you be in school?" the guy at the ticket window said.

"I homeschool."

"They let you watch *Planet of the Apes* for class these days, huh? You have it pretty good."

"Don't I know it," I said. School. It was the last thing on my mind. The bullying, eating lunch under the stairs, Angelina's stupid tricks, gum in the water fountain, Ronda's shoves—they all seemed so *nothing* now, so far away, as far away as the idea of going to college with Halley or going to school at all anymore. I was becoming one of them, the kids who disappeared.

Once I settled into the back of the theater and the lights went down I snuck Flip out of the backpack and he slept inside my hoodie. I set my phone to buzz me awake a little before the movie ended, and then I snuck into another movie and did the same thing, and then another after that, until three o'clock, and then we had to go. Even if Halley wasn't into being friends with me anymore, I wasn't about to let down Mrs. Lorentz. I was going to keep my promise.

40
TRAVELER BRIAN
AND THE TUNNEL OF LIGHT

"Ben, my Ben, what happened to you two?" Mrs. Lorentz said. "Those bags under your eyes. You look like you haven't slept in a month. What's that mark on your cheek?"

"How's Halley?"

"She was up crying all night. You didn't answer my question. That Rayburn character Halley told me about—did he hit you again?"

"It was a stop sign."

She folded her arms and frowned. "A stop sign?"

"I'm so embarrassed. I was looking at my phone while I was walking, and I walked right into the stop sign pole." I saw somebody do that once. "Aren't they waiting for us upstairs?"

They were too, the whole Read to Rufus gang, everybody except Halley. Flip gave out knuckle bumps and jumped up into Brian's lap. I had to keep this going, Flip and Read to

Rufus. It was the only thing that felt good now. The only thing that felt right. "What story are you going to read to Flip today, Bri?" I said.

"I forgot to pick one."

I reached into my backpack. It was my last book, the one Halley had left on the table at Housing Works.

"Fee, *Feathers*?" Brian said.

"You're awesome. This is another one where the ending is sad but happy."

"I better read it to Flip, then," Brian said. "He's waiting for me." And Brian read about the moments that last forever and ever. Hearing the words I almost felt like Halley was reading them to me the way she did the day before at Housing Works, when she was holding my hand.

And then suddenly she was. She was there, and not in a dream. She was a real-life angel this time. She sat next to me and rested her head on my shoulder and listened. She was wearing a soft gray beret, and it felt nice on my cheek. Everything felt perfect in that moment, being there with her and the kids and Mrs. Lorentz and Flip. I was so happy, I didn't worry about the future. It wasn't even on my mind.

We said good-bye to everybody, and then Mrs. Lorentz scooped up Flip and went downstairs to leave Halley and me alone. We hunkered in the safety of the nook behind the Dragonbreath bookcase. "I'm sorry," we both said at the same time. "Let's go walk Flip on the boardwalk and work on *The Magic Box*," I said.

"Can't, stupid doctor's appointment again. Text me tonight, after homework. We can work on it then."

"Thanks," I said.

"For what?"

"Not firing me."

I helped Mrs. Lorentz close up the library, sort of. I disabled the alarm to the alley door and left it unlocked. "You really do look pale, Ben. Here, take this for the ride home." She gave me an orange and a trail mix bar. "How are things back home anyway?"

"You know, settling in."

"Good," her mouth said, but her eyes said, I'm not even close to believing you.

"I better get back to the house for dinner," I said, before she could ask me any more questions.

"Watch those stop signs," she said.

"Yeah," I said, stumbling into the door frame on the way out, pretending to smack my face on it.

"My poor baby," Mrs. Lorentz said. "Let me see."

"I'm fine, I'm fine," I said. "Thanks." I headed for the train, faking like I was a little dazed. If I survived being a teenager, I was thinking I might have a shot at an acting career.

I waited behind the candy stand on the corner until she

left, and then I went into the alley and snuck back into the library. We were alone, me and Flip. We were safe. I read bits of lots of books. I think if there's a heaven it'll be my own private library. I walked along row after row of books and dragged my fingertips over their spines. In the twilight I felt the magic in them. They whispered to me, *Pick me. Do you want to know an awesome secret?*

When the sun was gone for good I read by my phone light. No way was I turning on the lights. The streetlights lit up part of the first floor, and I went there and stared into the silkscreened picture of the old Luna Park parachute tower that rose up from the young adult section. I swear I heard the screams and laughter of the people on the ride.

I had two tins of dog food in the backpack, and it actually didn't taste that bad. I found unopened ketchup packets in the garbage and added hot water from the sink. It warmed me up. I checked my phone and ignored the stream of texts from Aunt Jeanie until I couldn't anymore. She was worried sick. She called the school. Mrs. Pinto called the police. They were so mad at themselves, Leo and Jeanie, she said. Why didn't she think to get the number of the nice woman who took me to the hospital after I had that asthma attack? Please, please, please call *the house.* I texted her, *I'm ok. I need time to think. I feel so bad I'm worrying you. I'll call you when I figure things out.* I thought about what else to say, but I couldn't think of anything except I love you, and

I knew that would just make her uncomfortable. I blocked her after that, because I really didn't think I could stand to read all the sadness she was about to text my way. I was okay there in the library that night. I was with Flip, and I felt like we were really safe there, and I didn't want to be bummed out. I texted Halley.

BC: How was it at the doctor's?

HL: Just a blood test. Next chapter of The Magic Box?

BC: OK. Rayburn has secretly boarded our spaceship, The Golden Tower of Light.

HL: I knew it! The dreaded Rayburn! And?

BC: Flip sniffed him out. He caught Rayburn in the storage bay, where he was trying to steal the magic box.

HL: Yay Flip! Rayburn runs to the airlock where he docked his sneaky invisible ship. If Bruce and Helen don't let him take the box, he's going to whip out his laser sword and cut a hole in the window, and the release of air pressure will blow apart our ship of golden light and everything in it. Do they let him go?

BC: They can't. They need to get that magic box to Tess. Helen tells Rayburn, "Wait! You need the key!" Rayburn checks the lock, and he's laughing, cackling. The box was never locked at all!

HL: Uh, NO, you sneak. Mercurious locked it with the key made of sparks!

BC: He only pretended to! He wanted Helen and Bruce to be able to get to the magic and save themselves in case things got really bad, LIKE NOW. It's like he said, a truly great magician can never keep his magic secret. It's meant to be shared. So once and for all, what's inside the freaking box?

HL: Ask Rayburn. He's opening it!

I waited for her to keep going, and waited. Finally I texted, *And?!*

HL: Rayburn's crying. "This is the Greatest Treasure? OMG it's completely worthless." He totally passes out.

BC: What the freak? What's inside???

HL: Flip snatches the box from Rayburn's hands and sits on it and won't let Bruce and Helen look. Flip's not a biter, but don't push him. Now, how do Bruce and Helen take their revenge on Rayburn? I'll let you handle the gory part.

BC: I say they help him into a spare sleeping pod, pipe some awesome low-key rap into it and tell him to chill until they get to Mundum Nostrum. Once they deliver the magic, Tess will turn him into a half-decent humanoid.

HL: This is why I love you. You know there are no bad guys. OK, awesome story jam session, but—ahem—I didn't get any sleep last night. Must. Go. To. Bed. Gnight. ;0)

"I wish you could read, Flip. I'd ask you if you see what I see. The wink. She sent me the wink. Good joke, right, boy? Yup, ha." I had to look over that last text a few times to be sure it really did say what I though it did. "She actually loves me, Flip—as a friend, I mean, but still." He nipped my nose and did a wiggle worm into my hoodie.

We settled in on a couch in the back office, and I couldn't fall asleep, because I couldn't imagine what was inside that box. I cracked the window to let in some air, and it felt good. I breathed and breathed and breathed a little easier, and then I fell asleep.

I was only asleep a few minutes when Flip's growling woke me. The library was pure dark. The only thing darker was the silhouette of the very tall man standing over me. He drew something from his hip and aimed it at me, and then a thousandth of a second after I heard the click I was hit in the face by a golden tunnel of light.

41
THE MAN WHO COMES
TO TAKE YOU AWAY

"Son, just let me into your phone," the police lady said. The precinct was noisy and crowded, and they had me in a room way at the end of the hall. Hot as it was back there, Flip wouldn't come out from my hoodie pocket. "Tell you what," the cop said. "Just give me your name at least."

"I can't," I said. "We can't go back there."

"Where?"

"Please, just let us go. I'm begging you. We'll be okay, I swear."

"Sweetheart, I'm begging *you*. I only want to help you and your dog, okay? The emergency caseworker is on his way. In about five minutes, he's going to be here. If I don't know your name by then, he takes you away into protective custody. Now, they don't let dogs into the emergency housing facilities."

"I know."

"Your friend there goes to the pound."

"I know. I know. I don't know what to do." Flip kept cocking his head and licking my face.

"Please," she said, "just give me your name."

Somebody leaned into the room and said to her, "There's a guy outside who says he's here to pick him up."

The cop turned to me. "This is your last chance."

"Okay," I said. "Okay. Just promise you'll call Halley and give her my dog."

"Halley?"

"My friend. My best friend."

"Okay. Good. That's a deal. I'll call her. I'll get our little friend here to her myself. And if she doesn't want him, *I'll* take him home. I promise."

"You sure? You have dogs?"

"Two." She showed me a video on her phone. Her dogs were fat and wagging their tails like crazy because she was feeding them cheese puffs. She was my kind of cop.

"Okay, my name is—"

"Ben," somebody said. I looked up and there was Mercurious. He hugged me and told me it was okay, that everything was going to be okay.

42
THE MIDNIGHT MEETING

The clock ticked past midnight and into the month of October. We were sitting around the dining room table. Flip snored belly up in Halley's lap. Mrs. Lorentz ordered pizza but nobody ate. I told them everything—except the part about Leo slapping me. The part about him kicking Flip was enough, though, because when I finished talking, Mrs. Lorentz said, "Okay, you're staying here with us."

"I don't think it's that easy, ma'am," I said.

"Ben, please, I'm a librarian."

"Media specialist," Halley said.

"Either way, stop calling me ma'am."

"It's better than him wanting to send you the wink," Halley said.

I gave Halley *SHUT UP* eyes, and Halley said, "She doesn't even know what it means."

"The emoticon?" Mrs. Lorentz said. "Oh that's so sweet of you, Ben. You send me the wink any old time you want and I'll wink right back. We'll be total wink buddies, how fun!"

Halley gave me a look like, Wow, she's even dopier than you on this one. "You so totally have to stay here with us," she said. "You and Mommers—you two are gonna get along *great*. Yes, it's going to be truly fun to torture you."

"Ben," Mrs. Lorentz said, "I'm thinking you want to call your aunt."

She was going to be a weepy mess. She was going to make me talk to Leo too. I couldn't handle that. My brain was fried. I just needed to pass out. "Can you call her for me?"

"You poor baby. Okay, give me her number. You'll call her tomorrow."

Mercurious said, "Ben, let's get you and Flip set up for bed."

The couch in Mercurious's little home office folded out into a bed. Pictures of stars and galaxies covered the walls. Model planets and airplanes hung from the ceiling, and books were jammed every which way into their cases. He pulled a sparkly blanket off a model of a city, Luna Park 1905. *Dreamland at Night.* It was half built, but the golden tower was almost done. He'd strung miniature lights from the steeple to the smaller towers that surrounded it. The buildings were made of shiny paper. "Turn off the lights," he said. Flip's eyes glowed gold with the reflection. "For her birthday," Mercurious said. "For when she turns fourteen."

43

JEANIE

By the time I was awake the next morning, Mrs. Lorentz had a bunch of papers spread over the dining room table. She and Mercurious were reading through them. Halley was wrapped up in a blanket on the couch. She wore a bright pink wool cap with pink antlers. Flip hopped up into Halley's lap, raised his paw for a knuckle bump, yawned and rolled over for her to scratch his fat little stomach. "I just wish he felt more at home here," Halley said.

"How'd you sleep?" Mercurious said.

"Great," I said. I really did too. I slept so hard I didn't even dream.

"We had a very long talk, your aunt Jeanie and I," Mrs. Lorentz said. "Ben, we need to talk about that *stop sign* you ran into. Look at me. Come here." She held my face to the light to look at where Leo slapped me. There was hardly a mark anymore. I checked myself in the bathroom mirror first thing when I woke up. Mrs. Lorentz frowned. "Does your neck hurt? I need you to be absolutely honest with me."

"I'm okay. Really I am."

"I need to take a picture of your face."

"No, I don't want to make a big thing out of this," I said.

"It is a big thing. It's a very big thing. Hiding it will make it worse."

"It's not like they're ever going to bring another kid into that house. They were okay before I got there. Aunt Jeanie. I don't want to ruin her life."

"You're not. You didn't do anything wrong. The fact that Leo came forward and told Jeanie what happened—that's going to help him a lot. He'll get counseling anyway, and he should. He needs it. You're helping him get the help he needs."

"Doesn't feel that way."

"Ben, you can't go back to that house. Children's Services won't allow it. Now, there's a lot to sort through. I have the social worker coming here in a bit to inspect the apartment. They're running background checks on Michael and me, and we'll know in a few hours if we're going to get the preliminary okay to be foster caregivers. I expect we will. It helps that you and I have known each other for two years. Jeanie is coming over to meet us this afternoon. She only wants you to be happy. And more than anything she wants you to be safe. You're safe here, all right? You're safe with us. All that said, I want you to know that this is not something that can't be undone. You're not trapped here either, if you decide you don't want to stay. After Leo gets whatever counseling he needs, and if he's cleared to be your guardian, you can go back to live with Jeanie if you want to."

"I won't. We won't, me and Flip."

"Mom, seriously?" Halley said. "Why would he want to go back there?"

"I just want you to know your options. We're going to take this one day at a time, Ben, and we're going to follow your lead. Are you okay with that?"

I had to think for a second before I nodded. I wasn't used to calling the shots. I wasn't used to having options. I was almost excited, the way you feel after you see a movie you thought was going to be just okay, but it ended up being great.

Mercurious was looking at me and nodding. Halley cuddled Flip and said, "Everything's gonna be all right, Flip. Everything's gonna be okay."

"So we all agree that Ben is better off living here for the time being?" the social worker said. She turned to Aunt Jeanie. "You're sure you're okay with this?"

Aunt Jeanie was wearing a lot more makeup today. She stared into the center of the table, not at me when she said, "Am I sure, Ben?"

I couldn't get myself to look into her eyes when I nodded.

I looked to Halley instead. She smiled a little sadly and cuddled Flip.

The social worker showed Jeanie where she had to sign, and she did. She put down the pen. She still wasn't looking at me when she said, "Ben, can you walk me to my car? I have a little something for you."

It was a beautiful afternoon, and now I was glad to get a chance to talk with her. "I just wanted to thank you for everything."

"Stop, Ben," she said. She dabbed her eyes with a cotton ball to keep her mascara from running. "I wasn't in the Lorentzes' apartment for even a minute when I knew just how badly I had let you down. Had let Tess down."

"You didn't though."

"I can see why you would rather live with them. They're wonderful. They know how to do it."

"Do what?"

"Halley's spectacular. They did such a beautiful job with her. I just want you to be happy. I'm so sorry. I feel awful about everything. Here, sit in the car with me for a minute." We did and she took a small package out of the glove compartment and gave it to me. It was wrapped so perfectly I didn't want to tear the paper. "Save the ribbon," she said. "It's expensive, and you can use it again."

The paper folded away, and it was a framed picture. "I

want you to have this," she said. "It's my favorite of Tess, of the three of us all together."

Mom was in the middle. She had one arm over Jeanie's shoulders and the other over Laura's. They were all laughing, for real too. They wore Santa hats and they might even have been a little tipsy.

"Doesn't she look so beautiful there?" Jeanie said. "She had the loveliest smile, Tess did. Your mother, I mean. Your mom. Ben, can you ever forgive me?"

"For what? You tried to help me."

"That's how he was brought up. Spare the rod and spoil the child. Had I known he would hit you, I would have . . . I don't know. I would have done something to protect you. I've never known him to be violent. He says he's just not cut out to be a parent. Some people aren't. Please don't hate him."

"I don't," I said, which was a lie. Except maybe it wasn't. I don't know. Maybe I felt sorry for him. I definitely didn't like him.

"You're so forgiving. Tess always said you were special. Ridiculously special, is how she put it. I knew you were too, from the little bits of time we got to spend together the last couple of years, but you were good at hiding. You were so quiet. I thought you didn't like me."

"I do though. I do."

"These past few weeks, back at the house, I really wanted

to let you know you I loved you. I just didn't know how. I'm not going to give up, though, okay? I'm going to keep trying. I'm here for you, as much as you want me to be." She hugged me and then pushed me away. "Look at what I did. I got makeup on your shirt."

"It's okay."

"Go, before I start crying. I don't want my mascara to run." It was too late for that. I got out of the car. "Call me tomorrow, all right? Call me and let me know you're okay. We're going to see each other as much as you want, all right? I want to be in on all the beautiful things coming your way. Yes. All the beautiful things." Then she said the last thing as she was driving away. She wasn't looking at me, and her voice was soft, and she said it fast, but she said, "Love you."

I watched her Mercedes get small on the avenue. That car was so clean, and the sun glinted off it, and then it disappeared when she turned the corner. I studied the picture she gave me. Jeanie, Mom and Laura all looked so young. They looked like they weren't worried about anything, like nothing bad could happen, and they would always be this way, laughing, happy, together.

It was such a sunny, breezy day. Sometimes this old woman used to sell flowers on days like this, way down at the other end of the boardwalk. I walked fast down the street toward where she kept her cart. I felt the sun inside me, almost like I was about to float up from the pavement and maybe even fly, so high that I'd be able to see the whole city. The old woman was there, and for five bucks I got the nicest bunch of flowers, reds and purples and pinks. I practically ran home to give them to the Lorentzes. By the time I got back up into their apartment the social worker was gone. Mrs. Lorentz pulled me in for a hug. "I'm so happy you're here," she said. "So grateful." She took the flowers and went to the cabinet for a vase and said, "Go and get your room set up now."

44
CHEWIE

Mercurious had moved all his stuff out of his office into the dining room. I begged him not to, but he did it while I was at school. He left the cool stuff, the pictures of the galaxies, the model planes. I peeked under the sparkly wrap that covered the model of Luna Park 1905 Mercurious was building for Halley's birthday. He'd gotten a little further along. He'd laid down gold foil at the base of the tower and along the beach line. The foil was wrinkled in a pattern to make it look like an ocean filled with quiet little waves.

Above the model was a patch of empty corkboard wall. Mercurious had taken down his diagrams and sketches for the tricks he was working on for that big party he had coming up at the Museum of Natural History. I hung up my Chewie poster. I pushed in the tacks, wondering how long it would be before I had to pull them out again.

Halley came in with Flip and plunked on the bed. She watched me push in the tacks. "So you really are staying then."

"You don't seem too psyched," I said. She looked sad.

"I'm totally psyched. Especially since I have to do another round of chemo next week. It's only once a month, but I feel kind of crummy for a few days after. This way I can make you feel crummy too. I'm messing with you, Coffin. I'm just saying it'll be awesome that you're here. We can cheer each other up."

"How much longer do you have to take the medicine?"

"Not sure. Maybe a few more months, until I'm a hundred and eleven percent. I'll ask the doctor again tomorrow after we get the results from the blood test. That's gonna be one of the best parts about being better. No more bruises on my arms." She showed me the places where they took the blood. The bruises were different colors: yellow, brown, green, purple. She peeled off a Band-Aid, and the bruise there was almost black.

"It's really nice out," I said.

"Let's go to the beach and fly a kite." And that's what we did. It was sparkly purple with a gold tail.

45

THE RAINBOW GIRL
AND THE FLYING TRAPEZE

The next day I was pretty psyched coming home from school, not just because it was Friday but because Halley and I were going to work on *The Magic Box*. I was pretty close to threatening her that if she didn't tell me what was inside it, I wouldn't be friends with her anymore. If it could save a whole planet, the magic had to be something that could spread, like a song that made you feel taller when you heard it. My phone blipped.

Aunt Jeanie. It was a sticker of a cartoon cat waving its paw. I waved back to her with a dopey-looking dog. She wanted to take me to dinner next week. I was sort of afraid to sit down with her. I didn't want to know about Leo, about what was happening with him with the counseling or whatever. I just didn't want to think about him. To remember the way he kicked Flip. But I texted, *Sounds great*.

Halley and Flip were waiting for me on the steps outside the Lorentzes' apartment building. She was smiling but looked tired. She patted the step next to her, and I sat. "Mom's freaking out up there. Mercurious is trying to calm her down. I had to get outside, you know? See what you got yourself into, Coffin? Welcome to the drama."

"What'd I do?"

"Why do you always think it's you?"

"It just usually is, is all."

"Not this time." She took out her phone. The screen was chart after chart of all these numbers in columns with weird headings like *T-Cells* and *Alpha-fetoprotein*.

"What does it mean?" I said.

"It's back. Look, don't freak, because I'm not. I'm totally kicking this thing's butt. I am, Ben."

"You so totally are, I know," I said, but I didn't know anything.

"I knew just now for sure when the doctor called," Halley said, "but I *knew* the day of our bookstore tour. I woke up feeling different that morning. It's like this weird warmth in my lower back."

"Is that how it felt the first time, last winter?"

"No, that time I woke up with blood in my pee and this stomachache that wouldn't go away. I had to go straight into surgery. It was a six-pound tumor. I made the doctor show me a picture of it. I couldn't believe it was inside of me. It looked like a giant's fist, gray with black veins. So look, the chemotherapy I'm going to take this round is a brand-new medicine, and it's a lot stronger, which is awesome, because it's going to completely burn the bad stuff away. It's also going to make me feel pretty sick for a while—like sicker than I'd normally get. I have to start the chemo right away, tomorrow, so I need you to take me to Luna Park today."

"Right now?"

"We'll just bring Flip back upstairs, then we'll go. There's no better time. It's already October, and it'll be closed for the season by the time I'm back to a hundred and eleven percent. I want you to fly with me."

"Fly?"

She grinned. "We need to take a ride on the Boardwalk Flight."

It was basically a mix of skydiving and a slingshot that threw you two hundred feet into the air at a speed of sixty miles an hour. The attendant strapped us into the safety vests. "I probably should have told you, but I'm terrified of heights," Halley said.

"Which is why your heroine from *The Magic Box* is a trapeze artist," I said. "Makes perfect sense."

"It does, if you really think about it," she said. "I might barf all over you."

"This would have been good to know before we got on the ride."

The cable whipped us upward—and backward by our ankles—to the top of the tower. Halley screamed and laughed. "Holy ship, my stomach!"

"Oh boy."

"Do *not* let go of my hand, Ben Coffin!"

"I won't, I promise, even though you're breaking my fingers. Uh-oh, here we go." We swung down toward the boardwalk and then up toward the sun.

"Don't let me fly away! Hold me!"

"I am! I got you!"

"And I got *you*! Ben?"

"Halley?"

"We're flying! We really are! This is so freaking spectacular!" And it was. It was.

46
DON'T BE SCARED

We walked the boardwalk slowly and didn't say anything, and the sun was warm on our faces, and she smiled. She flipped her leg backward to kick me in the butt.

"What was that for?" I said.

"Don't be scared, okay?" she said. "Everything's going to be totally fine."

"I should be saying these things to you," I said.

"But I'm not scared. I swear I'm not. Look." She pointed into the funhouse mirror. It stretched us thin. We were aliens with big eyes and huge heads and we both looked like we were trying really hard not to look scared. Halley aimed her phone at the mirror and took a picture of us. The flash stayed in my eyes that night, especially when I shut them and tried to fall asleep.

Saturday morning breakfast, the four of us held hands. Halley prayed, "God, thank you for this meal. Thank you for us. I hope you get everybody here to see that nobody should stop living the heck out of life the next month or so. Each day is the best day from here on in." She opened her eyes. "Ben, I need you and Flip to keep Read to Rufus going the days I'm not feeling so great. We can't let it fall apart. That's the one thing that will make me mad. Flip, high four." He gave her one and surfed her lap. "Mom, look into his eyes. They're just like Harry's, right?" That was her dog who died. "What's he trying to tell us? Look. You see it, don't you? What *is* that?"

After, I helped Mrs. Lorentz wash the dishes. Out of nowhere she hugged me with wet dish gloves. "I don't know what we would do without you right now."

"She's totally going to beat this thing," I said.

"I know," Mrs. Lorentz said, but she didn't know either.

Flip and I delivered my coupons and met up with Mercurious at the church and watched him finish his magic lesson with the little kids. A girl tripped and cried, "My knee hurts." Mercurious sat her in a chair and sprinkled magic dust on her knee and made her pain vanish. "It works," she said.

"That's right," he said. He patted her head. "All better now."

We got into the sparkly purple SUV and got on the highway. I strapped Flip into the passenger seat, in my lap. "He slept with Halley last night," I said.

"Us too," Mercurious said. "At about three this morning he came scratching at the door."

"Sorry."

"For what? That's his job. Warm everybody up, right?"

We didn't listen to music, we didn't talk. The sky was white, too bright. Halley and her mom had to go earlier so Halley could get a port put into her chest, whatever a port was. Maybe twenty minutes into the ride, Mercurious said, "Ben? Thank you for being here. Without you, this would be unbearable."

47

SIRIUS

I expected more of a hospital-type place. We pulled into a strip mall right off the highway. The waiting room was pictures of horses and forests and this big one of a flower field. "Flip!" Halley said. Her beret that day was fuzzy orange.

Flip surfed and boxed for everybody in the waiting room and hopped into the lap of this little boy who was sitting next to Halley. "Ben, this is Franco. He's awesome."

He was also bald. He kissed Flip and said, "He has bad breath."

"We know," we all said.

The nurse came out. "Okay, Halley, ready to rock?"

Mrs. Lorentz hugged Halley.

"Mom, relax," Halley said.

"I am," Mrs. Lorentz said. "I *am*, sheesh."

"Can my friends come with me, Tall and Furry?" Halley said.

"Absolutely." The nurse put out his hand. "Jerry."

"This is Ben," Halley said. "He's smarter than he looks."

"He looks pretty smart to me," Jerry said.

Halley held my hand. She was shaking all over. We went into a small room with two recliners and a huge TV. Halley sank back into one of them, and Flip hopped up into her lap and yawned. I learned that dogs yawn when they're tired, sure, but also when they're nervous.

Jerry slid down Halley's shirt a little. The port was right under her collarbone, toward the middle of her chest. It looked like where you connect the air pump to a bike tire, except it was white plastic. Jerry attached a tube that went into a bag of fluid hanging from a metal hook in the wall. The stuff in the bag was clear. It looked like plain old water.

"Here we go, Halley," Jerry said. "Might feel a little cold at first." He unscrewed this little plastic ring in the middle of the tube. He dimmed the lights and clicked on the TV but left the sound off. He handed me the remote. "See you guys in half an hour," he said.

We stared at the TV. It was a Justice League cartoon.

"When last we saw our interstellar travelers Bruce, Helen, and Flip, they were nearing the planet of Mundum Nostrum," Halley said. "Well, now they're almost there. It's in the most beautiful place in the galaxy. So quiet out here. So pink and clean. We're flying right by Sirius now. We're swinging in so close it's all we can see. There's no sky, just the star. You can look right into it, and it doesn't hurt at all.

It burns cool and blue and even Rayburn can't be sad now. There's a breeze, whispery. It's Tess's voice. 'You're so close now,' she says. 'So close.' Ben? I'm not worried."

"Me either," I said.

"I didn't sleep so great with this hairy little bug kicking at me. I'm just gonna close my eyes for a bit, okay? Let's take a nap, the three of us." She closed her eyes. Flip closed his and burrowed under her sweatshirt and she smiled. "This dog," she said with her eyes still closed. "He is so freaking amazing." She looked healthy. Her cheeks were even pink that day. It just didn't make any sense. "You know what?" she said. "On second thought, can you find the music channel and dial up some rap?"

48
I ALWAYS WANTED TO
BE A VAMPIRE

She threw up in the car on the way home. I was in the back with her and held the bag. Flip didn't mind the smell. He cuddled right into her and wagged his tail. When we pulled up to the apartment, Mrs. Lorentz said, "He's a lifesaver, right Halley?"

"Good job, Flip," I said.

Halley rolled her eyes. "Again, she was talking about *you*, dope." She threw up as soon as we got into the apartment. I rubbed her back while she was bent over the toilet. Her fuzzy orange beret fell into the water. I took it out.

"Sorry," she said.

"I don't mind."

"No, that you have to see me like this. Puking. Bald. I'm lucky I have a totally gorgeous head."

"You do."

"Oh, I know. Yeah. I always wanted to be a vampire."

"I can't see you ripping apart somebody's neck to suck their blood."

"I wouldn't. I'd be a nice one. I'd be a medical lab techni cian and drink what they were going to throw away. I will soon, though."

"Become a lab technician?"

"Look like a vampire. You'll see, when I lose more weight. I might cry now. In sixth grade I was voted Best Hair. Me, Halley Lorentz. I'm sure to get into Harvard with that on my application. Okay, I'm actually *not* going to cry, it seems. Phew."

She leaned on me into her room and flopped down onto her bed. "Cover me up fast with all the blankets. Thanks. Ben, I stink and I'm gross, so Flip's the only one who can stay, okay? You're the only one, Flip. His eyes, Ben. See?"

I left them in there. Mrs. Lorentz was passed out on the couch with her arms over her eyes. Mercurious was making soup. "Need any help?" I said.

"You're doing just fine," he said. "On second thought, you can taste this for me."

"Tastes healthy."

He laughed, sort of. Mercurious had a very quiet laugh, more of a smile, the kind the superhero has at the end of the movie, when all is right with the world again. "I'm thinking this might be a little *too* healthy for you and me. How'd you like to order a pizza?"

"I'll go pick it up," I said. "I have to walk Flip anyway."

On the way there I texted Aunt Jeanie that I was going to have to postpone dinner. I had a really busy week coming up.

Halley slept straight through until the next morning. Her mom made her drink some cold peppermint tea with honey, and she threw it up. She slept. By four o'clock Sunday afternoon, she was up. She was too stiff to stay in bed, but too tired to work on *The Magic Box*. We played video games. Her phone buzzed with a text. It had been buzzing practically nonstop.

"They're all demanding to see me now. My friends from school. Yes, believe it or not, I am fantastically popular and just chock-*full* of friends. They've *been* demanding to see me, ever since that first trip to the emergency room last winter, but I keep blowing them off. I know that's mean, not letting them help me, but I can't see them right now, you know? I want to be a hundred and eleven percent. It's not because of the way I look. It's because of the way they'll look at me. That sadness in their eyes. That fear. You and Flip, you guys never look that way. Maybe you look a little sad, but you're not afraid for me."

She was right. I wasn't afraid for her. She was tough enough to handle anything. I was afraid for *me*. Of what it would be like without her, the world. It would be like a planet that lost its orbit and got chucked into space and everything's cold and you can't breathe. "I have a present for you," I said. "It's in the other room."

"Your room?"

"I'll be right back."

It was a rainbow-striped cap. I bought it on the street from the man who sold socks and phone cases by the subway. She put it on her head and checked herself out in the mirror. "I love you, Ben Coffin. I'm never taking it off, even after my hair grows back."

49
WHERE'S HALLEY?

"How's she doing?" Mold said Monday during lunch in our regular spot in the cafeteria.

"She's doing great," I said. The window was open and it was one of those days in early fall when the air forgets it's not summer anymore. Every fly in the city decided to get together that afternoon for a conference around the dumpster.

"I'd like to visit her," Chucky said. "Not to look at her butt. That wouldn't be right at this point."

"It wasn't right at the other point either," I said.

"Coffin, I'm thirteen. You'll understand when you get to be my age. I just want to thank her."

"For *what?*"

"I don't know. She was nice to me."

"She's not going anywhere. You'll see her when she gets better."

"I'd like to come to Read to Rufus again today, just in case.

Sorry. I didn't mean that. I'm sure she's going to be fine."

"Look, Chucky, maybe some other time. I'll talk with her about it. We'll see, okay?"

Angelina plunked down next to me and took one of my Chips Ahoy! Ronda stood behind her, arms folded. "Damon said you lost your mind," Angelina said with her mouth full of my cookie.

"What a brilliant observation by Damon," I said.

"You so did not just talk to me that way. Have you lost your mind?"

"Didn't we just establish that?" Halley inspired me to stand up for myself. The way she was standing up to her cancer. Not hers. It. I took out my phone and took a picture of Angelina. "Pinto said you need to steer clear. Go or I email this to her."

"You freaking geek. If I get suspended—"

"I seriously don't care," I said.

"Let's go," Ronda said.

Angelina got up. "Sorry about your pants," she said to me.

I rolled my eyes. "Okay, and why would you be sorry about my pants?"

"Seems you sat in some gum."

I stood up and sure enough my butt and the bench were attached by a long string of Juicy Fruit, it smelled like. "You're brilliant, Angelina," I said.

"Thank you."

"No, I mean seriously. You are *so* creative. The whole putting gum on somebody's seat thing? It's never been done before. How did you ever come up with such a dazzling idea? I mean, you are a genius."

"Smart enough not to sit on a wad of gum anyway." She was still laughing, like she was genuinely happy about messing me up.

"Shut up, Ange," Ronda said.

"No, seriously, isn't he like the hugest loser?"

"You know what, Caramello? Coffin's right. You're a freaking *genius.* You're not allowed to hang with me anymore." She shoved Angelina and headed off.

Angelina chased after her. "*I'm* not allowed to hang with *you?* You have it all backward, *Glom*ski."

"I hate her," Chucky said. "Seriously, why does Halley have to get cancer when it should be Angelina?"

"Chucky? Shut the freak up."

"What?"

"Why does *either* of them have to get it?" I couldn't erase it from my mind, the image of Halley's fuzzy orange beret floating in the toilet.

When I got to the library for Read to Rufus, Flip and Mercurious were there, but Mrs. Lorentz and Halley weren't. "Is she okay?" I said.

"She has a temperature," Mercurious said. "Are *you* okay?"

"Of course," I said.

"She wants us to take pictures. She says to tell everybody she'll be here next time for sure."

And that's what we did. Still, Brian asked, "But where is she? Why can't she be with us?"

Flip seemed confused too. He kept looking around the room for her.

When we got back to the apartment I showed her the pictures. She kept going through them. "I'm starting to feel better. I feel it working, the medicine, you know? I *feel* it. I'll be at the next one. I will, Ben."

"Oh, I know you will."

"For sure."

"For sure."

50
IT'S LIKE WHEN YOU BITE YOUR TONGUE

Halley barely said anything during Tuesday breakfast and she didn't eat. "Sweetheart, have some toast at least," Mrs. Lorentz said.

"I'm fine."

"I thought you were feeling better," her mom said.

"I was. But now that I know I'm going to be puking like a maniac in a few hours, I'd rather not waste food." Her second chemotherapy session was that afternoon.

"Halley," her mom said, and that was as far as she got.

"Mom, can't you just shut up for like two *seconds*." She pushed away from the table and stomped to her room and slammed the door. Flip scratched on it and she let him in.

It was weird, seeing her talk to her mom that way. It made me think she was really worried, which got me really worried. "Can I go with her to chemotherapy?" I said.

"No, you can help her by going to school and doing well on your social studies test," Mrs. Lorentz said.

I got back from school a little before Halley got home from chemotherapy. Again she went right into the bathroom and threw up. Again I rubbed her back while she puked. Nothing came up, just dry heaves. "Can you put my cap back on?" she said. She liked to wear it backward.

Flip wiggled between her and the toilet bowl and slumped and sighed.

"This is true friendship," she said.

"He's awesome," I said.

"Ben, how can you not know I'm talking about you? Idiot. I'm going to Read to Rufus tomorrow. I am." She heaved again, and then again.

I helped her to her bed. She crashed on it. I took her shoes off and put all her blankets on her. I left Flip with her and I didn't see her until right before I went to bed. I had to take Flip out for his last walk. I cracked the door to let him out, and I looked in to see if she was okay. Her mom was reading to her, but Halley was sleeping. Mrs. Lorentz came out with Flip. She walked with us. "Your aunt Jeanie called," she said. "She thought you were avoiding her, until I told her about Halley. Ben, are you avoiding her?"

"No. Maybe."

"I want you to go to dinner with her. I'd invite her over, but with Halley so sick, well, you know. When Halles is better, we'll have a party. I want Jeanie to be there, okay?"

"Okay."

"Meanwhile, can you give her a call? Please, for me, all right?"

Wednesday morning Halley was awake and dressed before I was. She was making Flip's breakfast. "I'm taking him for his walk," she said.

Her mom frowned. She put her hand on Halley's forehead. "Sit," she said.

"Mom—"

"Halley Lorentz, sit down. If your temperature's fine you can walk Flip." She went through this tray where we kept all Halley's medical stuff: the blood pressure cuff, the stethoscope, these pills to make her less queasy, these other pills to help with her headaches, a couple of thermometers. Mrs. Lorentz popped one under Halley's tongue.

"This isn't the butt one, right?" Halley said.

"Of *course* not. Sheesh."

"She's so not sure," Halley said to me.

We waited for the thermometer to stop rising. Flip poked Halley's leg with his nose to make her watch him do this trick where he stood on his hind legs and sort of moonwalked backward. Even in her crummy mood, she laughed. She took the thermometer out. "See? Perfect." She grabbed Flip's leash and ran out with him.

Mrs. Lorentz checked the thermometer and frowned. "Ben, go with her. Make sure she doesn't pass out in the middle of the freaking boardwalk," except she didn't say "freaking."

By the time I got to the elevator, she was gone. I took the stairs down to the lobby. She hadn't even made it to the front door. She and Flip were sitting on the bench by the mailboxes. I sat next to her. She was shaking. "Don't say anything," she said.

"I won't."

"I'm not scared."

"I know."

"This is just the medicine working. It's strong, so of course it's going to be knocking me out."

"I know."

"Yeah." She caught her breath. "He kisses me awake in the mornings, Flip."

"He does that."

"Uh-huh. It's too quiet here, but I'll tell you."

"Tell me what?"

"It's called rhabdomyosarcoma. There, I said it. Even the name sounds disgusting enough to make you want to puke, right? Sounds evil? Except it's not. I'm not saying it's good either. It's just like every other living thing, trying to survive. It's simply being what it is, which is a tumor that worms through your guts and then the rest of you like an exploded bowl of spaghetti. Or at least that's what the one they took out of me last winter was going to do. Nobody told me that, but I read it online, in one of the chat rooms. This boy a little older than me said that's what the tumor in him was up to. You want to know what it feels like too, right? Most times, I don't feel it. And then I do. This warmth that's almost a burn, and then it goes away. And then sometimes it's something *completely* different. Like last night it snuck up on me and pounced. You ever bite your tongue? It was like that, except all over my body. Now I'm sorry I talked about it. Talking about it gives it power. I need to keep my focus on the golden stuff. Let's go."

"Halley."

"Back upstairs, I mean. Let's go back upstairs. I have to go to bed. I'm freezing. Sorry Flip." She hung heavy on me in the elevator. "Ben, you don't have to say anything. There's nothing to say. Just hold my hand. Thanks. Your hand's almost warm. It feels really good."

51
FLIP'S MAGIC

She didn't make it to Read to Rufus that time either. Afterward I gathered everybody together, the kids, parents, and teachers. We walked to the beach. It was a beautiful day. We made a get-well video full of stuff we thought might make her laugh. The kids made goofy faces, inside-out eyelids, huge balls of fake snot made from chewed-up paper, dripping out of their noses. One of the teachers was a gymnast a long time ago, and she did a split and ripped her pants up the butt. One kid hid behind another except for her arms, so the kid in front looked like she had four arms. One of the dads spun his four-year-old daughter in circles and then put her down on the ground, and she was so dizzy she giggled and staggered around off balance like she was drunk. Flip thought she wanted to dance with him, so he did his moonwalk thing.

They all left video messages saying "Feel better" and "We miss you." Brian's video to her was, "Ben said you promised you'd watch me read again. If you come I'll give you a real long hug and I'll let you kiss me on the cheek, even though I already have a girlfriend."

I went back to the library and uploaded the videos and edited them. When I got back to the Lorentzes' Halley was still in bed but awake and sitting up. She was making a sketch of the Golden Tower of Light as it was about to dock with an antenna on top of Mundum Nostrum's tallest skyscraper.

"Hey," I said.

"Hey."

"It was awesome today."

"I'm sure."

"Everybody misses you." I handed her my phone. "We made a video for you."

She handed me her iPad. More charts, more numbers. "It means it isn't working, the chemotherapy. Not at all." She rolled away. "I have to go to sleep." I put my hand on her shoulder but she shrugged it off. She cried so hard I thought she'd die of shortness of breath. Flip wiggled into her arms and nudged her chin, and she started to calm down. She whispered things to him and then she got quiet and wiped her eyes and hugged him and he snuggled her, and I left them like that.

Mrs. Lorentz was on the phone, pacing up and down the kitchen. She said, "But what about the experimental drug?

You said it looked promising. Then there's still hope." Mercurious was in the dining room, working on the model of Luna Park 1905. I sat next to him. "I could use some help with this," he said. "You have time to give me a hand?"

"Sure," I said, and we worked on the model together. I painted the smaller buildings with gold dots and put flags on them. Mercurious was hanging a crescent moon.

The next morning I delivered my coupons alone. Flip was spending all his time with Halley now, and I was glad. When he was with her she was calm and smiled more.

The air was cold, and I whipped through my route and got the deliveries done before sunrise. By the time I was back at the apartment, Halley and Flip were at the breakfast table. She still looked pretty sick, but she was grinning. Flip kept pulling off her socks. She was watching the video we made for her. "I won't miss the next one," she said.

"I know," I said.

"Meanwhile, I need you to help Dad tomorrow night. It's the huge bar mitzvah at the Museum of Natural History. I was supposed to assist. I was going to try, but Mom wants me to rest up before we get into this new chemotherapy thing. Dad says not to ask you, that he'll be able to manage, because he knows the whole magician thing freaks you out. But I told him you're a big boy and ready to face your fears and you'd love to help him. He's unveiling a new illusion. He's been working on it for the past year. It'll be spectacular when he pulls it off. Congratulations, you've been promoted to magician's assistant." She snapped her fingers, and the sun just peeked over the horizon and nailed us with a gold beam.

"How'd you do that?" I said.

She spun the iPad around. It was on the weather page. Right at the top was sunrise: 6:55 a.m. Right above that was the time of day: 6:55 a.m. "I actually think I might be able to stomach half a waffle this morning," she said.

"Cool," I said, and I made us waffles.

That afternoon Aunt Jeanie picked me up and we headed out to the diner. "I don't want you to feel like you have to do this," I said. "You know, us hanging out because you think that's what Mom would want."

"But *I* want to. Do you?"

I nodded and forced myself to fake a smile.

She patted my hand, and then she took her hand away. "Yes. Well, Leo wanted me to, to tell you he's sorry. He really did. He really is."

I nodded. "How is he, like, doing?"

"Oh Ben, you're so sweet. I'm touched, really. He's going to be okay. I'll let him know you asked about him." She chewed her bottom lip for a bit. "Do you mind if I ask how Halley's doing?"

"No, not at all. She's doing great. Seriously. They're putting her on a new medicine, and it's going to do the trick."

"I'm sure," she said.

"It is. Really."

"Oh, I know."

52

HALLEY'S STARDUST
AND RAINBOW SNOW

Mercurious and I finished up our last rehearsal Friday afternoon in his workshop in the church basement. "Ready?" he said.

"I'm a little freaked, but I think I got it."

"A little freaked is good. We just need to fix you up with one last thing." He gave me a sparkly purple sweat suit.

We got there right as the museum closed, and the party started right after that. The guests packed into the Hall of Ocean Life. We'd set up the show the night before, and now all we could do was wait until after dinner, when Mercurious would pull off his grandest illusion yet.

The kid whose bar mitzvah it was came over and introduced himself and gave me the same gift bag his friends were getting. It had all the stuff I loved: vintage comics, a chronograph watch with a flashlight and about ten pounds of candy. He took me over to the buffet to make sure I ate. "I was really nervous to meet your dad," he said.

I didn't bother to correct him about the fact that Mercurious wasn't my dad. He was, well, Mercurious. "Why?"

"Ben, dude, he's totally famous. You're gonna be a magician too, right? You get to be at a party every night."

It really was an awesome party. Think of being able to run around the Museum of Natural History while eating mini pizzas and shooting your friends with laser guns. Then it was showtime.

The lights went down and I went to my spot in the video projection booth. Mercurious went out into the middle of the hall and the place went silent. "Jon, would you come up here? I'd like to introduce you to your guardian angel."

"I didn't know I had one," the bar mitzvah boy said.

"We all do. As you begin your journey into this next magical phase of your life, know that you always have someone looking out for you." Mercurious tapped Jon's shoulder, and Halley appeared, a miniature version of her, the way she looked almost a year ago, the first time I met her, at the library, when she was helping out behind the counter, and she rolled her eyes when I gave her *I, Robot* to check out for me. Here though, now, in the museum, her long, light brown hair was pulled back into a braided bun, with silver cords woven through. She wore a rainbow-colored gown with angel's wings.

Mercurious made Jon hold out his hand, and Halley fluttered down into his palm. She raised her own palm and blew stardust into Jon's face. She vanished and reappeared life-size on top of the ninety-four-foot model of the blue whale. She knelt down from the whale's fin and blew stardust. It rained from the ceiling onto the guests. It was snowing silver and pink and gold and emerald, and I remembered the time my mom wanted to go to the beach during a snowstorm. We bundled up and drank hot chocolate from a thermos, and the strangest thing happened. It was still snowing, but the sun came out, just for a minute, just long enough to turn the flakes every color of the rainbow.

Somebody called out to me from far away, like the voice was coming through radio static, and it was. It was Mercurious. *"Ben, can you hear me?"* He was on the private channel of our walkie-talkies.

"Ten-four, Mercurious."

"I just wanted to let you know that I think your mom's watching, and she's proud of you. We all are. Thank you, son. I really needed you here with me tonight." And I saw through the stardust that down on the floor, he was looking up at Halley's ghost, and the tear tracks were zigzags on his cheeks. I tried not to get too freaked out. I mean, if Mercurious was worried, then there definitely was a reason to worry now.

We finished loading up the projectors into Mercurious's SUV. "Put out your palm," he said. He put five hundred-dollar bills into it. "That's crazy," I said.

"That's your share."

"But all I did was play around on the iPad." It was like a video game. I moved Halley's image here and there and made sure the video projectors went on and off at the right times. "I had too much fun to make this much money."

"Ben, that's how it's supposed to be."

"Two questions. First, can you put this into my college fund?"

"I like the way you think. What else?"

"When can we do the next one?"

Flip met us at the door. Mrs. Lorentz wasn't far behind. She'd been crying but now she was smiling. "How'd it go?" she said.

"Awesome," I said. "How's Halley?"

"Awesome. Truly. Halley is absolutely amazing." She was talking to Mercurious when she said that last part. Mercurious frowned. "Go in and say hi, Ben," Mrs. Lorentz said. "She's been waiting up for you. She'll want to hear all about tonight."

Flip led me into her room and hopped onto her bed and yawned.

"How'd I do?" she said. "All the boys said I was hot, right? Let's see the gift bag." She chucked the comics and grabbed the flashlight watch and put it on. "While you were out making me fly around the Museum of Natural History, I figured out the next chapter of *The Magic Box*."

"Okay?"

"So as the Golden Tower of Light coasts into Mundum Nostrum, a series of miniature asteroids comes out of nowhere."

"They always do. Better activate the laser shields."

"Unfortunately, the laser shields aren't going to be enough this time. These asteroids are tiny but insidiously lethal. They snuck completely undetected into the ship's orbit and they're moving too fast. Think of a bag of frozen peas traveling at supersonic speed. They blow right through the laser shields and explode when they hit the Golden Tower of Light. The back of the ship is gone, completely shorn away. Now, in the *front* of the ship, Rayburn is tucked safely into his sleeping pod. Flip is tucked safely into the backpack on our hero Bruce's back. Bruce is secured to the ship by a golden tendril of light. Helen, on the other hand, was floating free in zero gravity when the asteroids hit. She's being sucked out of the ship, into the vacuum of space. So is the magic box. Helen grabs it and jams it into a crack in the fuselage just before she flies outward into the perfect infinity of the stars."

"Bruce goes with her—"

"No, Bruce stays with the ship."

"Absolutely *not*. Unacceptable. Bruce follows Helen—"

"Bruce has to bring the magic box to Tess. He has to deliver the Greatest Treasure and save the people of Mundum Nostrum. He has to keep on keeping on."

"But what if he doesn't want to, not without Helen?"

"He forces himself to realize how strong he is, how awesome. He's a traveler, like Tess always told him he was. That's what he's born to do. Halley will always be with Ben and Flip anyway. Helen, I mean. Helen will always be with them."

"How? Just explain to me how the frick Halley is with them when they're stuck on Mundum Nostrum and Halley's . . . just . . . *not*."

She held my hand. "I can't do it again, Ben. I can't be sick like that anymore. Me and Mom were on the phone with the doctors all night. This new drug they were thinking of is totally experimental. It has a twenty percent chance of giving me another three months. There's a fifty percent chance it will kill me in three days. There's a hundred percent chance it will make me sicker than I've ever felt in my life."

"What about other stuff, like surgery?"

"Not an option. Ben, they found it in my blood vessels. It's only a matter of time before it spreads everywhere."

"I don't know what to say."

"I don't either, really." She brushed the hair out of my eyes. "It's the weirdest thing. I mean, I knew back in the winter, after they took out the tumor, that the kind I have is the worst kind. But I really thought I was gonna beat it. The five-year survival rate in children under fourteen is thirty percent. Almost one in three. I thought I was going to be the one. I was so sure, I even started to feel bad about it. About being the one who lives when the other two would have to die. You ever wonder that? Why somebody has to die? Why we all do? It just seems so crazy." Flip pawed her to pet him. She did. "The doctor said now that I won't be on chemotherapy, I'll actually feel a little better for a little while. I'm not giving up, Ben Coffin, and you can't either. I don't know how many days I have left—fifty, thirty, seventy—but we're going to fight to be happy every minute we get to spend with each other. The happier we are now, the happier we'll always be when you remember me. I need you to have my back on this one."

"Okay," I said. "Okay, I do."

"Promise?"

"Swear." We locked pinkies.

"Good," she said. At first I thought it was weird, her being so calm after just finding out she was going to die sooner rather than later. But then I saw it wasn't calmness. She was just plain tired. Her eyelids were heavy and dark. She looked beat-up. "You look like you want to ask me something," she said.

I wanted to ask her lots of things. Like, Who could I be mad at? Seriously, why couldn't the cancer have an inventor, some psycho villain along the lines of Darth Sidious, somebody I could track down and beat the crud out of before I stabbed him in the heart with my laser sword, except how can you do that when the traitor doesn't have a heart? My biggest question was, Why couldn't it be me instead of her? "The magic box," I said. "Once and for all, what's inside?"

She mussed my hair a little, and just after she'd fixed it too. "I promise I won't leave you hanging. You'll find out soon enough."

53

MRS. SALVADOR AND PEACOCK FEATHERS

Halley never really bounced back from being tired from the chemotherapy. She slept a lot, but she wasn't nauseous anymore, and she said she wasn't in pain—most of the time. By the middle of October, though, they gave her pills to help her hurt less. Mrs. Lorentz made me and Mercurious stick to our schedules, and for me that meant school, homework, my coupon deliveries, Read to Rufus, and keeping up with Aunt Jeanie, which, to be honest, was the hardest thing. Or the second-hardest thing.

Mrs. Lorentz took a leave of absence from the library to take care of Halley. A nurse came for a few hours a day to help out too. She was super nice, Mrs. Salvador, and she loved to read to Halley. She was going for a degree in literature at the City College of New York, and that's why the agency paired her with us. Halley loved the way she read *Feathers*. She acted out the parts and did voices and stuff.

When Halley was sleeping, Mrs. Salvador and I talked. "How do you stand it?" I said. "Having to say good-bye to one patient, and then starting all over again?"

"It's a gift each time I meet someone new," she said. Flip took a break from cuddle duty to be with us and climbed into Mrs. Salvador's lap. He rolled belly up for a scratch and wagged his tail and yipped until she gave him what he wanted. "And anyway, they never really say good-bye. Right Flip?"

The third weekend of October Mercurious and I were on a long line at Costco with a cart full of stuff for Halley, ginger ale and bright plants for her windowsill. She liked to sit with her sketchbook and look out at the beach and Luna Park. We had other stuff in the cart too, lots of paper towels and sani wipes and yes, diapers. An old man on the next line had the same ones in his cart, and he looked like us, sort of like he couldn't believe any of this was actually happening.

"How did you guys meet?" I said to Mercurious.

"Penny and I? We were in the same library sciences program."

"What made you switch to magic?"

"I guess I never thought of it as a switch. You ever think about going into it? Library science? I think you'd be great at it. You're analytical and you have a huge heart."

Talking about what I wanted to do when I grew up felt

weird when my best friend was never going to grow up. "I'd like to be you," I said.

"A party magician?" he said doubtfully.

"A great guy."

"Ben, you're something else," he said, which is exactly what my mom used to say except she'd never tell me exactly what that something else was.

When we got back, Halley was feeling pretty good. She was sitting up at the window with Flip and bossing us around about where she wanted the flowers. We moved the model of Luna Park into her room. There wasn't much left to do before it'd be finished. We had to put in a walkway, so the people could get into the golden tower. Mercurious wanted to hang a few planets over it too, and a handful of stars. Mrs. Lorentz stuck fake peacock feathers into Halley's rainbow cap.

That night on my way to the kitchen for a midnight peanut butter and jelly and milk I found Mrs. Lorentz and Mercurious passed out on the couch with a photo album. They'd left the window open a crack and I could smell the ocean. They looked cold, so I put a blanket on them.

54
FRIENDS AND KITES

The texts and calls got to be too much, so she set aside a day to let everybody visit. She posted a sign on her door: NO CRYING. YES LAUGHING. Practically everybody got it backward.

They knew she had that sweet tooth, and they brought her cakes, cookies, and barrels of gummy bears, none of which she could eat because she'd pretty much stopped eating. They brought her stuffed animals, which Flip collected in a corner of her room, like they were his harem. Chucky brought flowers. "You think these are good enough? They're only from the deli. I wanted to get twelve but I was starving and if I didn't get a meatball parm I seriously would have died of starvation. I only had enough money left for like six."

"What are they?"

"Posies. Or maybe pansies, I don't know. Do I look like a horticulturalist?"

"You look like you're about to cry. Chucky, you better not."

"I *won't*, Coffin. Chill."

I brought him in. Halley said to Chucky, "You forgot your pocket protector."

"I try not to wear it at non-school events, except in extraordinary circumstances."

"Those being?"

"For instance if I'm somewhere that requires multiple pens. Sometimes I go to autograph shows, and the superhero or whoever steals your Bic. You were the first girl who didn't call me a dork." He cried. He gave her the flowers.

"Poppies," she said. She cried. "Chucky, can you give Ben and me a minute?"

He sobbed his way out.

"Get everybody out," she said. "I'm sorry, but I can't stand it. I'll say my good-byes on Facebook. I only want to be with you and Flip from here on in, Mom and Mercurious. And the Read to Rufus kids. I'm saying those good-byes in person, if it's the last thing I do."

"What's the difference, Mom? I mean, we're really worried about my cold getting worse at this point?"

"Let's try again," Mrs. Salvador said. She put the digital thermometer into Halley's ear.

It was one of those perfect October afternoons, deep blue sky and a beach wind that puffed up the ocean into whitecaps. The kites were all over the sky. Halley wanted to go out and watch.

Mrs. Salvador checked the thermometer. She frowned.

"Can't do it, Halles," her mom said. "I don't want to be the bad guy."

"Then don't be."

"You go outside on a day like today and it might be your last day."

"So? Why do you have to be such a freaking psycho about every little thing?"

"You know what? I'm sick of your nastiness to me. Go to your room until you remember how to talk to me."

"Fine." She went and shut the door as hard as she could, and we could still hear her crying and screaming "I hate you" over and over on the other side of it. Then Mrs. Lorentz started crying and Mrs. Salvador said, "Okay. Okay. Everybody breathe now."

"Ben?" Halley said from behind her door. "Ben!"

I went in. She was on her bed, facing the wall. Flip was dragging a stuffed animal across the floor to her. She reached back for me to grab her hand. "Promise me I'll get to be outside one last time."

"Promise."

"I guess having cancer doesn't make me immune from being a jerk now and again. Tell Mom I know I'm being an idiot."

55
WHOA

That third Wednesday of October was a warm day. Mrs. Lorentz wanted to drive Halley over to the library, but she wanted to walk. Mercurious sided with Halley and said they would meet us over there. I brought the wheelchair just in case. She made it a couple of blocks before she needed to use the chair. Still, she was psyched. She couldn't wait to see Brian. His teacher emailed Halley that Brian was close to reading at grade level now.

Mrs. Lorentz and Mrs. Salvador had wrapped up Halley in all her crazy colorful scarves. She gave them away to the kids. Brian read to her and Flip, and she got her hug and kiss on the cheek. The kids were cool. They didn't make her sad. They knew she was dying, but they said good-bye like they'd see her next week, and I swear they meant what they said, and I really wished I could be like them.

After, she wanted to ride down the boardwalk, just her,

me, and Flip. She wanted me to push the wheelchair fast. "Push, Coffin. *Push.* Faster. Yeah, like that. Woohoo!"

We were in her room, sunset. We worked on the model of Luna Park 1905, or I worked, and she watched. I fiddled with a string of lights that went from the top of the golden tower to one of the stars Mercurious had hung from the ceiling. Flip snored in her lap. "Ready for the last chapter of *The Magic Box*?" she said.

I'd been waiting for her to bring it up, or more like dreading it. I didn't want the story to end. "Ready," I said.

"Tess says, 'You've saved Mundum Nostrum, Ben. You and Flip. You brought the magic. Herein lies the cure to every malady, the fix for Rayburn's sadness, the peace that will help the people of Mundum Nostrum remember they are of one blood, brothers and sisters, friends forever. Go ahead and see for yourself, the Greatest Treasure.' Tess gives him the box. He opens it. He looks in. 'That's it?' he says. 'That's everything,' Tess says."

"And?" I said.

"And that's all," Halley said. "End of story."

"Uh, *no.* After dragging me and Flip all the way to Mundum Nostrum, you're telling me what's inside that box."

"Seriously, Coffin? You haven't figured it out yet? By the way, if you're ever going to kiss me, you might want to do it soon. For instance, now would be a good time."

"Way to distract me from trying to get you to tell me

once and for all what's inside the stupid box. Plus, I thought you said there's nothing better than friends."

"Forget what I said."

I kissed her. I felt her heartbeat in her lips. They were chapped, and then they got slippery. They were just like I'd dreamed, lit with sparks. All the while Flip snored right next to us in the upside-down flying squirrel pose. "Whoa," I said.

"Yeah, whoa. We're shaking like crazy, aren't we?"

"I can't stop my teeth from chattering."

"Was that your first kiss?" she said.

"Yours too?"

"Third. Ha. Be happy for me."

"Did I do it right?" I said. "Like, was it lame, ours, compared to the other two?"

"Kiss me again and I'll tell you."

"Halley?"

"Ben?"

"I totally freaking love you."

"Me freaking too."

I woke the next morning to Flip's barking and Halley's screaming and then Mrs. Lorentz's. I could barely hear Mercurious as he called 911, even though I was standing right next to him. Halley bunched up like a pill bug. "It's cold but it burns," she said. "My back, in the middle. Like somebody's hitting me."

The EMTs came and put her onto a stretcher. "My hat," she said. "My rainbow hat. Please." They went lights and sirens to the hospital. Mrs. Lorentz rode with her in the ambulance. By the time Mercurious and I got to the hospital a few minutes after the ambulance, she was on the operating table. She had to have emergency surgery because her kidneys were all blocked up and she couldn't pee. She never made it out of the surgery. One of the nurses said it was a blessing that she didn't drag on for the next few weeks, all drugged up and all but dead. Yes, that she died in her sleep was a gift. It sure didn't feel like one. Not at all. It was like with Mom all over again. I was so mad. She never told me what was inside the magic box.

56

GOOD-BYE FOR A WHILE

When we got back to the apartment Flip was waiting for me at the front door with one of Halley's dirty socks, I thought, but it was mine. "Flip," I said, and his tail flicked. I crouched and he crawled into my lap. I carried him into Mercurious's office and set him on the couch. I stared at my Chewie poster. Mrs. Lorentz and Mercurious came in. They sat on either side of me. Mrs. Lorentz kissed my forehead.

"Can Flip stay?" I said.

"What are you talking about?" she said.

"Everybody I love disappears. I can't figure out how to bring them back. I have to go now."

"What?"

"I'll remind you of her. It's just going to make you feel worse."

"Ben, reminding us of her is going to keep her alive," Mrs. Lorentz said. "How can you say these things to us? How can you not see that this is where you're supposed to be, you and Flip? We're not losing you too. We're *not*. My Ben. Oh God, please don't go. Please. We need each other. We really do. Michael, tell him. *Tell* him."

Mercurious put his arm over my shoulder. He went somewhere between hug and headlock, just like Mom used to. "She left something for you," he said. "Come on now, son." I followed him into Halley's room, and Flip followed me. We stood in front of her desk, in front of the model of Luna Park 1905 spread over it. We'd come so close to finishing it, just one last detail. I'd wanted to put some people in the top of the tower, a family looking out over the city, the ocean.

Mercurious opened the desk drawer and took out Halley's phone and gave it to me in its bright pink case. He patted my back and left his hand there for a bit, and then he left. The phone was tapped up to Halley's notepad. I sat in the desk chair and read the note written three days before, the time stamp said.

> Dear Ben,
>
> As awesome as our story of *The Magic Box* is, it's not as awesome as your story, and that's the one I want you to tell. Speaking of *The Magic Box* . . . It's right there, in the model, in *Dreamland at Night*. Mercurious snuck it in for me. Look at the Golden Tower of Light. You see the foundation there, the one the tower is built on? You can look inside now, Ben. Yup, there's the Greatest Treasure. I still can't believe you didn't figure it out. The secret was in Flip's big gold eyes all along.

Your mom knew too. It's why she picked you.

Take care of Mom and Dad for me, and give my books to

Housing Works.

Love forever and ever,

Rainbow Girl

I lifted the golden tower out of the model of Luna Park 1905. Beneath it was a wooden box, just big enough to keep a book safe. I opened the box. Inside was a mirror. I looked into it, and all I saw was me.

57
TRAVELERS AND MAGICIANS

My favorite thing about Halley Lorentz will always be this: Every time she hugged you it was like she hadn't seen you in a long, long time. I'll never forget the way she held hands either, cold and trembly and hard enough to make your fingers ache a little the next day. Frannie's teacher from *Feathers* was right after all. Some things never fade away.

It's a year later and I go to a different school now, one for science geeks. It's really competitive and I'm not, but otherwise it's awesome. I never fall asleep in class and nobody smacks me in the back of the head. The only fights I get into are about whether or not roentgenium can occur naturally in environments where the gravity is a hundred and eleven times stronger than it is on Earth. If I stay on track I have a shot at getting into a good engineering program for college. Then again I might just go ahead and be a waterslide tester. Most of all, I like working with Mercurious. Maybe I'll design rockets and roller coasters by day and be a magician at night.

Aunt Jeanie and I get together a couple of times a month. She's always giving me presents, really nice stuff from Macy's, and some of it's even stuff that I like to wear. Hoodies and jeans and stuff. I tell her I feel bad, her spending all this money, but she says I shouldn't worry because she gets it dirt-cheap with her discount. She never brings up Leo unless I ask, and I do once in a while. He isn't drinking and he's losing weight, she says. She never asks me if I want to see him, because she knows I don't. I want him to be okay, though. I really, really do.

This one sweater Jeanie got me—it's really preppy. I wear it when Flip and I do Read to Rufus. Brian is reading above grade level now, and he isn't afraid to be caught carrying around a book.

I posted *The Magic Box* on some of the story sites. All told it has a little over eleven hundred reviews so far. A few girls and one guy even wrote spinoffs of it and a few more were threatening to. That's all Halley ever wanted anyway. To give the story to a few people. I posted her sketches too, with the story. I listen to the audio tracks, the notes Halley talked into her phone. I loved the sound of her voice. I still love it, loud and husky and just plain true.

It's Saturday, and Flip and I meet up with Chucky at the basketball courts. We both totally blow and these bigger dudes kick us off the court, which is fine because my asthma is starting up and Chucky is sucking wind worse than me because he's been eating way too many donuts. "Want to come over for my sister's birthday party?" he says.

"Can't, have to help Mercurious. Which sister and how old, though?"

"Coffin, are you serious? I'm lucky if I can remember their names."

Mercurious and I head on over to the hospital. We're in the pediatric wing where the kids are all bunched up in this one room, and they're going *whoa* and *holy crud, did you see that?* The angel Halley makes her appearance and flutters around the room and kisses each one of them on the cheek. And then Mercurious calls me out from behind the video controls for the showstopper. It's an old trick, but the kids go bonkers for it. I take off my magic silver sombrero and put it on the table and tap it with my light saber. Flip pops out in his rabbit ears and surfs on over to the kids and knuckle bumps them. There's high-fours all around and all the kids are cracking up and in the corner Mom Lorentz is crying but more she's laughing too.

After the show it's such a nice night, way too nice to be inside. Flip and I head out. We stop off at that supermarket where the lady gave me the cheddar samples that brought us all together in the first place, and I actually *buy* some cheese, and Flip and I head to the beach to play chase.

At dusk we stroll down the boardwalk to Luna Park. The lights are coming on, millions of them. I'm falling hard into my dream, traveling into the past, to 1905. Somewhere in time it still exists, and an apprentice electrician and a magician watch a young woman swing on the trapeze high into the night sky, and they pray she'll be okay. In the middle of it all is the golden tower. Flip and I run up those winding stairs to the top, and I'm breathless. She's there. She really is. Mom. Laura's with her. Jeanie and, yes, Leo, and it's okay, I don't mind. Then there's the woman who regretted selling Flip for forty dollars, who trained Flip to be awesomeness. The bus driver who fed me. Jerry the chemotherapy nurse, Franco, Mrs. Salvador, Kayla, the Santa magician, even Rayburn. And then there's Halley. Halley most of all.

Flip leaps to greet her and gets his stinky tongue up into her mouth. She holds my hand and we turn to the ocean, and what a view. It's not just the past anymore that I see. It's the future too and it's now and it's everything and everyone I've ever met and will meet. I look out and see forever. Yes, Halley's with me. All I have to do is close my eyes and think of her.

ACKNOWLEDGMENTS

Thank you to Jodi Reamer, who's not only one of the nicest people I know in publishing but also one of the nicest people I know. Do NOT get into a fight with her, though. She'll totally kick your butt. Seriously, she's crazy strong and just plain crazy. Ditto for Alec Shane, who, in addition to being a great agent, is also a great guy. David Levithan, for hooking me up with The Blackbelt.

My Behind The Book crew for hooking me up with the amazing Patty McCormick. The phenomenal Andy Griffiths, for giving the book to the phenomenal Markus Zusak. The lovely Steph Stepan, for giving the book to the lovely Rebecca Stead. The incredibly kind Rick Margolis, for giving the book to The King, aka Gary Schmidt. The wonderful Jacqueline Woodson, for letting me quote *Feathers*, and, for reaching out to Jackie, the divine Nancy Paulsen, who also happens to have a divine singing voice. David Baldacci and Kristen for the nicest tweet and for so many hours of reading happiness—same goes for Timothy Zahn. (Harper Lee and *To Kill a* freaking *Mockingbird* are pretty good too.)

Mary Kate McDevitt and Dani Calotta for the ridiculously beautiful cover; Jasmin Rubero and Regina Castillo for making the inside just as ridiculously beautiful.

Namrata Tripathi, for her perfect notes, her generosity re the cover and for coming up with the most gorgeous title in concert with Ellen Cormier, who gave equally perfect notes, made me crack up (laughing), put up with my lame pranks and generally held my hand as this book made its way through production. Puffin Julia gave rockin' notes too, as did my pal Heather Alexander.

Lauri Hornik, for that final round of notes and the best hugs, for the hilarious late-night e-mails, for taking me to yummy places to eat and for just being so completely and totally awesome to me these many years.

Sheila Hennessey—I don't even know what to say about Sheila, except you know how Ben takes in scruffy little Flip off the street? That's what Sheila did with me. Hugs to Shark. Shout-out to Steve Kent, Doni Kay, JD, Colleen, Ev and Nicole too. Eileen and Dana, Kendra, Stacey B and Kathy D, Mary Raymond, Helen, Kim and Draga, Michael, Penny, Steph, Alaina and my Text peeps. Jen Loja was awesome with cover and title support. Erin, Emily, Alexis, Don, Felicia, Carmela, Venessa, Melinda, Courtney, Anna, Jackie, Jennifer, and Marisa. Steve Meltzer, did you move? How come I don't see you in Frank's anymore? I miss you Jess, Marie, Emily, Scottie, Donne, Sara, Alex.

For the very fun and very marathon phone calls, Shawn Goodman (great man), Gayle Forman (outrageously magnificent), Nan Mercado (guardian angel of punk writers, or at least this one) and my bud Barry Lyga, who also sold me his phone for half what he could have gotten for it on Swappa. Morgan Baden, for keeping Barry on a leash, albeit with limited effectiveness. Michael Northrop, Coe Booth (Coe, might I ask, what are you working on now?), Gordon Korman and the rest of the TARN revelers. Jess, Karlan, Claudio and LIT. Greg Neri, Melissa Walker, Matt de la Peña, Libba Bray, Paul Volponi, Ted Goeglein, Torrey "Brando" Maldonado, Allen Zadoff, and especially Elizabeth Hill and Scott Smith, an amazing friend.

Dad, for always reading; Mom, for always buying. General Kathleen Whelan for marshaling the troops. Baba for all those hours at the *hotokesama*, Kari for all those hours keeping us giggling.

My dogs, Ray (Liotta), Al (Pacino), Bobby (DeNiro), Marty (Scorsese), Nice Guy Eddie (from *Reservoir Dogs*, also the model for Flip. See him there, in the picture with Halley's hand and the magic square?), and my lovely, dainty little jackal MiMi (from *La Bohème*. We needed a lady to class up the joint).

My friends who invite me to their bookstores, libraries, detention centers, schools and crazy conferences, with particular—and particularly fun—craziness coming from that Texas librarian band and my Florida FAME peeps. JLG crew: love you all.

My friends who visit me every time I close my eyes and think of them.

My editor, Kate Harrison. Kate, your big-hearted and brilliant notes and letters, our calls and lunches and brainstorming sessions—every minute I get with you is the greatest treasure. Our collaborations are so fun I feel guilty getting paid for them. (Please don't tell Lauri I said that.) Thank you for keeping me around all these years. They mean everything to me—your guidance, your teaching, your friendship.

TWO NOTES: The Coney Island Library is a little different from the way I described it here, but it's a dream world for sure. You should go.

Alas, Boardwalk Flight closed in 2014, but it lives on in my heart and can in yours too. All you have to do is close your eyes and think of it, right? (Or, if you're lazy like me—I am—you can search Google images.)

TURN THE PAGE

FOR A GLIMPSE OF PAUL GRIFFIN'S

NEXT HEARTWARMING NOVEL

PART I

Fall

1. CALIFORNIA DREAMING

The day Marty came into my life started normally enough. Paloma Lee and I met up before school, in the courtyard, and strummed our guitars. This was a month into sixth grade, the first Friday of October.

Pal's guitar was covered in stickers. One was a Smurf playing a guitar. She had long, loopy black hair and shiny black eyes. Not the Smurf, Paloma. She'd sewn tiny bells to the cuffs of her jeans, and every time she tapped her foot she jingled. The wash-off tattoo on the back of her hand said *The Dream Is the Only Thing That's Real*.

If you go by that height-weight chart in the nurse's office, Pal was big for her age. If you ask me, she was perfect. Her size matched her spirit. I was big too, at least size wise. Six foot two and two hundred fifty pounds isn't even on the chart when you're eleven. Everybody kept begging me to try out for football. "Renzo, you'd be a killer," they said, but I had zero interest in killing anybody. I didn't think I'd like *getting* killed a whole bunch either.

3

"Lorenzo Ventura, look me in the eye," Pal said. "Why you so sad?"

"I'm not *sad*," I said. "I'm smiling, aren't I?"

"That's your liar's smile," she said.

She was right. This was the day Reggie and her piglets were being auctioned off. We took in Reggie that summer when our neighbor had to sell his farm quick, before the bank grabbed it. Reggie was pregnant, and I asked Mom if we could keep the babies. She said sure, I just had to win the lottery first, and then we'd have the money to feed them.

I picked at my guitar and tried to block out the movie running in my mind: Reggie in a truck bed packed with strangers headed for the butcher. I almost told Pal about it, but then she'd be sad too. So instead I said, "Come over later for Mavericks and s'mores."

Chasing Mavericks was our favorite movie, about this kid who dreams of surfing the raddest waves in the Pacific. It had cool music too.

"Can't," Pal said. "I promised Mrs. Nikita I'd let her streamer curl my hair and hang my picture in the window. If she doesn't start bringing in customers, she's out of business."

The wind blew road sand from last winter into my eyes. Our school was at the crossroads, where the train tracks cut up with the old cemetery road. It was one of those dusty patches where the sycamores stop and the weeds creep in.

The trees were bare already, gray. Fall came early to southwest Pennsylvania.

"California, Renz," Pal said.

"California, yup."

We were going to be street musicians and camp up in
the hills by the Hollywood sign. Then, when Pal got discovered, I'd be her guitar man and bodyguard, just so long as
I didn't have to punch anybody. We'd surf by day and write
songs all night. The dream was crazy, but our friendship
was real.

We met in kindergarten, in peewee folk band. Pal was
four when her mom caught one of those lung infections
that start out a tickle in your throat, and a week later you're
dead. My dad died before I was born. Pal and I were missing
half of who we were. When we were together, we were one
whole person.

"Quit being sad," Pal said.

"I'm *not*."

The bell rang to start school.

"What makes a hero?" Mr. Gianelli said.

Max Hawkes raised his hand.

"Mr. Hawkes?" Mr. G said.

"Can I go to the bathroom?" Max said.

"I hope so," Mr. G said. "Heroes. They're rare these days.
Or are they everywhere? Mr. Ventura?"

A picture of my dad came to me. Big grin, dressed in his Army uniform. He was the real reason I wanted to visit California someday. Mom had scattered his ashes in the Pacific. They'd gone out to Malibu for their honeymoon.

"Renzo?" Mr. G said.

"Heroes are rare," I said.

The combat medics have a saying: Heroes go to heaven. They have another saying too: Don't be a hero.

The bell rang, this time to end school.

"Wait," Mr. G said. "Your mission is to write about your hero, and why she or he is such."

Everybody groaned about homework on the weekend. My mind was on Reggie's piglets, sold and scattered by now, no brothers or sisters all of a sudden, no mom. If I kept thinking about it I'd well up, so I didn't, and I didn't.

2. THE BRONZE STAR

Somebody had gotten to our sign again.

COME RIGHT ON UP!

Maple Clutch Orchard
RoTTiNeST
"~~Juiciest~~ Freestone Peaches This Side of the
Kishux River"

Family Owned Since 1925

I headed uphill to the house for nail polish remover, the one thing that made permanent marker impermanent. Bella, our black Lab, didn't greet me at the door. She was two weeks from having yet another round of puppies, and she couldn't do much more than sleep in front of the wood stove. I wanted to take her up to the arbor for some air, but she wasn't in the den. I checked my room, and she wasn't there either.

The afternoon light was orange on the wall. I stood there a second, in front of my closet door, to soak in the quiet. Then, with that hero essay for Mr. G on my mind, I opened the door.

On the top shelf was my dad's Bronze Star in a picture frame.

AWARDED TO MARTIN ANTHONY VENTURA, FOR VALOR

His commander wrote, *"Sergeant Ventura crawled through twenty yards of crossfire to his platoon mate PFC Rajiv Bedi, who'd been hit by a sniper. Raj told Marty to high-tail out of there, since Marty was about to become a father in three months. Apparently Marty said, 'What kind of father would I be if I left my brother out here?'"*

I had pictures too. In one he's serenading Mom with his guitar. I never saw her smile that true in real life. In another, from the honeymoon, he's on a surfboard. He was big like me, and he rode it on his belly. I could hear him going "Woohoo!"

On the next shelf was a peach jar half full of guitar picks, one for each bar or wedding he played. He'd written the dates on them with fine-tip marker.

He'd kept a classic CD collection, Johnny Cash, Sarah Vaughan, Bruce Springsteen, Odetta. The boombox was speckled yellow and white. Mom saw him hang a flyer on the church bulletin board and hired him to paint the barn, even though it didn't need painting. Double Pop, my grandfather, told me that one, and all the other stories too.

Then there were the letters handwritten to me, before I was born. I must have read each fifty times.

Mom's truck chugged up the driveway, and the gravel *pop-pop-popped.*

I wasn't ready to be around her sadness just yet.

I snuck out the back door and forced myself down to the barn and Reggie's empty stall to rake out the straw.

Except it wasn't empty.

Bella'd had her puppies right there in Reggie's bedding. She was licking them clean. Those spiky-haired pups climbed over each other to get at Bella's milk. I ran up to the house for Double Pop.

3. THE RUNT

Ugliest puppies ever," Mom said. "Ugh, those stripes. One of John Mason's shepherds got at her again, the giant one, I bet you."

"Keeth," I said, which was short for *killer teeth*. I'd never seen him myself, but legend was he tore the throat out of a hunter who'd wandered onto Mason's property.

"That dog is the devil made flesh," Mom said. "What can you expect when his owner is Mason?"

"He called again," Double said. Mason was the condo king, and he wanted our land for a golf course.

"Daddy, I'll die before I sell to that man."

"I told him just that too." Double's grandparents started Maple Clutch, but if it was up to him we'd sell the place yesterday and move to the Carolinas, where your money stretched so much, you could wrap a dollar around a tree, he said. Double was a soldier too, Vietnam, shot in the knee. It locked up on him in the Pennsylvania winters.

"You stay, a, *way* from that half a wolf, Renzo, and I bet

10

you it is one too," Mom said. "I don't want you within a mile of Mason's property. You hear me?"

"Yup."

"'Yup.'"

"Yes, okay? I understand, sheesh."

"Lorenzo Ventura, don't you sheesh me."

"All right now," Double said.

"Here I'm sure to be up all night with that stack of bills, robbing Peter to pay Paul, and now this mess with the dog, throwing her litter early."

"You head on up to the house," Double said. "Me and Renzo, we got Bell and the pups covered."

"Striped puppies," Mom said. "I bet they don't sell for twenty dollars apiece." She marched off, but then she turned back, her eyes wet. "Sorry, Renz. I know it's not your fault."

"It's all right, Ma."

"It's not all right. None of it." She left fast.

"She's having a rough one tonight," I said.

"Yup," Double said, which is where I got it from. "The auction was harder on her than she thought it'd be." He patted my shoulder. His hand was a giant's but it landed on you softer than a sparrow. "I'll get the heaters and blankets, son. You break a bale and rake in some fresh straw."

I was smoothing out the bedding for the pups when I noticed one wasn't striped like the rest. He was brown and gold spots and getting stepped on by the other dogs.

11

Except he wasn't a dog.

He was the runt piglet Mom must have missed when she swept up Reggie and her brood for the auction.

Bella picked up that fuzzy little pig in her teeth and set him down in front of her. She looked at him, and then she looked at me.

All I could do was smile.

Bella sighed, and then she nudged that goofy-looking piglet downward so he could get his share of the milk.